LiTURGiCAL
HYMNS OLD & NEW

Compiled by
Robert Kelly
Sister Sheila McGovern SSL
Kevin Mayhew
Father Andrew Moore
Sister Louisa Poole SSL

Kevin
Mayhew

Important Copyright Information

We would like to remind users of this hymnal that the reproduction of any song texts without the permission of the copyright holder is illegal. Details of all copyright holders are clearly indicated above each song and full addresses can be found in the Acknowledgements section at the end of this book.

Some of the songs may be covered either by a Christian Copyright Licensing (CCL) licence or a Calamus licence. If you possess a CCL or Calamus licence, it is essential that you check your instruction manual to ensure that the song you wish to use is covered.

If you are *not* a member of CCL or Calamus, or the song you wish to reproduce is not covered by your licence, you must contact the copyright holder direct for their permission.

If you are interested in joining CCL or Calamus they can be contacted at the following addresses:

Christian Copyright Licensing (Europe) Ltd, P.O. Box 1339, Eastbourne, East Sussex, BN21 4YF.
Tel: 01323 417711, Fax: 01323 417722.

Calamus, 30 North Terrace, Mildenhall, Suffolk, IP28 7AB.
Tel: 01638 716579, Fax: 01638 510390.

First published in Great Britain in 1999 by
KEVIN MAYHEW LIMITED
Buxhall, Stowmarket
Suffolk IP14 3DJ

Compilation © Kevin Mayhew Ltd 1999

The following editions are available

People's copy (standard)	Catalogue No. 1413081	
	ISBN No. 1 84003 303 7	ISMN No. M 57004 570 9
People's copy (plastic)	Catalogue No. 1413082	
	ISBN No. 1 84003 318 5	ISMN No. M 57004 560 0
Melody/guitar	Catalogue No. 1413083	
	ISBN No. 1 84003 304 5	ISMN No. M 57004 501 3
Organ/choir	Catalogue No. 1413084	
	ISBN No. 1 84003 305 3	ISMN No. M 57004 502 0

Front cover design by Jonathan Stroulger
Printed and bound in Great Britain

CONTENTS

Copyright Information for Responsorial Psalms, Nos 900-1078

FOREWORD

The first edition of *Hymns Old and New* appeared in 1977. The principle underlying its production was simple: to offer in one, single, conveniently sized book, a selection of the hymns most used by Catholic communities in Britain and Ireland. The contents ranged from the stalwart songs of the traditional pre-Vatican II hymnals to the best of the new as discovered and tested by the series of *20th Century Folk Hymnals*.

By 1984 it was clear that a major revision of this basically sound idea was needed. Very little adjustment to the 'old' traditional material was needed, but by now the repertoire of 'new' material had broadened. This was largely due to the work of people like the late Brother Damian Lundy in encouraging young people to be brave enough to express their faith in song, and which had made the influential *Songs of the Spirit* series possible. There was also the papal visit of 1982, where the various public celebrations had opened the eyes of many parishes to the role that music could and should play in their liturgy. Not only did parishes and other communities seem to have developed an immense appetite for music for their celebrations, but they were demanding a wider repertoire of material, and expecting higher standards from the words. As a response to these pastoral demands, *Hymns Old and New with Supplement* was published. It was the first popular hymnal to offer a scriptural index, and to equip parishes to be able to sing the Responsorial Psalm for every Sunday and major feast. This edition soon became, and for many years has remained, Britain's best-selling hymnal.

A decade later seemed an opportune moment to offer a new edition. There was, of course, the need to include the good new material that had been emerging in the rest of Europe and the United States. The result, *Hymns Old and New, New Century Edition*, was also a far more elegant product, thanks to the improvements in computer-based music-setting which did not exist ten years earlier. The somewhat summary scriptural index of its predecessor was now far more generous, matching the growing realisation that scripture should be the primary source for what we proclaim in song in our liturgies. This edition's main innovation, though, was to try and serve those parishes whose musical repertoire was almost exclusively traditional material by offering 'hymns for the Lectionary': a comprehensive range of new texts, explicitly constructed on the scripture readings for the Sundays and feasts – but all singable to traditional hymn-tunes.

The need so clearly felt to renew the material for our celebrations is a healthy one, because it is a sign of the Church's vitality. Quite naturally, parishes and communities are now looking for the pastoral tool that will take them and their celebrations forward into the third millennium. This latest edition of the series is designed to serve that purpose. It has consciously taken the best insights and initiatives of its predecessors, and added another very important one. The basic title *Hymns Old and New* has gained the significant adjective '*Liturgical*'. Parishes are now more discerning in the material they choose for their celebrations: they are demanding songs that have clear and coherent connections with the scripture texts that are proclaimed; the people are reclaiming the parts of the Mass and the celebration of the sacraments that belong to them by wanting – as they should – to sing them; it is, happily, becoming standard practice for the Responsorial Psalm to be sung. These are all profoundly 'liturgical' aspirations, and this book is designed to satisfy them.

Robert Kelly
Sister Sheila McGovern SSL
Kevin Mayhew
Father Andrew Moore
Sister Louisa Poole SSL

LITURGICAL
HYMNS OLD & NEW

MUSIC FOR THE MASS

1 A New People's Mass (Gregory Murray)

Penitential Rite

Lord, have mer - cy. Lord, have mer - cy. Christ, have mer - cy.

Christ, have mer - cy. Lord, have mer - cy. Lord, have mer - cy.

Gloria

Glo - ry to God in the high - est, and peace to his peo - ple on earth. Lord God,

hea - ven - ly King, al - migh - ty God and Fa - ther, we wor - ship you, we

give you thanks, we praise you for your glo - ry. Lord Je - sus Christ, on - ly

Son of the Fa - ther, Lord God, Lamb of God, you take a - way the sins of the

world, have mer - cy on us; you are seat - ed at the right hand of the Fa -

ther, re - ceive our prayer. For you a - lone are the Ho - ly One,

you a - lone are the Lord, you a - lone are the Most High, Je - sus Christ,

with the Ho - ly Spi - rit, in the glo - ry of God the Fa - ther. A - men.

Sanctus

Ho - ly, ho - ly, ho - ly Lord. God of pow - er and might, hea - ven and earth are full of your

glo - ry. Ho - san - na in the high - est. Bles - sed is he who comes in the

name of the Lord. Ho - san - na in the high - est.

Memorial Acclamation

Christ has died, Christ is ri - sen, Christ will come a - gain.

Great Amen

A - men.

Agnus Dei

Lamb of God, you take a - way the sins of the world:

1st & 2nd times have mer - cy on us. *3rd time* grant us peace.

2 A Simple Mass (Andrew Moore)

Penitential Rite

Lord, have mer - cy. Lord, have mer- cy. Christ, have mer - cy.

Christ, have mer - cy. Lord, have mer - cy. Lord, have mer - cy.

Gloria

Glo - ry to God in the high - est, and peace to his peo - ple on earth.

Lord God, heav'n - ly King, al - migh - ty God and Fa - ther, we wor- ship you, we give you

thanks, we praise you for your glo - ry, we praise you for your glo - ry.

Lord Je - sus Christ, on- ly Son of the Fa - ther, Lord God, Lamb of God, you take a - way the

sins of the world: have mer - cy on us; you are seat- ed at the right hand of the

Fa - ther: re - ceive our prayer. For you a- lone are the Ho - ly One, you a- lone are the

Lord, you a-lone are the Most High, Je-sus Christ, with the Ho-ly

Spi-rit, in the glo-ry of God the Fa-ther. A-men. A-men.

Sanctus

Ho-ly, ho-ly, ho-ly Lord, God of pow-er and God of might,

hea-ven and earth are full of your glo-ry. Ho-san-na in the

high-est. Ho-san-na in the high-est. Bless-ed is he who

comes in the name of the Lord. Bless-ed is he who comes in the name of the

Lord. Ho-san-na in the high-est, ho-san-na in the high-est.

Memorial acclamation

Dy-ing, you de-stroyed our death, ris-ing, you re-

stored our life. Lord Je-sus, come in glo-ry.

Agnus Dei

Lamb of God, you take a-way the sins of the world: have

mer-cy on us. Lamb of God, you take a-way the

sins of the world: have mer-cy on us. Lamb of God, you

take a-way the sins of the world: grant us peace.

3 Mass of the Spirit (Kevin Mayhew)

Penitential Rite

Lord, have mer - cy. Lord, have mer - cy. Lord, have mer - cy.

Christ, have mer - cy. Christ, have mer - cy. Christ, have mer - cy.

Lord, have mer - cy. Lord, have mer - cy. Lord, have mer - cy.

Gloria

Glo - ry to God in the high - est, and peace to his peo - ple on earth.

Lord God, hea - ven - ly King, al - migh - ty God and Fa - ther, we wor - ship you, we

give you thanks, we praise you for your glo - ry. Lord Je - sus Christ, on - ly Son of the

Fa - ther, Lord God, Lamb of God, you take a - way the sin of the world: have

mer - cy on us; you are seat - ed at the right hand of the Fa - ther: re - ceive our

prayer. For you a - lone are the Ho - ly One, you a - lone are the

Lord, you a - lone are the Most High, Je - sus Christ, with the Ho - ly Spi - rit,

in the glo - ry of God the Fa - ther. A - men, a - men.

Sanctus

Ho - ly,   ho - ly,   ho - ly Lord,   God of pow - er and might,

hea - ven and earth are   full   of your glo - ry. Ho - san - na in the high - est.

Bless - ed is   he   who comes   in the name of the Lord. Ho - san - na in the high - est.

Agnus Dei

Lamb of God,   you take a - way the   sins   of the world: have mer - cy on   us.

Lamb of God,   you take a - way the   sins   of the world: have mer - cy on   us.

Lamb of God,   you take a - way the   sins   of the world: grant us   peace.

4 Mass of the Bread of Life (Margaret Rizza)

Penitential Rite

Lord, have mer - cy. Lord, have mer - cy.   Lord, have mer - cy.   Lord, have   mer - cy.

Christ, have mer - cy. Christ, have mer - cy. Christ, have mer - cy.   Christ, have   mer - cy.

rall. al fine

Lord, have mer - cy. Lord, have mer - cy.   Lord, have mer - cy.   Lord, have   mer - cy.

Agnus Dei

Je - sus, Lamb of God, Je - sus, Lamb of God, you take a – way the sins of the world: have

mer - cy on us. Je - sus, Lamb of God, Je - sus, Lamb of God, you take a – way the

sins of the world: have mer - cy on us. Je - sus, Lamb of God, Je - sus, Lamb of God, you

take a – way the sins of the world: grant us your peace, grant us your peace.

5 Missa de Angelis (Plainsong)

Penitential Rite

Ky - ri - e, e – le - i - son.

Chris - te, e – le - i - son.

Ky - ri - e, e – le - i - son.

Ky - ri - e, e – le - i - son.

Gloria

Glo - ri - a in ex - cel - sis De - o, et in ter - ra pax ho - mi - ni - bus bo - næ vo - lun - ta - tis.

Lau - da - mus te, be - ne - di - ci - mus te, a - dor - a - mus te,

glo - ri - fi - ca - mus te, gra - ti - as a - gi - mus ti - bi prop - ter mag - nam glo - ri - am tu - am,

Do - mi - ne De - us, Rex cæ - le - stis, De - us Pa - ter om - ni - po - tens. Do - mi - ne Fi - li un - i - ge - ni - te,

Je - su Chris - te. Do - mi - ne De - us, Ag - nus De - i, Fi - li - us Pa - tris,

6 Mass XVIII (Plainsong)

Penitential Rite

Ky – ri – e, e – le – i – son. Chris – te, e – le – i – son.

Ky – ri – e, e – le – i – son. Ky – ri – e, e – le – i – son.

Sanctus

San – ctus, san – ctus, san – ctus Do – mi – nus De – us sa – ba – oth.

Ple – ni sunt cæ – li et ter – ra glo – ri – a tu – a. Ho – san – na in ex – cel – sis.

Be – ne – di – ctus qui ve – nit in no – mi – ne Do – mi – ni. Ho – san – na in ex – cel – sis.

Agnus Dei

A – gnus De – i, qui tol – lis pec – ca – ta mun – di: mi – se – re – re no – bis.

A – gnus De – i, qui tol – lis pec – ca – ta mun – di: do – na no – bis pa – cem.

7 The 'American' Eucharist (adapted from the Liturgy by Sandra Joan Billington)

Kyrie, Sanctus, Agnus Dei © McCrimmon Publishing Co. Ltd.
Gospel and Memorial acclamations © Kevin Mayhew Ltd.

Penitential Rite

1. Lord, have mercy; Lord, have mercy
   on your servants, Lord, have mercy.
   God almighty, just and faithful,
   Lord, have mercy; Lord, have mercy.

2. Christ, have mercy; Christ, have mercy;
   gift from heaven, Christ, have mercy.
   Light of truth and light of justice,
   Christ, have mercy; Christ, have mercy.

3. Lord, have mercy; Lord, have mercy;
   on your servants, Lord, have mercy.
   God almighty, just and faithful,
   Lord, have mercy; Lord, have mercy.

Gospel acclamation
(adapted from the Liturgy by Robert B. Kelly)

Alleluia, alleluia,
Let us praise Christ, our Lord Jesus.
Alleluia, let us praise him,
now among us in his Gospel.

Sanctus

1. Holy, holy, holy, holy,
   Lord of hosts. You fill with glory
   all the earth and all the heavens.
   Song hosanna, sing hosanna.

2. Blest and holy, blest and holy,
   he who comes now in the Lord's name.
   In the highest sing hosanna,
   in the highest sing hosanna.

Memorial acclamation
(adapted from the Liturgy by Robert B. Kelly)

When we eat this bread you give us,
and we drink this cup you left us,
we proclaim your death, Lord Jesus,
till you come again in glory.

Agnus Dei

1. Jesus, Lamb of God, have mercy,
   bearer of our sins, have mercy. *(Repeat)*

2. Saviour of the world, Lord Jesus,
   may your peace be always with us. *(Repeat)*

8 The 'Hopwood' Mass
(adapted from the Liturgy by Terence Collins)
© 1978 Kevin Mayhew Ltd.

Penitential Rite

1. Father of all, O Lord, have mercy. *(x2)*
   Father of all, have mercy on us.
   Father of all, be ever near us.

2. Saviour of all, O Christ, have mercy. *(x2)*
   Saviour of all, have mercy on us.
   Saviour of all, be ever near us.

3. Spirit of all, O Lord, have mercy. *(x2)*
   Spirit of all, have mercy on us.
   Spirit of all, be ever near us.

Sanctus

1. Holy are you, Lord of creation!
   Holy are you, Lord God of angels!
   Holy are you, God of all people!
   Heaven and earth proclaim your glory.

2. Glory to you! Your name is holy.
   Blessèd is he who comes in your name!
   Glory to him! We sing his praises.
   Heaven and earth proclaim your glory.

Angus Dei

1. O Lamb of God, you bore our sinning.
   O Lamb of God, you bore our dying.
   O Lamb of God, your peace be with us.

9 The 'Israeli' Mass (adapted from the Liturgy by Anthony Hamson)
© McCrimmon Publishing Co. Ltd.

Penitential Rite

1. Lord, have mercy. Lord, have mercy.
   Lord, have mercy on us all.
   Lord, have mercy. Lord, have mercy.
   Lord, have mercy on us all.

2. Christ, have mercy. Christ, have mercy.
   Christ, have mercy on us all.
   Christ, have mercy. Christ, have mercy.
   Christ, have mercy on us all.

3. Lord, have mercy. Lord, have mercy.
   Lord, have mercy on us all.
   Lord, have mercy. Lord, have mercy.
   Lord, have mercy on us all.

Sanctus

1. Holy, holy, holy, holy,
   Lord of pow'r, Lord of might.
   Heav'n and earth are filled with glory.
   Sing hosanna evermore.

2. Blest and holy, blest and holy,
   he who comes from God on high.
   Raise your voices, sing his glory,
   praise his name for evermore.

Angus Dei

1. Lamb of God, you take away the sin,
   the sin of all the world:
   give us mercy, give us mercy,
   give us mercy, Lamb of God.

2. Lamb of God, you take away the sin,
   the sin of all the world:
   give us mercy, give us mercy,
   give us mercy, Lamb of God.

3. Lamb of God, you take away the sin,
   the sin of all the world:
   grant us peace, Lord; grant us peace, Lord;
   grant us peace, Lamb of God.

10 Lord, have mercy (de Angelis: Alan Rees)

Lord, have mer - cy. Lord, have mer - cy. Lord, have mer - cy.

Christ, have mer - cy. Christ, have mer - cy. Christ, have mer - cy.

Lord, have mer - cy. Lord, have mer - cy. Lord, have mer - cy.

11 Lord, have mercy (Orbis Factor: Alan Rees)

King eternal, creator of the world,
  have mercy.

Christ, light of the world, bestower of life,
  have mercy.

Loving Saviour, take away our sins
  and have mercy.

Lord, have mer - cy.

Christ, have mer - cy.

Lord, have mer - cy.

12 Lord, have mercy (Alme Pater: Alan Rees)

You were sent to heal the contrite.

You came to call sinners.

You are seated at the right hand of the
  Father.

Lord, have mer - cy.

Christ, have mer - cy.

Lord, have mer - cy.

13 Kyrie eleison (Haugen)

Ky- ri- e, e - le - i - son. Chris - te, e -

le - i - son. Ky- ri - e, e - le - i - son.

1. Lord Jesus, you come to gather the nations
   into the peace of God's kingdom.
2. You come in word and sacrament to
   strengthen us in holiness.
3. You will come in glory with salvation for
   your people.

14 Lord, have mercy (Malcolm Archer)

Lord, have mer-cy. Lord, have mer-cy. Christ, have mer-cy.

Christ, have mer-cy. Lord, have mer-cy. Lord, have mer-cy.

15 Lord, have mercy (Gordon Rock)

1. Lord, have mer-cy on us all. Lord, have mer-cy on us all.

Lord, have mer-cy, Lord, have mer-cy, Lord, have mer-cy on us all.

2. Christ, have mercy . . .   3. Lord, have mercy . . .

16 Kyrie eleison (Margaret Rizza)

Ky - ri - e, e - le - i - son. Chri - ste, e - le - i - son. Ky - ri - e, ex - au - di nos,

Do - mi - ne. Ky - ri - e, e - le - i - son. Chri - ste, e - le - i - son.

Ky - ri - e, e - le - i - son. Chri - ste, ex - au - di nos, Do - mi - ne.

Ky - ri - e, Ky - ri - e, Do - mi - ne, Do - mi - ne, Do - mi - ne!

17 Kyrie (Colin Mawby)

Ky - ri - e, Chri - ste,

Ky - ri - e, e - le - i - son.

Continued overleaf

Or

Lord, have mer - cy. Christ, have mer - cy.

Lord have mer - cy, have mer - cy.

18 Kyrie 7 (Taizé)
© Ateliers et Presses de Taizé

Ky - ri - e, Ky - ri - e, e - le - i - son. *(hum under the invocations)*

19 Lord, have mercy (Friedrich Filitz)
© 1997 Kevin Mayhew Ltd.

1. Lord, have mer - cy on us, hear us as we pray; Lord, have mer - cy on us, take our sin a - way.

2. Christ, have mercy on us,
   hear us as we pray;
   Christ, have mercy on us,
   take our sin away.

3. Lord, have mercy on us,
   hear us as we pray;
   Lord, have mercy on us,
   take our sin away.

Text: Michael Forster (b. 1946)

20 Coventry Gloria
© 1981, 1982 Peter Jones/OCP Publications

Glory to God, glory in the highest, peace to his people, peace on earth.

Glo - ry to God, glo - ry in the high - est, peace to his peo - ple, peace on earth.

Lord God, heavenly King, almighty God and Father.

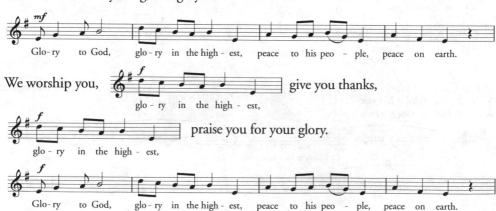

Glo - ry to God, glo - ry in the high - est, peace to his peo - ple, peace on earth.

We worship you,

glo - ry in the high - est,

give you thanks,

glo - ry in the high - est,

praise you for your glory.

Glo - ry to God, glo - ry in the high - est, peace to his peo - ple, peace on earth.

Lord Jesus Christ, only Son of the Father, Lord God, Lamb of God, you take away the sin

of the world: have mercy on us,  you are seated at the

have mer - cy on us;

right hand of the Father: receive our prayer,

re - ceive our prayer.

Glory to God, glory in the highest, peace to his people, peace on earth.

Glo - ry to God, glo - ry in the high - est, peace to his peo - ple, peace on earth.

For you alone are the Holy One, you alone are the Lord, you alone are the Most High,
Jesus Christ, with the Holy Spirit, in the glory of God, the glory of God the Father.

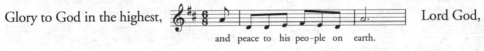

Glo - ry to God, glo - ry in the high - est, peace to his peo - ple, peace on earth.

21 Gloria (Alan Rees)
© 1992 Kevin Mayhew Ltd.

Glory to God in the highest, 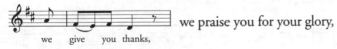 Lord God,

and peace to his peo - ple on earth.

heavenly King,  we worship you,

al - migh - ty God and Fa - ther,

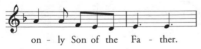 we praise you for your glory,

we give you thanks,

we praise you for your glo - ry. Lord Jesus Christ,

on - ly Son of the Fa - ther.

Lord God, Lamb of God, you take away the sin of the

Lord God, Lamb of God,

world; have mercy on us, You who sit at the Father's right

have mer - cy on us.

hand: receive our prayer, For you alone are the Holy One,

re - ceive our prayer.

Continued overleaf

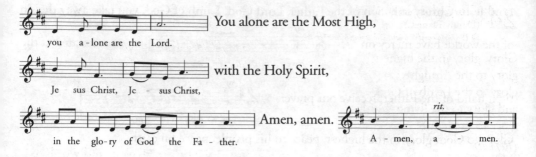

You alone are the Most High,
you a-lone are the Lord.

with the Holy Spirit,
Je-sus Christ, Je-sus Christ,

Amen, amen.
in the glo-ry of God the Fa-ther.

rit.
A - men, a - men.

22 Glory to God (Malcolm Archer)
© 1995 Kevin Mayhew Ltd.

Glo-ry to God in the high - est, and peace to his peo-ple on earth. Lord God,

heav'n-ly King, al-migh-ty God and Fa-ther, we wor-ship you, we give you thanks, we

praise you for your glo-ry. Lord Je-sus Christ, on-ly Son of the Fa-ther, Lord God, Lamb of God, you

take a-way the sins of the world: have mer-cy on us; you are seat-ed at the

right hand of the Fa-ther; re-ceive our prayer. For you a-lone are the Ho-ly One,

you a-lone are the Lord, you a-lone are the Most High, Je-sus Christ, with the

rall.
Ho-ly Spi-rit, in the glo-ry of God the Fa-ther. A - men.

23 Gloria 3 (Taizé)
© Ateliers et Presses de Taizé

This setting may be sung as a canon with entries as indicated.

Glo - ri - a, glo - ri - a in ex - cel - sis De - o!

Glo - ri - a, glo - ri - a, al - le - lu - ia, al - le - lu - ia!

24 Glory, glory in the highest
(Danny Daniels)

Glory, glory in the highest;
glory to the Almighty;
glory to the Lamb of God,
and glory to the living Word;
glory to the Lamb!

(Repeat)

Men	I give glory,
Women	glory,
Men	glory,
Women	glory,
Men	glory,
All	glory to the Lamb. *(Repeat)*
Last time	I give glory to the Lamb.

25 Gloria (Mike Anderson)

Gloria, gloria, in excelsis Deo.
Gloria, gloria, in excelsis Deo.

1. Lord God, heavenly King,
   peace you bring to us;
   we worship you, we give you thanks,
   we sing our song of praise.

2. Jesus, Saviour of all,
   Lord God, Lamb of God,
   you take away our sins,
   O Lord, have mercy on us all.

3. At the Father's right hand,
   Lord receive our prayer,
   for you alone are the Holy One,
   and you alone are Lord.

4. Glory, Father and Son,
   glory, Holy Spirit,
   to you we raise our hands up high,
   we glorify your name.

26 Gloria (George Salazar, trans. Paul Inwood)

Glory! Glory! Glory to God!
Glory! Glory! Glory to God!

1. Glory to God in the heights of the
   heavens.
   Peace to God's people, all people on
   earth.

2. Son of the Father, all glory and worship;
   praise and thanksgiving to you,
   Lamb of God.

3. You take away the sin of the world;
   have mercy on us, receive our prayer.

4. Seated in pow'r at the right of the Father,
   Jesus alone is the Lord, the Most High.

5. And with the Spirit of love everlasting,
   reigning in glory for ever. Amen.

27 Gloria (Francis Duffy)

Gloria, gloria in excelsis Deo;
gloria, gloria in excesis Deo.

1. Glory to God in the <u>high</u>est,
   and <u>peace</u> to his people on <u>earth</u>.
   Lord God, heavenly <u>King</u>,
   al<u>might</u>y <u>God</u> and <u>Father</u>,
   <u>we</u> worship you, we give you <u>thanks</u>,
   we <u>praise</u> you for your glory.

2. Lord Jesus Christ, only Son of the <u>Father</u>,
   Lord God, Lamb of <u>God</u>,
   you take away the sin of the <u>world</u>:
   have mercy on <u>us</u>;
   you are seated at the right hand
       of the <u>Father</u>:
   receive our <u>prayer</u>.

3. For you alone are the <u>Holy</u> One,
   you alone are the <u>Lord</u>,
   you alone are the Most <u>High</u>,
   Jesus <u>Christ</u>,
   with the Holy <u>Spirit</u>,
   in the glory of God the <u>Father</u>.

28 Lourdes Gloria
© 1998 Kevin Mayhew Ltd.

Gloria, gloria in excelsis Deo.
Gloria, gloria in excelsis Deo.

1. Glory to <u>God</u> <u>in</u> the <u>highest</u>, <u>and</u> <u>peace</u>
   to his <u>people</u> on <u>earth</u>.
   <u>Lord</u> God, heavenly <u>King</u>, almighty <u>God</u>
   and <u>Father</u>,
   <u>we</u> worship you, we give you <u>thanks</u>, we
   <u>praise</u> you for your <u>glory</u>.

2. Lord Jesus <u>Christ</u>, only <u>Son</u> of the <u>Father</u>.
   <u>Lord</u> <u>God</u>, <u>Lamb</u> of God.
   <u>you</u> take away the sin of the <u>world</u>: have
   <u>mercy</u> on <u>us</u>;
   <u>you</u> are seated at the <u>right</u> hand of the
   Father: re<u>ceive</u> our <u>prayer</u>.

3. For you a<u>lone</u> are the <u>Holy</u> <u>One</u>, <u>you</u>
   <u>alone</u> are the <u>Lord</u>.
   <u>you</u> alone are the Most <u>High</u>, <u>Jesus</u>
   <u>Christ</u>, <u>with</u> the Holy <u>Spirit</u>, in the
   glory of God the <u>Father</u>. <u>Amen</u>.

29 Sing to God a song of glory
(Francesca Leftley)
© 1978 Kevin Mayhew Ltd.

1. Sing to God a song of glory,
   peace he brings to all on earth.
   Worship we the King of heaven;
   praise and bless his holy name.

   Glory, glory, sing his glory.
   Glory to our God on high.

2. Sing to Christ, the Father's loved one,
   Jesus, Lord and Lamb of God:
   hear our prayer, O Lord, have mercy,
   you who bear the sins of all.

3. Sing to Christ, the Lord and Saviour,
   seated there at God's right hand:
   hear our prayer, O Lord, have mercy,
   you alone the Holy One.

4. Glory sing to God the Father,
   glory to his only Son,
   glory to the Holy Spirit,
   glory to the Three in One.

30 Peruvian Gloria
© 1976 Kevin Mayhew Ltd.

1. Glory to God, glory to God,
   glory to the Father.
   Glory to God, glory to God,
   glory to the Father.
   To him be glory for ever.
   To him be glory for ever.
   Alleluia, amen,
   alleluia, amen,
   alleluia, amen,
   alleluia, amen.

2. Glory to God, glory to God,
   Son of the Father.
   Glory to God, glory to God,
   Son of the Father.
   To him be glory for ever.
   To him be glory for ever.
   Alleluia, amen.
   Alleluia, amen,
   alleluia, amen,
   alleluia, amen.

3. Glory to God, glory to God,
   glory to the Spirit.
   Glory to God, glory to god,
   Son of the Spirit.
   To him be glory for ever.
   To him be glory for ever.
   Alleluia, amen.
   Alleluia, amen,
   alleluia, amen,
   alleluia, amen.

31 Country Gardens Gloria
(Michael Forster) © 1995, 1999 Kevin Mayhew Ltd.

1. Glory to God, to God in the height,
   bringing peace to ev'ry nation.
   Lord God almighty, Father and King,
   and the author of salvation.
   'Glory!' let the people sing,
   let the whole creation ring,
   telling out redemption's story,
   as we worship your name
   with thankful songs of praise
   for the love that is your glory.

2. Jesus, the Father's one holy Son,
   all creation bows before you.
   You are the God, the God we acclaim,
   and we worship and adore you.
   Lamb of God, to you we pray,
   you who take our sin away,
   mercy, grace and truth revealing.
   At the right hand of God,
   receive our humble prayer
   for forgiveness, hope and healing.

3. You, Jesus Christ, alone are the Lord,
   by your own eternal merit;
   sharing by right the glory of God
   in the presence of the Spirit.
   You alone are Lord Most High,
   you alone we glorify,
   reigning over all creation.
   To the Father, the Son
   and Spirit, Three in One,
   be eternal acclamation!

32 Ash Grove Gloria (Michael Forster)
© 1995 Kevin Mayhew Ltd.

1. Sing glory to God
   in the height of the heavens,
   salvation and peace
   to his people on earth;
   our King and our Saviour,
   our God and our Father,
   we worship and praise you
   and sing of your worth.

   Creation unites in the pow'r of the Spirit,
   in praise of the Father,
   through Jesus, the Son.
   So complex, so simple,
   so clear, so mysterious,
   our God ever three yet eternally one.

2. Lord Jesus, the Christ,
   only Son of the Father,
   the Lamb who has carried
   our burden of shame,

now seated on high
in the glory of heaven,
have mercy upon us
who call on your name.

3. For you, only you,
   we acknowledge as holy,
   we name you alone
   as our Saviour and Lord;
   you only, O Christ,
   with the Spirit exalted,
   at one with the Father
   for ever adored.

33 Advent Alleluia (Michael Joncas)
© 1981, 1983 New Dawn Music

Prepare the way of the Lord,
make straight his paths:
all people shall see the salvation of God.

or

A virgin will give birth to a Son;
a virgin will give birth to a Son;
his name will be Emanuel: God is with us.

34 Allcluia (Richard Lloyd)
© 1995 Kevin Mayhew Ltd.

Speak, Lord, your servant is listening:
you have the message of eternal life.
or
The Word was made flesh
and lived among us;
to all who did accept him
he gave power to become children of God.

35 Scottish Alleluia (Frances M. Kelly)

Praise to you, Lord Jesus Christ!
Alleluia! You bring us healing!

Other texts may be substituted for 'You bring us healing!' to reflect the gospel reading:

Light for our darkness!
Way to the Father!
Shepherd eternal!
Strength in our weakness!
Word here among us!

36 Irish Alleluia (Traditional)

This may be sung unaccompanied as a round.

37 Celtic Alleluia (Fintan O'Carroll)

38 Eightfold Alleluia (Unknown)

39 Easter Alleluia (Plainsong)

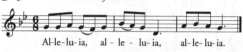

40 Alleluia 7 (Jaques Berthier)

41 Alleluia (Malcolm Archer)

42 Alleluia (Plainsong)

43 Alleluia (Andrew Moore No. 1)

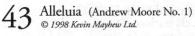

Al-le-lu-ia, al-le-lu-ia, al-le-lu-ia.

44 Alleluia (Andrew Moore No. 2)

Al-le-lu-ia, al-le-lu-ia, al-le-lu-ia.

45 Alleluia (Estelle White)

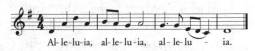

Al-le-lu-ia. (Al-le-lu-ia.)

Your word is true, help us to listen, Lord.

46 Alleluia (Andrew Moore No. 3)

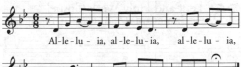

Al-le-lu-ia, al-le-lu-ia, al-le-lu-ia,

al-le-lu-ia, al-le-lu-ia, al-le-lu-ia.

47 Alleluia (Laurence Bevenot)

Al-le-lu-ia, al-le-lu-ia,

al-le-lu-ia.

48 Alleluia (Damian Lundy)

Al-le-lu-ia, al-le-lu-ia,

al-le-lu-ia.

Easter

Lord Jesus, you are risen from the dead:
you are our companion on the road of life,
and we know you in the breaking of the
bread.

Advent and Christmas

Lord Jesus, Word of God made man for us,
you reveal your glory to our broken world,
and we worship you. Come again in glory!

Pentecost

Lord Jesus, you are at the Father's side:
you have sent your Spirit to renew our joy,
and we praise you. Come again in glory!

49 Alleluia! Magnificat!

Al-le-lu-ia, al-le-lu-ia! Al-le-lu-
ia, al-le-lu-ia! Al-le-lu-
ia, al-le-lu-ia! Al-le-lu-ia!

50 Alleluia: We will hear your word
(Joe Wise) © GIA Publications Inc.

Al-le-lu-ia,
al-le-lu-ia,
al-le-lu-ia, al-le-
Fine
lu-ia, al-le-lu-ia.
We will hear your Word, one in love; we will
live your Word, one in love; we will
D.C.
spread your Word, one in love.

51 Halle, halle, halle (Traditional)

Hal-le, hal-le, hal - le - lu-
jah! Hal-le, hal-le, hal - le -
lu - jah! Hal-le, hal-le, hal-
- le - lu - jah! Hal-le -
lu-jah, hal-le-lu - jah!

52 Sing praises to the Lord
(Christopher Walker)

© 1985 Christopher Walker/OCP Publications

*This acclamation may be sung by a cantor
with the congregation joining in each
'alleluia', or by everyone throughout.*

1. Sing praises to the Lord, alleluia,
   Sing praise to greet the Word, alleluia.
   The Word is a sign
   of God's wisdom and love,
   alleluia, alleluia.

2. God's truth can set us free, alleluia,
   Christ Jesus is the key, alleluia.
   Our ears hear the Word,
   but it lives in our hearts,
   alleluia, alleluia.

3. We listen to your voice, alleluia,
   we praise you and rejoice, alleluia.
   Your Spirit is with us,
   she breathes in your Word:
   Alleluia, alleluia.

4. Sing Praises to the Lord, alleluia,
   sing praise to greet the Word, alleluia.
   Creator and Son with the Spirit adored:
   alleluia, alleluia.

53 Lent and Holy Week Gospel Acclamation (Damian Lundy)

© 1979 Kevin Mayhew Ltd.

Praise to you, Lord, praise to you, Lord,
praise to you, Lord.

Lord Jesus, obedient to the Father's will,
you became a slave, enduring death for us.
Now you reign as Lord. Come again in
glory!

54 Lent and Holy Week Gospel Acclamation (James Walsh)

© Rev James Walsh

Glo-ry and praise to you, O Christ!
Glo-ry and praise to you, O Christ!

55 Lent and Holy Week Gospel Acclamation (Andrew Moore)

© 1995 Kevin Mayhew Ltd.

Praise to you, O Christ,
King of e-ter-nal glo - ry!
Praise to you, O Christ,
King of e-ter-nal glo - ry!

Lent

From the bright cloud,
the Father's voice was heard:
'This is my Son, the Beloved.
Listen to him!'

Holy Week

Christ was humbler yet,
even to accepting death, death on a cross.
But God raised him high and gave him
the name which is above all names.

56 Credo 3 (Plainsong)

Cre-do in un-um De - um, Pa - trem om-ni-po-ten-tem, fac-tor-em cæ-li et ter-ræ,

vi-si-bi-li-um o - mni-um, et in-vi-si-bi - li-um. Et in u-num Do-mi-num Je-sum Chri-stum,

Fi-li-um De-i u-ni-ge-ni-tum, et ex pa-tre na - tum an-te om-ni-a sæ - cu-la. De-um de De-o,

lu-men de lu-mi-ne, De-um ve-rum de De-o ve-ro, ge-ni-tum non fa - ctum, con-sub-stan-ti-a-lem Pa-tri:

per quem om-ni-a fa-cta sunt. Qui pro-pter nos ho-mi-nes, et pro-pter nos-tram sa-lu-tem

de-scen-dit de cæ-lis. Et in-car-na-tus est de Spi-ri-tu San - cto ex Ma-ri-a Vir-gi-ne:

et ho-mo fa-ctus est. Cru-ci-fi - xus et-i-am pro no - bis sub Pon-ti-o Pi-la-to,

pas-sus et se-pul - tus est. Et re-sur-re-xit ter-ti-a di - e, se-cun-dum Scri-ptu - ras,

et as-cen-dit in cæ - lum: se-det ad dex-te-ram Pa - tris. Et i-te-rum ven-tu-rus est cum glo-ri-a,

ju-di-ca-re vi-vos et mor-tu-os: cu-jus reg-ni non e-rit fi-nis. Et in Spi-ri-tum San-ctum, Do-mi-num,

et vi-vi-fi-can-tem: qui ex Pa-tre Fi-li-o-que pro-ce-dit. Qui cum Pa-tre et Fi-li-o

si-mul a-do-ra-tur, et con-glo-ri-fi-ca-tur: qui lo-cu-tus est per Pro-phe-tas.

Et u-nam, san-ctam cath-o-li-cam et a-po-sto-li-cam Ec-cle-si-am. Con-fi-te-or un-um ba - pti-sma

in re-mis-si-o-nem pec-ca-to-rum. Et ex-spe-cto re-sur-re-cti-o-nem mor-tu-o-rum.

Et vi - tam ven-tu-ri sæ-cu - li. A - - - men.

57 Lourdes Credo (Jean-Paul Lécot)
© Jean-Paul Lécot

Cre - do, cre - do, cre - do, A - men!

I believe in God the Fa - ther, Cre - ator of heaven and earth.

I believe in Jesus his Son, who was made man, who died and rose a - gain.

I believe in the Ho - ly Spirit, who gives life to the Church.

58 We believe (Gerry Fitzpatrick)
© 1986 Kevin Mayhew Ltd.

1. Do you believe in God the Father
   almighty, creator of heav'n and earth?

After each verse the people sing:

We be-lieve, we do be-lieve.

2. Do you believe in Jesus Christ,
   his only Son, our Lord,
   who was born of the Virgin Mary,
   was crucified, died and was buried?

3. Do you believe in Jesus Christ,
   who rose from the dead,
   and is now seated
   at the right hand of the Father?

4. Do you believe in the Holy Spirit,
   the holy Catholic Church,
   the communion of saints?

5. Do you believe in the forgiveness of sins,
   the resurrection of the body,
   and the life everlasting?

59 Holy, holy, holy (James MacMillan)
© 1997 Boosey & Hawkes Music Publishers Ltd.

Ho - ly, ho - ly, ho - ly Lord, God of pow'r and might. Heav'n and earth are full of your glo - ry. Ho - san - na in the high - est. Bles - sed is he, O bles - sed is he who comes in the name of the Lord. Ho - san - na in the high - est. Ho - san - na in the high - est.

60 Holy, holy, holy (Celtic Liturgy: Christopher Walker)

1. Ho - ly, ho - ly, ho - ly Lord, God of pow-er and might,

heav-en and earth are full of your glo-ry. Ho-san-na, ho-san-na in the

high-est. 2. Bles-sed is he who comes in the name of the Lord. Ho-

san-na in the high-est, ho-san-na in the high-est.

61 Sanctus (Noel Donnelly)

Ho - ly, ho - ly, ho - ly Lord, God of pow'r and might, heav-en and earth are

full of your glo-ry. Ho san - na in the high - est. Bles-sed is he who

comes in the name of the Lord. Ho - san - na in the high - est.

62 Holy, holy, holy (Deutsche Messe: Franz Schubert)

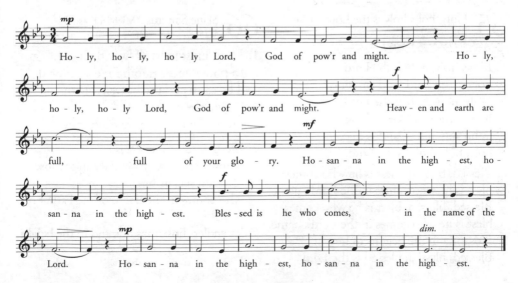

Ho - ly, ho - ly, ho - ly Lord, God of pow'r and might. Ho - ly,

ho - ly, ho - ly Lord, God of pow'r and might. Heav - en and earth are

full, full of your glo - ry. Ho - san - na in the high - est, ho -

san - na in the high - est. Bles - sed is he who comes, in the name of the

Lord. Ho - san - na in the high - est, ho - san - na in the high - est.

63 Sanctus (Taizé)
© Ateliers et Presses de Taizé

San-ctus, san-ctus, san-ctus Do-mi-nus De-us Sa-ba-oth, De-us Sa-ba-oth.

64 Lourdes Sanctus (Jean-Paul Lécot)
© 1988 Kevin Mayhew Ltd.

Refrain ... *Fine*

Ho - ly, ho - ly, ho - ly Lord, God of pow'r and might!

1. Full of your glo - ry are heav'n and earth, God of pow'r and might.

2. Bles - sed is he who comes a - mong us in the name of the Lord.

3. Ho - san - na in the high - est!

65 Holy, holy, holy is the Lord (John Ballantine)
© 1984 Kevin Mayhew Ltd.

1. Holy, holy, holy is the Lord,
   holy is the Lord God almighty!
   Holy, holy, holy is the Lord,
   holy is the Lord God almighty!
   Who was and is, and is to come;
   holy, holy, holy is the Lord.

2. Blessèd, blessèd, blest is he who comes,
   blest is he who comes in the Lord's name.
   Blessèd, blessèd, blest is he who comes,
   blest is he who comes in the Lord's name.
   Hosanna in the heights of heav'n.
   Blessèd, blessèd, blessèd is the Lord.

66 Slane Sanctus (Michael Forster)
© 1995, 1999 Kevin Mayhew Ltd.

1. Holy, most holy, all holy the Lord,
   in power and wisdom for ever adored.
   The earth and the heavens are full of
      your love;
   our joyful hosannas re-echo above.

2. Blessèd, most blessèd is he
   whose life makes us whole, and whose
      death sets us free:
   who comes in the name of the Father of
      light,
   let endless hosannas resound in the height.

67 Ash Grove Sanctus (Michael Forster)
© 1999 Kevin Mayhew Ltd.

O holy, most holy,
the God of creation,
For ever exalted
in pow'r and great might.
The earth and the heavens
are full of your glory.
Hosanna, hosanna
and praise in the height!
How blessèd is he
who is sent to redeem us,
Who puts ev'ry fear
and injustice to flight;
who comes in the name
of the Lord as our Saviour.
Hosanna, hosanna
and praise in the height!

68 Christ has died (Celtic Liturgy:
Christopher Walker)
© 1982 Christopher Walker/OCP Publications

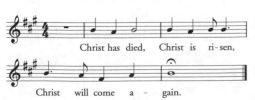

69 Christ has died (Philip Duffy)
© 1979 Philip Duffy

70 Christ has died (Noel Donnelly)
© 1986 Kevin Mayhew Ltd.

Let us proclaim the myst'ry of faith.

71 Christ has died (David Hill)
© 1999 Kevin Mayhew Ltd.

72 Christ has died (Joe Wise)
© 1970 GIA Publications Inc.

73 Dying you destroyed our death
(Philip Duffy) © 1999 Kevin Mayhew Ltd.

Dy - ing you de - stroyed our death,
ri - sing you re - stored our life. Lord
Je - sus, come in glo - ry, Lord
Je - sus, come in glo - ry.

74 When we eat this bread (Irish melody)

When we eat this bread and
drink this cup, we pro - claim your
death, Lord Je - sus, un - til you
come in glo - ry, un -
til you come in glo - ry.

75 When we eat this bread
(James MacMillan)
© 1997 Boosey & Hawkes Music Publishers Ltd.

When we eat this
bread and drink this cup we pro -
claim your death, Lord Je -
sus, un - til you come in

glo - ry, un - til you
come in glo - ry.

76 When we eat this bread (Richard Proulx)
© GIA Publications Inc.

When we eat this
bread and drink this cup, we pro -
claim your death, Lord Je - sus, un -
til you come in glo - ry.

77 Great Amen (Kevin Mayhew)
© 1986 Kevin Mayhew Ltd.

A - men, a - men,
a - men.

78 Great Amen (Jean-Paul Lécot)
© 1988 Kevin Mayhew Ltd.

Through him, with him, in him,

A - men.

in the unity of the Holy Spirit,

a - men.

All glory and honour is yours, almighty
Father, for ever and ever,

a - men.

79 Great Amen (Plainsong)

A - men.

80 Great Amen (David Hill)
© 1999 Kevin Mayhew Ltd.

A - men.

A - men.

81 Great Amen (Richard Proulx)
© GIA Publications Inc.

A - men, a -

men, a - men, a -

men.

82 Great Amen (South African) R. B. Kelly
© 1999 Kevin Mayhew Ltd.

Ho-nour and glory, a - men!

Ho-nour and glo - ry, a - men!

A - men! A - men!

Ho-nour and glo - ry, a - men!

83 Our Father (Estelle White)
© 1974 Kevin Mayhew Ltd.

Our Fa - ther, who art in hea - ven, hal - lowed be thy name; thy

king-dom come; thy will be done on earth as it is in hea - ven. Give us this day our

dai - ly bread; and for - give us our tres-pas-ses as we for-give those who tres-pass a-gainst us; and

lead us not in - to temp - ta - tion, but de - liv - er us from e - vil.

Doxology

For the king - dom, the pow'r and the glo - ry are yours, now and for e - ver.

84 Our Father (Julian Wiener)

Our Father, who art in heaven, hallowed be thy name; thy kingdom come; thy will be done on earth as it is in heaven. Give us this day our daily bread; and forgive us our trespasses as we forgive those who trespass against us; and lead us not into temptation, but deliver us from all that is evil.

Doxology

For the kingdom, the pow'r and the glory are yours, now and for ever. A - men.

85 Our Father (Rimsky-Korsakov, adapted by Joseph Gelineau and Robert B. Kelly)

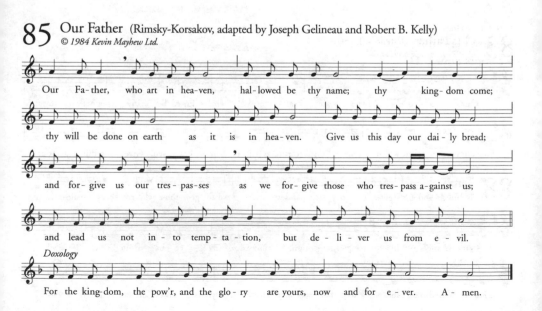

Our Father, who art in heaven, hallowed be thy name; thy kingdom come; thy will be done on earth as it is in heaven. Give us this day our daily bread; and forgive us our trespasses as we forgive those who trespass against us; and lead us not into temptation, but deliver us from evil.

Doxology

For the kingdom, the pow'r, and the glory are yours, now and for ever. A - men.

86 'Echo' Our Father (Jacqueline Emery)
© 1978 Kevin Mayhew Ltd.

The priest or cantor sings each line,
repeated by all.

Our Father,
who art in heaven,
hallowed be thy name,
hallowed be thy name;
thy kingdom come,
thy will be done
upon the earth
as it is in heav'n.
Give us this day
our daily bread
and forgive us
our trespasses,
as we forgive,
forgive those
who trespass
against us;
and lead us not
into temptation,
but deliver us
from evil.

Doxology
For the kingdom,
the pow'r and the glory
are yours now
and for ever, amen.

87 Our Father (Caribbean)

1. Our Father, who art in heaven,
   hallowed be thy name.
   Thy kingdom come, thy will be done,
   hallowed be thy name. (x2)

2. On earth as it is in heaven.
   hallowed be thy name.
   Give us this day our daily bread,
   hallowed be thy name. (x2)

3. Forgive us our trespasses,
   hallowed be thy name.
   as we forgive those who trespass against us.
   hallowed be thy name. (x2)

4. Lead us not into temptation,
   hallowed be thy name.
   but deliver us from all that is evil.
   hallowed be thy name. (x2)

Doxolgy
5. For thine is the kingdom, the power, and
       the glory,
   hallowed be thy name.
   for ever, and for ever and ever.
   hallowed be thy name. (x2)

6. Amen, amen, it shall be so.
   hallowed be thy name.
   Amen, amen, it shall be so.
   hallowed be thy name. (x2)

88 Lamb of God (Gerry Fitzpatrick)
© 1986 Kevin Mayhew Ltd.

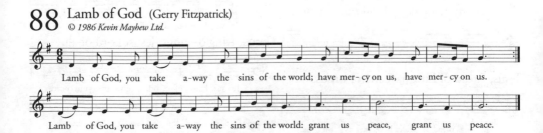

Lamb of God, you take a-way the sins of the world; have mer-cy on us, have mer-cy on us.

Lamb of God, you take a-way the sins of the world: grant us peace, grant us peace.

89 Lamb of God (Malcolm Archer)

Lamb of God, you take a-way the sins of the world: have mer - cy, have mer - cy on us. Lamb of God, you take a-way the sins of the world: grant us, grant us peace.

90 Lamb of God (Alan Rees)

Lamb of God, you take a-way the sins of the world: have mer - cy on us.

Lamb of God, you take a-way the sins of the world: grant us peace.

91 Jesus, Lamb of God (Paul Inwood)

Jesus, Lamb of God, have mercy on us.

Je - sus, Lamb of God, have mer - cy on us.

Jesus, Word made flesh, bearer of our sins:

Je - sus, Lamb of God, have mer - cy on us.

Jesus, Bread of Life, have mercy on us.

Je - sus, Bread of Life, have mer - cy on us.

Jesus, Morning Star; Jesus, Prince of Peace:

Je - sus, Bread of Life, have mer - cy on us.

Jesus, Lamb of God, have mercy on us.

Je - sus, Lamb of God, have mer - cy on us.

Jesus, King of kings; Jesus, Lord of all:

Je - sus, Lamb of God, give us your peace.

92 Jesus, Lamb of God (Philip Duffy)

Jesus, Lamb of God, have mercy on us.

Je - sus, Lamb of God, have mer-cy on us.

God's beloved Son, Saviour of us all.

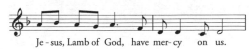

Je - sus, Lamb of God, have mer-cy on us.

Bearer of our sins, have mercy on us:

Bear-er of our sins, have mer-cy on us.

Healer of our wounds, comfort of our ills:

Bear-er of our sins, have mer-cy on us.

Jesus, Lamb of God, have mercy on us.

Je - sus, Lamb of God, have mer-cy on us.

Christ, eternal priest, Shepherd of the flock:

Je - sus, Lamb of God, have mer-cy on us.

Hope of those who fail, rest for those who toil;

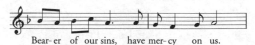

Bear-er of our sins, have mer-cy on us.

Solace of the sick, comfort in distress:

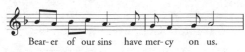

Bear-er of our sins have mer-cy on us.

Jesus, Lamb of God, give us your peace:

Je - sus, Lamb of God, give us your peace.

God's beloved Son, promise now fulfilled,

Je - sus, Lamb of God, give us your peace.

93 O Lamb of God (Michael Forster)

1. O Lamb of God, come cleanse our hearts
   and take our sin away.
   O Lamb of God, your grace impart,
   and let our guilty fear depart,
   have mercy, Lord, we pray,
   have mercy, Lord, we pray.

2. O Lamb of God, our lives restore,
   our guilty souls release.
   Into our lives your Spirit pour
   and let us live for evermore
   in perfect heav'nly peace,
   in perfect heav'nly peace.

LITURGICAL

HYMNS OLD & NEW

HYMNS AND SONGS

94
Carey Landry
© 1977 North American Liturgy Resources

Abba, Abba, Father, you are the potter,
we are the clay, the work of your hands.

1. Mould us, mould us and fashion us
   into the image of Jesus, your Son,
   of Jesus your Son.

2. Father, may we be one in you,
   as he is in you and you are in him,
   and you are in him.

3. Glory, glory and praise to you,
   glory and praise to you for ever, amen,
   for ever, amen.

95
Damian Lundy
© 1982 Kevin Mayhew Ltd.

1. Abba Father, from your hands
   the living waters flow.
   In your love you give me joy,
   joy so I may grow.
   Abba Father, from your hands
   the living waters flow.

2. Jesus, Saviour, from your wounds
   the living waters flow.
   In your love you give me peace,
   peace so I may grow.
   Jesus, Saviour, from your wounds
   the living waters flow.

3. Holy Spirit, from your pow'r
   the living waters flow.
   In your love you give me pow'r,
   pow'r so I may grow.
   Holy Spirit, from your pow'r
   the living waters flow.

4. Alleluia! From your life
   the living waters flow.
   In your love you give me joy,
   joy so I may grow.
   Alleluia! From your life
   the living waters flow.

96
Virginia Vissing
© 1974, 1998 Sisters of St Mary of Namur

1. Abba, Father, send your Spirit.
   Glory, Jesus Christ. *(Repeat)*

   Glory, hallelujah, glory, Jesus Christ!
   Glory, hallelujah, glory, Jesus Christ!

2. I will give you living water . . .

3. If you seek me you will find me . . .

4. If you listen you will hear me . . .

5. Come, my children, I will teach you . . .

6. I'm your shepherd, I will lead you . . .

7. Peace I leave you, peace I give you . . .

8. I'm your life and resurrection . . .

9. Glory, Father, glory, Spirit . . .

97
Henry Francis Lyte

1. Abide with me,
   fast falls the eventide;
   the darkness deepens;
   Lord, with me abide:
   when other helpers fail,
   and comforts flee,
   help of the helpless,
   O abide with me.

2. Swift to its close
   ebbs out life's little day;
   earth's joys grow dim,
   its glories pass away;
   change and decay
   in all around I see;
   O thou who changest not,
   abide with me.

3. I need thy presence
   ev'ry passing hour;
   what but thy grace can foil
   the tempter's pow'r?

Continued overleaf

Who like thyself my guide
and stay can be?
Through cloud and sunshine,
Lord, abide with me.

4. I fear no foe
with thee at hand to bless;
ills have no weight,
and tears no bitterness.
Where is death's sting?
Where, grave, thy victory?
I triumph still,
if thou abide with me.

5. Hold thou thy cross
before my closing eyes;
shine through the gloom,
and point me to the skies;
heav'n's morning breaks,
and earth's vain shadows flee;
in life, in death, O Lord,
abide with me.

98 14th-century Latin, trans. Ruth Fox Hume
© 1964, 1986 GIA Publications Inc.

1. A child is born in Bethlehem, alleluia,
therefore rejoice, Jerusalem, alleluia,
alleluia.

Our joyful hearts we raise.
Christ is born, O come adore him
in new-found songs of praise.

2. The babe who lies upon the straw, alleluia,
will rule the world for evermore, alleluia,
alleluia.

3. Upon this joyful holy night, alleluia,
we bless your name, O Lord of light,
alleluia, alleluia.

4. We praise you, Holy Trinity, alleluia,
adoring you eternally, alleluia,
alleluia.

99 Denis E. Hurley
© The Archdiocese of Durban, South Africa

1. Across the years there echoes still
the Baptist's bold assertion:
the call of God to change of heart,
repentance and conversion.

2. The word that John more boldly spoke
in dying, than in living,
now Christ takes up, as he proclaims
a Father all-forgiving.

3. The erring son he welcomes home
when all is spent and squandered.
He lovingly pursues the sheep
that from the flock has wandered.

4. Forgive us, Lord, all we have done
to you and one another.
So often we have gone our way,
forgetful of each other.

5. Forgetful of the cross they bear
of hunger, want, oppression –
grant, Lord, that we may make amends,
who humbly make confession.

100 John Francis Wade

1. Adeste fideles, læti triumphantes;
venite, venite in Bethlehem;
natum videte regem angelorum:

venite adoremus, venite adoremus,
venite adoremus Dominum.

2. Deum de Deo, lumen de lumine,
gestant puellæ viscera:
Deum verum, genitum, non factum:

3. Cantet nunc Io! Chorus angelorum:
cantet nunc aula cælestium;
Gloria in excelsis Deo!

4. Ergo qui natus die hodierna,
Jesu tibi sit gloria:
Patris æterni Verbum caro factum!

101 Venerable Bede, trans. 'Lutheran Book of Worship'
(1978)

1. A hymn of glory let us sing!
New hymns throughout the world
shall ring.
Alleluia! Alleluia!

Christ, by a road before untrod,
ascends unto the throne of God.

Alleluia! (x5)

2. The holy apostolic band
upon the Mount of Olives stand.
Alleluia! Alleluia!
And with his faithful followers see
their Lord ascend in majesty.

3. To whom the shining angels cry,
'Why stand and gaze upon the sky?'
Alleluia! Alleluia!
'This is the Saviour!' Thus they say,
'This is his glorious triumph day!'

4. O risen Christ, ascended Lord,
all praise to you let earth accord:
Alleluia! Alleluia!
You are, while endless ages run,
with Father and with Spirit one.

102 Hayward Osborne, based on the Canticle of Daniel
©1975 Josef Weinberger Ltd.

1. All creation, bless the Lord.
Earth and heaven, bless the Lord.
Spirits, powers, bless the Lord.
Praise him for ever.
Sun and moon, bless the Lord.
Stars and planets, bless the Lord.
Dews and showers, bless the Lord.
Praise him for ever.

2. Winds and breezes, bless the Lord.
Spring and autumn, bless the Lord.
Winter, summer, bless the Lord.
Praise him for ever.
Fire and heat, bless the Lord.
Frost and cold, bless the Lord.
Ice and snow, bless the Lord.
Praise him for ever.

3. Night and daytime, bless the Lord.
Light and darkness, bless the Lord.
Clouds and lightning, bless the Lord.
Praise him for ever.

All the earth, bless the Lord.
Hills and mountains, bless the Lord.
Trees and flowers, bless the Lord.
Praise him for ever.

4. Springs and rivers, bless the Lord.
Seas and oceans, bless the Lord.
Whales and fishes, bless the Lord.
Praise him for ever.
Birds and insects, bless the Lord.
Beasts and cattle, bless the Lord.
Let all creatures bless the Lord.
Praise him for ever.

5. Let God's people bless the Lord.
Men and women, bless the Lord.
All creation, bless the Lord.
Praise him for ever.
Let God's people bless the Lord.
Men and women, bless the Lord.
All creation, bless the Lord.
Praise him for ever.

103 William Henry Draper, alt.
© J. Curwen & Sons Ltd.

1. All creatures of our God and King,
lift up your voice and with us sing
alleluia, alleluia!
Thou burning sun with golden beam,
thou silver moon with softer gleam:

*O praise him, O praise him,
alleluia, alleluia, alleluia!*

2. Thou rushing wind that art so strong,
ye clouds that sail in heav'n along,
O praise him, alleluia!
Thou rising morn, in praise rejoice,
ye lights of evening, find a voice:

3. Thou flowing water, pure and clear,
make music for thy Lord to hear,
alleluia, alleluia!
Thou fire so masterful and bright,
that givest us both warmth and light:

Continued overleaf

4. Dear mother earth, who day by day
   unfoldest blessings on our way,
   O praise him, alleluia!
   The flow'rs and fruits that in thee grow,
   let them his glory also show.

5. All you with mercy in your heart,
   forgiving others, take your part,
   O sing ye, alleluia!
   Ye who long pain and sorrow bear,
   praise God and on him cast your care:

6. And thou, most kind and gentle death,
   waiting to hush our latest breath,
   O praise him, alleluia!
   Thou leadest home the child of God,
   and Christ our Lord the way hath trod:

7. Let all things their Creator bless,
   and worship him in humbleness,
   O praise him, alleluia!
   Praise, praise the Father, praise the Son,
   and praise the Spirit, Three in One.

104 Hubert J. Richards, based on Psalm 99
    © 1996 Kevin Mayhew Ltd.

Alleluia, alleluia. *Alleluia, alleluia.*
Alleluia, *alleluia.*

1. All the earth, sing out to the Lord.
   Serve the Lord with joy in your heart;
   come into his presence with song.

2. Come and bring your gifts to the Lord.
   Come before him, singing his praise;
   he is Lord, and he is our God.

3. God is good, his love never ends;
   he is always true to his word,
   he is faithful, age upon age.

105 Donald Fishel. © 1973 Word of God Music
    Administered by CopyCare

Alleluia, alleluia,
give thanks to the risen Lord,
alleluia, alleluia, give praise to his name.

1. Jesus is Lord of all the earth.
   He is the King of creation.

2. Spread the good news o'er all the earth.
   Jesus has died and is risen.

3. We have been crucified with Christ.
   Now we shall live for ever.

4. God has proclaimed the just reward:
   'Life for us all, alleluia!'

5. Come, let us praise the living God,
   joyfully sing to our Saviour.

106 Michael Cockett, based on Psalm 145
    © McCrimmon Publishing Co Ltd.

Alleluia, alleluia!
I will praise the Father for all of my life,
I will sing to my God as long as I live.
Alleluia, alleluia, alleluia!

1. Do not place all your trust in
   a woman or man: they cannot save.
   Their schemes will all perish
   when they yield up their breath
   at the end of their days.

2. But so happy are those who
   will trust in their God: they will find help.
   For God is the maker
   of the heavens and earth
   and of all that these hold.

3. All the searchers for justice,
   for freedom, for love, God will fulfil.
   The widow, the orphan,
   and the blind and the lame
   in his love are restored.

107 Jean-Paul Lécot, based on Psalms 110, 111, 117, 118
    © 1998 Kevin Mayhew Ltd.

Alleluia! Alleluia! Alleluia!

1. Let us sing of the Lord, alleluia!
   Let us give praise to his name for evermore.

2. We give thanks to the Lord, for he is good;
   his loving kindness endures eternally.

3. All the works of the Lord proclaim his love;
   he is the source of contentment
        for his friends.

108 Hubert J. Richards, based on Psalms 102 and 104
© 1995 Kevin Mayhew Ltd.

Alleluia, alleluia, alleluia.

1. Praise God, who forgives all our sins
   and heals us of ev'rything evil;
   he rescues our life from the grave
   and clothes us in mercy and love.

2. Our God is all kindness and love,
   so patient and rich in compassion;
   not treating us as we deserve:
   not paying us back for our sins.

3. As heaven is high over earth,
   so strong is his love for his people.
   As far as the east from the west,
   so far he removes all our sins.

4. As fathers take pity on sons,
   we know God will show us compassion;
   for he knows of what we are made:
   no more than the dust of the earth.

109 Christina Wilde, based on Luke 1:46-55
© 1999 Kevin Mayhew Ltd.

Alleluia! Alleluia! Alleluia!

1. Sing with gladness, my soul, and praise
   the Lord,
   let my spirit rejoice in God my Saviour.

2. He has honoured me in my lowliness,
   and all people to come shall call me
   blessèd.

3. The Almighty has shown his pow'r in me,
   and his mercy is known by all his people.

4. He has brought down the mighty and
   the proud,
   and exalted on high the poor and humble.

5. He has satisfied all the hungry ones,
   but has sent back the wealthy
   empty-handed.

6. He protected his servant, Israel,
   as he promised to Abraham, our father.

7. Praise the Father, the Spirit and the Son,
   God who was, who is now and ever
   shall be.

110 William Chatterton Dix

1. Alleluia, sing to Jesus,
   his the sceptre, his the throne;
   alleluia, his the triumph,
   his the victory alone:
   hark, the songs of peaceful Sion
   thunder like a mighty flood:
   Jesus, out of ev'ry nation,
   hath redeemed us by his blood.

2. Alleluia, not as orphans
   are we left in sorrow now;
   alleluia, he is near us,
   faith believes, nor questions how;
   though the cloud from sight received him
   when the forty days were o'er,
   shall our hearts forget his promise,
   'I am with you evermore'?

3. Alleluia, bread of angels,
   here on earth our food, our stay;
   alleluia, here the sinful
   come to you from day to day.
   Intercessor, friend of sinners,
   earth's redeemer, plead for me,
   where the songs of all the sinless
   sweep across the crystal sea.

4. Alleluia, King eternal,
   he the Lord of lords we own;
   alleluia, born of Mary,
   earth his footstool, heav'n his throne;
   he within the veil has entered
   robed in flesh, our great High Priest;
   he on earth both priest and victim
   in the Eucharistic Feast.

111 Mike Anderson
© 1980 Kevin Mayhew Ltd.

Alleluia (x4)

1. Thank you for fathers,
   the men on this earth!
   Thank you for mothers,
   who gave us our birth!

Continued overleaf

Thank you for children,
their smiles and their tears!
Thank you for helping us
conquer our fears!

2. Praise for the mountains,
the hills and ravines;
praise for the rivers,
the brooks and the streams;
praise for the oceans,
the sand and the sea;
praise for the natural beauties we see!

3. Sing of the blossoms
that flow'r on the trees;
sing of the wind,
and the calm and the breeze;
sing of the autumn,
and winter and spring;
sing of the sunshine
the summer will bring!

4. Thank you for giving
the life that we know!
Praise for the honesty
we all must show.
Sing against tyrants
and despots and greed.
Love be our message
and peace be our creed!

112 William John Sparrow-Simpson, alt.
© *Novello & Co. Ltd.*

1. All for Jesus! All for Jesus!
This our song shall ever be;
for we have no hope nor Saviour
if we have not hope in thee.

2. All for Jesus! thou wilt give us
strength to serve thee hour by hour;
none can move us from thy presence
while we trust thy love and pow'r.

3. All for Jesus! at thine altar
thou dost give us sweet content;
there, dear Saviour, we receive thee
in thy holy sacrament.

4. All for Jesus! thou hast loved us,
all for Jesus! thou hast died,
all for Jesus! thou art with us,
all for Jesus, glorified!

5. All for Jesus! All for Jesus!
This the Church's song shall be,
till at last the flock is gathered
one in love, and one in thee.

113 St Theodulph of Orleans,
trans. John Mason Neale

All glory, laud and honour,
to thee, Redeemer King,
to whom the lips of children
made sweet hosannas ring.

1. Thou art the King of Israel,
thou David's royal Son,
who in the Lord's name comest,
the King and blessed one.

2. The company of angels
are praising thee on high,
and mortals, joined with all things
created, make reply.

3. The people of the Hebrews
with palms before thee went:
our praise and prayer and anthems
before thee we present.

4. To thee before thy passion
they sang their hymns of praise:
to thee now high exalted
our melody we raise.

5. Thou didst accept their praises,
accept the prayers we bring,
who in all good delightest,
thou good and gracious king.

114 Damian Lundy
© *1979 Kevin Mayhew Ltd.*

All glory to you, Redeemer and Lord,
the true Son of God.

1. Lord Jesus Christ, to you be glory,
alleluia.
For you reign with your Father,
alleluia.

2. Lord Jesus Christ, to you be glory . . .
   You were born of the virgin . . .

3. Lord Jesus Christ, to you be glory . . .
   You fought evil and conquered . . .

4. Lord Jesus Christ, to you be glory . . .
   Risen Lord, we acclaim you . . .

5. Lord Jesus Christ, to you be glory . . .
   You have ransomed God's people . . .

6. Lord Jesus Christ, to you be glory . . .
   You have made us God's children . . .

7. Lord Jesus Christ, to you be glory . . .
   Lead us all to your kingdom . . .

115
Peter Watcyn-Jones
© 1978, 1999 Kevin Mayhew Ltd.

1. All God's people, here together,
   worship the King!
   For his love will last for ever,
   worship the King!
   Through life's struggles he'll be with us,
   he'll be guiding, watching o'er us.
   We rejoice, sing hallelujah,
   worship the King!

2. All God's people, pray together,
   peace to the world,
   loving brother, loving sister,
   peace to the world!
   God is love and God is kindness,
   he will guide us through the darkness.
   We rejoice, sing hallelujah,
   peace to the world.

3. All God's people, love each other,
   glory to God!
   Though we die we live for ever,
   glory to God!
   We will enter life eternal,
   chosen, blessed, for ever praising.
   We rejoice, sing hallelujah,
   glory to God!

116
Edward Perronet, adapted by Michael Forster
© 1999 Kevin Mayhew Ltd.

1. All hail the pow'r of Jesus' name,
   let angels prostrate fall;
   bring forth the royal diadem

   and crown him, crown him, crown him,
   crown him Lord of all.

2. Crown him, all martyrs of your God,
   who from his altar call;
   praise him whose way of pain you trod,
   and crown him . . .

3. O prophets faithful to his word,
   in matters great and small,
   who made his voice of justice heard,
   now crown him . . .

4. All sinners, now redeemed by grace,
   who heard your Saviour's call,
   now robed in light before his face,
   O crown him . . .

5. Let every tribe and every race
   who heard the freedom call,
   in liberation, see Christ's face,
   and crown him . . .

6. Let every people, every tongue
   to him their heart enthral:
   lift high the universal song
   and crown him . . .

117
Tricia Richards
© 1987 Kingsway's Thankyou Music

1. All heav'n declares
   the glory of the risen Lord.
   Who can compare
   with the beauty of the Lord?
   For ever he will be
   the Lamb upon the throne.
   I gladly bow the knee
   and worship him alone.

2. I will proclaim
   the glory of the risen Lord.
   Who once was slain
   to reconcile us all to God.

Continued overleaf

For ever you will be
the Lamb upon the throne.
I gladly bow the knee
and worship you alone.

118 Graham Kendrick, based on Philippians 3:8-12
©1993 *Make Way Music*

1. All I once held dear, built my life upon,
   all this world reveres, and wars to own,
   all I once thought gain I have
       counted loss;
   spent and worthless now, compared
       to this.

   Knowing you, Jesus, knowing you,
   there is no greater thing.
   You're my all, you're the best,
   you're my joy, my righteousness,
   and I love you, Lord.

2. Now my heart's desire is to know
       you more,
   to be found in you and known as yours.
   To possess by faith what I could not earn,
   all-surpassing gift of righteousness.

3. Oh, to know the pow'r of your risen life,
   and to know you in your sufferings.
   To become like you in your death,
       my Lord,
   so with you to live and never die.

119 Robert Bridges, based on 'Meine Hoffnung stehet
feste' by Joachim Neander
© *Oxford University Press*

1. All my hope on God is founded;
   he doth still my trust renew.
   Me through change and chance
       he guideth,
   only good and only true.
   God unknown, he alone
   calls my heart to be his own.

2. Human pride and earthly glory,
   sword and crown betray his trust;
   what with care and toil he buildeth,
   tow'r and temple, fall to dust.
   But God's pow'r, hour by hour,
   is my temple and my tow'r.

3. God's great goodness aye endureth,
   deep his wisdom, passing thought:
   splendour, light and life attend him,
   beauty springeth out of naught.
   Evermore, from his store,
   new-born worlds rise and adore.

4. Still from earth to God eternal
   sacrifice of praise be done,
   high above all praises praising
   for the gift of Christ his Son.
   Christ doth call one and all:
   ye who follow shall not fall.

120 Roy Turner
© *1984 Kingsway's Thankyou Music*

1. All over the world the Spirit is moving,
   all over the world,
   as the prophets said it would be.
   All over the world there's a mighty
       revelation
   of the glory of the Lord,
   as the waters cover the sea.

2. All over this land the Spirit is
       moving . . .

3. All over the Church the Spirit is
       moving . . .

4. All over us all the Spirit is
       moving . . .

5. Deep down in my heart the Spirit
   is moving . . .

121

William Kethe

1. All people that on earth do dwell,
   sing to the Lord with cheerful voice;
   him serve with fear, his praise forth tell,
   come ye before him and rejoice.

2. The Lord, ye know, is God indeed,
   without our aid he did us make;
   we are his folk, he doth us feed
   and for his sheep he doth us take.

3. O enter then his gates with praise,
   approach with joy his courts unto;
   praise, laud and bless his name always,
   for it is seemly so to do.

4. For why? the Lord our God is good:
   his mercy is for ever sure;
   his truth at all times firmly stood,
   and shall from age to age endure.

5. To Father, Son and Holy Ghost,
   the God whom heav'n and earth adore,
   from us and from the angel-host
   be praise and glory evermore.

122

Sebastian Temple
© 1967 OCP Publications

1. All that I am, all that I do,
   all that I'll ever have, I offer now to you.
   Take and sanctify these gifts
   for your honour, Lord.
   Knowing that I love and serve you
   is enough reward.
   All that I am, all that I do,
   all that I'll ever have I offer now to you.

2. All that I dream, all that I pray,
   all that I'll ever make I give to you today.
   Take and sanctify these gifts
   for your honour, Lord.
   Knowing that I love and serve you
   is enough reward.
   All that I am, all that I do,
   all that I'll ever have I offer now to you.

123

Lucien Deiss, based on Psalm 99
© 1965 World Library Publications

All the earth proclaim the Lord,
sing your praise to God.

1. Serve you the Lord,
   heart filled with gladness.
   Come into his presence, singing for joy.

2. Know that the Lord is our creator.
   Yes, he is our Father, we are his own.

3. We are the sheep of his green pasture,
   for we are his people; he is our God.

4. Enter his gates bringing thanksgiving.
   O enter his courts while singing his praise.

5. Our Lord is good, his love enduring,
   his Word is abiding now with us all.

6. Honour and praise be to the Father,
   the Son, and the Spirit, world without end.

124

Susan Sayers, based on Psalm 97
© 1995 Kevin Mayhew Ltd.

All the ends of the earth have seen
the salvation of our God.

1. Let us sing a new song to the Lord
   for the wonderful things he has done;
   by his holy and powerful arm,
   his salvation is brought to us all.

2. His salvation is known on the earth,
   all the nations can see he is just;
   he will never neglect to be true
   to the people he knows as his own.

3. Ev'ry part of creation has seen
   the salvation our God has bestowed.
   Let the earth shout aloud to our God,
   and the universe ring with delight.

4. O sing songs to our God with the harp,
   and with music sing praise to the Lord;
   let the horn and the trumpet give voice,
   we acknowledge the Lord who is King.

125 Cecil Frances Alexander

All things bright and beautiful,
all creatures great and small,
all things wise and wonderful,
the Lord God made them all.

1. Each little flow'r that opens,
   each little bird that sings,
   he made their glowing colours,
   he made their tiny wings.

2. The purple-headed mountain,
   the river running by,
   the sunset and the morning
   that brightens up the sky.

3. The cold wind in the winter,
   the pleasant summer sun,
   the ripe fruits in the garden,
   he made them every one.

4. The tall trees in the greenwood,
   the meadows for our play,
   the rushes by the water,
   to gather ev'ry day.

5. He gave us eyes to see them,
   and lips that we might tell
   how great is God Almighty.
   who has made all things well.

126 Lucien Deiss, based on Psalm 65
© 1965 World Library Publications Inc.

All you nations,
sing out your joy to the Lord;
alleluia, alleluia.

1. Joyfully shout, all you on earth,
   give praise to the glory of God;
   and with a hymn
   sing out his glorious praise; alleluia!

2. Lift up your hearts, sing to your God:
   tremendous his deeds on the earth!
   Vanquished your foes,
   struck down by power and might; alleluia!

3. Let all the earth kneel in his sight,
   extolling his marvellous fame;
   honour his name,
   in highest heaven give praise; alleluia!

4. Come forth and see all the great works
   that God has brought forth by his might;
   fall on your knees
   before his glorious throne; alleluia!

5. Parting the seas with might and power,
   he rescued his people from shame;
   let us give thanks
   for all his merciful deeds; alleluia!

6. His eyes keep watch on all the earth,
   his strength is forever renewed;
   and let no one rebel
   against his commands; alleluia!

7. Tested are we by God the Lord,
   as silver is tested by fire;
   burdened with pain,
   we fall ensnared in our sins; alleluia!

8. Over our heads wicked ones rode,
   we passed through the fire and the flood;
   then, Lord, you brought
   your people into your peace; alleluia!

9. Glory and thanks be to the Father;
   honour and praise to the Son;
   and to the Spirit,
   source of life and of love; alleluia!

127 18th century-Latin, trans. Edward Caswall, alt.
© 1999 Kevin Mayhew Ltd.

1. All you who seek a comfort sure
   in trouble and distress,
   whatever sorrow vex the mind,
   or guilt the soul oppress.

2. Jesus, who gave himself for you
   upon the cross to die,
   opens to you his sacred heart;
   O, to that heart draw nigh.

3. You hear how kindly he invites;
   you hear his words so blest:
   'All you that labour, come to me,
   and I will give you rest.'

4. What meeker than the Saviour's heart?
   As on the cross he lay,
   it did his murderers forgive,
   and for their pardon pray.

5. Jesus, the joy of saints on high,
   the hope of sinners here,
   attracted by those loving words
   to you I lift my prayer.

6. Wash then my wounds in that dear blood
   which forth from you does flow;
   by grace a better hope inspire,
   and risen life bestow.

128 Hermann the Lame

Alma redemptoris mater,
quæ pervia cæli porta manes,
et stella maris, succurre cadenti,
surgere qui curat populo:
tu quæ genuisti, natura mirante,
tuum sanctum Genitorem:
virgo prius ac posterius,
Gabrielis ab ore sumens illud Ave,
peccatorum miserere.

129 Vincent Stuckey Stratton Coles, alt. Michael Forster. © 1999 Kevin Mayhew Ltd.

1. Almighty Father, Lord most high,
   creating all, and filling all,
   your name we praise and magnify,
   for all our needs on you we call.

2. We offer to you of your own,
   ourselves and all that we can bring,
   in bread and cup before you shown,
   our universal offering.

3. Were we to offer all we own,
   our wealth combined could not suffice.
   Yet all has value through your love
   and Christ's atoning sacrifice.

4. By this command in bread and cup,
   his body and his blood we plead;
   what on the cross he offered up
   is here our sacrifice indeed.

5. For all your gifts of life and grace,
   here we your servants humbly pray
   that you would look upon the face
   of your anointed Son today.

130 Unknown, alt.

1. Almighty Father, take this bread
   thy people offer thee;
   where sins divide us, take instead
   one fold and family.

2. The wine we offer soon will be
   Christ's blood, redemption's price;
   receive it, Holy Trinity,
   this holy sacrifice.

3. O God, by angels' choirs adored,
   thy name be praised on earth;
   on all may be that peace outpoured
   once promised at his birth.

131 vs 1-4 John Newton, alt.; v 5 John Rees

1. Amazing grace! How sweet the sound
   that saved a wretch like me.
   I once was lost, but now I'm found;
   was blind, but now I see.

2. 'Twas grace that taught my heart to fear,
   and grace my fears relieved.
   How precious did that grace appear
   the hour I first believed.

3. Through many dangers, toils and snares
   I have already come.
   'Tis grace that brought me safe thus far,
   and grace will lead me home.

Continued overleaf

4. The Lord has promised good to me,
   his word my hope secures;
   he will my shield and portion be
   as long as life endures.

5. When we've been there a thousand years,
   bright shining as the sun,
   we've no less days to sing God's praise
   than when we first begun.

132 William Blake

1. And did those feet in ancient time
   walk upon England's mountains green?
   And was the holy Lamb of God
   on England's pleasant pastures seen?
   And did the countenance divine
   shine forth upon our clouded hills?
   And was Jerusalem builded here
   among those dark satanic mills?

2. Bring me my bow of burning gold!
   Bring me my arrows of desire!
   Bring me my spear! O clouds unfold!
   Bring me my chariot of fire!
   I will not cease from mental fight,
   nor shall my sword sleep in my hand,
   till we have built Jerusalem
   in England's green and pleasant land.

133 v 1 unknown, based on John 13:34-35; vs 2-4 Aniceto Nazareth, based on John 15 and 1 Cor. 13
© 1984, 1999 Kevin Mayhew Ltd.

A new commandment I give unto you:
that you love one another as I have loved you,
that you love one another as I have loved you.

1. By this shall all know
   that you are my disciples
   if you have love one for another. *(Repeat)*

2. You are my friends
   if you do what I command you.
   Without my help you can do nothing.
   (Repeat)

3. I am the true vine,
   my Father is the gard'ner.
   Abide in me: I will be with you. *(Repeat)*

4. True love is patient,
   not arrogant nor boastful;
   love bears all things, love is eternal.
   (Repeat)

134 James Chadwick

1. Angels we have heard in heaven
   sweetly singing o'er our plains;
   and the mountain tops in answer
   echoing their joyous strains.

   Gloria in excelsis Deo.

2. Shepherds, why this exultation?
   Why your rapturous strain prolong?
   Tell us of the gladsome tidings
   which inspire your joyous song.

3. Come to Bethlehem, and see him
   o'er whose birth the angels sing:
   come, adore, devoutly kneeling,
   Christ the Lord, the new-born King.

4. See him in a manger lying
   whom the choir of angels praise!
   Mary, Joseph, come to aid us
   while our hearts in love we raise.

135 James Chadwick

1. Angels we have heard on high
   sweetly singing o'er our plains,
   and the mountains in reply
   echo still their joyous strains.

   Gloria in excelsis Deo.

2. Shepherds, why this jubilee?
   Why your rapturous strain prolong?
   Say, what may your tidings be,
   which inspire your heavenly song.

3. Come to Bethlehem and see
   him whose birth the angels sing:
   come, adore on bended knee
   th'infant Christ, the new-born King.

4. See within a manger laid,
   Jesus, Lord of heav'n and earth!
   Mary, Joseph, lend your aid
   to celebrate our Saviour's birth.

136
Vorreformatorisch (Cologne 1599),
cento paraphrased by Anthony G. Petti

1. A noble flow'r of Judah
   from tender roots has sprung,
   a rose from stem of Jesse,
   as prophets long had sung;
   a blossom fair and bright,
   that in the midst of winter
   will change to dawn our night.

2. The rose of grace and beauty
   of which Isaiah sings
   is Mary, virgin mother,
   and Christ the flow'r she brings.
   By God's divine decree
   she bore our loving Saviour
   who died to set us free.

3. To Mary, dearest mother,
   with fervent hearts we pray:
   grant that your tender infant
   will cast our sins away,
   and guide us with his love
   that we shall ever serve him
   and live with him above.

137
Psalm 99, Grail translation
© The Grail, England

Arise, come to your God,
sing him your songs of rejoicing!

1. Cry out with joy to the Lord,
      all the earth.
   Serve the Lord with gladness.
   Come before him, singing for joy.

2. Know that he, the Lord, is God.
   He made us, we belong to him,
   we are his people, the sheep of his flock.

3. Go within his gates, giving thanks.
   Enter his courts with songs of praise.
   Give thanks to him and bless his name.

4. Indeed, how good is the Lord,
   eternal his merciful love;
   he is faithful from age to age.

5. Give glory to the Father Almighty,
   to his Son, Jesus Christ, the Lord,
   to the Spirit who dwells in our hearts.

138
Michael Forster, based on Isaiah 60:1-6
© 1993 Kevin Mayhew Ltd.

1. Arise to greet the Lord of light,
   you people of his choice.
   In uncreated glory bright,
   he bursts upon our inward sight.
   And bids the heart rejoice,
   and bids the heart rejoice!

2. Towards his light shall kings be drawn
   this majesty to see;
   and in the brightness of the dawn
   shall see the world in hope reborn,
   in justice full and free,
   in justice full and free.

3. The holy light in Judah's skies
   calls sages from afar.
   The hope of kings they recognise
   which, in the virgin mother's eyes,
   outshines the guiding star,
   outshines the guiding star.

4. This majesty for long concealed
   from longing human sight,
   in Jesus Christ is now revealed,
   and God's eternal promise sealed
   in love's unending light,
   in love's unending light.

139

Estelle White
© 1976, 1999 Kevin Mayhew Ltd.

1. As bread my Lord comes to me,
   though I am unworthy.
   He heals me, body and soul,
   and sets my spirit free.

   For he is my Saviour and my God:
   yes, he is my Saviour and my God.

2. I am far nearer to him
   than the air I breathe.
   With joy I welcome him home;
   he satisfies my heart's need.

3. The still, small voice that I hear,
   always is reminding
   my soul of love and of peace,
   that passes understanding.

140

Anne Conway, based on Isaiah 55
© 1984 Kevin Mayhew Ltd.

1. As earth that is dry
   and parched in the sun
   lies waiting for rain,
   my soul is a desert,
   arid and waste;
   it longs for your word, O Lord.

   Come to the waters, all you who thirst,
   come, now, and eat my bread.

2. Though you have no money,
   come, buy my corn
   and drink my red wine.
   Why spend precious gold
   on what will not last?
   Hear me, and your soul will live.

3. As one on a journey
   strays from the road
   and falls in the dark,
   my mind is a wand'rer,
   choosing wrong paths
   and longing to find a star.

4. The Lord is your light,
   the Lord is your strength,
   turn back to him now,
   for his ways are not
   the ways you would choose,
   and his thoughts are always new.

5. As rain from the mountains
   falls on the land
   and brings forth the seed,
   the word of the Lord
   sinks deep in our hearts,
   creating the flow'r of truth.

141

Maria Parkinson
© 1978 Kevin Mayhew Ltd.

1. As I kneel before you,
   as I bow my head in prayer,
   take this day, make it yours
   and fill me with your love.

   Ave, Maria, gratia plena,
   Dominus tecum, benedicta tu.

2. All I have I give you,
   ev'ry dream and wish are yours;
   mother of Christ, mother of mine,
   present them to my Lord.

3. As I kneel before you,
   and I see your smiling face,
   ev'ry thought, ev'ry word
   is lost in your embrace.

142

Martin Nystrom, based on Psalm 42:1-2
© 1983 Restoration Music Ltd.
Administered by Sovereign Music UK

1. As the deer pants for the water,
   so my soul longs after you.
   You alone are my heart's desire
   and I long to worship you.

   You alone are my strength, my shield,
   to you alone may my spirit yield.
   You alone are my heart's desire
   and I long to worship you.

2. I want you more than gold or silver,
   only you can satisfy.
   You alone are the real joy-giver
   and the apple of my eye.

3. You're my friend and you are my brother,
   even though you are a king.
   I love you more than any other,
   so much more than anything.

143

John Daniels
© 1979 Word's Spirit of Praise Music
Administered by CopyCare

As we are gathered, Jesus is here;
one with each other, Jesus is here;
joined by the Spirit, washed in the blood,
part of the body, the church of God.
As we are gathered, Jesus is here;
one with each other, Jesus is here.

144

William Chatterton Dix

1. As with gladness men of old
   did the guiding star behold,
   as with joy they hailed its light,
   leading onward, beaming bright;
   so, most gracious Lord, may we
   evermore be led to thee.

2. As with joyful steps they sped,
   to that lowly manger-bed,
   there to bend the knee before
   him whom heav'n and earth adore,
   so may we with willing feet
   ever seek thy mercy-seat.

3. As their precious gifts they laid,
   at thy manger roughly made,
   so may we with holy joy,
   pure, and free from sin's alloy,
   all our costliest treasures bring,
   Christ, to thee our heav'nly King.

4. Holy Jesu, ev'ry day
   keep us in the narrow way;
   and, when earthly things are past,
   bring our ransomed souls at last
   where they need no star to guide,
   where no clouds thy glory hide.

5. In the heav'nly country bright
   need they no created light,
   thou its light, its joy, its crown,
   thou its sun which goes not down;
   there for ever may we sing
   alleluias to our King.

145

Jacopone da Todi, trans. Edward Caswall

1. At the cross her station keeping,
   stood the mournful mother weeping,
   close to Jesus to the last.

2. Through her heart, his sorrow sharing,
   all his bitter anguish bearing,
   now at length the sword has passed.

3. O, how sad and sore distressed
   was that mother highly blest,
   of the sole-begotten One.

4. Christ above in torment hangs;
   she beneath beholds the pangs
   of her dying glorious Son.

5. Is there one who would not weep,
   whelmed in miseries so deep,
   Christ's dear mother to behold?

6. Can the human heart refrain
   from partaking in her pain,
   in that mother's pain untold?

7. Bruised, derided, cursed, defiled,
   she beheld her tender child,
   all with bloody scourges rent.

8. For the sins of his own nation,
   saw him hang in desolation,
   till his spirit forth he sent.

9. O thou mother! Fount of love!
   Touch my spirit from above,
   make my heart with thine accord.

10. Make me feel as thou hast felt;
    make my soul to glow and melt
    with the love of Christ my Lord.

11. Holy Mother, pierce me through,
    in my heart each wound renew
    of my Saviour crucified.

12. Let me share with thee his pain
    who for all my sins was slain,
    who for me in torments died.

Continued overleaf

13. Let me mingle tears with thee,
    mourning him who mourned for me,
    all the days that I may live.

14. By the cross with thee to stay,
    there with thee to weep and pray,
    this I ask of thee to give.

146 'Ad regias Agni dapes', trans. Robert Campbell

1. At the Lamb's high feast we sing
   praise to our victorious King,
   who hath washed us in the tide
   flowing from his piercèd side;
   praise we him, whose love divine
   gives his sacred blood for wine,
   gives his body for the feast,
   Christ the victim, Christ the priest.

2. Where the paschal blood is poured,
   death's dark angel sheathes his sword;
   faithful hosts triumphant go
   through the wave that drowns the foe.
   Praise we Christ, whose blood was shed,
   paschal victim, paschal bread;
   with sincerity and love
   eat we manna from above.

3. Mighty victim from above,
   conqu'ring by the pow'r of love;
   thou hast triumphed in the fight,
   thou hast brought us life and light.
   Now no more can death appal,
   now no more the grave enthral:
   thou hast opened paradise,
   and in thee thy saints shall rise.

4. Easter triumph, Easter joy,
   nothing now can this destroy;
   from sin's pow'r do thou set free
   souls new-born, O Lord, in thee.
   Hymns of glory and of praise,
   risen Lord, to thee we raise;
   holy Father, praise to thee,
   with the Spirit, ever be.

147 Caroline Maria Noel

1. At the name of Jesus
   ev'ry knee shall bow,
   ev'ry tongue confess him
   King of glory now;
   'tis the Father's pleasure
   we should call him Lord,
   who, from the beginning,
   was the mighty Word.

2. At his voice creation
   sprang at once to sight,
   all the angels' faces,
   all the hosts of light,
   thrones and dominations,
   stars upon their way,
   all the heav'nly orders
   in their great array.

3. Humbled for a season,
   to receive a name
   from the lips of sinners
   unto whom he came,
   faithfully he bore it,
   spotless to the last,
   brought it back victorious
   when from death he passed.

4. Bore it up triumphant
   with its human light,
   through all ranks of creatures
   to the central height,
   to the throne of Godhead,
   to the Father's breast,
   filled it with the glory
   of that perfect rest.

5. In your hearts enthrone him;
   there let him subdue
   all that is not holy,
   all that is not true;
   crown him as your captain
   in temptation's hour;
   let his will enfold you
   in its light and pow'r.

6. Truly, this Lord Jesus
shall return again,
with his Father's glory,
with his angel train;
for all wreaths of empire
meet upon his brow,
and our hearts confess him
King of glory now.

148
Michael Forster
© 1992 Kevin Mayhew Ltd.

1. At your feet, great God, we offer
bread, the sign of hope we share;
all the fullness of creation
in the feast that you prepare.
Christ our host, in risen splendour,
gives us food beyond compare.

2. Now, in humble adoration,
drawn by grace, we offer here
wine that speaks of love's oblation,
life from death and hope from fear.
Sharing in his cup of sorrow,
our Redeemer we revere.

3. Here, most holy God, we offer,
with the saints in full accord,
hearts and gifts for your acceptance,
broken dreams to be restored.
All creation cries for healing;
you alone such grace afford!

149
'Sister M'

1. Ave Maria, O maiden, O mother,
fondly thy children are calling on thee;
thine are the graces unclaimed by another,
sinless and beautiful star of the sea.

Mater amabilis, ora pro nobis,
pray for thy children who call upon thee,
ave sanctissima, ave purissima,
sinless and beautiful star of the sea.

2. Ave Maria, the night shades are falling,
softly, our voices arise unto thee;
earth's lonely exiles for succour are calling,
sinless and beautiful star of the sea.

3. Ave Maria, thy children are kneeling,
words of endearment are murmured
to thee;
softly thy spirit upon us is stealing,
sinless and beautiful star of the sea.

150
Unknown, 12th century

Ave, Regina cælorum!
Ave, Domina angelorum!
Salve radix, salve porta,
ex qua mundo lux est orta.
Gaude Virgo gloriosa,
super omnes speciosa:
vale, o valde decora,
et pro nobis Christum exora.

151
Traditional

Ave verum corpus, natum ex Maria virgine;
vere passum, immolatum in cruce
pro homine.
Cujus latus perforatum unda fluxit
et sanguine;
esto nobis prægustatum mortis in examine.
O Jesu dulcis! O Jesu pie! O Jesu fili Mariae.

152
Marty Haugen
© 1983 GIA Publications Inc.

1. Awake, awake and greet the new morn,
for angels herald its dawning,
sing out your joy, for now he is born,
behold, the child of our longing.
Come as a baby weak and poor,
to bring all hearts together,
he opens wide the heav'nly door
and lives now inside us for ever.

2. To us, to all in sorrow and fear,
Emmanuel comes a-singing,
his humble song is quiet and near,
yet fills the earth with its ringing;
music to heal the broken soul
and hymn of loving kindness,
the thunder of his anthems roll
to shatter all hatred and blindness.

Continued overleaf

3. In darkest night his coming shall be,
   when all the world is despairing,
   as morning light so quiet and free,
   so warm and gentle and caring.
   Then shall the mute break forth in song,
   the lame shall leap in wonder,
   the weak be raised above the strong,
   and weapons be broken asunder.

4. Rejoice, rejoice, take heart in the night,
   though dark the winter and cheerless,
   the rising sun shall crown you with light,
   be strong and loving and fearless;
   love be our song and love our prayer,
   and love our endless story,
   may God fill ev'ry day we share,
   and bring us at last into glory.

153 John Raphael Peacey, based on Ephesians 5:6-20
© Revd M. J. Hancock

1. Awake, awake: fling off the night!
   for God has sent his glorious light;
   and we who live in Christ's new day
   must works of darkness put away.

2. Awake and rise, in Christ renewed,
   and with the Spirit's pow'r endued.
   The light of life in us must glow,
   and fruits of truth and goodness show.

3. Let in the light; all sin expose
   to Christ, whose life no darkness knows.
   Before his cross for guidance kneel;
   his light will judge and, judging, heal.

4. Awake, and rise up from the dead,
   and Christ his light on you will shed.
   Its pow'r will wrong desires destroy,
   and your whole nature fill with joy.

5. Then sing for joy, and use each day;
   give thanks for everything alway.
   Lift up your hearts; with one accord
   praise God through Jesus Christ our Lord.

154 Dan Schutte
© 1981 Daniel L. Schutte and New Dawn Music

1. Awake from your slumber!
   Arise from your sleep!
   A new day is dawning
   for all those who weep.
   The people in darkness
   have seen a great light.
   The Lord of our longing
   has conquered the night.

   Let us build the city of God,
   may our tears be turned into dancing!
   For the Lord, our light and our love,
   has turned the night into day.

2. We are sons of the morning,
   we are daughters of day.
   The one who has loved us
   has brightened our way.
   The Lord of all kindness
   has called us to be
   a light for his people
   to set their hearts free.

3. God is light; in him there is no darkness.
   Let us walk in his light,
   his children, one and all.
   O comfort my people,
   make gentle your words.
   Proclaim to my city
   the day of her birth.

4. O city of gladness,
   now lift up your voice!
   Proclaim the good tidings
   that all may rejoice!

155 Original text: William James Kirkpatrick
Alternative text (vs 2 and 3): Michael Forster
Alternative verses © 1996 Kevin Mayhew Ltd.

1. Away in a manger, no crib for a bed,
   the little Lord Jesus laid down his
        sweet head.
   The stars in the bright sky
   looked down where he lay,
   the little Lord Jesus,
   asleep on the hay.

2. The cattle are lowing, the baby awakes,
but little Lord Jesus no crying he makes.
I love thee, Lord Jesus!
Look down from the sky,
and stay by my side
until morning is nigh.

3. Be near me Lord Jesus; I ask thee to stay
close by me for ever, and love me, I pray.
Bless all the dear children
in thy tender care,
and fit us for heaven,
to live with thee there.

Alternative version:

1. Away in a manger, no crib for a bed,
the little Lord Jesus laid down his
   sweet head.
The stars in the bright sky
looked down where he lay,
the little Lord Jesus,
asleep on the hay.

2. The cattle are lowing, they also adore
the little Lord Jesus who lies on the straw.
I love you, Lord Jesus,
I know you are near
to love and protect me
till morning is here.

3. Be near me, Lord Jesus; I ask you to stay
close by me for ever, and love me, I pray.
Bless all the dear children
in your tender care,
prepare us for heaven,
to live with you there.

156 'Simphonia Sirenum', trans. Ronald Arbuthnott Knox. © *Burns and Oates Ltd.*

1. Battle is o'er, hell's armies flee:
raise we the cry of victory
with abounding joy resounding,
alleluia, alleluia.

2. Christ who endured the shameful tree,
o'er death triumphant welcome we,
our adoring praise outpouring,
alleluia, alleluia.

3. On the third morn from death rose he,
clothed with what light in heav'n shall be,
our unswerving faith deserving,
alleluia, alleluia.

4. Hell's gloomy gates yield up their key,
paradise door thrown wide we see;
never-tiring be our choiring,
alleluia, alleluia.

5. Lord, by the stripes men laid on thee,
grant us to live from death set free,
this our greeting still repeating,
alleluia, alleluia.

157 Graham Kendrick © *1993 Make Way Music*

1. Beauty for brokenness, hope for despair,
Lord, in the suff'ring, this is our prayer:
bread for the children, justice, joy, peace,
sunrise to sunset your kingdom increase.

God of the poor, friend of the weak,
give us compassion we pray;
melt our cold hearts, let tears fall like rain,
come, change our love from a spark to a flame.

2. Shelter for fragile lives, cures for their ills,
work for the craftsmen, trade for
   their skills.
Land for the dispossessed, rights for
   the weak,
voices to plead the cause of those who
   can't speak.

3. Refuge from cruel wars, havens from fear,
cities for sanctu'ry, freedoms to share.
Peace to the killing fields, scorched earth
   to green,
Christ for the bitterness, his cross for pain.

4. Rest for the ravaged earth,
   oceans and streams,
plundered and poisoned, our future,
   our dreams.
Lord, end our madness, carelessness, greed;
make us content with the things that
   we need.

Continued overleaf

5. Lighten our darkness, breathe on this
   flame,
   until your justice burns brightly again;
   until the nations learn of your ways,
   seek your salvation and bring you
     their praise.

158
W. R. Lawrence, based on Matthew. 5:3-12
© 1988 Kevin Mayhew Ltd.

Be blessed, pure of heart,
you will see your God.

1. The poor in spirit will be blessed;
   it is to them that God's kingdom belongs.

2. The meek and patient will be blessed;
   they will succeed and inherit the earth.

3. All those who suffer will be blessed;
   they will be comforted in their distress.

4. All those who thirst for what is right
   will be blessed and be given their fill.

5. The merciful will all be blessed;
   they will have mercy and love shown
     to them.

6. The clean of heart will all be blessed;
   they will be given the vision of God.

7. Those making peace will all be blessed;
   they will be known as the children of God.

8. Those suff'ring in the cause of right
   will all be blessed in the kingdom
     of heav'n.

159
'Te Lucis ante terminum', trans. Dom Ralph Wright.
© Dom Ralph Wright

1. Before the light of evening fades
   we pray, O Lord of all,
   that by your love we may be saved
   from ev'ry grievous fall.

2. Repel the terrors of the night
   and Satan's pow'r of guile,
   impose a calm and restful sleep
   that nothing may defile.

3. Most holy Father, grant our prayer
   through Christ your only Son,
   that in your Spirit we may live
   and praise you ever one.

160
Damian Lundy, based on Psalm 50
© 1997 Kevin Mayhew Ltd.

Behold the Lamb of God, the Holy One!
Behold the Lord who died to take our sin.

1. In your great tenderness forgive my sin.
   My guilt is known to you, my Lord!

2. My sin is constantly before my eyes,
   so wash me whiter than the snow.

3. Give me your joy and take away
     my shame,
   and fill my body with new life.

4. Create in me, O Lord, a heart renewed,
   and keep me always pure and clean.

5. Do not deprive me of your spirit, Lord,
   open my lips to sing your praise!

6. I come to offer you a sacrifice:
   the broken heart you have made new.

161
Michael Forster, based on Isaiah 11:1-10
© 1993 Kevin Mayhew Ltd.

1. Behold the Saviour of the nations
   shall spring from David's royal line,
   to rule with mercy all the peoples,
   and judge with righteousness divine!

2. He shall delight in truth and wisdom,
   with justice for the meek and poor,
   and reconcile his whole creation,
   where beasts of prey shall hunt no more.

3. Here may his word, with hope abounding,
   unite us all in peace and love,
   to live as one with all creation,
   redeemed by mercy from above.

4. Prepare the way with awe and wonder;
   salvation comes on judgement's wing,
   for God will purify his people,
   and 'Glory!' all the earth shall sing.

162
Horatius Bonar, based on 1 John 4:7

1. Beloved, let us love: for love is of God;
   in God alone love has its true abode.

2. Beloved, let us love: for those who love,
   they only, are his children from above.

3. Beloved, let us love: for love is rest,
   and those who do not love cannot
     be blessed.

4. Beloved, let us love: for love is light,
   and those who do not love still live
     in night.

5. Beloved, let us love: for only thus
   shall we see God, the Lord who first
     loved us.

163
Anne Conway
© 1984 Kevin Mayhew Ltd.

1. Be still and know I am with you,
   be still, I am the Lord.
   I will not leave you orphans,
   I leave with you my world. Be one.

2. You fear the light may be fading,
   you fear to lose your way.
   Be still, and know I am near you.
   I'll lead you to the day and the sun.

3. Be glad the day you have sorrow,
   be glad, for then you live.
   The stars shine only in darkness,
   and in your need I give my peace.

164
Unknown, based on Psalm 45

1. Be still and know that I am God. *(x3)*

2. I am the Lord that healeth thee. *(x3)*

3. In thee, O Lord, I put my trust. *(x3)*

165
David J. Evans
© 1986 Kingsway's Thankyou Music

1. Be still, for the presence of the Lord,
   the Holy One, is here.
   Come, bow before him now,
   with reverence and fear.
   In him no sin is found,
   we stand on holy ground.
   Be still, for the presence of the Lord,
   the Holy One, is here.

2. Be still, for the glory of the Lord
   is shining all around;
   he burns with holy fire,
   with splendour he is crowned.
   How awesome is the sight,
   our radiant King of light!
   Be still, for the glory of the Lord
   is shining all around.

3. Be still, for the power of the Lord
   is moving in this place;
   he comes to cleanse and heal,
   to minister his grace.
   No work too hard for him,
   in faith receive from him.
   Be still, for the power of the Lord
   is moving in this place.

166
Katherina von Schlegel, trans. Jane L. Borthwick, alt.

1. Be still, my soul: the Lord is at your side;
   bear patiently the cross of grief and pain;
   leave to your God to order and provide;
   in ev'ry change he faithful will remain.
   Be still, my soul: your best, your
     heav'nly friend,
   through thorny ways, leads to a joyful end.

2. Be still, my soul: your God will undertake
   to guide the future as he has the past.
   Your hope, your confidence let nothing
     shake,
   all now mysterious shall be clear at last.
   Be still, my soul: the tempests still obey
   his voice, who ruled them once on Galilee.

Continued overleaf

3. Be still, my soul: the hour is hastening on
when we shall be for ever with the Lord,
when disappointment, grief and fear
are gone,
sorrow forgotten, love's pure joy restored.
Be still, my soul: when change and tears
are past,
all safe and blessèd we shall meet at last.

167 'O sola magnarum urbium' by Clemens Prudentius, trans. Edward Caswall, alt. Michael Forster. © 1999 Kevin Mayhew Ltd.

1. Bethlehem, of noblest cities
none can once with you compare;
you alone the Lord from heaven
did for us incarnate bear.

2. Fairer than the sun at morning
was the star that told his birth,
to the lands their God announcing,
veiled in human form on earth.

3. Guided by its shining glory
did the eastern kings appear;
see them bend, their gifts to offer,
for a greater King is here.

4. Solemn things of mystic meaning!
incense shows God's presence here,
gold proclaims his sovereign kingship,
myrrh foreshadows death and tears.

5. Holy Jesus, in your brightness
to the gentile world displayed,
with the Father and the Spirit
endless praise to you be paid.

168 Irish 8th century, trans. Mary Byrne and Eleanor Hull. © Copyright control

1. Be thou my vision, O Lord of my heart,
naught be all else to me save that thou art;
thou my best thought in the day and
the night,
waking or sleeping, thy presence my light.

2. Be thou my wisdom, be thou my
true word,
I ever with thee and thou with me, Lord;
thou my great Father, and I thy true heir;
thou in me dwelling, and I in thy care.

3. Be thou my breastplate, my sword for
the fight,
be thou my armour, and be thou
my might,
thou my soul's shelter, and thou my
high tow'r,
raise thou me heav'nward, O Pow'r of
my pow'r.

4. Riches I need not, nor all the
world's praise,
thou mine inheritance through all my days;
thou, and thou only, the first in my heart,
high King of heaven, my treasure thou art!

5. High King of heaven, when battle is done,
grant heaven's joy to me, O bright
heav'n's sun;
Christ of my own heart, whatever befall,
still be my vision, O Ruler of all.

169 Bob Gillman © 1977 Kingsway's Thankyou Music

Bind us together, Lord,
bind us together with cords
that cannot be broken.
Bind us together, Lord,
bind us together, Lord,
bind us together in love.

1. There is only one God,
there is only one King.
There is only one Body,
that is why we sing:

2. Fit for the glory of God,
purchased by his precious Blood,
born with the right to be free:
Jesus the vict'ry has won.

3. We are the fam'ly of God,
   we are his promise divine,
   we are his chosen desire,
   we are the glorious new wine.

170 Frances Jane van Alstyne (Fanny J. Crosby)

1. Blessed assurance, Jesus is mine:
   O what a foretaste of glory divine!
   Heir of salvation, purchase of God;
   born of his Spirit, washed in his blood.

   This is my story, this is my song,
   praising my Saviour all the day long.

2. Perfect submission, perfect delight,
   visions of rapture burst on my sight;
   angels descending, bring from above
   echoes of mercy, whispers of love.

3. Perfect submission, all is at rest,
   I in my Saviour am happy and blest;
   watching and waiting, looking above,
   filled with his goodness, lost in his love.

171 Hubert J. Richards, based on Psalm 95
© *1996 Kevin Mayhew Ltd.*

Blessed be God for ever, amen. (x3)

1. Come, sing a new song to the Lord;
   come, sing to the Lord, all the earth,
   and ring out your praises to God.

2. Come, tell of all his wondrous deeds,
   come, thank him for all he has done,
   and offer your gifts to the Lord.

3. Let all creation shout for joy;
   come worship the Lord in his house,
   the Lord who made heaven and earth.

172 Michael Forster, based on Ephesians 1:3-14
© *1996 Kevin Mayhew Ltd.*

1. Bless'd be the God of Jesus Christ,
   Father of our redeeming Lord:
   he who has bless'd us by his grace
   with gifts that heav'n alone affords.

2. Chosen in Christ, by God's good will,
   before the earth was set in place,
   called to be children of his love,
   and holy stand before his face:

3. We have redemption through his blood,
   pardon by his abundant grace,
   blessing eternal from above,
   by Christ made known in time and space.

4. Wisdom and insight of our God
   make known the myst'ry of his ways;
   to him all things of heav'n and earth
   shall gather on the final day.

5. In him the gospel truth is known,
   his word of wholeness is revealed.
   All who believe and trust in him
   are with the Holy Spirit sealed.

6. This is the pledge that we receive,
   sign of redemption as his own;
   then shall the heav'ns and earth unite
   to make his praise and glory known.

173 Mike Anderson
© *1999 Kevin Mayhew Ltd.*

Bless the Lord, my soul!
Bless the Lord, my soul!
Let all that is within me praise his name!
(Repeat)

1. Praise the Lord on cymbals,
   praise the Lord on drums,
   praise the Lord
   for all that he has done.

2. Praise the Lord on trumpet,
   praise the Lord in song,
   praise him all
   who stand before his throne.

3. Praise him for his mercy,
   praise him for his pow'r,
   praise him for
   his love which conquers all.

174 vs 1, 3 John Keeble, vs 2, 4
William John Hall's 'Psalms and Hymns', alt.

1. Blest are the pure in heart,
   for they shall see our God;
   the secret of the Lord is theirs,
   their soul is Christ's abode.

2. The Lord who left the heav'ns
   our life and peace to bring,
   to dwell in lowliness with us,
   our pattern and our King.

3. Still to the lowly soul
   he doth himself impart,
   and for his dwelling and his throne
   chooseth the pure in heart.

4. Lord, we thy presence seek;
   may ours this blessing be:
   give us a pure and lowly heart,
   a temple meet for thee.

175 Aniceto Nazareth, based on the Roman Missal
© 1984 Kevin Mayhew Ltd.

1. Blest are you, Lord, God of all creation,
   thanks to your goodness
   this bread we offer:
   fruit of the earth, work of our hands,
   it will become the bread of life.

   Blessed be God! Blessed be God!
   Blessed be God for ever! Amen! (Repeat)

2. Blest are you, Lord, God of all creation,
   thanks to your goodness
   this wine we offer:
   fruit of the earth, work of our hands,
   it will become the cup of life.

176 Hubert J. Richards, based on the Roman Missal
© 1996 Kevin Mayhew Ltd.

1. Blest are you, Lord of creation,
   you provide the bread we offer,
   fruit of your earth and work of our hands.

   Blest be the Lord for ever, Amen. (Repeat)

2. Blest are you, Lord of creation,
   you provide the wine we offer,
   fruit of your earth and work of our hands.

3. Blest are you, Lord of creation,
   look with favour on our off'rings,
   pour out your Spirit over these gifts.

177 Michael Forster
© 1999 Kevin Mayhew Ltd.

1. Blest are you, O God, Creator;
   through your goodness, bread we share,
   by the earth conceived and given,
   made with human skill and care.
   Common food, by grace made holy,
   bread of life to us will be.
   This will be the feast of heaven,
   blest be God eternally.

2. Blest are you, O God, Creator;
   by your grace we bring you wine,
   work of human hands combining
   with the goodness of the vine;
   cup of blessing yet of sorrow,
   cup of life and love to be;
   sign of covenant eternal;
   blest be God eternally.

3. Blest are you, O God, Creator;
   Light of lights and Pow'r of pow'rs,
   yet in humble love accepting
   gifts from hands as poor as ours.
   In our gifts our lives are given,
   by your grace Christ's life to be.
   In the giving and receiving,
   blest be God eternally.

178 Dan Schutte, based on Psalm 91
© 1976 Daniel L. Schutte and New Dawn Music

Blest be the Lord; blest be the Lord,
the God of mercy, the God who saves.
I shall not fear the dark of night,
nor the arrow that flies by day.

1. He will release me from
   the nets of all my foes.
   He will protect me from their
       wicked hands.
   Beneath the shadow of his wings
   I will rejoice
   to find a dwelling place secure.

2. I need not shrink before
   the terrors of the night,
   nor stand alone before the light of day.
   No harm shall come to me,
   no arrow strike me down,
   no evil settle in my soul.

3. Although a thousand strong
   have fallen at my side,
   I'll not be shaken with the Lord at hand.
   His faithful love is all
   the armour that I need
   to wage my battle with the foe.

179 Geoffrey Ainger
© 1964 Stainer & Bell Ltd.

1. Born in the night, Mary's child,
   a long way from your home;
   coming in need, Mary's child,
   born in a borrowed room.

2. Clear shining light, Mary's child,
   your face lights up our way;
   light of the world, Mary's child,
   dawn on our darkened day.

3. Truth of our life, Mary's child,
   you tell us God is good;
   prove it is true, Mary's child,
   go to your cross of wood.

4. Hope of the world, Mary's child,
   you're coming soon to reign;
   King of the earth, Mary's child,
   walk in our streets again.

180 Luke Connaughton MARRA
© McCrimmon Publishing Co. Ltd.

1. Bread from the earth, wine from the soil,
   Adam made of clay:
   bring to the Lord – sing to the Lord! –
   gifts of red and gold.
   Red is the wine, royal and rich,
   golden gleams the wheat.

2. Fashioned from dust, what can you give,
   Adam, weak and poor?
   Bring to the Lord – sing to the Lord! –
   what he gave to you:
   spirit of flame, mastering mind,
   body fine and proud.

3. Cry on his name, worship your God,
   all who dwell on earth.
   Bring to the Lord – sing to the Lord! –
   heart and voice and will.
   Father and Son, Spirit most high,
   worship Three in One.

181 John L. Bell and Graham Maule. © 1989 WGRG, Iona
Community (Wild Goose Publications 1989)

1. Bread is blessed and broken,
   wine is blessed and poured:
   take this and remember
   Christ the Lord.

2. Share the food of heaven
   earth cannot afford.
   Here is grace in essence –
   Christ the Lord.

3. Know yourself forgiven,
   find yourself restored,
   meet a friend for ever –
   Christ the Lord.

4. God has kept his promise
   sealed by sign and word:
   here, for those who want him –
   Christ the Lord.

182
Edwin Hatch, alt. the Editors
© 1999 Kevin Mayhew Ltd.

1. Breathe on me, breath of God,
   fill me with life anew,
   that as you love, so I may love,
   and do what you would do.

2. Breathe on me, breath of God
   until my heart is pure:
   until my will is one with yours
   to do and to endure.

3. Breathe on me, breath of God,
   fulfil my heart's desire,
   until this earthly part of me
   glows with your heav'nly fire.

4. Breathe on me, breath of God,
   so shall I never die,
   but live with you the perfect life
   of your eternity.

183
Estelle White
© 1982 Kevin Mayhew Ltd.

1. Breath of God, O Holy Spirit, *(x3)*
   breathe on us now.

2. Comforter in time of sorrow, *(x3)*
   give us your peace.

3. Fount of joy and of all beauty, *(x3)*
   come, fill our minds.

4. Light divine and flame eternal, *(x3)*
   burn in us now.

5. Promise of our Saviour, Jesus, *(x3)*
   speak through us now.

184
'Victoriae Paschali Laudes', attributed to Wipo of
Burgundy (11th century), trans. Walter Kirkham Blount

1. Bring, all ye dear-bought nations, bring,
   your richest praises to your King,
   alleluia, alleluia,
   that spotless Lamb, who more than due,
   paid for his sheep, and those sheep you,

   alleluia!

2. That guiltless Son, who bought
      your peace,
   and made his Father's anger cease,
   alleluia, alleluia,
   then, life and death together fought,
   each to a strange extreme were brought.

3. Life died, but soon revived again,
   and even death by it was slain,
   alleluia, alleluia.
   Say, happy Magdalen, O, say,
   what didst thou see there by the way?

4. 'I saw the tomb of my dear Lord,
   I saw himself, and him adored,
   alleluia, alleluia,
   I saw the napkin and the sheet,
   that bound his head and wrapped his feet.'

5. 'I heard the angels witness bear,
   Jesus is ris'n; he is not here,
   alleluia, alleluia;
   go, tell his foll'wers they shall see
   thine and their hope in Galilee.'

6. We, Lord, with faithful hearts and voice,
   on this thy rising day rejoice,
   alleluia, alleluia.
   O thou, whose power o'ercame the grave,
   by grace and love us sinners save.

185
A Sister of Notre Dame

1. Bring flow'rs of the rarest,
   bring blossoms the fairest,
   from garden and woodland
   and hillside and dale;
   our full hearts are swelling,
   our glad voices telling
   the praise of the loveliest
   flow'r of the vale.

   *O Mary, we crown thee
   with blossoms today,
   Queen of the angels
   and Queen of the May.*

2. Their lady they name thee,
their mistress proclaim thee.
O, grant that thy children
on earth be as true,
as long as the bowers
are radiant with flowers
as long as the azure
shall keep its bright hue.

3. Sing gaily in chorus,
the bright angels o'er us
re-echo the strains
we begin upon earth;
their harps are repeating
the notes of our greeting,
for Mary herself is
the cause of our mirth.

186 Richard Gillard

1. Brother, sister, let me serve you,
let me be as Christ to you;
pray that I may have the grace to
let you be my servant, too.

2. We are pilgrims on a journey,
fellow trav'llers on the road;
we are here to help each other
walk the mile and bear the load.

3. I will hold the Christlight for you
in the night-time of your fear;
I will hold my hand out to you,
speak the peace you long to hear.

4. I will weep when you are weeping;
when you laugh, I'll laugh with you.
I will share your joy and sorrow
till we've seen this journey through.

5. When we sing to God in heaven,
we shall find such harmony,
born of all we've know together
of Christ's love and agony.

6. Brother, sister, let me serve you,
let me be as Christ to you;
pray that I may have the grace to
let you be my servant, too.

187 Steven Fry

By his grace we are redeemed,
by his blood we are made clean,
and we now can know him face to face.
By his pow'r we have been raised,
hidden now in Christ by faith,
we will praise the glory of his grace.

188 Frederick William Faber

1. By the blood that flowed from thee
in thy grievous agony;
by the traitor's guileful kiss,
filling up thy bitterness;

Jesus, Saviour, hear our cry;
thou wert suff'ring once as we:
now enthroned in majesty
countless angels sing to thee.

2. By the cords that, round thee cast,
bound thee to the pillar fast,
by the scourge so meekly borne,
by the purple robe of scorn.

3. By the thorns that crowned thy head;
by the sceptre of a reed;
by thy foes on bended knee,
mocking at thy royalty.

4. By the people's cruel jeers;
by the holy women's tears;
by thy footsteps, faint and slow,
weighed beneath thy cross of woe.

5. By thy weeping mother's woe;
by the sword that pierced her through,
when in anguish standing by,
on the cross she saw thee die.

189

Robert B. Kelly
© 1999 Kevin Mayhew Ltd.

By the cross we are marked for life!
We are chosen as God's people!
To this Tree of life we are branched by Christ,
and its fruit will last forever.

1. Made in the image
   and the likeness of the one true God,
   we are the daughters
   and the sons of God, our Father.
   But, for a tree and its fruit,
   we turned against him,
   we chose to clothe ourselves
   in selfishness and shame.

2. Made in our image
   and the likeness of humanity,
   Christ came from God
   and taught us how to call him 'Father'!
   Then, by the Tree,
   did he lead us to the Garden,
   where God awaits in welcome
   if we're clothed in Christ.

190

Based on Psalm 137
© Copyright control

1. By the waters, the waters of Babylon,
   we sat down and wept,
       and wept for thee, Zion;
   we remember thee, remember thee,
   remember thee, Zion.

2. On the willows, the willows of Babylon,
   we hung up our harps,
       our harps, for thee, Zion;
   how can we sing, can we sing,
   sing of thee, Zion?

3. There our captors,
       our captors from Babylon,
   tried to make us sing, to sing of thee, Zion;
   but we could not sing, we could not sing,
   we could not sing, Zion.

191

James G. Johnson
© James G. Johnson, Eighth Day Creations Music

Called to be servants, called to be sons,
called to be daughters, we're called to be one.
Called into service, called to be free;
you are called to be you,
and I'm called to be me.

1. Children, come with wide open eyes.
   Look at the water; you have been baptised.
   You're free from the slav'ry
   that bound you to sin,
   so live now as children
   in the kingdom of heav'n.

2. We are saints! Forgiveness is sure,
   not of ourselves, but the cross
       Christ endured.
   We're free from the law that said
   'You must provide!'
   We're free to be servants;
   we're called, we're baptised.

3. Jesus closed the dark pit of death.
   He has breathed on us with his
       holy breath.
   He gives us the faith
   to respond to his News.
   We're free to show mercy,
   to love, to be bruised.

192

Eddie Espinosa, based on Isaiah 64:8
© 1982 Mercy/Vineyard Publishing/
Music Services/CopyCare

Change my heart, O God,
make it ever true;
change my heart, O God,
may I be like you.
You are the potter, I am the clay;
mould me and make me:
this is what I pray.

193

Mary MacDonald, trans. Lachlan MacBean
© Copyright control

1. Child in the manger, infant of Mary;
   outcast and stranger, Lord of all;
   child who inherits all our transgressions,
   all our demerits on him fall.

2. Once the most holy child of salvation
   gently and lowly lived below;
   now as our glorious mighty Redeemer,
   see him victorious o'er each foe.

3. Prophets foretold him, infant of wonder;
   angels behold him on his throne;
   worthy our Saviour of all their praises;
   happy for ever are his own.

194

Adapted from 'St Patrick's Breastplate' by James Quinn
© 1969 Geoffrey Chapman, an imprint of Cassell plc

1. Christ be beside me, Christ be before me,
   Christ be behind me, King of my heart.
   Christ be within me, Christ be below me,
   Christ be above me, never to part.

2. Christ on my right hand,
       Christ on my left hand,
   Christ all around me, shield in the strife.
   Christ in my sleeping,
       Christ in my sitting,
   Christ in my rising, light of my life.

3. Christ be in all hearts thinking about me.
   Christ be in all tongues telling of me.
   Christ be the vision in eyes that see me,
   in ears that hear me, Christ ever be.

195

John E. Bowers
© John E. Bowers

Christians, lift up your hearts,
and make this a day of rejoicing;
God is our strength and song;
glory and praise to his name!

1. This is the house of the Lord,
   where seekers and finders are welcome;
   enter its gates with your praise,
   fill all its courts with your song:

2. All those baptised into Christ
   share the glory of his resurrection,
   dying with him unto sin,
   walking in newness of life:

3. Here God's life-giving word
   once more is proclaimed to his people,
   uplifting those who are down,
   challenging all with its truth:

4. Those who are burdened with sin
   find here the joy or forgiveness,
   laying their sins before Christ,
   pardon and peace their reward:

5. Summoned by Christ's command
   his people draw near to his table,
   gladly to greet their Lord,
   known in the breaking of bread:

6. Strong and alert in his grace,
   God's people are one in their worship;
   kept by his peace they depart,
   ready for serving their Lord:

196

Ivor J. E. Daniel
© Burns & Oates Ltd.

1. Christ is King of earth and heaven!
   Let his subjects all proclaim,
   in the splendour of his temple,
   honour to his holy name.

2. Christ is King! No soul created
   can refuse to bend the knee
   to the God made man who reigneth,
   as 'twas promised, from the tree.

3. Christ is King! Let humble sorrow
   for our past neglect atone,
   for the lack of faithful service
   to the Master whom we own.

4. Christ is King! Let joy and gladness
   greet him; let his courts resound
   with the praise of faithful subjects
   to his love in honour bound.

Continued overleaf

5. Christ is King! In health and sickness,
   till we breathe our latest breath,
   till we greet in highest heaven,
   Christ the victor over death.

197 'Urbs beata Jerusalem', 7th century,
trans. John Mason Neale, alt.

1. Christ is made the sure foundation,
   Christ the head and cornerstone,
   chosen of the Lord, and precious,
   binding all the Church in one,
   holy Zion's help for ever,
   and her confidence alone.

2. To this temple, where we call you,
   come, O Lord of hosts, today;
   you have promised loving kindness,
   hear your servants as we pray,
   bless your people now before you,
   turn our darkness into day.

3. Here the cry of all your people,
   what they ask and hope to gain;
   what they gain from you, for ever
   with your chosen to retain,
   and hereafter in your glory
   evermore with you to reign.

4. Praise and honour to the Father,
   praise and honour to the Son,
   praise and honour to the Spirit,
   ever Three and ever One,
   One in might and One in glory
   while unending ages run.

198 John L. Bell and Graham Maule
© 1989 WGRG, Iona Community

1. Christ's is the world in which we move,
   Christ's are the folk we're summoned
      to love,
   Christ's is the voice which calls us to care,
   and Christ is the one who meets us here.

   To the lost Christ shows his face;
   to the unloved he gives his embrace;
   to those who cry in pain or disgrace,
   Christ makes with his friends a
      touching place.

2. Feel for the people we most avoid,
   strange or bereaved or never employed;
   feel for the women, and feel for the men
   who fear that their living is all in vain.

3. Feel for the parents who've lost their child,
   feel for the women whom men
      have defiled,
   feel for the baby for whom there's
      no breast,
   and feel for the weary who find no rest.

4. Feel for the lives by life confused,
   riddled with doubt, in loving abused;
   feel for the lonely heart, conscious of sin,
   which longs to be pure but fears to begin.

199 'Victimae Paschali Laudes', attributed to Wipo of
Burgundy (11th century), trans. Jane Elizabeth
Leeson, alt.

1. Christ the Lord is ris'n today!
   Christians, haste your vows to pay,
   offer ye your praises meet
   at the paschal victim's feet;
   for the sheep the Lamb hath bled,
   sinless in the sinner's stead.
   Christ the Lord is ris'n on high;
   now he lives, no more to die.

2. Christ, the victim undefiled,
   God and sinners reconciled
   when in strange and awful strife
   met together death and life;
   Christians, on this happy day,
   haste with joy your vows to pay.
   Christ the Lord is ris'n on high;
   now he lives, no more to die.

3. Say, O wond'ring Mary, say,
   what thou sawest on thy way,
   'I beheld, where Christ had lain,
   empty tomb and angels twain,
   I beheld the glory bright
   of the rising Lord of light;
   Christ my hope is ris'n again;
   now he lives, and lives to reign.'

4. Christ who once for sinners bled,
   now the first-born from the dead,
   throned in endless might and power,
   lives and reigns for evermore.
   Hail, eternal hope on high!
   Hail, thou King of victory!
   Hail, thou Prince of life adored!
   Help and save us, gracious Lord.

200 Michael Saward
© *Michael Saward/Jubilate Hymns*

1. Christ triumphant, ever reigning,
   Saviour, Master, King.
   Lord of heav'n, our lives sustaining,
   hear us as we sing:

   Yours the glory and the crown,
   the high renown, th'eternal name.

2. Word incarnate, truth revealing,
   Son of Man on earth!
   Pow'r and majesty concealing
   by your humble birth:

3. Suff'ring servant, scorned, ill-treated,
   victim crucified!
   Death is through the cross defeated,
   sinners justified:

4. Priestly King, enthroned for ever
   high in heav'n above!
   Sin and death and hell shall never
   stifle hymns of love:

5. So, our hearts and voices raising
   through the ages long,
   ceaselessly upon you gazing,
   this shall be our song:

201 Robert B. Kelly
© *1999 Kevin Mayhew Ltd.*

Christus vincit, Christus regnat,
Christus imperat.

1. Christ has delivered us from the
       dominion of darkness
   and transferred us to the kingdom of his
       beloved Son:

in Christ, we gain our freedom,
in him, the forgiveness of our sins.

2. Christ is the image of the unseen God,
   he is the first-born of all creation:
   in Christ, all things were created,
       in heaven and on earth,
   all things, visible and invisible.

3. In Christ, all things were created,
   through him and for him.
   Christ is, and was before all things,
   all things are held in unity by Christ.

4. The Church is the Body of Christ,
   he is its head:
   he is the beginning,
   the first-born from the dead.

5. In Christ all the fullness of God was
       pleased to dwell,
   and through Christ to reconcile all things
       to himself;
   to reconcile everything in heaven or
       on earth,
   making peace by the blood of the cross.

202 Sue McClellan/John Paculabo/Keith Ryecroft
© *1974 Kingsway's Thankyou Music*

1. Colours of day dawn into the mind,
   the sun has come up, the night is behind.
   Go down in the city, into the street,
   and let's give the message
   to the people we meet.

   So light up the fire and let the flame burn,
   open the door, let Jesus return,
   take seeds of his Spirit, let the fruit grow,
   tell the people of Jesus, let his love show.

2. Go through the park, on into the town;
   the sun still shines on; it never goes down.
   The light of the world is risen again;
   the people of darkness
   are needing our friend.

Continued overleaf

3. Open your eyes, look into the sky,
the darkness has come, the sun came to die.
The evening draws on, the sun disappears,
but Jesus is living,
and his Spirit is near.

203

Aniceto Nazareth, based on Scripture
© 1984 Kevin Mayhew Ltd.

Come and be filled as you sit at my table,
quenching your thirst
as you drink of my wine;
bringing the mem'ry of my dying and rising
into your bloodstream
which is mingled with mine.

1. This is the bread
that has come down from heaven.
This is my blood
for the life of the world.

2. He leads us out
of the power of darkness
and brings us safe
to his kingdom of life.

3. No longer I,
but now Christ lives within me.
I live by faith
in the Son of God.

4. For those in Christ
there is no condemnation.
He sets them free
through the Spirit he sends.

5. Thus shall the world
know you are my disciples,
if you can love,
and if you can forgive.

204

David Haas
© 1985 GIA Publications Inc.

Come and be light for our eyes;
be the air we breathe,
be the voice we speak!
Come, be the song we sing,
be the path we seek!

1. Your life was given; food for all people,
body and blood, new life in our midst!
Death is no longer, life is our future,
Jesus, Messiah; name of all names!

2. We hold your presence; risen for ever!
Your Name now names us people of God!
Filled with your vision, people of mission,
healing, forgiving; light for the world!

3. Lead us to justice, light in the darkness;
singing, proclaiming Jesus is Lord!
Teach us to speak, and help us to listen
for when your truth and our
dreams embrace!

205

v 1 unknown, vs 2-6 Damian Lundy
© 1978 Kevin Mayhew Ltd

1. Come and go with me
to my Father's house,
to my Father's house,
to my Father's house.
Come and go with me
to my Father's house,
where there's joy, joy, joy.

2. It's not very far
to my Father's house . . .

3. There is room for all
in my Father's house . . .

4. Ev'rything is free
in my Father's house . . .

5. Jesus is the way
to my Father's house . . .

6. Jesus is the light
in my Father's house . . .

206

Andy Carter
© 1977 Kingsway's Thankyou Music

Come and praise him, royal priesthood.
Come and worship, holy nation.
Worship Jesus, our Redeemer.
He is risen, King of glory.

207

Gregory Norbert, based on Hosea
© 1972 The Benedictine Foundation of the State of
Vermont, Inc.

1. Come back to me with all your heart,
   don't let fear keep us apart.
   Trees do bend, though straight and tall;
   so must we to others' call.

   Long have I waited for your
   coming home to me
   and living deeply our new life.

2. The wilderness will lead you
   to your heart where I will speak.
   Integrity and justice with
   tenderness you shall know.

3. You shall sleep secure with peace;
   faithfulness will be your joy.

208

Unknown, alt.

Come, come, come to the manger,
children, come to the children's King;
sing, sing, chorus of angels,
star of morning o'er Bethlehem sing.

1. He lies 'mid the beasts of the stall,
   who is Maker and Lord of us all;
   the wintry wind blows cold and dreary,
   see, he weeps, the world is weary;
   Lord, have pity and mercy on me!

2. He leaves all his glory behind,
   to be Saviour of all humankind,
   with grateful beasts his cradle chooses,
   thankless world his love refuses;
   Lord, have pity and mercy on me!

3. To the manger of Bethlehem come,
   to the Saviour Emmanuel's home;
   the heav'nly hosts above are singing,
   set the Christmas bells a-ringing;
   Lord, have pity and mercy on me!

209

'Discendi, amor santo' by Bianco da Siena,
trans. Richard F. Littledale, alt.

1. Come down, O Love divine,
   seek thou this soul of mine,
   and visit it with thine own ardour glowing;
   O Comforter, draw near,
   within my heart appear,
   and kindle it, thy holy flame bestowing.

2. O let it freely burn,
   till earthly passions turn
   to dust and ashes in its heat consuming;
   and let thy glorious light
   shine ever on my sight,
   and clothe me round, the while my
      path illuming.

3. Let holy charity
   mine outward vesture be,
   and lowliness become mine inner clothing;
   true lowliness of heart,
   which takes the humbler part,
   and o'er its own shortcomings weeps
      with loathing.

4. And so the yearning strong,
   with which the soul will long,
   shall far outpass the pow'r of human
      telling;
   nor can we guess its grace,
   till we become the place
   wherein the Holy Spirit makes
      his dwelling.

210

'Veni, Creator Spiritus', ascribed to
Rabanus Maurus, trans. unknown.

1. Come, Holy Ghost, Creator, come
   from thy bright heav'nly throne,
   come, take possession of our souls,
   and make them all thine own.

2. Thou who art called the Paraclete,
   best gift of God above,
   the living spring, the living fire,
   sweet unction and true love.

Continued overleaf

3. Thou who art sev'nfold in thy grace,
   finger of God's right hand;
   his promise, teaching little ones
   to speak and understand.

4. O guide our minds with thy blest light,
   with love our hearts inflame;
   and with thy strength, which ne'er decays,
   confirm our mortal frame.

5. Far from us drive our deadly foe;
   true peace unto us bring;
   and through all perils lead us safe
   beneath thy sacred wing.

6. Through thee may we the Father know,
   through thee th'eternal Son,
   and thee the Spirit of them both,
   thrice-blessèd Three in One.

7. All glory to the Father be,
   with his co-equal Son:
   the same to thee, great Paraclete,
   while endless ages run.

211
Michael Forster
© 1992 Kevin Mayhew Ltd.

1. Come, Holy Spirit, come!
   Inflame our souls with love,
   transforming ev'ry heart and home
   with wisdom from above.
   O let us not despise
   the humble path Christ trod,
   but choose, to shame the worldly-wise,
   the foolishness of God.

2. All-knowing Spirit, prove
   the poverty of pride,
   by knowledge of the Father's love
   in Jesus crucified.
   And grant us faith to know
   the glory of that sign,
   and in our very lives to show
   the marks of love divine.

3. Come with the gift to heal
   the wounds of guilt and fear,
   and to oppression's face reveal
   the kingdom drawing near.
   Where chaos longs to reign,
   descend, O holy Dove,
   and free us all to work again
   the miracle of love.

4. Spirit of truth, arise;
   inspire the prophet's voice:
   expose to scorn the tyrant's lies,
   and bid the poor rejoice.
   O Spirit, clear our sight,
   all prejudice remove,
   and help us to discern the right,
   and covet only love.

5. Give us the tongues to speak,
   in ev'ry time and place,
   to rich and poor, to strong and weak,
   the word of love and grace.
   Enable us to hear
   the words that others bring,
   interpreting with open ear
   the special song they sing.

6. Come, Holy Spirit, dance
   within our hearts today,
   our earthbound spirits to entrance,
   our mortal fears allay.
   And teach us to desire,
   all other things above,
   that self-consuming holy fire,
   the perfect gift of love!

212
Mike Anderson, based on Psalm 95
© 1982 Kevin Mayhew Ltd.

*Come, let us raise a joyful song to the Lord,
a shout of triumph!
Come, let us raise a joyful song to the Lord,
and give him thanks!*

1. The furthest places on the earth
   are in his hands.
   He made them, and we sing his praise.

2. The seas and waters on the earth
are in his hands.
He made them, and we sing his praise.

3. The hills and valleys on the earth
are in his hands.
He made them, and we sing his praise.

4. All living creatures on the earth
are in his hands.
He made them, and we sing his praise.

5. And we his people on the earth
are in his hands.
He saved us, and we sing his praise.

213 Damian Lundy
© 1986 Kevin Mayhew Ltd.

1. Come, Lord Jesus, come, Lord Jesus,
come, Lord Jesus, come again.

   Come, Lord Jesus, come again.

2. Born of Mary, *(x3)*
come again.

3. Slain to save us, *(x3)*
come again.

4. Raised to new life, *(x3)*
come again.

5. At God's right hand, *(x3)*
come again.

6. Send your Spirit, *(x3)*
come again.

7. Come in glory, *(x3)*
come again.

214 Kevin Mayhew
© 1974, 1976 Kevin Mayhew Ltd.

1. Come, Lord Jesus, come.
Come, take my hands,
take them for your work.
Take them for your service, Lord.
Take them for your glory, Lord.
Come, Lord Jesus, come.
Come, Lord Jesus, take my hands.

2. Come, Lord Jesus, come.
Come, take my eyes,
may they shine with joy.
Take them for your service, Lord.
Take them for your glory, Lord.
Come, Lord Jesus, come.
Come, Lord Jesus, take my eyes.

3. Come, Lord Jesus, come.
Come, take my lips,
may they speak your truth.
Take them for your service, Lord.
Take them for your glory, Lord.
Come, Lord Jesus, come.
Come, Lord Jesus, take my lips.

4. Come, Lord Jesus, come.
Come, take my feet,
may they walk your path.
Take them for your service, Lord.
Take them for your glory, Lord.
Come, Lord Jesus, come.
Come, Lord Jesus, take my feet.

5. Come, Lord Jesus, come.
Come, take my heart,
fill it with your love.
Take it for your service, Lord.
Take it for your glory, Lord.
Come, Lord Jesus, come.
Come, Lord Jesus, take my heart.

6. Come, Lord Jesus, come.
Come take my life,
take it for your own.
Take it for your service, Lord.
Take it for your glory, Lord.
Come, Lord Jesus, come.
Come, Lord Jesus, take my life.

215 George Herbert

1. Come, my Way, my Truth, my Life:
such a way as gives us breath;
such a truth as ends all strife;
such a life as killeth death.

Continued overleaf

2. Come, my Light, my Feast, my Strength:
such a light as shows a feast;
such a feast as mends in length;
such a strength as makes his guest.

3. Come, my Joy, my Love, my Heart:
such a joy as none can move;
such a love as none can part;
such a heart as joys in love.

216 Sister Mary of St Philip

1. Come, O divine Messiah!
The world in silence waits the day
when hope shall sing its triumph,
and sadness flee away.

Sweet Saviour, haste: come, come to earth:
dispel the night, and show thy face,
and bid us hail the dawn of grace.
Come, O divine Messiah!
The world in silence waits the day
when hope shall sing its triumph,
and sadness flee away.

2. O thou, whom nations sighed for,
whom priests and prophets long foretold,
wilt break the captive fetters,
redeem the long-lost fold.

3. Shalt come in peace and meekness,
and lowly will thy cradle be:
all clothed in human weakness
shall we thy Godhead see.

217 Marty Haugen
© 1985 GIA Publications Inc.

1. Come, O God of all the earth:
Come to us, O righteous one;
come, and bring our love to birth:
in the glory of your Son.

Sing out, earth and skies!
Sing of the God who loves you!
Raise your joyful cries!
Dance to the life around you!

2. Come, O God of wind and flame:
fill the earth with righteousness;
teach us all to sing your name:
may our lives your love confess.

3. Come, O God of flashing light:
twinkling star and burning sun;
God of day and God of night:
in your light we all are one.

4. Come, O God of snow and rain:
shower down upon the earth;
come, O God of joy and pain:
God of sorrow, God of mirth.

5. Come, O justice, come, O peace:
come and shape our hearts anew;
come and make oppression cease:
bring us all to life to you.

218 Charles Wesley, based on Haggai 2:7, alt. the Editors

1. Come, O long expected Jesus,
born to set your people free;
from our fears and sins release us;
free us from captivity.

2. Israel's strength and consolation,
you the hope of all the earth,
dear desire of ev'ry nation,
come, and save us by your birth!

3. Born your people to deliver;
born a child and yet a King!
Born to reign in us for ever,
now your gracious kingdom bring.

4. By your own eternal Spirit
rule in all our hearts alone;
by your all-sufficient merit,
raise us to your glorious throne.

219 Patricia Morgan and Dave Bankhead
©1984 Kingsway's Thankyou Music

Come on and celebrate
his gift of love, we will celebrate
the Son of God who loved us
and gave us life.

We'll shout your praise, O King,
you give us joy nothing else can bring;
we'll give to you our offering
in celebration praise.

Come on and celebrate, celebrate,
celebrate and sing,
celebrate and sing to the King. *(Repeat)*

220 Psalm 116 versified by James Quinn
© *1969 Geoffrey Chapman, an imprint of Cassell plc.*

1. Come, praise the Lord, the almighty,
   the King of all nations!
   Tell forth his fame, O ye peoples,
   with loud acclamations!
   His love is sure;
   faithful his word shall endure,
   steadfast through all generations!

2. Praise to the Father most gracious,
   the Lord of creation!
   Praise to his Son, the Redeemer,
   who wrought our salvation!
   O heav'nly Dove,
   praise to thee, fruit of their love,
   giver of all consolation!

221 Joseph Gelineau and Robert B. Kelly, based on Isaiah
35 and 40 and Baruch 5

Come, prepare the way of the Lord!
Open wide the gates of your heart!
For the Saviour comes,
and all will see the salvation of God.

1. Cast off the rags that speak of sadness!
   God means to crown you with his gladness!
   Wear his integrity with pride,
   God himself casts sorrow aside!

2. Tell the faint-hearted, tell the fearful,
   no need to worry, God will save you!
   God comes, salvation in his hand,
   leads you to the new Promised Land!

3. See them laid low, the hills and mountains.
   Valleys are filled, becoming great plains.
   We are no longer left to roam,
   God himself will shepherd us home.

4. Those who were blind now see God's glory,
   those who were deaf now hear God's story.
   Those who were hungry eat their fill,
   those once lame now cannot keep still!

5. Fresh water irrigates the dry land,
   flowers now grow in what was dead sand.
   Earth now lies ready for the grain,
   earth is ripe for planting the vine!

222 Noel Donnelly, based on Psalm 129
© *Noel S. Donnelly*

Come to me and I shall give you rest.

1. From the depths I call to you.
   Listen, Lord, and hear my pleading.

2. Love and mercy flow from you,
   Lord of life and kind Redeemer.

3. In the dark I hope for you,
   you are light of new day dawning.

4. Weak and frail we come to you,
   God of love and new beginning.

223 Gregory Norbert, based on Psalm 22 and Matthew
11:28-30. © *1971 The Benedictine Foundation of the
State of Vermont, Inc.*

Come to me,
all who labour and are heavy burdened,
and I shall give you rest.
Take up my yoke and learn from me,
for I am meek and humble of heart.
And you'll find rest for your souls.
Yes, my yoke is easy and my burden is light.

The Lord is my shepherd,
I shall never be in need.
Fresh and green are the meadows
where he gives me rest.

224
Gerard Markland
© 1998 Kevin Mayhew Ltd.

1. Come to me, come, my people;
   learn from me, be humble of heart.

2. I your Lord, I your master;
   learn from me, be humble of heart.

3. Follow me to my Father;
   learn from me, be humble of heart.

4. In my death, in my rising;
   learn from me, be humble of heart.

5. Be transformed by my Spirit;
   learn from me, be humble of heart.

6. Glory be to my Father;
   learn from me, be humble of heart.

225
Michael Forster
Text © 1999 Kevin Mayhew Ltd.

Come to the table of the Lord,
sinners by faith and grace restored;
taste here what earth cannot afford,
alleluia!

1. How I rejoiced when Jesus said,
   'Come to my table, share my bread,
   where souls and bodies both are fed.'

2. 'This is my body, giv'n to be
   broken for you eternally:
   do this when you remember me.'

3. 'This is my lifeblood, flowing free,
   shed for the world eternally:
   do this when you remember me.'

226 Henry Alford

1. Come, ye thankful people, come,
   raise the song of harvest-home!
   All is safely gathered in,
   ere the winter storms begin;
   God, our maker, doth provide
   for our wants to be supplied;
   come to God's own temple, come;
   raise the song of harvest-home!

2. We ourselves are God's own field,
   fruit unto his praise to yield;
   wheat and tares together sown,
   unto joy or sorrow grown;
   first the blade and then the ear,
   then the full corn shall appear:
   grant, O harvest Lord, that we
   wholesome grain and pure may be.

3. For the Lord our God shall come,
   and shall take his harvest home,
   from his field shall purge away
   all that doth offend, that day;
   give his angels charge at last
   in the fire the tares to cast,
   but the fruitful ears to store
   in his garner evermore.

4. Then, thou Church triumphant, come,
   raise the song of harvest-home;
   all be safely gathered in,
   free from sorrow, free from sin,
   there for ever purified
   in God's garner to abide:
   come, ten thousand angels, come,
   raise the glorious harvest-home!

227
Anthony D'Souza, based on Isaiah 40
© 1984 Kevin Mayhew Ltd.

'Comfort, comfort my people,'
says the Lord, your God.
'Cry out loud to Jerusalem,
God has pardoned you!'

1. Ev'ry valley shall be filled,
   ev'ry mount and hill laid low.

2. In the desert make a path
   for the Lord Emmanuel.

3. For the glory of the Lord
   soon shall be revealed to me.

228

Michael Hodgetts
© Michael Hodgetts

1. Creator of the day and night,
   who turned the darkness into light
   and charged us to proclaim the Word,
   whom we have touched and seen
      and heard.

   The glory that you gave the Son,
   he gives to us, to make us one.

2. Your kingdom in a mystery,
   began with twelve in Galilee,
   through whom the Son would teach
      and cure;
   whose fruit would ripen and endure.

3. At Pentecost, with wind and flame,
   you sent the Spirit in his name,
   to make the Church a present Christ;
   anointed Prophet, King and Priest.

4. And when your purpose is complete,
   the Son of Man will take his seat;
   and Christ will be identified
   with these, the least, for whom he died.

229

Matthew Bridges

1. Crown him with many crowns,
   the Lamb upon his throne;
   hark, how the heav'nly anthem drowns
   all music but its own:
   awake, my soul, and sing
   of him who died for thee,
   and hail him as thy matchless King
   through all eternity.

2. Crown him the Virgin's Son,
   the God incarnate born,
   whose arm those crimson trophies won
   which now his brow adorn;
   fruit of the mystic Rose,
   as of that Rose the Stem,
   the Root, whence mercy ever flows,
   the Babe of Bethlehem.

3. Crown him the Lord of love;
   behold his hands and side,
   rich wounds, yet visible above,
   in beauty glorified:
   no angel in the sky
   can fully bear that sight,
   but downward bends each burning eye
   at mysteries so bright.

4. Crown him the Lord of peace,
   whose pow'r a sceptre sways
   from pole to pole, that wars may cease,
   absorbed in prayer and praise:
   his reign shall know no end,
   and round his piercèd feet
   fair flow'rs of paradise extend
   their fragrance ever sweet.

5. Crown him the Lord of years,
   the Potentate of time,
   Creator of the rolling spheres,
   ineffably sublime.
   All hail, Redeemer, hail!
   for thou hast died for me;
   thy praise shall never, never fail
   throughout eternity.

230

'Omni die dic Mariae' ascribed to St. Bernard of
Cluny (12th century), trans. Henry Bittleston

1. Daily, daily, sing to Mary,
   sing my soul, her praises due;
   all her feasts, her actions worship,
   with her heart's devotion true.
   Lost in wond'ring contemplation
   be her majesty confessed:
   call her mother, call her virgin,
   happy mother, virgin blest.

2. She is mighty to deliver;
   call her, trust her lovingly.
   When the tempest rages round thee,
   she will calm the troubled sea.
   Gifts of heaven she has given,
   noble lady, to our race:
   she, the queen, who decks her subjects,
   with the light of God's own grace.

Continued overleaf

3. Sing, my tongue, the virgin's trophies,
who for us her Maker bore;
for the curse of old inflicted,
peace and blessings to restore.
Sing in songs of praise unending,
sing the world's majestic queen;
weary not, nor faint in telling
all the gifts she gives to men.

4. All my senses, heart, affections,
strive to sound her glory forth;
spread abroad, the sweet memorials,
of the virgin's priceless worth.
Where the voice of music thrilling,
where the tongues of eloquence,
that can utter hymns beseeming
all her matchless excellence?

5. All our joys do flow from Mary,
all then join her praise to sing;
trembling, sing the virgin mother,
mother of our Lord and King,
while we sing her awful glory,
far above our fancy's reach,
let our hearts be quick to offer
love the heart alone can teach.

231 Mike Anderson
© 1999 Kevin Mayhew Ltd.

Dance in your Spirit,
we dance in your Spirit,
we dance in your Spirit of joy! (Repeat)

1. Jesus, you showed us the way to live,
and your Spirit sets us free,
free now to sing, free to dance and shout,
'Glory, glory' to your name.

2. Jesus, you opened your arms for us,
but we nailed them to a cross;
but you are risen and now we live,
free from, free from ev'ry fear.

3. Your Spirit brings peace and gentleness,
kindness, self-control and love,
patience and goodness and faith and joy,
Spirit, Spirit fill us now.

232 James Quinn
© Geoffrey Chapman, an imprint of Cassell plc.

1. Day is done, but love unfailing
dwells ever here;
shadows fall, but hope prevailing
calms ev'ry fear;
Loving Father, none forsaking,
take our hearts, of love's own making,
watch our sleeping, guard our waking,
be always near!

2. Dark descends, but light unending
shines through our night;
you are with us, ever lending
new strength to sight;
one in love, your truth confessing,
one in hope of heaven's blessing,
may we see, in love's possessing,
love's endless light!

3. Eyes will close, but you, unsleeping,
watch by our side;
death may come: in love's safe keeping
still we abide.
God of love, all evil quelling,
sin forgiving, fear dispelling,
stay with us, our hearts indwelling,
this eventide!

233 Michael Forster
© 1993 Kevin Mayhew Ltd.

1. Day of wrath and day of wonder,
whence hope has fled!
See the body torn asunder,
blood freely shed.
Stripped of majesty we saw him,
human sight recoiled before him,
yet it was our sorrows tore him;
for us he bled.

2. Day of hope and day of glory,
though unperceived!
See redemption's dreadful story,
long, long conceived.

Evil pow'rs, in downfall lying,
knowing death itself is dying,
hear the voice triumphant crying,
'All is achieved!'

3. Day of majesty and splendour,
here ends the race!
Christ, our Priest, our soul's defender,
us will embrace.
He who walked this earth before us,
tried and tempted, yet victorious,
calls us to the kingdom glorious,
O perfect grace!

234 John Greenleaf Whittier

1. Dear Lord and Father of mankind,
forgive our foolish ways!
Re-clothe us in our rightful mind,
in purer lives thy service find,
in deeper rev'rence praise,
in deeper rev'rence praise.

2. In simple trust like theirs who heard,
beside the Syrian sea,
the gracious calling of the Lord,
let us, like them, without a word,
rise up and follow thee,
rise up and follow thee.

3. O Sabbath rest by Galilee!
O calm of hills above,
where Jesus knelt to share with thee
the silence of eternity,
interpreted by love!
Interpreted by love!

4. Drop thy still dews of quietness,
till all our strivings cease;
take from our souls the strain and stress,
and let our ordered lives confess
the beauty of thy peace,
the beauty of thy peace.

5. Breathe through the heats of our desire
thy coolness and thy balm;
let sense be dumb, let flesh retire;
speak through the earthquake,
wind and fire,
O still small voice of calm!
O still small voice of calm!

235 Estelle White
© 1978 Kevin Mayhew Ltd.

1. Deep calls to deep,
and my soul finds no resting place but him.
He is my God,
the yearnings of my heart his touch
can still.

And each rare moment
that I've felt his presence,
I shall remember and forever cherish.

2. Deep calls to deep,
and at his feast I am a welcome guest.
He gives me food,
the hunger of my soul is laid to rest.

3. Deep calls to deep,
for he created me to be his own.
He understands,
the joy and pain of life he too has known.

236 Fiona MacLeod

Deep peace of the running wave to you,
deep peace of the flowing air to you,
deep peace of the quiet earth to you,
deep peace of the shining stars to you,
deep peace of the Son of peace to you.

237 Mike Anderson
© 1999 Kevin Mayhew Ltd.

1. Deep within my heart I know Jesus
loves me,
deep within my heart I know he loves me.
Guilt and shame are conquered in his name,
and I'm alive now.
Deep within my heart I know he loves me.

Continued overleaf

2. Deep within my heart I know I'm forgiven,
deep within my heart I know that I'm free.
Free from sin, a new life to begin,
and I'm alive now.
Deep within my heart I know that I'm free.

3. Deep within my heart Jesus' love is healing,
deep within my heart he is healing me.
Tears like rain are flooding out the pain,
and I'm alive now.
Deep within my heart he is healing me.

238 George Ratcliffe Woodward
© SPCK

1. Ding dong, merrily on high!
In heav'n the bells are ringing;
ding dong, verily the sky
is riv'n with angels singing.

Gloria, hosanna in excelsis!
Gloria, hosanna in excelsis!

2. E'en so here below, below,
let steeple bells be swungen,
and io, io, io,
by priest and people sungen.

3. Pray you, dutifully prime
your matin chime, ye ringers;
may you beautifully rhyme
your evetime song, ye singers.

239 Traditional

Dona nobis, nobis pacem,
dona nobis pacem.
Dona nobis pacem (x4)

Translation: Give us peace

240 Gerard Markland, based on Isaiah 43:1-4
© 1978 Kevin Mayhew Ltd.

Do not be afraid, for I have redeemed you.
I have called you by your name;
you are mine.

1. When you walk through the waters,
I'll be with you.
You will never sink beneath the waves.

2. When the fire is burning
all around you,
you will never be consumed by the flames.

3. When the fear of loneliness
is looming,
then remember I am at your side.

4. When you dwell in the exile
of the stranger,
remember you are precious in my eyes.

5. You are mine, O my child,
I am your Father,
and I love you with a perfect love.

241 Michael Marchal
© 1973 ICEL

Dying you destroyed our death:
rising you restored our life.
Lord Jesus, Lord Jesus, come in glory!

1. May Christ who died for you
lead you into his kingdom;
may Christ who died for you
lead you this day into Paradise.

2. May Christ, the Good Shepherd,
lead you home today,
and give you a place within his flock.

*2. May Christ, the Good Shepherd,
take you on his shoulders
and bring you home,
bring you home today.

3. May the angels lead you into Paradise:
may the martyrs come to welcome you
and take you to the Holy City,
the new and eternal Jerusalem.

4. May the choirs of angels
come to meet you,
may the choirs of angels
come to meet you
where Lazarus is poor no longer,
may you have eternal life in Christ.

*4. May the choirs of angels
   come to meet you,
   may the choirs of angels
   come to meet you
   and with all God's children
   may you have eternal life in Christ.

* *Alternative children's verses*

242 Willard F. Jabusch
© *1998 Willard F. Jabusch*

Enter in the wilderness, the Lord is coming,
in the desert make the highway straight.
Ev'ry valley shall be lifted up before him,
ev'ry mountain levelled at his feet.

1. God comes, run out to meet him;
   God comes, hurry to greet him;
   God comes, try to be ready,
   for the King is on his way. So,

2. Christ comes, now we will heed him;
   Christ comes, all of us need him;
   Christ comes, hope of the nations,
   Son of justice, Prince of Peace. So,

3. Look up, bonds cut asunder;
   look up, waiting in wonder;
   look up, soon you will see him,
   Christ the Lord is on his way. So,

243 William Whiting, alt.

1. Eternal Father, strong to save,
   whose arm doth bind the restless wave,
   who bidd'st the mighty ocean deep
   its own appointed limits keep:
   O hear us when we cry to thee
   for those in peril on the sea.

2. O Saviour, whose almighty word
   the winds and waves submissive heard,
   who walkedst on the foaming deep,
   and calm, amid its rage, didst sleep:
   O hear us when we cry to thee
   for those in peril on the sea.

3. O sacred Spirit, who didst brood
   upon the waters dark and rude,
   and bid their angry tumult cease,
   and give, for wild confusion, peace:
   O hear us when we cry to thee
   for those in peril on the sea.

4. O Trinity of love and pow'r,
   our brethren shield in danger's hour.
   From rock and tempest, fire and foe,
   protect them whereso'er they go,
   and ever let there rise to thee
   glad hymns of praise from land and sea.

244 Kevin Nichols, based on 'Crux fidelis'
© *Kevin Nichols*

1. Faithful Cross, sustain your burden,
   do not splinter, do not crack,
   though the load of all our sorrows hangs,
   a dead-weight on your back;
   upright on the hill of sadness
   in the gale of evil's pow'r,
   hold him strongly, hold him gently
   at his covenanted hour.

2. Nameless in the forest mounting,
   shoot and sapling, branch and tree,
   felled dismembered, planed and jointed
   for this day's dark mystery.
   Gibbet, infamous, ennobled
   by this death and by this birth,
   hold your cross-grained branches open
   harbour for a shipwrecked earth.

3. When, the noontide darkness ending,
   he whom you have borne is dead,
   in his mother's arms laid gently
   you are left untenanted;
   sharp against the soul's horizon
   still uphold us, shining tree,
   emblem of the Saviour's passion
   standard of his victory.

245
Aniceto Nazareth, based on Psalm 61
© 1984 Kevin Mayhew Ltd.

Faith in God can move the mountains,
trust in him can calm the sea.
He's my fortress, he's my stronghold,
he's the rock who rescues me.

1. Lord, you are my refuge,
   never let me be ashamed.
   In your justice rescue me,
   turn to me and hear my prayer.

2. You are my salvation,
   from oppression set me free.
   Ever since my childhood,
   you have been my only hope.

3. Bitter troubles burden me,
   but you fill me with new life.
   From the grave you raise me up,
   so my tongue will sing your praise.

246
Frederick William Faber

1. Faith of our fathers, living still
   in spite of dungeon, fire and sword;
   O, how our hearts beat high with joy
   whene'er we hear that glorious word!

   Faith of our fathers! Holy Faith!
   We will be true to thee till death,
   we will be true to thee till death.

2. Our fathers, chained in prisons dark,
   were still in heart and conscience free;
   how sweet would be their children's fate,
   if they, like them, could die for thee!

3. Faith of our fathers, Mary's prayers
   shall win our country back to thee;
   and through the truth that comes
       from God
   this land shall then indeed be free.

4. Faith of our fathers, we will love
   both friend and foe in all our strife,
   and preach thee too, as love knows how,
   by kindly words and virtuous life.

247
A. J. Newman

1. Father and life-giver,
   grace of Christ impart;
   he, the Word incarnate,
   food for mind and heart.
   Children of the promise,
   homage now we pay;
   sacrificial banquet
   cheers the desert way.

2. Wine and bread the symbols,
   love and life convey,
   offered by your people,
   work and joy portray.
   All we own consigning,
   nothing is retained;
   tokens of our service,
   gifts and song contain.

3. Transformation wondrous,
   water into wine;
   mingled in the Godhead
   we are made divine.
   Birth into his body
   brought us life anew,
   total consecration,
   fruit from grafting true.

4. Christ, the head, and members
   living now as one,
   offered to the Father
   by this holy Son;
   and our adoration
   purified we find,
   through the Holy Spirit
   breathing in mankind.

248
Gerard Markland, based on Psalm 138
© 1998 Kevin Mayhew Ltd.

Father God, gentle Father God,
my Lord of consolation,
I lift up my heart to you.

1. O Lord, you search me,
   you know me, my ev'ry move.
   My thoughts you read from afar,
   all my ways lie there before you.

2. My heart, my innermost being
   was made by you.
   My body, secretly formed in the womb
   was always with you.

3. What place, what heavens could
   hide me away from you.
   Were I to fly to the ends of the sea,
   your hand would guide me.

4. Your works, your knowledge, your love
   are beyond my mind.
   My Lord, I thank you for these
   and the wonder of my being.

5. O Lord, come search me, come find
   what is in my mind,
   that I may never stray far
   from your path of life eternal.

249 Ian Smale
© 1984 Kingsway's Thankyou Music

Father God,
I wonder how I managed to exist
without the knowledge of your parenthood
and your loving care.
But now I am your child,
I am adopted in your family
and I can never be alone,
'cause, Father God, you're there beside me.
I will sing your praises,
I will sing your praises,
I will sing your praises,
for evermore.

250 Frank Andersen
© Word of Life International

1. Father, in my life I see,
   you are God who walks with me.
   You hold my life in your hands;
   close beside you I will stand.
   I give all my life to you:
   help me, Father, to be true.

2. Jesus, in my life I see
   you are God who walks with me.
   You hold my life in your hands;
   close beside you I will stand.
   I give all my life to you:
   help me, Jesus, to be true.

3. Spirit, in my life I see
   you are God who walks with me.
   You hold my life in your hands;
   close beside you I will stand.
   I give all my life to you:
   help me, Spirit, to be true.

251 Jenny Hewer
© 1975 Kingsway's Thankyou Music

1. Father, I place into your hands
   the things I cannot do.
   Father, I place into your hands
   the things that I've been through.
   Father, I place into your hands
   the way that I should go,
   for I know I always can trust you.

2. Father, I place into your hands
   my friends and family.
   Father, I place into your hands
   the things that trouble me.
   Father I place into your hands
   the person I would be,
   for I know I always can trust you.

3. Father, we love to see your face,
   we love to hear your voice,
   Father, we love to sing your praise
   and in your name rejoice.
   Father, we love to walk with you
   and in your presence rest,
   for we know we always can trust you.

4. Father, I want to be with you
   and do the things you do.
   Father, I want to speak the words
   that you are speaking too.
   Father, I want to love the ones
   that you will draw to you,
   for I know that I am one with you.

252 Terrye Coelho. © 1972 Maranatha!
Music. Administered by CopyCare

1. Father, we adore you,
   lay our lives before you.
   How we love you!

2. Jesus, we adore you . . .

3. Spirit, we adore you . . .

253 James Walsh
© James Walsh, O.S.B. OCP Publications

Father, we come to you,
   God of all pow'r and might.
Show us your glory: give us your life.
Father, we come to you,
   God of all pow'r and might.
Show us your glory: give us your life.
You have united us,
   bound us in love and peace:
God in the midst of us, holy, unseen.
Blessed is he who comes,
   piercing our night of sin.
Open your hearts to him.
   Great is his name.
Bread of life shared with us,
   body of Christ the Lord,
broken and died for us: life for the world.
Father, we come to you,
   God of all pow'r and might.
Show us your glory: give us your life.
Blessed is he who comes,
   piercing our night of sin.
Open our hearts to you:
   great is your name.
Open our hearts to you:
   great is your name!

254 Donna Adkins. © 1976 Maranatha!
Music. Administered by CopyCare

1. Father, we love you,
   we worship and adore you,
   glorify your name in all the earth.

Glorify your name, glorify your name,
glorify your name in all the earth.

2. Jesus, we love you . . .

3. Spirit, we love you . . .

255 John Samuel Bewley Monsell, alt.

1. Fight the good fight with all thy might;
   Christ is thy strength, and Christ thy right;
   lay hold on life, and it shall be
   thy joy and crown eternally.

2. Run the straight race through God's
      good grace,
   lift up thine eyes and seek his face;
   life with its way before us lies;
   Christ is the path, and Christ the prize.

3. Cast care aside, lean on thy guide;
   his boundless mercy will provide;
   trust, and thy trusting soul shall prove
   Christ is its life, and Christ its love.

4. Faint not nor fear, his arms are near;
   he changeth not, and thou art dear;
   only believe, and thou shalt see
   that Christ is all in all to thee.

256 Peter Kearney. © 1971 J. Albert & Son Pty Ltd.,
assigned to B. Feldman & Co. Ltd.

1. Fill my house unto the fullest,
   eat my bread and drink my wine.
   The love I bear is held from no one.

   All I own and all I do I give to you.

2. Take my time unto the fullest,
   find in me the trust you seek,
   and take my hands to you outreaching.

3. Christ our Lord with love enormous
   from the cross his lesson taught:
   'Show love to all, as I have loved you.'

4. Join with me as one in Christ-love,
   may our hearts all beat as one,
   and may we give ourselves completely.

257 Timothy Dudley-Smith
© *Timothy Dudley-Smith*

1. Fill your hearts with joy and gladness,
   sing and praise your God and mine!
   Great the Lord in love and wisdom,
   might and majesty divine!
   He who framed the starry heavens
   knows and names them as they shine.
   Fill your hearts with joy and gladness,
   sing and praise your God and mine!

2. Praise the Lord, his people, praise him!
   Wounded souls his comfort know.
   Those who fear him find his mercies,
   peace for pain and joy for woe;
   humble hearts are high exalted,
   human pride and pow'r laid low.
   Praise the Lord, his people, praise him!
   Wounded souls his comfort know.

3. Praise the Lord for times and seasons,
   cloud and sunshine, wind and rain;
   spring to melt the snows of winter
   till the waters flow again;
   grass upon the mountain pastures,
   golden valleys thick with grain.
   Praise the Lord for times and seasons,
   cloud and sunshine, wind and rain.

4. Fill your hearts with joy and gladness,
   peace and plenty crown your days!
   Love his laws, declare his judgements,
   walk in all his words and ways;
   he the Lord and we his children,
   praise the Lord, all people, praise!
   Fill your hearts with joy and gladness,
   peace and plenty crown your days!

258 John Henry Newman

1. Firmly I believe and truly
   God is three, and God is one,
   and I next acknowledge duly
   manhood taken by the Son.

2. And I trust and hope most fully
   in the Saviour crucified;
   and each thought and deed unruly
   do to death, as he has died.

3. Simply to his grace and wholly
   light and life and strength belong;
   and I love supremely, solely,
   him the holy, him the strong.

4. And I hold in veneration,
   for the love of him alone,
   Holy Church, as his creation,
   and her teachings, as his own.

5. Adoration aye be given,
   with and through th'angelic host,
   to the God of earth and heaven,
   Father, Son and Holy Ghost.

259 Michael Cockett
© 1978 *Kevin Mayhew Ltd.*

Follow me, follow me,
leave your home and family,
leave your fishing nets and boats
upon the shore.
Leave the seed that you have sown,
leave the crops that you've grown,
leave the people you have known
and follow me.

1. The foxes have their holes
   and the swallows have their nests,
   but the Son of Man
   has no place to lie down.
   I do not offer comfort,
   I do not offer wealth,
   but in me will all happiness be found.

2. If you would follow me,
   you must leave old ways behind.
   You must take my cross and
   follow on my path.
   You may be far from loved ones,
   you may be far from home,
   but my Father will welcome you at last.

Continued overleaf

3. Although I go away
   you will never be alone,
   for the Spirit will be
   there to comfort you.
   Though all of you may scatter,
   each follow his own path,
   still the Spirit of love will lead you home.

260 William Walsham How

1. For all the saints
   who from their labours rest,
   who thee by faith
   before the world confessed,
   thy name, O Jesus,
   be for ever blest.

   Alleluia, alleluia!

2. Thou wast their rock,
   their fortress and their might;
   thou, Lord, their captain
   in the well-fought fight;
   thou in the darkness drear
   their one true light.

3. O may thy soldiers,
   faithful, true and bold,
   fight as the saints
   who nobly fought of old,
   and win, with them,
   the victor's crown of gold.

4. O blest communion!
   fellowship divine!
   we feebly struggle,
   they in glory shine;
   yet all are one in thee,
   for all are thine.

5. And when the strife is fierce,
   the warfare long,
   steals on the ear
   the distant triumph song,
   and hearts are brave again,
   and arms are strong.

6. The golden evening
   brightens in the west;
   soon, soon to faithful
   warriors cometh rest;
   sweet is the calm of
   paradise the blest.

7. But lo! There breaks
   a yet more glorious day;
   the saints triumphant
   rise in bright array:
   the King of glory
   passes on his way.

8. From earth's wide bounds,
   from ocean's farthest coast,
   through gates of pearl
   streams in the countless host,
   singing to Father,
   Son and Holy Ghost.

261 Fred Pratt Green
© Stainer & Bell Ltd

1. For the fruits of his creation,
   thanks be to God;
   for his gifts to ev'ry nation,
   thanks be to God;
   for the ploughing, sowing, reaping,
   silent growth while we are sleeping,
   future needs in earth's safe keeping,
   thanks be to God.

2. In the just reward of labour,
   God's will is done;
   in the help we give our neighbour,
   God's will is done;
   in our world-wide task of caring
   for the hungry and despairing,
   in the harvests we are sharing,
   God's will is done.

3. For the harvests of his Spirit,
   thanks be to God;
   for the good we all inherit,
   thanks be to God;

for the wonders that astound us,
for the truths that still confound us,
most of all, that love has found us,
thanks be to God.

262
Fred Kaan
© 1968 Stainer & Bell Ltd.

1. For the healing of the nations,
   Lord, we pray with one accord;
   for a just and equal sharing
   of the things that earth affords.
   To a life of love in action
   help us rise and pledge our word.

2. Lead us, Father, into freedom,
   from despair your world release;
   that, redeemed from war and hatred,
   all may come and go in peace.
   Show us how through care and goodness
   fear will die and hope increase.

3. All that kills abundant living,
   let it from the earth be banned;
   pride of status, race or schooling
   dogmas that obscure your plan.
   In our common quest for justice
   may we hallow life's brief span.

4. You, creator-God, have written
   your great name on humankind;
   for our growing in your likeness
   bring the life of Christ to mind;
   that by our response and service
   earth its destiny may find.

263
James Quinn
© Geoffrey Chapman, a division of Cassell plc.

1. Forth in the peace of Christ we go;
   Christ to the world with joy we bring;
   Christ in our minds, Christ on our lips.
   Christ in our hearts, the world's true King.

2. King of our hearts, Christ makes us kings;
   kingship with him his servants gain;
   with Christ, the Servant-Lord of all,
   Christ's world we serve to share Christ's
   reign.

3. Priests of the world, Christ send us forth
   this world of time to consecrate,
   our world of sin by grace to heal,
   Christ's world in Christ to re-create.

4. Prophets of Christ, we hear his word:
   he claims our minds, to search his ways,
   he claims our lips, to speak his truth,
   he claims our hearts, to sing his praise.

5. We are his Church, he makes us one:
   here is one hearth for all to find,
   here is one flock, one Shepherd-King,
   here is one faith, one heart, one mind.

264
George Hunt Smyttan, adapted by Michael Forster.
© 1999 Kevin Mayhew Ltd.

1. Forty days and forty nights
   you were fasting in the wild;
   forty days and forty nights,
   tempted still, yet unbeguiled.

2. Sunbeams scorching all the day,
   chilly dew-drops nightly shed,
   prowling beasts about your way,
   stones your pillow, earth your bed.

3. Let us your endurance share,
   and from earthly greed abstain,
   with you vigilant in prayer,
   with you strong to suffer pain.

4. Then if evil on us press,
   flesh or spirit to assail,
   Victor in the wilderness,
   help us not to swerve or fail.

5. So shall peace divine be ours;
   holy gladness, pure and true:
   come to us, angelic powers,
   such as ministered to you.

6. Keep, O keep us, Saviour dear,
   ever constant by your side,
   that with you we may appear
   at th'eternal Eastertide.

265

Susan Sayers
© 1995 Kevin Mayhew Ltd.

For you my soul is thirsting, O Lord,
for you my soul is thirsting, O Lord,
for you my soul is thirsting.

1. You are my God, it is you that I seek.
   I am thirsting for you;
   just as a land that is weary and parched,
   longs my body for you.

2. Day after day I will watch in your house.
   You are glory and pow'r;
   better than life is your love for your child,
   I shall sing to your praise.

3. All my life long I will bless you, my God,
   lift my hands in your name;
   richly my soul will be feasted with love,
   I shall praise you with joy.

4. I will remember you, Lord, when I sleep.
   I will watch through the night;
   you are my help and with you I am safe
   in the shade of your wing.

266

Damian Lundy
© 1982 Kevin Mayhew Ltd.

Freedom for my people!
Freedom for my people!
Call them to liberty!
Alleluia! Healing!
Liberation for a new creation!
Set all my people free!

1. Moses was the man I called
   to liberty;
   sent him back to Pharaoh's court
   to set my people free.
   He led all my people out to liberty,
   calling them to leave that land
   of their slavery.

2. Through the desert they were led
   to liberty:
   with the manna they were fed
   so they could be free.

And I gave my law to them for liberty,
so that they might live in peace
and in unity.

3. Oh, when will my people know
   how to be free?
   All my prophets tried to show:
   the people would not see.
   So I gave my only Son, precious to me;
   on the cross he hung in pain
   for your liberty.

4. Jesus rose on Easter Day
   to liberty.
   He will never go away –
   he will set you free!
   Never will he die again! He is with me,
   and we have begun our reign
   with his victory!

(after vs 4 and 5)
Gloria! Alleluia!
Gloria! Alleluia!
Sing of his victory! Alleluia!
Gloria! Alleluia!
Gloria! Alleluia!
Set all my people free!

5. I'm your God and you are mine:
   now you are free!
   Eat my bread and drink my wine!
   Come and follow me!
   You will know my Spirit's love and you
   will see
   power coming from above
   to set all people free!

267

Graham Kendrick
© 1983 Kingsway's Thankyou Music

1. From heav'n you came, helpless babe,
   entered our world, your glory veiled;
   not to be served but to serve,
   and give your life that we might live.

   This is our God, the Servant King,
   he calls us now to follow him,
   to bring our lives as a daily offering
   of worship to the Servant King.

2. There in the garden of tears,
   my heavy load he chose to bear;
   his heart with sorrow was torn.
   'Yet not my will but yours,' he said.

3. Come see his hands and his feet,
   the scars that speak of sacrifice,
   hands that flung stars into space,
   to cruel nails surrendered.

4. So let us learn how to serve,
   and in our lives enthrone him;
   each other's needs to prefer,
   for it is Christ we're serving.

268 Michael Forster, based on the Didaché
© 1992 Kevin Mayhew Ltd.

1. From many grains, once scattered far
     and wide,
   each one alone, to grow as best it may,
   now safely gathered in and unified,
   one single loaf we offer here today.
   So may your Church, in ev'ry time
     and place,
   be in this meal united by your grace.

2. From many grapes, once living on
     the vine,
   now crushed and broken under
     human feet,
   we offer here this single cup of wine:
   the sign of love, unbroken and complete.
   So may we stand among the crucified,
   and live the risen life of him who died.

3. From many places gathered, we are here,
   each with a gift that we alone can bring.
   O Spirit of the living God, draw near,
   make whole by grace our broken offering.
   O crush the pride that bids us stand alone;
   let flow the love that makes our spirits one.

269 Sister M. Teresine, based on Psalm 129

1. From the depths we cry to thee,
   God of sov'reign majesty!
   Hear our chants and hymns of praise;
   bless our Lent of forty days.

2. Though our consciences proclaim
   our transgressions and our shame,
   cleanse us, Lord, we humbly plead,
   from our sins of thought and deed.

3 Lord, accept our Lenten fast
   and forgive our sinful past,
   that we may partake with thee
   in the Easter mystery.

270 Graham Kendrick
©1988 Make Way Music

1. From the sun's rising unto the sun's setting,
   Jesus our Lord, shall be great in the earth;
   and all earth's kingdoms shall be
     his dominion,
   all of creation shall sing of his worth.

   Let ev'ry heart, ev'ry voice,
   ev'ry tongue join with spirits ablaze;
   one in his love, we will circle the world
   with the song of his praise.
   O let all his people rejoice,
   and let all the earth hear his voice.

2. To ev'ry tongue, tribe and nation he
     sends us,
   to make disciples, to teach and baptise.
   For all authority to him is given;
   now, as his witnesses, we shall arise.

3. Come, let us join with the Church from
     all nations,
   cross ev'ry border, throw wide ev'ry door;
   workers with him as he gathers his harvest,
   till earth's corners our Saviour adore.

271

Michael Forster
© 1992 Kevin Mayhew Ltd.

1. From the very depths of darkness
   springs a bright and living light;
   out of falsehood and deceit
   a greater truth is brought to sight;
   in the halls of death, defiant,
   life is dancing with delight!
   The Lord is risen indeed!

   Christ is risen! Hallelujah! (x3)
   The Lord is risen indeed!

2. Jesus meets us at the dawning
   of the resurrection day;
   speaks our name with love, and gently
   says that here we may not stay:
   'Do not cling to me, but go to all
   the fearful ones and say,
   "The Lord is risen indeed!" '

3. So proclaim it in the high-rise,
   in the hostel let it ring;
   make it known in Cardboard City,
   let the homeless rise and sing:
   'He is Lord of life abundant,
   and he changes everything;
   the Lord is risen indeed!'

4. In the heartlands of oppression,
   sound the cry of liberty;
   where the poor are crucified,
   behold the Lord of Calvary;
   from the fear of death and dying,
   Christ has set his people free;
   the Lord is risen indeed!

5. To the tyrant, tell the gospel
   of a love he's never known
   in his guarded palace tomb,
   condemned to live and die alone:
   'Take the risk of love and freedom;
   Christ has rolled away the stone!
   The Lord is risen indeed!'

6. When our spirits are entombed
   in mortal prejudice and pride;
   when the gates of hell itself
   are firmly bolted from inside;
   at the bidding of his Spirit,
   we may fling them open wide;
   The Lord is risen indeed!.

272

Jean Holloway
© 1994 Kevin Mayhew Ltd.

Gather around, for the table is spread,
welcome the food and rest!
Wide is our circle, with Christ at the head,
he is the honoured guest.
Learn of his love, grow in his grace,
pray for the peace he gives;
here at this meal, here in this place,
know that his Spirit lives!
Once he was known
in the breaking of bread,
shared with a chosen few;
multitudes gathered
and by him were fed,
so will he feed us too.

273

Christine McCann
© 1978 Kevin Mayhew Ltd.

1. Gifts of bread and wine, gifts we've offered,
   fruits of labour, fruits of love, taken,
   offered, sanctified, blessed and broken;
   words of one who died;

   'Take my body, take my saving blood.'
   Gifts of bread and wine: Christ our Lord.

2. Christ our Saviour, living presence here,
   as he promised while on earth:
   'I am with you for all time,
   I am with you in this bread and wine.'

3. To the Father, with the Spirit,
   one in union with the Son,
   for God's people, joined in prayer,
   faith is strengthened by the food we share.

274
Traditional

1. Give me joy in my heart, keep me praising,
   give me joy in my heart, I pray.
   Give me joy in my heart, keep my praising,
   keep me praising till the end of day.

   Sing hosanna! Sing hosanna!
   Sing hosanna to the King of kings!
   Sing hosanna! Sing hosanna!
   Sing hosanna to the King!

2. Give me peace in my heart,
   keep me resting . . .

3. Give me love in my heart,
   keep me serving . . .

4. Give me oil in my lamp,
   keep me burning . . .

275
Michael Forster, based on Psalm 117
© 1997 Kevin Mayhew Ltd.

1. Give thanks to God, for he is good,
   his love will never end.
   To our eternal Saviour
   let songs of praise ascend.
   Let all his people say with joy,
   'His love will never end.'

   Sing alleluia! Praise the Lord! Alleluia!
   Sing alleluia! Praise the Lord!

2. The Lord has triumphed gloriously,
   his hand has raised me high.
   Now I shall tell his wonders,
   and never shall I die.
   Let all his people sing with joy,
   'His hand has raised me high.'

3. The stone the builders cast aside
   is now the cornerstone,
   a work by which God's glory
   and faithfulness are shown.
   Let all his people sing with joy,
   'He is our cornerstone.'

276
Henry Smith. © 1978 Integrity's Hosanna! Music
Administered by Kingsway's Thankyou Music

Give thanks with a grateful heart,
give thanks to the Holy One,
give thanks because he's given
Jesus Christ, his Son.
And now let the weak say, 'I am strong',
let the poor say, 'I am rich',
because of what the Lord has done for us.
And now let the weak say, 'I am strong',
let the poor say, 'I am rich',
because of what the Lord has done for us.

277
Peter Gonsalves, based on Psalm 33
© 1984 Kevin Mayhew Ltd.

Glorify the Lord, glorify the Lord,
glorify the Lord with me!

1. I sought the Lord and he answered me,
   from all my terrors he has set me free.
   Come join with me
   and bless his holy name.

2. Look at the Lord, do not be ashamed,
   he will deliver those who call his name.
   The poor have called,
   the Lord has heard their plea.

3. O taste and see that the Lord is good.
   Happy are those who put their trust
      in him.
   So fear the Lord
   and you will know no want.

278
Sebastian Temple
© 1967 OCP Publications

1. Glorious God, King of creation,
   we praise you, we bless you,
   we worship you in song.
   Glorious God in adoration,
   at your feet we belong.

   Lord of life, Father almighty,
   Lord of hearts, Christ the King.
   Lord of love, Holy Spirit,
   to whom we homage bring.

Continued overleaf

2. Glorious God, magnificent, holy,
   we love you, adore you,
   and come to you in pray'r.
   Glorious God, mighty, eternal,
   we sing your praise ev'rywhere.

279 Dan Schutte, based on Psalm 65, 66
© 1976 Daniel L. Schutte and New Dawn Music

Glory and praise to our God,
who alone gives light to our days.
Many are the blessings he bears
to those who trust in his ways.

1. We, the daughters and sons of him
   who built the valleys and plains,
   praise the wonders our God has done
   in ev'ry heart that sings.

2. In his wisdom he strengthens us,
   like gold that's tested in fire.
   Though the power of sin prevails,
   our God is there to save.

3. Ev'ry moment of ev'ry day
   our God is waiting to save,
   always ready to seek the lost,
   to answer those who pray.

4. God has watered our barren land
   and sent his merciful rain.
   Now the rivers of life run
   full for anyone to drink.

280 'Viva, viva, Gestù', 18th century,
trans. Edward Caswall, alt.

1. Glory be to Jesus
   who in bitter pains,
   poured for me the lifeblood
   from his sacred veins.

2. Grace and life eternal
   in that blood I find:
   blest be his compassion,
   infinitely kind.

3. Blest, through endless ages,
   be the precious stream
   which, from endless torment,
   did the world redeem.

4. There the fainting spirit
   drinks of life her fill;
   there, as in a fountain,
   laves herself at will.

5. Abel's blood for vengeance
   pleaded to the skies,
   but the blood of Jesus
   for our pardon cries.

6. Oft as it is sprinkled
   on our guilty hearts
   Satan in confusion
   terror-struck departs.

7. Oft as earth exulting
   wafts its praise on high
   angel hosts rejoicing,
   make their glad reply.

8. Lift, then, all your voices,
   swell the mighty flood;
   louder still and louder,
   praise the precious blood.

281 John Greally. © The Trustees for Roman
Catholic Purposes Registered

1. Glory to thee, Lord God!
   In faith and hope we sing.
   Through this completed sacrifice
   our love and praise we bring.
   We give thee for our sins
   a price beyond all worth,
   which none could ever fitly pay
   but this thy Son on earth.

2. Here is the Lord of all,
   to thee in glory slain;
   of worthless givers, worthy gift,
   a victim without stain.
   Through him we give thee thanks,
   with him we bend the knee,
   in him be all our life, who is
   our one true way to thee.

3. So may this sacrifice
   we offer here this day,
   be joined with our poor lives in all
   we think and do and say.

By living true to grace,
for thee and thee alone,
our sorrows, labours, and our joys
will be his very own.

282 Thomas Ken

1. Glory to thee, my God, this night
   for all the blessings of the light;
   keep me, O keep me, King of kings,
   beneath thine own almighty wings.

2. Forgive me, Lord, for thy dear Son,
   the ill that I this day have done,
   that with the world, myself and thee,
   I, ere I sleep, at peace may be.

3. Teach me to live, that I may dread
   the grave as little as my bed;
   teach me to die, that so I may
   rise glorious at the aweful day.

4. O may my soul on thee repose,
   and with sweet sleep mine eyelids close;
   sleep that may me more vig'rous make
   to serve my God when I awake.

5. Praise God, from whom all blessings flow;
   praise him, all creatures here below;
   praise him above, ye heav'nly host;
   praise Father, Son and Holy Ghost.

283 Book of Hours

God be in my head,
and in my understanding;
God be in mine eyes,
and in my looking;
God be in my mouth,
and in my speaking;
God be in my heart,
and in my thinking;
God be at mine end,
and at my departing.

284 Harold Riley

1. God everlasting,
   wonderful and holy,
   Father most gracious,
   we who stand before thee
   here at thine altar,
   as thy Son has taught us,
   come to adore thee.

2. Countless the mercies
   thou has lavished on us,
   source of all blessing
   to all creatures living;
   to thee we render,
   for thy love o'erflowing,
   humble thanksgiving.

3. Now in remembrance
   of our great Redeemer,
   dying on Calv'ry,
   rising and ascending,
   through him we offer
   what he ever offers,
   sinners befriending.

4. Strength to the living,
   rest to the departed,
   grant, Holy Father,
   through this pure oblation:
   may the life-giving bread
   for ever bring us
   health and salvation.

285 Jean-Paul Lécot, based on Luke 1:46-55, trans. Michael Hodgetts. © 1974 Michael Hodgetts

God fills me with joy, alleluia.
His holy presence is my robe, alleluia.

1. My soul, now glorify the Lord
   who is my Saviour.
   Rejoice, for who am I,
   that God has shown me favour.

2. The world shall call me blest
   and ponder on my story.
   In me is manifest
   God's greatness and his glory.

Continued overleaf

3. For those who are his friends,
   and keep his laws as holy,
   his mercy never ends,
   and he exalts the lowly.

4. But by his power the great,
   the proud, the self-conceited,
   the kings who sit in state,
   are humbled and defeated.

5. He feeds the starving poor,
   he guards his holy nation,
   fulfilling what he swore
   long since in revelation.

6. Then glorify with me
   the Lord who is my Saviour:
   one holy Trinity
   for ever and for ever.

286

Carol Owens. © 1972 Bud John Songs/EMI Christian Music Publishing. Administered by CopyCare

1. God forgave my sin in Jesus' name.
   I've been born again in Jesus' name.
   And in Jesus' name I come to you
   to share his love as he told me to.

   He said: 'Freely, freely you have received;
   freely, freely give.
   Go in my name, and because you believe,
   others will know that I live.'

2. All pow'r is giv'n in Jesus' name,
   in earth and heav'n in Jesus' name.
   And in Jesus' name I come to you
   to share his pow'r as he told me to.

3. God gives us life in Jesus' name,
   he lives in us in Jesus' name.
   And in Jesus' name I come to you
   to share his peace as he told me to.

287

Ascribed to St Thomas Aquinas, trans. Gerard Manley Hopkins, alt.

1. Godhead here in hiding,
   whom I do adore,
   masked by these bare shadows,
   shape and nothing more,
   see, Lord, at thy service
   low lies here a heart
   lost, all lost in wonder
   at the God thou art.

2. Seeing, touching, tasting
   are in thee deceived;
   how, says trusty hearing,
   that shall be believed?
   What God's Son hath told me,
   take for truth I do;
   truth himself speaks truly,
   or there's nothing true.

3. On the cross thy Godhead
   made no sign to men;
   here thy very manhood
   steals from human ken;
   both are my confession,
   both are my belief;
   and I pray the prayer
   of the dying thief.

4. I am not like Thomas,
   wounds I cannot see,
   but can plainly call thee
   Lord and God as he;
   this faith each day deeper
   be my holding of,
   daily make me harder
   hope and dearer love.

5. O thou our reminder
   of Christ crucified,
   living Bread, the life of
   us for whom he died,
   lend this life to me then,
   feed and feast my mind,
   there be thou the sweetness
   man was meant to find.

6. Jesu, whom I look at
   shrouded here below,
   I beseech thee send me
   what I long for so,
   some day to gaze on thee

face to face in light
and be blest for ever
with thy glory's sight.

288
John L. Bell and Graham Maule

1. God, in the planning and purpose of life,
hallowed the union of husband and wife:
this we embody where love is displayed,
rings are presented and promises made.

2. Jesus was found, at a similar feast,
taking the roles of both water and priest,
turning the worldly towards the divine,
tears into the laughter and water to wine.

3. Therefore we pray that his Spirit preside
over the wedding of bridegroom
   and bride,
fulfilling all that they've hoped will
   come true,
lighting with love all they dream of and do.

4. Praise then the Maker, the Spirit, the Son,
source of the love through which two are
   made one.
God's is the glory, the goodness and grace
seen in this marriage and known in
   this place.

289
Traditional

1. God is love, and the one who lives in love
lives in God, and God lives in him.
God is love, and the one who lives in love
lives in God, and God lives in her.
And we have come to know
and have believed
the love which God has for us.
God is love, and all those who live in love
live in God, and God lives in them.

2. God is hope . . .

3. God is peace . . .

4. God is joy . . .

290
Percy Dearmer

1. God is love: his the care,
tending each, ev'rywhere.
God is love, all is there!
Jesus came to show him,
that we all might know him!

Sing aloud, loud, loud!
Sing aloud, loud, loud!
God is good! God is truth!
God is beauty! Praise him!

2. None can see God above;
we can share life and love;
thus may we Godward move,
seek him in creation,
holding ev'ry nation.

3. Jesus lived on the earth,
hope and life brought to birth
and affirmed human worth,
for he came to save us
by the truth he gave us.

4. To our Lord praise we sing,
light and life, friend and King,
coming down, love to bring,
pattern for our duty,
showing God in beauty.

291
Timothy Dudley-Smith, based on Psalm 62

1. God is my great desire,
his face I seek the first;
to him my heart and soul aspire,
for him I thirst.
As one in desert lands,
whose very flesh is flame,
in burning love I lift my hands
and bless his name.

2. God is my true delight,
my richest feast his praise,
through silent watches of the night,
through all my days.

Continued overleaf

To him my spirit clings,
on him my soul is cast;
beneath the shadow of his wings
he holds me fast.

3. God is my strong defence
in ev'ry evil hour;
in him I face with confidence
the tempter's pow'r.
I trust his mercy sure,
with truth and triumph crowned:
my hope and joy for evermore
in him are found.

292
Michael Forster
© 1993 Kevin Mayhew Ltd.

1. God of eternal light,
your promises we claim;
as Abram's heirs,
we recognise the honour of your name.
Our sacrifice accept,
our lives of faith inspire,
and ev'ry fearful heart
transform with purifying fire.

2. High on the mountain side
your glory was revealed,
and yet, that great mysterious light
a deeper truth concealed!
What fearful shadows still
those sights and sounds portray:
a dreadful kind of majesty
that words cannot convey!

3. Christ, from the heav'ns descend,
eternal life make known,
and all our mortal bodies change
to copies of your own.
Your great and glorious light
creation then shall see,
when truth and peace are all around,
and justice flowing free!

293
Edmund Vaughan, alt.

1. God of mercy and compassion,
look with pity upon me;
Father, let me call thee Father,
'tis thy child returns to thee.

Jesus, Lord, I ask for mercy,
knowing it is not in vain:
all my sins I now detest them,
help me not to sin again.

2. Only by thy grace and mercy
may I hope for heav'n above,
where the Saints rejoice for ever
in a sea of boundless love.

3. See our Saviour, bleeding, dying
on the cross of Calvary;
to that cross my sins have nailed him,
yet he bleeds and dies for me.

294
Michael Forster
© 1993 Kevin Mayhew Ltd.

1. God of the covenant,
yours is the Word of salvation,
moving the heart to repentance
and true adoration.
Blood is the seal,
pow'rful to cleanse and to heal,
sprinkled on all your creation.

2. God of the covenant,
known in the breaking and pouring,
body and blood of the Saviour,
creation restoring:
here we prepare,
Christ, in your passion to share,
humbly your presence adoring.

3. God of the covenant,
yours is the Word of salvation
bearing the terrible cost
of the world's liberation.
Freedom at last!
Christ through the curtain has passed.
God is at one with creation!

295

Michael Forster
© 1993 Kevin Mayhew Ltd.

1. God of the Passover,
   Author and Lord of salvation,
   gladly we gather to bring
   you our heart's adoration;
   ransomed and free,
   called and commissioned to be
   signs of your love for creation.

2. Here we remember that evening
   of wonder enthralling,
   myst'ry of passion divine,
   and betrayal appalling.
   Breaking the bread,
   'This is my body,' he said,
   'do this, my passion recalling.'

3. God of the Eucharist,
   humbly we gather before you
   and, at your table,
   for pardon and grace we implore you.
   Under the cross,
   counting as profit our loss,
   safe in its shade, we adore you.

296

Traditional

1. God rest you merry, gentlemen,
   let nothing you dismay,
   for Jesus Christ our Saviour
   was born on Christmas day,
   to save us all from Satan's pow'r
   when we were gone astray:

   O tidings of comfort and joy,
   comfort and joy,
   O tidings of comfort and joy.

2. In Bethlehem, in Jewry,
   this blessèd babe was born,
   and laid within a manger,
   upon this blessèd morn;
   the which his mother Mary
   did nothing take in scorn.

3. From God, our heav'nly Father,
   a blessèd angel came,
   and unto certain shepherds
   brought tidings of the same,
   how that in Bethlehem was born
   the Son of God by name.

4. 'Fear not,' then said the angel,
   'let nothing ye affright,
   this day is born a Saviour,
   of virtue, pow'r and might;
   by him the world is overcome
   and Satan put to flight.'

5. The shepherds at those tidings
   rejoicèd much in mind,
   and left their flocks a-feeding,
   in tempest, storm and wind,
   and went to Bethlehem straightway
   this blessèd babe to find.

6. But when to Bethlehem they came,
   whereat this infant lay,
   they found him in a manger,
   where oxen feed on hay;
   his mother Mary kneeling,
   unto the Lord did pray.

7. Now to the Lord sing praises,
   all you within this place,
   and with true love and fellowship
   each other now embrace;
   this holy tide of Christmas
   all others doth deface.

297

Alan Dale and Hubert J. Richards
© 1982 Kevin Mayhew Ltd.

1. God's Spirit is in my heart.
   He has called me and set me apart.
   This is what I have to do,
   what I have to do.

Continued overleaf

He sent me to give
the Good News to the poor,
tell pris'ners that they are pris'ners no more,
tell blind people that they can see,
and set the down trodden free,
and go tell ev'ry one the news
that the kingdom of God has come,
and go tell ev'ryone the news
that God's kingdom has come.

2. Just as the Father sent me,
so I'm sending you out to be
my witnesses throughout the world,
the whole of the world.

3. Don't carry a load in your pack,
you don't need two shirts on your back.
A workman can earn his own keep,
can earn his own keep.

4. Don't worry what you have to say,
don't worry because on that day
God's Spirit will speak in your heart,
will speak in your heart.

298

Michael Forster
© 1999 Kevin Mayhew Ltd.

1. Going home, moving on,
through God's open door;
hush, my soul, have no fear,
Christ has gone before.
Parting hurts, love protests,
pain is not denied;
yet, in Christ, life and hope
span the great divide.
Going home, moving on,
through God's open door;
hush, my soul, have no fear,
Christ has gone before,
Christ has gone before.

2. No more guilt, no more fear,
all the past is healed:
broken dreams now restored,
perfect grace revealed.
Christ has died, Christ is ris'n,
Christ will come again:

death destroyed, life restored,
love alone shall reign.
Going home, moving on,
through God's open door;
hush, my soul, have no fear,
Christ has gone before,
Christ has gone before.

299

Aniceto Nazareth
© 1984 Kevin Mayhew Ltd.

Go in peace to be Christ's body.
Go in peace, proclaim his Word.
You have shared his dying and his rising.
Go in peace, Christ lives in you.

1. But our treasure is in earthen vessels,
proving we are weak and need
God's strength.
Bearing in our flesh the death of Jesus,
we must show his life at work in us.

2. Though our outer nature may
seem wasted,
daily is the inner self renewed.
For the love of Jesus Christ controls us,
since we know that one man died for all.

300

John Mason Neale, alt.

1. Good Christians, all, rejoice
with heart and soul and voice!
Give ye heed to what we say:
News! News! Jesus Christ is born today;
ox and ass before him bow,
and he is in the manger now:
Christ is born today, Christ is born today!

2. Good Christians all, rejoice
with heart and soul and voice!
Now ye hear of endless bliss:
Joy! Joy! Jesus Christ was born for this.
He hath opened heaven's door,
and we are blest for evermore:
Christ was born for this,
Christ was born for this.

3. Good Christians all, rejoice
   with heart and soul and voice!
   Now ye need not fear the grave:
   Peace! Peace! Jesus Christ was born to save;
   calls you one, and calls you all,
   to gain his everlasting hall:
   Christ was born to save,
   Christ was born to save.

301 John Mason Neale, alt.

1. Good King Wenceslas looked out
   on the feast of Stephen,
   when the snow lay round about,
   deep, and crisp, and even;
   brightly shone the moon that night,
   though the frost was cruel,
   when a poor man came in sight,
   gath'ring winter fuel.

2. 'Hither, page, and stand by me,
   if thou know'st it, telling,
   yonder peasant, who is he,
   where and what his dwelling?'
   'Sire, he lives a good league hence,
   underneath the mountain,
   right against the forest fence,
   by Saint Agnes' fountain.'

3. 'Bring me flesh, and bring me wine,
   bring me pine logs hither:
   thou and I will see him dine,
   when we bring him thither.'
   Page and monarch, forth they went,
   forth they went together;
   through the rude wind's wild lament,
   and the bitter weather.

4. 'Sire, the night is darker now,
   and the wind blows stronger;
   fails my heart, I know not how;
   I can go no longer.'
   'Mark my footsteps good, my page;
   tread thou in them boldly:
   thou shalt find the winter's rage
   freeze thy blood less coldly.'

5. In his master's steps he trod,
   where the snow lay dinted;
   heat was in the very sod
   which the Saint had printed.
   Therefore, Christians all, be sure,
   wealth or rank possessing,
   ye who now will bless the poor,
   shall yourselves find blessing.

302 Traditional

Go, tell it on the mountain,
over the hills and ev'rywhere,
go, tell it on the mountain
that Jesus Christ is born.

1. While shepherds kept their watching
   o'er wand'ring flocks by night,
   behold, from out of heaven,
   there shone a holy light.

2. And lo, when they had seen it,
   they all bowed down and prayed;
   they travelled on together
   to where the babe was laid.

3. When I was a seeker,
   I sought both night and day:
   I asked my Lord to help me
   and he showed me the way.

4. He made me a watchman
   upon the city wall,
   and, if I am a Christian,
   I am the least of all.

303 Marie Lydia Pereira
© 1976 Kevin Mayhew Ltd.

1. Go, the Mass is ended,
   children of the Lord.
   Take his Word to others
   as you've heard it spoken to you.
   Go, the Mass is ended,
   go and tell the world
   the Lord is good, the Lord is kind,
   and he loves ev'ryone.

Continued overleaf

2. Go, the Mass is ended,
take his love to all.
Gladden all who meet you,
fill their hearts with hope and courage.
Go, the Mass is ended,
fill the world with love,
and give to all what you've received –
the peace and joy of Christ.

3. Go, the Mass is ended,
strengthened in the Lord,
lighten ev'ry burden,
spread the joy of Christ around you.
Go, the Mass is ended,
take his peace to all.
This day is yours to change the world –
to make God known and loved.

304 Lucien Deiss, adapted from Ezekiel 36:26 and Jeremiah 31: 31-34. © 1965, 1966, 1968, 1973 World Library Publications, a division of J. S. Paluch Co. Inc.

Grant to us, O Lord, a heart renewed;
recreate in us your own Spirit, Lord!

1. Behold, the days are coming,
says the Lord our God,
when I will make a new covenant
with the house of Israel.

2. Deep within their being
I will implant my law;
I will write it on their hearts.

3. I will be their God,
and they shall be my people.

4. And for all their faults
I will grant forgiveness;
nevermore will I remember their sins.

305 Francesca Leftley
© 1976 Kevin Mayhew Ltd.

1. Grant us* your peace, Lord,
shelter us from harm, Lord,
grant us your peace, Lord,
shield us with your love.

* or 'them'; 'her'; 'him' as appropriate

Just as a mother *(father)*
cares for her *(his)* children
grant us your peace, Lord,
shield us with your love.

2. Grant us your strength, Lord,
shelter us from harm, Lord,
grant us your strength, Lord,
shield us with your love.
From dusk till daybreak,
each waking moment,
grant us your strength, Lord,
shield us with your love.

306 Aniceto Nazareth, based on the Psalms
© 1984 Kevin Mayhew Ltd.

Great indeed are your works, O Lord,
now and evermore! (Repeat)

1. The universe, night and day,
tells of all your wonders.
You are our life and our light:
we shall praise you always.

2. You are the path which we tread,
you will lead us onward.
From ev'ry corner of earth
all the nations gather.

3. You lead them all by the hand
to the heav'nly kingdom.
Then, at the end of all times,
you will come in glory.

307 William Williams,
trans. Peter Williams and others

1. Guide me, O thou great Redeemer,
pilgrim through this barren land;
I am weak, but thou art mighty,
hold me with thy pow'rful hand:
Bread of Heaven, Bread of Heaven,
feed me till I want no more,
feed me till I want no more.

2. Open now the crystal fountain,
   whence the healing stream doth flow;
   let the fire and cloudy pillar
   lead me all my journey through;
   strong deliv'rer, strong deliv'rer,
   be thou still my strength and shield,
   be thou still my strength and shield.

3. When I tread the verge of Jordan,
   bid my anxious fears subside;
   death of death, and hell's destruction,
   land me safe on Canaan's side;
   songs of praises, songs of praises,
   I will ever give to thee,
   I will ever give to thee.

308 Sister Agnes

1. Hail, glorious Saint Patrick,
   dear saint of our isle,
   on us thy poor children
   bestow a sweet smile;
   and now thou art high
   in the mansions above,
   on Erin's green valleys
   look down in thy love.

   On Erin's green valleys (x3)
   look down in thy love.

2. Hail, glorious Saint Patrick,
   thy words were once strong
   against Satan's wiles and
   an infidel throng;
   not less is thy might
   where in heaven thou art;
   O, come to our aid,
   in our battle take part.

3. In the war against sin,
   in the fight for the faith,
   dear saint, may thy children
   resist unto death;

may their strength be in meekness,
in penance, in prayer,
their banner the Cross
which they glory to bear.

4. Thy people, now exiles
   on many a shore,
   shall love and revere thee
   till time be no more;
   and the fire thou has kindled
   shall ever burn bright,
   its warmth undiminished,
   undying its light.

5. Ever bless and defend the sweet
   land of our birth,
   where the shamrock still blooms
   as when thou wert on earth,
   and our hearts shall yet burn,
   wheresoever we roam,
   for God and Saint Patrick,
   and our native home.

309 John Lingard

1. Hail, Queen of heav'n, the ocean star,
   guide of the wand'rer here below;
   thrown on life's surge, we claim thy care;
   save us from peril and from woe.
   Mother of Christ, star of the sea,
   pray for the wand'rer, pray for me.

2. O gentle, chaste and spotless maid,
   we sinners make our prayers through thee;
   remind thy Son that he has paid
   the price of our iniquity.
   Virgin most pure, star of the sea,
   pray for the sinner, pray for me.

3. Sojourners in this vale of tears,
   to thee, blest advocate, we cry;
   pity our sorrows, calm our fears,
   and soothe with hope our misery.
   Refuge in grief, star of the sea,
   pray for the mourner, pray for me.

Continued overleaf

4. And while to him who reigns above,
   in Godhead One, in persons Three,
   the source of life, of grace, of love,
   homage we pay on bended knee,
   do thou, bright Queen, star of the sea,
   pray for thy children, pray for me.

310
Patrick Brennan
© Burns & Oakes Ltd.

1. Hail, Redeemer, King divine!
   Priest and Lamb, the throne is thine,
   King, whose reign shall never cease.
   Prince of everlasting peace.

   Angels, saints and nations sing:
   'Praised be Jesus Christ, our King,
   Lord of life, earth, sky and sea.
   King of love on Calvary.'

2. King whose name creation thrills,
   rule our minds, our hearts, our wills,
   till in peace each nation rings
   with thy praises, King of kings.

3. King most holy, King of truth,
   guide the lowly, guide the youth;
   Christ thou King of glory bright,
   be to us eternal light.

4. Shepherd-King, o'er mountains steep,
   homeward bring the wand'ring sheep,
   shelter in one royal fold
   states and kingdoms, new and old.

311
Charles Wesley, Thomas Cotterill and others, alt.

1. Hail the day that sees him rise, *alleluia!*
   to his throne above the skies; *alleluia!*
   Christ the Lamb, for sinners giv'n, *alleluia!*
   enters now the highest heav'n! *alleluia!*

2. There for him high triumph waits;
   lift your heads, eternal gates!
   He hath conquered death and sin;
   take the King of Glory in!

3. Circled round with angel-pow'rs,
   their triumphant Lord and ours;
   wide unfold the radiant scene,
   take the King of Glory in!

4. Lo, the heav'n its Lord receives,
   yet he loves the earth he leaves;
   though returning to his throne,
   calls the human race his own.

5. See, he lifts his hands above;
   see, he shows the prints of love;
   hark, his gracious lips bestow
   blessings on his Church below.

6. Still for us he intercedes,
   his prevailing death he pleads;
   near himself prepares our place,
   he the first-fruits of our race.

7. Lord, though parted from our sight,
   far above the starry height,
   grant our hearts may thither rise,
   seeking thee above the skies.

8. Ever upward let us move,
   wafted on the wings of love;
   looking when our Lord shall come,
   longing, sighing after home.

312
Michael Forster
© 1993 Kevin Mayhew Ltd.

1. Hail the risen Lord, ascending
   to his holy Father's side,
   angels lost in awe and wonder
   now acclaim the Lord who died.
   Alleluia, alleluia,
   Christ triumphant, glorified!

2. He who once, from royal splendour,
   came to share our state of blame,
   now ascends in clouds of glory
   to the heights from which he came.
   Alleluia, alleluia,
   Christ for evermore the same!

3. He will grant his praying servants,
   from the riches of his power,
   grace to live as risen people
   in this present watching hour.
   Alleluia, alleluia,
   God on us his blessings shower.

4. Now he bids us tell his story,
   where the lost and fearful roam:
   he will come again triumphant,
   and will lead his people home.
   Alleluia, alleluia,
   Maranatha! Come, Lord, come!

313 'Ave, maris stella' 9th century,
trans. Edward Caswall

1. Hail, thou star of ocean, portal of the sky,
   ever virgin mother of the Lord most high.
   O by Gabriel's 'Ave', uttered long ago,
   Eva's name reversing, 'stablish peace below.

2. Break the captive's fetters, light on
        blindness pour,
   all our ills expelling, ev'ry bliss implore.
   Show thyself a mother; offer him our sighs,
   who for us incarnate did not thee despise.

3. Virgin of all virgins, to thy shelter take us;
   gentlest of the gentle, chaste and gentle
        make us.
   Still, as on we journey, help our
        weak endeavour;
   till with thee and Jesus we rejoice for ever.

4. Through the highest heaven,
        to th'almighty Three,
   Father, Son and Spirit, One same glory be.

314 Paraphase of Psalm 71 by James Montgomery

1. Hail to the Lord's anointed,
   great David's greater son!
   Hail, in the time appointed,
   his reign on earth begun!

He comes to break oppression,
to set the captive free;
to take away transgression,
and rule in equity.

2. He comes with succour speedy
   to those who suffer wrong;
   to help the poor and needy,
   and bid the weak be strong;
   to give them songs for sighing,
   their darkness turn to light,
   whose souls, condemned and dying,
   were precious in his sight.

3. He shall come down like showers
   upon the fruitful earth,
   and love, joy, hope, like flowers,
   spring in his path to birth:
   before him on the mountains
   shall peace the herald go;
   and righteousness in fountains
   from hill to valley flow.

4. Kings shall fall down before him,
   and gold and incense bring;
   all nations shall adore him,
   his praise all people sing;
   to him shall prayer unceasing
   and daily vows ascend;
   his kingdom still increasing,
   a kingdom without end.

5. O'er ev'ry foe victorious,
   he on his throne shall rest,
   from age to age more glorious,
   all-blessing and all-blest;
   the tide of time shall never
   his covenant remove;
   his name shall stand for ever;
   that name to us is love.

315 Latin 14th century, trans. by H. N. Oxenham
© Copyright control

1. Hail, true Body, born of Mary,
   by a wondrous virgin birth.
   You who on the cross were offered
   to redeem us all on earth.

Continued overleaf

2. You whose side became a fountain
   pouring forth your precious blood,
   give us now, and at our dying,
   your own self to be our food.

   O kindest Jesu, O gracious Jesu,
   O Jesu, blessed Mary's Son.

316
'Vox clara ecce intonat' 6th century,
trans. Edward Caswall

1. Hark! a herald voice is calling:
   'Christ is nigh!' it seems to say;
   'Cast away the dreams of darkness,
   O ye children of the day!'

2. Startled at the solemn warning,
   let the earth-bound soul arise;
   Christ, her sun, all sloth dispelling,
   shines upon the morning skies.

3. Lo, the Lamb, so long expected,
   comes with pardon down from heav'n;
   let us haste, with tears of sorrow,
   one and all to be forgiv'n.

4. So when next he comes with glory,
   wrapping all the earth in fear,
   may he then, as our defender,
   on the clouds of heav'n appear.

5. Honour, glory, virtue, merit,
   to the Father and the Son,
   with the co-eternal Spirit,
   while unending ages run.

317
Charles Wesley, George Whitefield, Martin Madan
and others, alt.

1. Hark, the herald-angels sing
   glory to the new-born King;
   peace on earth and mercy mild,
   God and sinners reconciled:
   joyful, all ye nations rise,
   join the triumph of the skies,
   with th'angelic host proclaim,
   'Christ is born in Bethlehem.'

   Hark, the herald-angels sing
   glory to the new-born King.

2. Christ, by highest heav'n adored,
   Christ, the everlasting Lord,
   late in time behold him come,
   offspring of a virgin's womb!
   Veiled in flesh the Godhead see,
   hail, th'incarnate Deity!
   Pleased as man with us to dwell,
   Jesus, our Emmanuel.

3. Hail, the heav'n-born Prince of Peace!
   Hail, the Sun of Righteousness!
   Light and life to all he brings,
   ris'n with healing in his wings;
   mild he lays his glory by,
   born that we no more may die,
   born to raise us from the earth,
   born to give us second birth.

318
Susan Sayers, based on Psalm 50
© 1989 Kevin Mayhew Ltd.

Have mercy on us,
O Lord, for we have sinned. (Repeat)

1. O God, in your kindness,
   have mercy on me,
   and in your compassion
   blot out my offence.
   O wash me, O wash me
   from all of my guilt,
   until you have cleansed me from sin.

2. For all my offences
   I know very well,
   I cannot escape from
   the sight of my sin.
   Against you, O Lord,
   only you, have I sinned,
   and done what is wrong in your eyes.

3. A pure heart create
   in your servant, O Lord;
   a steadfast and trustworthy
   spirit in me.
   O cast me not out
   from your presence, I pray,
   and take not your spirit from me.

4. Restore to me, Lord,
   all the joy of your help;
   sustain me with fervour,
   sustain me with zeal.
   Then open my lips,
   and my mouth shall declare
   the praise of my Lord and my God.

319
Marty Haugen
© GIA Publications Inc.

Healer of our ev'ry ill,
light of each tomorrow,
give us peace beyond our fear,
and hope beyond our sorrow.

1. You who know our fears and sadness,
   grace us with your peace and gladness.
   Spirit of all comfort: fill our hearts.

2. In the pain and joy beholding,
   how your grace is still unfolding.
   Give us all your vision: God of love.

3. Give us strength to love each other,
   ev'ry sister, ev'ry brother.
   Spirit of all kindness: be our guide.

4. You who know each thought and feeling,
   teach us all your way of healing.
   Spirit of compassion: fill each heart.

320
Francesca Leftley
© 1999 Kevin Mayhew Ltd.

1. Healer of the sick,
   Lord Jesus, Son of God;
   Lord, how we long for you:
   walk here among us.

Bind up our broken lives,
comfort our broken hearts,
banish our hidden fears.
Lord, come with power,
bring new light to the blind,
bring peace to troubled minds,
hold us now in your arms, set us free now.

2. Bearer of our pain,
   Lord Jesus, Lamb of God;
   Lord, how we cry to you:
   walk here among us.

3. Calmer of our fears,
   Lord Jesus, Prince of Peace;
   Lord, how we yearn for you:
   walk here among us.

4. Saviour of the world,
   Lord Jesus, mighty God;
   Lord, how we sing to you:
   walk here among us.

321
Anthony D'Souza, based on Psalm 60
© 1984 Kevin Mayhew Ltd.

Hear my cry, O Lord, my God,
listen to my prayer;
from earth's end I call to you
when my heart is faint.

1. Set me high on a rock;
   you are my refuge, O Lord.

2. Let me stay in your tent;
   safe in the shade of your wings.

3. I will echo your praise;
   pay my vows day after day.

322
Graham Kendrick
© 1996 Make Way Music

	Refrain 1
Cantor	*Hear our cry, O hear our cry:*
All	*'Jesus, come!'*
Cantor	*Hear our cry, O hear our cry:*
All	*'Jesus, come!'*
All	1. The tide of prayer is rising, a deeper passion burning – *Refrain 1 above*
All	2. We lift our eyes with longing to see your kingdom coming – *Refrain 1 above, then:*

Continued overleaf

Refrain 2

Cantor/All *Whoever is thirsty, come now*
and drink the waters of life.

Cantor/All *'Jesus, come!' 'Jesus, come!'*

All 3. The streets of teeming cities
cry out for healing rivers –
Refrain 1

All 4. Refresh them with your
presence, give grace for deep
repentance –
Refrain 1, then *Refrain 2*

All 5. Tear back the shroud of
shadows that covers all the
peoples –
Refrain 1

All 6. Revealing your salvation in ev'ry
tribe and nation –
Refrain 1, then *Refrain 2*

323 Michael Forster
© 1993 Kevin Mayhew Ltd.

1. Heaven is open wide,
and Christ in glory stands,
with all authority endowed
and set at God's right hand.
Above the world of noise
extends his reign of peace,
and all the blood of martyrs calls
our angry ways to cease.

2. Heaven is open wide,
and perfect love we see
in God's eternal self revealed:
the blessèd Trinity.
Christ for the church has prayed,
that we may all be one,
and share the triune grace whereby
creation was begun.

3. Heaven is open wide,
and Christ in glory stands:
the Source and End, the First and Last,
with justice in his hands.
Let all the thirsty come
where life is flowing free,
and Christ, in splendour yet unknown,
our morning star will be.

324 Traditional

1. He brings us into his banqueting table,
his banner over me is love; *(x3)*
his banner over me is love.

2. The one way to peace
is the power of the cross . . .

3. He builds his Church
on a firm foundation . . .

4. In him we find a new creation . . .

5. He lifts us up to heavenly places . . .

325 Unknown

1. He is Lord, he is Lord.
He is risen from the dead and he is Lord.
Ev'ry knee shall bow, ev'ry tongue confess
that Jesus Christ is Lord.

2. He is King, he is King,
He is risen from the dead and he is King.
Ev'ry knee shall bow, ev'ry tongue confess
that Jesus Christ is King.

3. He is love, he is love.
He is risen from the dead and he is love.
Ev'ry knee shall bow, ev'ry tongue confess
that Jesus Christ is love.

326 Willard F. Jabusch
© 1998 Willard F. Jabusch

1. He is risen, tell the story
to the nations of the night;
from their sin and from their blindness,
let them walk in Easter light.
Now begins a new creation,
now has come our true salvation,
Jesus Christ, the Son of God!

2. Mary goes to tell the others
   of the wonders she has seen;
   John and Peter come a-running –
   what can all this truly mean?
   O Rabboni, Master holy,
   to appear to one so lowly!
   Jesus Christ, the Son of God!

3. He has cut down death and evil,
   he has conquered all despair;
   he has lifted from our shoulders
   all the weight of anxious care.
   Risen Brother, now before you,
   we will worship and adore you,
   Jesus Christ, the Son of God!

4. Now get busy, bring the message,
   so that all may come to know
   there is hope for saint and sinner,
   for our God has loved us so.
   Ev'ry church bell is a-ringing,
   ev'ry Christian now is singing,
   Jesus Christ, the Son of God!

327

Marty Haugen
© 1982 GIA Publications Inc.

1. Here in this place, new light is streaming,
   now is the darkness vanished away;
   see in this space,
   our fears and our dreamings,
   brought here to you in the light of
      this day.
   Gather us in, the lost and forsaken,
   gather us in, the blind and the lame;
   call to us now, and we shall awaken.
   We shall arise at the sound of your name.

2. We are the young, our lives are a myst'ry,
   we are the old who yearn for your face;
   we have been sung
   throughout all of hist'ry,
   called to be light to the whole human race.

Gather us in, the rich and the haughty,
gather us in, the proud and the strong;
give us a heart so meek and so lowly,
give us the courage to enter the song.

3. Here we will take the wine and the water,
   here we will take the bread of new birth;
   here you shall call
   your sons and your daughters,
   call us anew to be salt for the earth.
   Give us to drink the wine of compassion,
   give us to eat the bread that is you;
   nourish us well, and teach us to fashion
   lives that are holy and hearts that are true.

4. Not in the dark of buildings confining,
   not in some heaven, light years away,
   but here in this place
   the new light is shining,
   now is the kingdom, now is the day.
   Gather us in and hold us for ever,
   gather us in and make us your own;
   gather us in, all peoples together,
   fire of love in our flesh and our bone.

328

Graham Kendrick
© 1991 Make Way Music

1. Here is bread, here is wine,
   Christ is with us, he is with us.
   Break the bread, taste the wine,
   Christ is with us here.

   In this bread there is healing,
   in this cup is life for ever.
   In this moment, by the Spirit,
   Christ is with us here.

2. Here is grace, here is peace.
   Christ is with us, he is with us;
   know his grace, find his peace,
   feast on Jesus here.

3. Here we are, joined in one,
   Christ is with us, he is with us;
   we'll proclaim, till he comes,
   Jesus crucified.

329 Estelle White
© 1976 Kevin Mayhew Ltd.

1. Here's a child for you, O Lord,
   we shall cherish, we shall care.
   We'll be faithful to your Word,
   for we want this child to share
   your love-light.

2. May he (she) hold his (her) head up high,
   graceful, joyful, strong of limb.
   May his (her) eyes be clear and bright,
   seeing beauty in all things
   that you've made.

3. We were young ourselves, O Lord,
   we were eager, we were fresh
   like the op'ning buds of spring,
   and we wanted happiness
   in your way.

4. Then, at times, we went astray,
   we were foolish, we were weak,
   and the innocence we had
   vanished like the trace of feet
   when snow melts.

5. But we come, O Lord and King,
   at your bidding, and we pray
   that the precious gift we bring
   will grow stronger every day
   in your love.

6. By the water poured out here
   and your promise, we believe,
   he (she) will master every fear,
   and at last will come to see
   your Godhead.

330 Traditional

1. He's got the whole world in his hand. *(x4)*

2. He's got you and me, brother . . .

3. He's got you and me, sister . . .

4. He's got the little tiny baby . . .

5. He's got ev'rybody here . . .

331 Percy Dearmer after John Bunyan
© Oxford University Press

1. He who would valiant be
   'gainst all disaster,
   let him in constancy
   follow the Master.
   There's no discouragement
   shall make him once relent
   his first avowed intent
   to be a pilgrim.

2. Who so beset him round
   with dismal stories,
   do but themselves confound –
   his strength the more is.
   No foes shall stay his might,
   though he with giants fight:
   he will make good his right
   to be a pilgrim.

3. Since, Lord, thou dost defend
   us with thy Spirit,
   we know we at the end
   shall life inherit.
   Then fancies flee away!
   I'll fear not what men say,
   I'll labour night and day
   to be a pilgrim.

332 Michael Forster
© 1993 Kevin Mayhew Ltd.

1. Holy God, of righteous glory,
   see your people gathered here,
   in a solemn congregation,
   your forgiving word to hear.
   God of love and slow to anger,
   gracious, longing to restore,
   hear your priests and people calling,
   give us grace to sin no more.

2. We confess the pride we suffer,
   needs which none can satisfy:
   how we love the praise of mortals,
   swift to flow'r and quick to die.
   Let us find rewards eternal
   as we quietly seek your face,
   and our open, public living
   witness only to your grace.

3. Free us from our self-bound living,
   better witnesses to be,
   to the world by grace appealing,
   telling forth the mystery:
   how creation's pure Redeemer
   walked among us undefiled,
   by his deathless love proclaiming,
   God with us is reconciled.

333
Adaptation of a 4th century hymn by Ambrose.
Ascribed to Ignaz Franz, trans. Clarence Walworth

1. Holy God, we praise thy name;
   Lord of all, we bow before thee.
   All on earth thy sceptre own,
   all in heaven above adore thee.
   Infinite thy vast domain,
   everlasting is thy reign.

2. Hark, the loud celestial hymn,
   angel choirs above are raising;
   cherubim and seraphim,
   in unceasing chorus praising,
   fill the heavens with sweet accord,
   holy, holy, holy Lord.

3. Holy Father, Holy Son,
   Holy Spirit, three we name thee,
   while in essence only one
   undivided God we claim thee;
   and adoring bend the knee,
   while we own the mystery.

4. Spare thy people, Lord, we pray,
   by a thousand snares surrounded;
   keep us without sin today;
   never let us be confounded.
   Lo, I put my trust in thee,
   never, Lord, abandon me.

334
Michael Forster
© 1996 Kevin Mayhew Ltd.

1. Holy God, your pilgrim people
   by you were fed,
   through the vast and dreadful desert
   guided and led;
   water from the rock face pouring,
   hope to ev'ry heart restoring,
   sets the failing spirit soaring,
   life from the dead!

2. Living bread for mortals broken,
   gift from above,
   live in us the life eternal,
   perfect in love.
   Come, the word of wholeness bringing,
   where our fearful souls are clinging;
   and of life abundant singing,
   all fear remove.

3. One the bread and one the chalice,
   one work of grace;
   one the church of Christ, united
   in his embrace.
   One the gospel of salvation,
   for the wholeness of creation;
   Christ is poured in ev'ry nation,
   and ev'ry race.

335
Jimmy Owens. © 1972 Bud John Songs/EMI Christian
Music Publishing. Administered by CopyCare

1. Holy, holy, holy, holy.
   Holy, holy, holy Lord God almighty;
   and we lift our hearts before you
   as a token of our love,
   holy, holy, holy, holy.

2. Gracious Father, gracious Father,
   we are glad to be your children,
       gracious Father;
   and we lift our heads before you
   as a token of our love,
   gracious Father, gracious Father.

Continued overleaf

3. Risen Jesus, risen Jesus,
   we are glad you have redeemed us,
        risen Jesus;
   and we lift our hands before you
   as a token of our love,
   risen Jesus, risen Jesus.

4. Holy Spirit, Holy Spirit,
   come and fill our hearts anew, Holy Spirit;
   and we lift our voice before you
   as a token of our love,
   Holy Spirit, Holy Spirit.

5. Hallelujah, hallelujah,
   hallelujah, hallelujah, hallelujah;
   and we lift our hearts before you
   as a token of our love,
   hallelujah, hallelujah.

336 Unknown

1. Holy, holy, holy is the Lord,
   holy is the Lord God almighty.
   Holy, holy, holy is the Lord,
   holy is the Lord God almighty:
   who was, and is, and is to come;
   holy, holy, holy is the Lord.

2. Jesus, Jesus, Jesus is the Lord,
   Jesus is the Lord God almighty: *(Repeat)*
   who was, and is, and is to come;
   Jesus, Jesus, Jesus is the Lord.

3. Worthy, worthy, worthy is the Lord,
   worthy is the Lord God almighty: *(Repeat)*
   who was, and is and is to come;
   worthy is the Lord God almighty.

4. Glory, glory, glory to the Lord,
   glory to the Lord God almighty: *(Repeat)*
   who was, and is, and is to come;
   glory, glory, glory to the Lord.

For liturgical version (Sanctus) see no. 65

337 Reginald Heber

1. Holy, holy, holy!
   Lord God almighty!
   Early in the morning
   our song shall rise to thee;

holy, holy, holy!
Merciful and mighty!
God in three persons,
blessed Trinity!

2.* Holy, holy, holy!
   All the saints adore thee,
   casting down their golden crowns
   around the glassy sea;
   cherubim and seraphim
   falling down before thee,
   which wert, and art,
   and evermore shall be.

3. Holy, holy, holy!
   Though the darkness hide thee,
   though the eye made blind by sin
   thy glory may not see,
   only thou art holy,
   there is none beside thee,
   perfect in pow'r,
   in love, and purity.

4. Holy, holy, holy!
   Lord God almighty!
   All thy works shall praise thy name,
   in earth and sky and sea;
   holy, holy, holy!
   Merciful and mighty!
   God in three persons,
   blessèd Trinity!

* May be omitted

338 Michael Forster
© *1993 Kevin Mayhew Ltd.*

1. Holy Jesus, in our likeness born,
   a human home to share,
   you knew a father's kindness
   and a loving mother's care,
   by your ever-present mercy,
   may we catch this vision fair,
   may we catch this vision fair!

2. Look with kindness and compassion
   on each mortal family.
   Give us joy in one another,
   touching here eternity!

Saviour, hold your many people
in the sweetest harmony,
in the sweetest harmony.

3. May we live for one another,
growing through life's ev'ry stage,
with protection for the youngest
and respect for greater age;
all a common value sharing,
what a holy heritage,
what a holy heritage!

339 Damian Lundy
© 1987 Kevin Mayhew Ltd.

1. Holy Mary, you were chosen
by the Father, the God of life,
joyfully responding,
you became a mother.
Pray now for us, and show a mother's love.

2. Holy Mary, you were chosen,
called to carry the Son of God.
Gratefully responding,
you became his mother.
Pray now for us, and show a mother's love.

3. Holy Mary, you were chosen
so the Spirit could work in you.
Faithfully responding,
you became God's mother.
Pray now for us, and show a mother's love.

4. Holy Mary, you were chosen,
all God's children are blessed in you.
Joyfully responding,
you became our mother,
Pray now for us, and show a mother's love.

340 Brian Foley
© 1971 Faber Music Ltd.

1. Holy Spirit, come, confirm us
in the truth that Christ makes known;
we have faith and understanding
through your promised light alone.

2. Holy Spirit, come, console us,
come as Advocate to plead;
loving Spirit from the Father,
grant in Christ the help we need.

3. Holy Spirit, come renew us,
come yourself to make us live;
holy through your loving presence,
holy through the gifts you give.

4. Holy Spirit, come, possess us,
you the love of Three in One,
Holy Spirit of the Father,
Holy Spirit of the Son.

341 Ascribed to Stephen Langton,
trans. Edward Caswall

1. Holy Spirit, Lord of light,
from the clear celestial height,
thy pure beaming radiance give;
come, thou Father of the poor,
come with treasures which endure;
come, thou light of all that live!

2. Thou, of all consolers best,
thou, the soul's delightsome guest,
dost refreshing peace bestow:
thou in toil art comfort sweet;
pleasant coolness in the heat;
solace in the midst of woe.

3. Light immortal, light divine,
visit thou these hearts of thine,
and our inmost being fill:
if thou take thy grace away,
nothing pure in us will stay;
all his good is turned to ill.

4. Heal our wounds, our strength renew;
on our dryness pour thy dew;
wash the stains of guilt away;
bend the stubborn heart and will;
melt the frozen, warm the chill;
guide the steps that go astray.

Continued overleaf

5. Thou, on those who evermore
thee confess and thee adore,
in thy sev'nfold gifts descend:
give them comfort when they die;
give them life with thee on high;
give them joys that never end.

342
John Glynn
© 1976 Kevin Mayhew Ltd.

1. Holy Spirit of fire,
flame everlasting, so bright and clear,
speak this day in our hearts.
Lighten our darkness and purge us of fear,
Holy Spirit of fire.

The wind can blow or be still,
or water be parched by the sun.
A fire can die into dust:
but here the eternal Spirit of God
tells us a new world's begun.

2. Holy Spirit of love,
strong are the faithful who trust your pow'r.
Love who conquers our will,
teach us the words of the gospel of peace,
Holy Spirit of love.

3. Holy Spirit of God,
flame everlasting, so bright and clear,
speak this day in our hearts.
Lighten our darkness and purge us of fear,
Holy Spirit of God.

343
Jean-Paul Lécot, trans. W. R. Lawrence, alt.
© 1988 Kevin Mayhew Ltd.

1. Holy Virgin, by God's decree,
you were called eternally;
that he could give his Son to our race.
Mary, we praise you, hail full of grace.

Ave, ave, ave, Maria.

2. By your faith and loving accord,
as the handmaid of the Lord,
you undertook God's plan to embrace.
Mary, we thank you, hail, full of grace.

3. Joy to God you gave and expressed,
of all women none more blessed,
when in our flesh your Son took his place.
Mary, we love you, hail, full of grace.

4. Refuge for your children so weak,
sure protection all can seek.
Problems of life you help us to face.
Mary, we trust you, hail, full of grace.

5. To our needy world of today
love and beauty you portray,
showing the path to Christ we must trace.
Mary, our mother, hail, full of grace.

344
Carl Tuttle. © 1985 Mercy/Vineyard Publishing Music
Services. Administered by CopyCare

1. Hosanna, hosanna,
hosanna in the highest! *(Repeat)*

Lord, we lift up your name,
with hearts full of praise;
be exalted, O Lord, my God!
Hosanna in the highest!

2. Glory, glory,
glory to the King of kings! *(Repeat)*

345
Unknown

How great is our God,
how great is his name!
How great is our God,
for ever the same!

1. He rolled back the waters
of the mighty Red Sea,
and he said: 'I'll never leave you.
Put your trust in me.'

2. He sent his Son, Jesus,
to set us all free,
and he said: 'I'll never leave you.
Put your trust in me.'

3. He gave us his Spirit,
and now we can see.
And he said: 'I'll never leave you.
Put your trust in me.'

346

v 1 Leonard E. Smith Jnr, based on Isaiah 52, 53; vs 2-4 unknown. © 1974 Kingsway's Thankyou Music

1. How lovely on the mountains
   are the feet of him
   who brings good news, good news,
   announcing peace,
   proclaiming news of happiness:
   our God reigns, our God reigns.

   Our God reigns. (x4)

2. You watchmen, lift your voices
   joyfully as one,
   shout for your King, your King!
   See eye to eye,
   the Lord restoring Zion:
   our God reigns, our God reigns.

3. Wasteplaces of Jerusalem,
   break forth with joy!
   We are redeemed, redeemed.
   The Lord has saved
   and comforted his people:
   our God reigns, our God reigns.

4. Ends of the earth, see
   the salvation of our God!
   Jesus is Lord, is Lord!
   Before the nations,
   he has bared his holy arm:
   our God reigns, our God reigns.

347

Michael Perry
© 1980 Mrs B. Perry/Jubilate Hymns

1. How shall they hear the word of God
   unless the truth is told?
   How shall the sinful be set free,
   the sorrowful consoled?
   To all who speak the truth today
   impart your Spirit, Lord, we pray.

2. How shall they call to God for help
   unless they have believed?
   How shall the poor be given hope,
   the prisoner reprieved?
   To those who help the blind to see
   give light and love and clarity.

3. How shall the gospel be proclaimed
   that sinners may repent?
   How shall the world find peace at last
   if heralds are not sent?
   So send us, Lord, for we rejoice
   to speak of Christ with life and voice.

348

David Konstant
© 1976 Kevin Mayhew Ltd.

1. I am the bread of life.
   You who come to me will never be hungry.
   I will raise you up, I will raise you up,
   I will raise you up to eternal life.
   I am the bread of life.

2. I am the spring of life.
   You who hope in me will never be thirsty.
   I will raise you up, I will raise you up,
   I will raise you up to eternal life.
   I am the spring of life.

3. I am the way of life.
   You who follow me will never be lonely.
   I will raise you up, I will raise you up,
   I will raise you up to eternal life.
   I am the way of life.

4. I am the truth of life.
   You who look for me will never
      seek blindly.
   I will raise you up, I will raise you up,
   I will raise you up to eternal life.
   I am the truth of life.

5. I am the life of life.
   You who die with me will never die vainly.
   I will raise you up, I will raise you up,
   I will raise you up to eternal life.
   I am the life of life.

349

Suzanne Toolan
© 1966 GIA Publications Inc.

1. I am the bread of life.
   You who come to me shall not hunger;
   and who believe in me shall not thirst.
   No one can come to me
   unless the Father beckons.

And I will raise you up,
and I will raise you up,
and I will raise you up on the last day.

2. The bread that I will give
   is my flesh for the life of the world,
   and if you eat of this bread,
   you shall live for ever,
   you shall live for ever.

3. Unless you eat
   of the flesh of the Son of Man,
   and drink of his blood,
   and drink of his blood,
   you shall not have life within you.

4. I am the resurrection,
   I am the life.
   If you believe in me,
   even though you die,
   you shall live for ever.

5. Yes, Lord, I believe
   that you are the Christ,
   the Son of God,
   who has come
   into the world.

350

Aniceto Nazareth, based on the Gospel of John
© 1984 Kevin Mayhew Ltd.

1. I am the Light,
   bringing you out of darkness,
   so come, take my light to the world.
   I am the Bread you must
   feed to the hungry,
   the wine that must fill ev'ry heart.
   Foxes have holes, birds have their nests,
   but the Son of Man has no place to rest.

   Come, follow me; be the light of the nations.
   Leave your nets and come, follow me.

2. I am the Life
   that must change ev'ry life
   and the Way that must alter your ways.
   I am the Truth and my word
   is the cross you must take
   if you want to be free.
   Foxes have holes, birds have their nests,
   but the Son of Man has no place to rest.

3. I am the Sower,
   come, work in my vineyard, my field.
   Tend my vines, sow the grain.
   And should it fall to the ground,
   it can only spring up
   with new life, hundredfold.
   Foxes have holes, birds have their nests,
   but the Son of Man has no place to rest.

4. I am the Shepherd,
   come into the sheepfold
   to help feed my lambs, feed my sheep.
   Bring back the straying,
   and bind up their wounds, and rejoice
   when you've found what was lost.
   Foxes have holes, birds have their nests,
   but the Son of Man has no place to rest.

351

William Young Fullerton, alt.
© Copyright control

1. I cannot tell
   how he whom angels worship
   should stoop to love
   the peoples of the earth,
   or why as shepherd
   he should seek the wand'rer
   with his mysterious promise
   of new birth.
   But this I know,
   that he was born of Mary,
   when Bethl'em's manger
   was his only home,
   and that he lived at
   Nazareth and laboured,
   and so the Saviour,
   Saviour of the world, is come.

2. I cannot tell
   how silently he suffered,
   as with his peace
   he graced this place of tears,
   or how his heart
   upon the cross was broken,
   the crown of pain
   to three and thirty years.

But this I know,
he heals the broken-hearted,
and stays our sin,
and calms our lurking fear,
and lifts the burden
from the heavy laden,
for yet the Saviour,
Saviour of the world, is here.

3. I cannot tell
how he will win the nations,
how he will claim
his earthly heritage,
how satisfy
the needs and aspirations
of east and west,
of sinner and of sage.
But this I know,
all flesh shall see his glory,
and he shall reap
the harvest he has sown,
and some glad day
his sun shall shine in splendour
when he the Saviour,
Saviour of the world, is known.

4. I cannot tell
how all the lands shall worship,
when, at his bidding,
ev'ry storm is stilled,
or who can say
how great the jubilation
when ev'ry heart
with perfect love is filled.
But this I know,
the skies will thrill with rapture,
and myriad, myriad
human voices sing,
and earth to heav'n,
and heav'n to earth, will answer:
'At last the Saviour,
Saviour of the world, is King!'

352
Sydney Carter
© 1974 Stainer & Bell Ltd.

1. I come like a beggar
with a gift in my hand,
I come like a beggar
with a gift in my hand.

By the hungry I will feed you,
by the poor I make you rich,
by the broken I will mend you,
tell me, which one is which?

2. I come like a prisoner
to set you free . . .

3. The need of another is the gift that
I bring . . .

4. I come like a beggar,
what you do for my sake
is the wine that I offer you,
the bread that I break.

353
Sydney Carter
© 1963 Stainer & Bell Ltd.

1. I danced in the morning
when the world was begun,
and I danced in the moon
and the stars and the sun,
and I came down from heaven
and I danced on the earth,
at Bethlehem
I had my birth.

Dance then, wherever you may be,
I am the Lord of the Dance, said he,
and I'll lead you all, wherever you may be,
and I'll lead you all in the dance, said he.

2. I danced for the scribe
and the Pharisee,
but they would not dance
and they wouldn't follow me.
I danced for the fishermen,
for James and John –
they came with me
and the dance went on.

Continued overleaf

3. I danced on the Sabbath
and I cured the lame;
the holy people,
they said it was a shame.
They whipped and they stripped
and they hung me on high,
and they left me there
on a cross to die.

4. I danced on a Friday
when the sky turned black –
it's hard to dance
with the devil on your back.
They buried my body,
and they thought I'd gone,
but I am the dance,
and I still go on.

5. They cut me down
and I leapt up high;
I am the life
that'll never, never die;
I'll live in you
if you'll live in me –
I am the Lord
of the Dance, said he.

354

John Foley, based on Romans 8:31-39. © 1975 John B. Foley, S. J. and New Dawn Music

If God is for us, who can be against,
if the Spirit of God has set us free? (Repeat)

1. I know that nothing in this world
can ever take us from his love.

2. Nothing can take us from his love,
poured out in Jesus, the Lord.

3. And nothing present or to come
can ever take us from his love.

4. I know that neither death nor life
can ever take us from his love.

355

Damian Lundy, based on 1 Corinthians 13 © 1998 Kevin Mayhew Ltd.

If I am lacking love,
then I am nothing, Lord.
On love I set my heart;
my joy and my reward.

1. Without love my words ring hollow,
my intentions are disgraced,
all my sacrifices empty,
ev'ry hope and pray'r misplaced.

2. Love is patient, love is kindly,
never jealous, never proud;
not conceited, nor ill-mannered,
never selfish, never rude.

3. Love is gracious and forgiving,
taking no delight in sin;
love rejoices in the truth,
will not lose heart will not give in.

4. I know love is everlasting;
other gifts will pass away.
Only faith and hope and love
will never die, will ever stay.

5. God is bountiful in giving;
all his gifts are my desire,
but I set my heart on love.
May his love set my heart on fire!

356

Michael Forster, based on the Good Friday Reproaches. © Kevin Mayhew Ltd.

1. I give you love, and how do you repay?
When you were slaves I strove to set
you free;
I led you out from under Pharaoh's yoke,
but you led out your Christ to Calvary.

My people, tell me, what is my offence?
What have I done to harm you? Answer me!

2. For forty years I was your constant guide.
I fed you with my manna from on high.
I led you out to live in hope and peace,
but you led out my only Son to die.

3. With cloud and fire I marked the
desert way,
I heard your cries of rage and calmed
your fear.
I opened up the sea and led you through,
but you have opened Christ with nail
and spear.

4. When in distress you cried to me for food,
   I sent you quails in answer to your call,
   and saving water from the desert rock,
   but to my Son you offered bitter gall.

5. I gave you joy when you were in despair,
   with songs of hope, I set your hearts
       on fire;
   crowned you with grace, the people of
       my choice,
   but you have crowned my Christ with
       thorny briar.

6. When you were weak, exploited and
       oppressed,
   I heard you cry and listened to your plea.
   I raised you up to honour and renown,
   but you have raised me on a shameful tree.

357
Michael Joncas
© 1979 New Dawn Music

I have loved you with an everlasting love,
I have called you, and you are mine. (Repeat)

1. Seek the face of the Lord and long for him:
   he will bring you his light and his peace.

2. Seek the face of the Lord and long for him:
   he will bring you his joy and his hope.

3. Seek the face of the Lord and long for him:
   he will bring you his care and his love.

358
John Wyse, alt.

1. I'll sing a hymn to Mary,
   the mother of my God,
   the virgin of all virgins,
   of David's royal blood.
   O teach me, holy Mary,
   a loving song to frame,
   when wicked ones blaspheme thee,
   to love and bless thy name.

2. O noble Tower of David,
   of gold and ivory,
   the Ark of God's own promise,
   the gate of heav'n to me,
   to live and not to love thee,
   would fill my soul with shame;
   when wicked ones blaspheme thee,
   I'll love and bless thy name.

3. The saints are high in glory,
   with golden crowns so bright;
   but brighter far is Mary,
   upon her throne of light.
   O that which God did give thee,
   let mortal ne'er disclaim;
   when wicked ones blaspheme thee,
   I'll love and bless thy name.

4. But in the crown of Mary,
   there lies a wondrous gem,
   as queen of all the angels,
   which Mary shares with them:
   no sin hath e'er defiled thee,
   so doth our faith proclaim;
   when wicked ones blaspheme thee,
   I'll love and bless thy name.

359
Aniceto Nazareth, based on Psalm 42
© 1984 Kevin Mayhew Ltd.

I'll turn my steps to the altar of God,
I'll turn my steps to the gladness of my life.

1. Show your justice in pleading my cause,
   let me walk in the way of your laws.

2. Lead me on with your power and strength,
   then my courage will never be spent.

3. Fill my heart with your truth and
       your light
   as I enter with joy in your sight.

4. Holy praises of God will I sing;
   I will trust and will hope in my King.

5. Glory be to the Father, the Son
   and the Spirit, while endless years run.

360

1. Immaculate Mary!
   Our hearts are on fire;
   that title so wondrous
   fills all our desire.

   Ave, ave, ave Maria!

2. We pray for God's glory,
   may his kingdom come!
   We pray for his vicar,
   our father, and Rome.

3. We pray for our mother
   the Church upon earth,
   and bless, sweetest lady,
   the land of our birth.

4. For poor, sick, afflicted
   thy mercy we crave;
   and comfort the dying,
   thou light of the grave.

5. In grief and temptation,
   in joy or in pain,
   we'll ask thee, our mother,
   nor seek thee in vain.

6. In death's solemn moment,
   our mother, be nigh;
   as children of Mary,
   O teach us to die.

7. And crown thy sweet mercy
   with this special grace,
   and worship in heaven
   God's ravishing face.

8. To God be all glory
   and worship for aye;
   to God's virgin mother
   an endless Ave.

361
Walter Chalmers Smith, based on 1 Timothy 1:17

1. Immortal, invisible,
   God only wise,
   in light inaccessible hid
   from our eyes,
   most blessed, most glorious,
   the Ancient of Days,
   almighty, victorious,
   thy great name we praise.

2. Unresting, unhasting,
   and silent as light,
   nor wanting, nor wasting,
   thou rulest in might;
   thy justice like mountains
   high soaring above
   thy clouds which are fountains
   of goodness and love.

3. To all life thou givest,
   to both great and small;
   in all life thou livest,
   the true life of all;
   we blossom and flourish
   as leaves on the tree,
   and wither and perish;
   but naught changeth thee.

4. Great Father of glory,
   pure Father of light,
   thine angels adore thee,
   all veiling their sight;
   all laud we would render,
   O help us to see
   'tis only the splendour
   of light hideth thee.

362
Kevin Nichols
© 1976 Kevin Mayhew Ltd.

1. In bread we bring you, Lord,
   our bodies' labour.
   In wine we offer you our spirits' grief.
   We do not ask you, Lord,
   who is my neighbour,
   but stand united now,
   one in belief.
   O we have gladly heard
   your Word, your holy Word,
   and now in answer, Lord,
   our gifts we bring.
   Our selfish hearts make true,
   our failing faith renew,
   our lives belong to you, our Lord and King.

2. The bread we offer you
   is blessed and broken,
   and it becomes for us our spirits' food.
   Over the cup we bring
   your Word is spoken;
   make it your gift to us,
   your healing blood.
   Take all that daily toil
   plants in our hearts' poor soil,
   take all we start and spoil,
   each hopeful dream,
   the chances we have missed,
   the graces we resist,
   Lord, in thy Eucharist, take and redeem.

363

Michael Forster, based on St Gregory the Great
© 1999 Kevin Mayhew Ltd.

1. In company with Christians past,
   we keep the vigil, watch and pray,
   and with the tempted Christ,
   reject the superficial, easy way.

2. We will not turn our stones to bread,
   or from the temple's heights be hurled;
   nor look for cheap success within
   the ways and values of the world.

3. Forgive us, Lord, the times we fail
   to keep that promise day by day,
   and give us grace to follow you
   on faith's more costly, rocky way.

4. Then lead us on to find once more
   the glory veiled but never lost:
   the image of our God in us,
   restored by grace at such a cost!

5. O perfectly related God,
   eternal Father, Spirit, Son,
   renew us in the Covenant
   that makes your many people one.

6. Then move us on from fast to feast,
   where life and wholeness are restored,
   and you, in triune majesty
   are honoured, worshipped and adored.

364

Trans. from the Polish by Edith Margaret Gellibrand
Reed. © Copyright control

1. Infant holy, infant lowly,
   for his bed a cattle stall;
   oxen lowing, little knowing
   Christ the babe is Lord of all.
   Swift are winging angels singing,
   nowells ringing, tidings bringing,
   Christ the babe is Lord of all,
   Christ the babe is Lord of all.

2. Flocks were sleeping, shepherds keeping
   vigil till the morning new;
   saw the glory, heard the story,
   tidings of a gospel true.
   Thus rejoicing, free from sorrow,
   praises voicing, greet the morrow,
   Christ the babe was born for you,
   Christ the babe was born for you.

365

Christina Georgina Rossetti

1. In the bleak mid-winter
   frosty wind made moan,
   earth stood hard as iron,
   water like a stone;
   snow had fallen, snow on snow,
   snow on snow,
   in the bleak mid-winter, long ago.

2. Our God, heav'n cannot hold him
   nor earth sustain;
   heav'n and earth shall flee away
   when he comes to reign.
   In the bleak mid-winter
   a stable place sufficed
   the Lord God almighty, Jesus Christ.

3. Enough for him, whom cherubim
   worship night and day,
   a breastful of milk,
   and a mangerful of hay:
   enough for him, whom angels
   fall down before,
   the ox and ass and camel which adore.

Continued overleaf

4. Angels and archangels
   may have gathered there,
   cherubim and seraphim
   thronged the air;
   but only his mother
   in her maiden bliss
   worshipped the beloved with a kiss.

5. What can I give him,
   poor as I am?
   If I were a shepherd
   I would bring a lamb;
   if I were a wise man
   I would do my part,
   yet what I can I give him:
   give my heart.

366
Estelle White
© 1978 Kevin Mayhew Ltd.

1. In the love of God and neighbour
   we are gathered at his table:
   gifts of bread and wine will become
   a sign of the love our Father gave us,
   through the Son who came to save us,
   by the Spirit blest.

2. So we offer our tomorrows,
   all our present joys and sorrows,
   ev'ry heart and will, talent, gift and skill.
   For the riches we've been given
   to the Trinity of heaven
   we give thanks and praise.

367
Graham Kendrick
©1986 Kingsway's Thankyou Music

1. In the tomb so cold they laid him,
   death its victim claimed.
   Pow'rs of hell, they could not hold him;
   back to life he came!

   Men   *Christ is risen!*
   Women   *Christ is risen!*
   Men   *Death has been conquered.*
   Women   *Death has been conquered.*
   Men   *Christ is risen!*
   Women   *Christ is risen!*
   All   *He shall reign for ever.*

2. Hell had spent its fury on him,
   left him crucified.
   Yet, by blood, he boldly conquered,
   sin and death defied.

3. Now the fear of death is broken,
   love has won the crown.
   Pris'ners of the darkness listen,
   walls are tumbling down.

4. Raised from death to heav'n ascending,
   love's exalted King.
   Let his song of joy, unending,
   through the nations ring!

368
Michael Cockett, adapted from 'Ubi Caritas'
© McCrimmon Publishers

1. Into one we all are gathered
   through the love of Christ.
   Let us then rejoice with gladness.
   In him we find love.
   Let us fear and love the living God,
   and love and cherish humankind.

   Where charity and love are, there is God.

2. Therefore, when we are together
   in the love of Christ,
   let our minds know no division,
   strife or bitterness;
   may the Christ our God be in our midst.
   Through Christ our Lord all love is found.

3. May we see your face in glory,
   Christ our loving God.
   With the blessèd saints of heaven
   give us lasting joy.
   We will then possess true happiness,
   and love for all eternity.

369
Francesca Leftley
© 1978 Kevin Mayhew Ltd.

1. In you, my God,
   may my soul find its peace;
   you are, my refuge,
   my rock and my strength,

calming my fears
with the touch of your love.
Here in your presence
my troubles will cease.

2. In you, my God,
may my soul find its joy;
you are the radiance,
the song of my heart,
drying my tears
with the warmth of your love.
Here in your presence
my troubles will cease.

3. In you, my God,
may my soul find its rest;
you are the meaning,
the purpose of life,
drawing me near
to the fire of your love,
safe in your presence
my yearning will cease.

370 Damian Lundy, based on Psalm 120
© 1978 Kevin Mayhew Ltd.

In your coming and going God is with you.
He will keep you in safety night and day.

1. You raise your eyes and you look at
the mountains;
you cry aloud to the hills,
'Come and help me!'
Now, see our God is on his way;
he will stay beside you night and day.

2. His arm outstretched to protect you
in danger,
he never sleeps all the time he is watching.
He is the maker of the skies,
but he knows your name,
he hears your cries.

3. His loving care shelters you like a shadow,
to keep you safe from the evil around you.
He shields you from the burning sun,
and the moon at night will do no harm.

371 Unknown

I received the living God,
and my heart is full of joy.
I received the living God,
and my heart is full of joy.

1. He has said: I am the Bread,
kneaded long to give you life;
you who will partake of me
need not ever fear to die.

2. He has said: I am the Way,
and my Father longs for you;
so I come to bring you home
to be one with him anew.

3. He has said: I am the Truth;
if you follow close to me
you will know me in your heart,
and my word shall make you free.

4. He has said: I am the Life
far from whom no thing can grow,
but receive this living bread,
and my Spirit you shall know.

372 Stephen Dean. © 1993 Stephen Dean
OCP Publications

I saw streams of water flowing
from the temple's right side,
healing pow'r and life bestowing
from the one who had died:
Alleluia, alleluia,
from our Saviour glorified.

1. Into day from deepest night,
out of darkness into light,
Christ our Saviour comes once more,
opens up salvation's door!

2. He has healed us with his blood,
led us safe through Jordan's flood,
on the further bank we stand,
gazing on the promised land!

3. He has raised us from the grave,
from the Red Sea's mighty wave;
dead to sin we rise with Christ,
paschal Lamb now sacrificed.

373

Michael Forster, based on Revelation 21
© 1999 Kevin Mayhew Ltd.

I saw the holy city,
from the opened heav'n descending.
God's gift of new Jerusalem on earth,
and prepared as a bride
to meet her husband,
adorned for her great day.

1. Now the home of God
   is made upon the earth,
   he will dwell among his people
   and be with them.

2. He will wipe away the tears
   from every eye,
   and no more will death be known,
   that is his promise.

3. No more mourning, no more pain,
   and no more tears,
   for the former things
   have passed away for ever.

4. Praise the Father, Son and Spirit,
   Three in One,
   God who was, and who is now,
   and ever shall be.

374

Richard Beaumont
© 1974, 1998 Sisters of St Mary of Namur

I sing a song to you, Lord,
a song of love and praise.
All glory be to you, Lord,
through everlasting days.

1. Holy, holy, holy,
   mighty Lord and God.
   He who was and is now,
   and who is to come.

2. Worthy is the slain Lamb,
   honour him and praise.
   We rejoice with gladness,
   sing our love today.

3. He has used his power,
   has begun his reign.
   So rejoice, you heavens,
   and proclaim his name.

4. Shine your light on us, Lord,
   let us know your way.
   Be our guide for ever,
   make us yours today.

375

Edmund Hamilton Sears, alt.

1. It came upon the midnight clear,
   that glorious song of old,
   from angels bending near the earth
   to touch their harps of gold:
   'Peace on the earth, goodwill to all,
   from heav'ns all gracious King!'
   The world in solemn stillness lay
   to hear the angels sing.

2. Still through the cloven skies they come,
   with peaceful wings unfurled;
   and still their heav'nly music floats
   o'er all the weary world:
   above its sad and lowly plains
   they bend on hov'ring wing;
   and ever o'er its Babel-sounds
   the blessèd angels sing.

3. Yet with the woes of sin and strife
   the world has suffered long;
   beneath the angel-strain have rolled
   two thousand years of wrong;
   and warring humankind hears not
   the love-song which they bring;
   O hush the noise of mortal strife,
   and hear the angels sing!

4. And ye, beneath life's crushing load,
   whose forms are bending low,
   who toil along the climbing way
   with painful steps and slow:
   look now! for glad and golden hours
   come swiftly on the wing;
   O rest beside the weary road,
   and hear the angels sing.

5. For lo, the days are hast'ning on,
   by prophets seen of old,
   when with the ever-circling years
   comes round the age of gold;

when peace shall over all the earth
its ancient splendours fling,
and all the world give back the song
which now the angels sing.

376
Dan Schutte, based on Isaiah 6
© 1981 Daniel L. Schutte and New Dawn Music

1. I, the Lord of sea and sky,
   I have heard my people cry.
   All who dwell in dark and sin
   my hand will save.
   I who made the stars of night,
   I will make their darkness bright.
   Who will bear my light to them?
   Whom shall I send?

   Here I am, Lord. Is it I, Lord?
   I have heard you calling in the night.
   I will go, Lord, if you lead me.
   I will hold your people in my heart.

2. I, the Lord of snow and rain,
   I have borne my people's pain.
   I have wept for love of them.
   They turn away.
   I will break their hearts of stone,
   give them hearts for love alone.
   I will speak my word to them.
   Whom shall I send?

3. I, the Lord of wind and flame,
   I will tend the poor and lame.
   I will set a feast for them.
   My hand will save.
   Finest bread I will provide
   till their hearts be satisfied.
   I will give my life to them.
   Whom shall I send?

377
Noel Donnelly, based on John 13 and 14
© 1986 Kevin Mayhew Ltd.

I, the Servant-Lord, serve you;
serve one another.
Love and service are the signs
you are my disciples.

1. Jesus rose from table,
   put a tow'l around him,
   poured some water in a dish,
   knelt before his friends.

2. In the manner of a slave
   Jesus washed their feet.
   One by one he came to them,
   all who were at supper.

3. With the towel he wiped their feet –
   Judas too – and Peter.
   'Do you understand,' he said,
   'this is my example.'

4. 'Happiness will come to you
   if you serve each other.
   I, the Lord, have washed your feet;
   be each other's servant.'

5. 'Trust in God and trust in me;
   let no heart be troubled.
   I'll prepare a place for you,
   I will come back for you.'

6. Thomas said, 'What do you mean?
   Which way are you going?'
   'Through the darkness follow me;
   I go to the Father.'

7. 'Way and truth and life am I.
   Learn my way as servant.
   Love each other as I do;
   serve me in each other.'

8. 'Let us see the Father, Lord.'
   Philip asked of Jesus.
   'He is in me,' Jesus said,
   'I am in the Father.'

9. 'I in you and you in me,
   we are one together.
   Father, may we all be one,
   serving one another.'

10. 'If you love me, keep my word.
    Thus my Father loves you.
    We shall make our home in you.
    You shall live for ever.'

Continued overleaf

11. 'I have said these things to you
while I still am with you.
In my name the Spirit comes,
sent soon from my Father.'

12. 'My own peace I give to you,
not of this world's giving.
Fear must not constrain your heart.
My own peace I leave you.'

378
John Glynn
© 1976 Kevin Mayhew Ltd.

1. I watch the sunrise lighting the sky,
casting its shadows near.
And on this morning, bright though it be,
I feel those shadows near me.

   But you are always close to me,
   following all my ways.
   May I be always close to you,
   following all your ways, Lord.

2. I watch the sunlight shine through
      the clouds,
warming the earth below.
And at the mid-day, life seems to say:
'I feel your brightness near me.'
For you are always . . .

3. I watch the sunset fading away,
lighting the clouds with sleep.
And as the evening closes its eyes,
I feel your presence near me.
For you are always . . .

4. I watch the moonlight guarding the night,
waiting till morning comes.
The air is silent, earth is at rest –
only your peace is near me.
Yes, you are always . . .

379
Gerard Markland
© 1978 Kevin Mayhew Ltd.

I will be with you wherever you go.
Go now throughout the world!
I will be with you in all that you say.
Go now and spread my word!

1. Come, walk with me on stormy waters.
Why fear? Reach out, and I'll be there.

2. And you, my friend, will you now
      leave me,
or do you know me as your Lord?

3. Your life will be transformed with power
by living truly in my name.

4. And if you say: 'Yes, Lord, I love you,'
then feed my lambs and feed my sheep.

380
Susan Sayers
© 1996 Kevin Mayhew Ltd.

I will bless the Lord at all times. (x2)

1. Ev'rywhere I am, ev'rywhere I go,
I will praise the living God.
In ev'ryone I meet,
in ev'rything I see,
I will sing your praise, O Lord.

2. When I was in pain, when I lived in fear,
I was calling out to him.
He rescued me from death,
he wiped my tears away,
I will sing your praise, O Lord.

3. Trust him with your life,
      trust him with today,
come and praise the Lord with me;
O come and know his love,
O taste and understand,
let us sing your praise, O Lord.

381
Leona von Brethorst
© 1976 Maranatha! Music/CopyCare

I will enter his gates
with thanksgiving in my heart,
I will enter his courts with praise,
I will say this is the day
that the Lord has made,
I will rejoice for he has made me glad.
He has made me glad, he has made me glad,
I will rejoice for he has made me glad.
He has made me glad, he had made me glad,
I will rejoice for he has made me glad.

382

Carey Landry, based on Isaiah 49: 15-16
© 1983 North American Liturgy Resources

1. I will never forget you, my people;
I have carved you on the palm of
my hand.
I will never forget you;
I will not leave you orphaned.
I will never forget my own.

2. Does a mother forget her baby?
Or a woman the child within her womb?
Yet even if these forget,
yes, even if these forget,
I will never forget my own.

383

Noel and Tricia Richards
© 1990 Kingsway's Thankyou Music

I will seek your face, O Lord; (x4)

1. Lord, how awesome is your presence.
Who can stand in your light?
Those why by your grace and mercy
are made holy in your sight.

2. I will dwell in your presence
all the days of my life;
there to gaze upon your glory,
and to worship only you.

384

Damian Lundy, based on Psalm 146
© 1978 Kevin Mayhew Ltd.

I will sing a song, a song to please our God,
a song from all his people.

1. For he builds us a city of peace,
and he calls us together as one.

2. We were scattered, but he called us home;
broken-hearted but now we are whole.

3. We are healed – he has bound up
our wounds,
he who calls all the stars by their names.

4. He is God of the world that he made,
he is God of the poor that he helps.

5. How he covers the heavens with clouds!
How he clothes mountain valleys
with green!

6. He sends food to young ravens in need,
he will come if you wait for his love.

7. To the Father and Son sing a song,
to the Spirit who fills us with life.

385

Max Dyer
© 1974 Celebration/Kingsway's Thankyou Music

1. I will sing, I will sing
a song unto the Lord. *(x3)*
Alleluia, glory to the Lord.

Allelu, alleluia, glory to the Lord. (x3)
Alleluia, glory to the Lord.

2. We will come, we will come
as one before the Lord. *(x3)*
Alleluia, glory to the Lord.

3. If the Son, if the Son
shall make you free, *(x3)*
you shall be free indeed.

4. They that sow in tears
shall reap in joy. *(x3)*
Alleluia, glory to the Lord.

5. Ev'ry knee shall bow
and ev'ry tongue confess *(x3)*
that Jesus Christ is Lord.

6. In his name, in his name
we have the victory. *(x3)*
Alleluia, glory to the Lord.

386

Noel Donelly, based on Psalm 115
© Noel Donnelly

I will walk in the presence of God.

1. I trusted when I felt afflicted,
I walk in the sight of the Lord,
and even in the face of death
I will walk in the presence of God.

Continued overleaf

2. Your servant, Lord, is ever trusting.
   My bonds you have loosened with care.
   I offer thanks and sacrifice,
   I will walk in the presence of God.

3. My vows to God I keep with gladness,
   I dwell in the house of my Lord.
   My promises I will fulfil.
   I will walk in the presence of God.

387 'De Contemptu Mundi' by St. Bernard of Cluny, 12th century, trans. John Mason Neale

1. Jerusalem the golden,
   with milk and honey blest,
   beneath thy contemplation
   sink heart and voice oppressed.
   I know not, ah, I know not
   what joys await us there,
   what radiancy of glory,
   what bliss beyond compare.

2. They stand, those halls of Zion,
   all jubilant with song,
   and bright with many angels,
   and all the martyr throng;
   the prince is ever with them,
   the daylight is serene;
   the pastures of the blessèd
   are decked in glorious sheen.

3. There is the throne of David;
   and there, from care released,
   the shout of them that triumph,
   the song of them that feast;
   and they, who with their leader
   have fully run the race,
   are robed in white for ever
   before their Saviour's face.

4. O sweet and blessèd country,
   the home of God's elect!
   O sweet and blessèd country,
   that eager hearts expect!
   Jesus, in mercy, bring us
   to that dear land of rest;
   who art, with God the Father
   and Spirit, ever blest.

388 John L. Bell and Graham Maule
© 1989 WGRG, Iona Community

1. Jesus calls us here to meet him as,
   through word and song and prayer,
   we affirm God's promised presence
   where his people live and care.
   Praise the God who keeps his promise;
   praise the Son who calls us friends;
   praise the Spirit who, among us,
   to our hopes and fears attends.

2. Jesus call us to confess him
   Word of life and Lord of All,
   sharer of our flesh and frailness
   saving all who fail or fall.
   Tell his holy human story;
   tell his tales that all may hear;
   tell the world that Christ in glory
   came to earth to meet us here.

3. Jesus calls us to each other:
   found in him are no divides.
   Race and class and sex and language –
   such are barriers he derides.
   Join the hand of friend and stranger;
   join the hands of age and youth;
   join the faithful and the doubter
   in their common search for truth.

4. Jesus calls us to his table,
   rooted firm in time and space,
   where the Church in earth and heaven
   finds a common meeting place.
   Share the bread and wine, his body;
   share the love of which we sing;
   share the feast for saints and sinners
   hosted by our Lord and King.

389 'Lyra Davidica'

1. Jesus Christ is ris'n today, alleluia!
   our triumphant holy day, alleluia!
   who did once, upon the cross, alleluia!
   suffer to redeem our loss, alleluia!

2. Hymns of praise then let us sing, alleluia!
   unto Christ, our heav'nly King, alleluia!
   who endured the cross and grave, alleluia!
   sinners to redeem and save, alleluia!

3. But the pains that he endured, alleluia!
   our salvation have procured; alleluia!
   now above the sky he's King, alleluia!
   where the angels ever sing, alleluia!

390 John L. Bell and Graham Maule. © *1988 WGRG.*
Iona Community, from the 'Enemy of Apathy'
collection Wild Goose Publications, 1988.

1. Jesus Christ is waiting,
   waiting in the streets:
   no one is his neighbour,
   all alone he eats.
   Listen, Lord Jesus,
   I am lonely too;
   make me, friend or stranger,
   fit to wait on you.

2. Jesus Christ is raging,
   raging in the streets
   where injustice spirals
   and all hope retreats.
   Listen, Lord Jesus,
   I am angry too;
   in the kingdom's causes
   let me rage with you.

3. Jesus Christ is healing,
   healing in the streets
   curing those who suffer,
   touching those he greets.
   Listen, Lord Jesus,
   I have pity too;
   let my care be active,
   healing just like you.

4. Jesus Christ is dancing,
   dancing in the streets,
   where each sign of hatred
   his strong love defeats.

Listen, Lord Jesus,
I feel triumph too;
on suspicion's graveyard,
let me dance with you.

5. Jesus Christ is calling,
   calling in the streets,
   'Come and walk faith's tightrope,
   I will guide your feet.'
   Listen, Lord Jesus,
   let my fears be few;
   walk one step before me,
   I will follow you.

391 Delores Dufner, OSB
© *1992, 1996 Sisters of the Order of St. Benedict*

Jesus, ever-flowing fountain,
give us water from your well.
In the gracious gift you offer
there is joy no tongue can tell.

1. Come to me, all pilgrims thirsty,
   drink the water I will give.
   If you knew what gift I offer,
   you would come to me and live.

2. Come to me, all trav'lers weary,
   come that I may give you rest.
   Drink the cup of life I offer;
   at this table be my guest.

3. Come to me, believers burdened,
   find refreshment in this place.
   If you knew the gift I offer,
   you would turn and seek my face.

4. Come to me, repentant sinners;
   leave behind your guilt and shame.
   If you knew divine compassion,
   you would turn and call my name.

5. Come to me distressed and needy;
   I would be your trusted friend.
   If you seek the gift I offer,
   come, your open hands extend.

Continued overleaf

6. Come to me abandoned, orphaned;
   lonely ways no longer roam.
   If you knew the gift I offer,
   you would make in me your home.

392 Frederick William Faber

1. Jesus, gentlest Saviour,
   God of might and power,
   thou thyself art dwelling
   in us at this hour.
   Nature cannot hold thee,
   heav'n is all too strait
   for thine endless glory,
   and thy royal state.

2. Yet the hearts of children,
   hold what worlds cannot,
   and the God of wonders
   loves the lowly spot.
   Jesus, gentlest Saviour,
   thou art in us now,
   fill us full of goodness,
   till our hearts o'erflow.

3. Pray the prayer within us
   that to heaven shall rise;
   sing the song that angels
   sing above the skies;
   multiply our graces,
   chiefly love and fear;
   and, dear Lord, the chiefest,
   grace to persevere.

393 Frederick William Faber

1. Jesus is God! The solid earth,
   the ocean broad and bright,
   the countless stars, the golden dust,
   that strew the skies at night,
   the wheeling storm, the dreadful fire,
   the pleasant wholesome air,
   the summer's sun, the winter's frost,
   his own creations were.

2. Jesus is God! The glorious bands
   of golden angels sing
   songs of adoring praise to him,
   their Maker and their King.
   He was true God in Bethlehem's crib,
   on Calv'ry's cross, true God,
   he who in heav'n eternal reigned,
   in time on earth abode.

3. Jesus is God! Let sorrow come,
   and pain and ev'ry ill;
   all are worthwhile, for all are meant
   his glory to fulfil;
   worthwhile a thousand years of life
   to speak one little word,
   if by our Credo we might own
   the Godhead of our Lord.

394 David J. Mansell
© 1982 Springtide/Word's Spirit of Praise

1. Jesus is Lord!
   Creation's voice proclaims it,
   for by his pow'r each tree and flow'r
   was planned and made.
   Jesus is Lord! The universe declares it;
   sun, moon and stars in heaven cry:
   Jesus is Lord!

   Jesus is Lord! Jesus is Lord!
   Praise him with alleluias
   for Jesus is Lord!

2. Jesus is Lord!
   Yet from his throne eternal
   in flesh he came to die in pain
   on Calv'ry's tree.
   Jesus is Lord! From him all life proceeding,
   yet gave his life a ransom
   thus setting us free.

3. Jesus is Lord!
   O'er sin the mighty conqu'ror,
   from death he rose and all his foes
   shall own his name.
   Jesus is Lord! God sends his Holy Spirit
   to show by works of power
   that Jesus is Lord.

395

Damian Lundy
© 1982 Kevin Mayhew Ltd.

1. Jesus is Lord! In love he came
   to glorify the Father's name.
   To die, to rise, and in that hour
   release the Spirit's healing power.
   Alleluia! Alleluia!

2. Jesus is Lord! He'll come again,
   in empty hearts take up his reign;
   where living springs of water flow
   in desert land, new orchards grow.

3. Jesus is Lord! Be still for he
   will come with healing, quietly.
   Deep in your heart, you'll hear his voice,
   and in that stillness you'll rejoice.

4. Jesus is Lord! Be glad and know
   he is the way by which we go
   into our Father's home to share
   the joyful welcome waiting there.

5. Jesus is Lord! His victory
   the deaf will hear, the blind will see,
   and from their graves the dead will rise,
   with saints and angels crowd the skies.

396

'Adoro te devote' ascribed to St. Thomas Aquinas,
trans. James Quinn. © *Geoffrey Chapman, an imprint
of Cassell plc.*

1. Jesus, Lord of glory,
   clothed in heaven's light,
   here I bow before you,
   hidden from my sight.
   Lord to whom my body,
   mind and heart belong,
   mind and heart here falter,
   Love so deep so strong.

2. Here distrust, my spirit,
   eye and tongue and hand,
   trust faith's ear and listen,
   hear and understand.
   Hear the voice of Wisdom,
   speaking now to you;
   when God's Word has spoken,
   what can be more true?

3. Once you hid your glory,
   Jesus crucified,
   now you hide your body,
   Jesus glorified.
   When you come in judgement,
   plain for all to see,
   God and man in splendour,
   Lord, remember me.

4. Once you showed to Thomas wounded
   hands and side.
   Here I kneel adoring,
   faith alone my guide.
   Help me grow in faith,
   Lord, grow in hope and love,
   living by your Spirit,
   gift of God above.

5. Here I see your dying,
   Jesus, victim-priest,
   here I know your rising,
   host and guest and feast.
   Let me taste your goodness,
   manna from the skies,
   feed me, heal me, save me,
   food of Paradise.

6. Heart of Jesus, broken,
   pierced and open wide,
   wash me in the water
   flowing from your side.
   Jesus' blood so precious
   that one drop could free
   all the world from evil,
   come and ransom me.

7. How I long to see you,
   Jesus, face to face,
   how the heart is thirsting,
   living spring of grace.
   Show me soon your glory,
   be my great reward,
   be my joy for ever,
   Jesus, gracious Lord.

397 Frederick William Faber

1. Jesus, my Lord, my God, my all,
   how can I love thee as I ought?
   And how revere this wondrous gift
   so far surpassing hope or thought?

   Sweet Sacrament, we thee adore;
   O make us love thee more and more.

2. Had I but Mary's sinless heart
   to love thee with, my dearest King,
   O, with what bursts of fervent praise
   thy goodness, Jesus, would I sing!

3. Ah, see, within a creature's hand
   the vast Creator deigns to be,
   reposing, infant-like, as though
   on Joseph's arm, or Mary's knee.

4. Thy body, soul and Godhead, all;
   O mystery of love divine!
   I cannot compass all I have,
   for all thou hast and art are mine.

5. Sound, sound, his praises higher, still,
   and come, ye angels, to our aid;
   'tis God, 'tis God, the very God
   whose pow'r both us and angels made.

398 Nadia Hearn. © *1974 Scripture in Song, a division of Integrity Music. Administered by Kingsway's Thankyou Music*

Jesus, Name above all names,
beautiful Saviour, glorious Lord,
Emmanuel, God is with us,
blessed Redeemer, living Word.

399 Damian Lundy
© *1988 Kevin Mayhew Ltd.*

1. Jesus rose on Easter Day,
   alleluia, now we pray.
   Resurrexit, let us say,
   for he is Lord and mighty God for ever.

2. He has conquered death and sin.
   All God's people now begin
   singing praises unto him.
   for he is Lord and mighty God for ever.

3. 'Alleluia' is our cry,
   for he lives, no more to die.
   Glory be to God on high,
   for he is Lord and mighty God for ever.

4. Alleluia! May we know
   all the joy which long ago
   set the Easter sky aglow;
   for he is Lord and mighty God for ever.

5. Alleluia! Let us be
   filled with love, our hearts set free
   as we praise his victory,
   for he is Lord and mighty God for ever.

400 11th century, trans. Edward Caswall, alt.
© *1999 Kevin Mayhew Ltd.*

1. Jesu, the very thought of thee
   with sweetness fills my breast;
   but sweeter far thy face to see,
   and in thy presence rest.

2. No voice can sing, no heart can frame,
   nor can the mind recall,
   a sweeter sound than thy blest name,
   O Saviour of us all.

3. O hope of ev'ry contrite heart,
   O joy of all the meek,
   to those who fall, how kind thou art,
   how good to those who seek!

4. But what to those who find? Ah, this
   no tongue nor pen can show;
   the love of Jesus, what it is
   none but his lovers know.

5. Jesu, our only joy be thou,
   as thou our prize wilt be,
   Jesu, be thou our glory now,
   and through eternity.

401

Keith D. Pearson, based on John 1 and 3
© 1996 Keith D. Pearson

1. Jesus, the Word, has lived among us,
   sharing his fullness, truth and grace,
   God's only Son, the Father's loved one
   reveals him to the human race.
   Jesus, the Word, has lived among us
   sharing his fullness, truth and grace.

2. He was with God from the beginning
   and through him all things came to be.
   He lightens darkness, conquers evil,
   gives life for living, glad and free.
   He was with God from the beginning
   and through him all things came to be.

3. Sing praise to God who sent Christ Jesus
   to be his sign of endless love;
   sent him to live his life among us,
   lifting our hearts to things above.
   Sing praise to God who sent Christ Jesus
   to be his sign of endless love!

402

Michael Forster
©1997 Kevin Mayhew Ltd.

A hymn for the Stations of the Cross

1. Jesus, who condemns you?
   Who cries 'Crucify'?
   Priest or politician?
   Jesus, is it I?

2. Heavy, oh too heavy,
   weighs a world of hate;
   Christ, be our Redeemer,
   Jesus, bear the weight.

3. Perfect in obedience
   to your Father's call,
   Christ, creation's glory,
   shares creation's fall.

4. Where the humble suffer,
   and the proud deride,
   Mary, blessed Mother,
   calls us to your side.

5. Christ, our only Saviour,
   you must bear the loss;
   yet give us compassion,
   let us bear the cross.

6. Christ, where now you suffer,
   in each painful place,
   let each act of kindness
   still reveal your face.

7. Mortal flesh exhausted,
   tortured sinews fail,
   yet the spirit triumphs,
   and the will prevails.

8. Still the faithful women
   stand beside the way,
   weeping for the victims
   of the present day.

9. Bowed beneath the burden
   of creation's pain,
   Saviour, be beside us
   when we fall again.

10. Church of God, resplendent
    in the robes of pow'r,
    be the Saviour's body,
    share his triumph hour!

11. All the pow'rs of evil
    join to strike the nail;
    patience and compassion
    silently prevail.

12. Lonely and forsaken,
    in this dying breath,
    love alone can bear him
    through the veil of death.

13. Arms that cradled Jesus,
    both at death and birth,
    cradle all who suffer
    in the pains of earth.

14. Christ, who came with nothing
    from your Mother's womb,
    rest in destitution,
    in a borrowed tomb.

15. Broken but triumphant,
    birthing gain from loss,
    let us share your glory,
    let us share your cross.

403

Dan Schutte
© 1992 Daniel L. Schutte/OCP Publications

Join in the dance of the earth's jubilation!
This is the feast of the love of God.
Shout from the heights
to the ends of creation:
Jesus the Saviour is risen from the grave!

1. Wake, O people, sleep no longer:
   greet the breaking day!
   Christ, Redeemer, Lamb and Lion,
   turns the night away!

2. All creation, like a mother,
   labours to give birth.
   Soon the pain will be forgotten,
   joy for all the earth.

3. Now our shame becomes our glory
   on this holy tree.
   Now the reign of death is ended;
   now we are set free!

4. None on earth, no prince or power,
   neither death nor life,
   nothing now can ever part us
   from the love of Christ!

5. Love's triumphant day of vict'ry
   heaven opens wide.
   On the tree of hope and glory
   death itself has died!

6. Christ for ever, Lord of ages,
   love beyond our dreams:
   Christ our hope of heaven's glory,
   all that yet will be!

404

Isaac Watts, based on Psalm 97, alt.

1. Joy to the world! The Lord is come;
   let earth receive her King;
   let ev'ry heart prepare him room,
   and heav'n and nature sing,
   and heav'n and nature sing,
   and heav'n and heav'n and nature sing.

2. Joy to the earth! The Saviour reigns;
   let us our songs employ;
   while fields and floods, rocks,
       hills and plains
   repeat the sounding joy,
   repeat the sounding joy,
   repeat, repeat the sounding joy.

3. He rules the world with truth and grace,
   and makes the nations prove
   the glories of his righteousness,
   and wonders of his love,
   and wonders of his love,
   and wonders, and wonders of his love.

405

Jean-Paul Lécot based on Psalm 32, trans.
W. R. Lawrence. © 1988 Kevin Mayhew Ltd.

Jubilate Deo, cantate Domino! (Repeat)

1. All of you who accept to be
   servants of God,
   by your songs of joy praise him
   now and evermore.

2. To the Lord offer thanks
   and give praise to his name;
   sing aloud new songs to proclaim
   his mighty power.

3. For the Word of the Lord
   is both faithful and sure;
   all the things he does
   show his justice, truth and love.

4. All creation is filled
   with the love of the Lord;
   everything that is
   was created through the Word.

5. May the People of God
   in all ages be bless'd;
   day by day his grace
   is outpoured upon us all.

6. May our hearts never waver,
   but trust in the Lord;
   he, the living God,
   is both merciful and good.

7. May your love,
   Lord, be with us in all that we do;
   all our hope and longing
   we humbly place in you.

406
Fred Dunn
© 1977 Kingsway's Thankyou Music

Jubilate, ev'rybody,
serve the Lord in all your ways and
come before his presence singing;
enter now his courts with praise.
For the Lord our God is gracious,
and his mercy everlasting.
Jubilate, jubilate, jubilate, Deo!

407
Lucien Deiss, based on 2 Timothy 2:8-11
© 1965 World Library Publications, a division of
J. S. Paluch Co. Inc.

Keep in mind
that Jesus Christ has died for us
and is risen from the dead.
He is our saving Lord, he is joy for all ages.

1. If we die with the Lord,
   we shall live with the Lord.

2. If we endure with the Lord,
   we shall reign with the Lord.

3. In him hope of glory,
   in him all our love.

4. In him our redemption,
   in him all our grace.

5. In him our salvation,
   in him all our peace.

408
George Herbert

1. King of glory, King of peace,
   I will love thee;
   and, that love may never cease,
   I will move thee.
   Thou hast granted my appeal,
   thou hast heard me;
   thou didst note my ardent zeal,
   thou hast spared me.

2. Wherefore with my utmost art,
   I will sing thee,
   and the cream of all my heart
   I will bring thee.
   Though my sins against me cried,
   thou didst clear me,
   and alone, when they replied,
   thou didst hear me.

3. Sev'n whole days, not one in sev'n,
   I will praise thee;
   in my heart, though not in heav'n,
   I can raise thee.
   Small it is, in this poor sort
   to enrol thee:
   e'en eternity's too short
   to extol thee.

409
Naomi Batya and Sophie Conty
© 1980 Maranatha! Music/CopyCare

King of kings and Lord of lords,
   glory, hallelujah. *(Repeat)*
Jesus, Prince of Peace,
   glory, hallelujah. *(Repeat)*

410
Chris Bowater
© 1988 Sovereign Lifestyle Music Ltd.

Lamb of God, Holy One,
Jesus Christ, Son of God,
lifted up willingly to die;
that I the guilty one may know
the blood once shed
still freely flowing,
still cleansing, still healing.
I exalt you, Jesus, my sacrifice,
I exalt you, my Redeemer and my Lord.
I exalt you, worthy Lamb of God,
and in honour I bow down before
   your throne.

411

Psalm 147, Grail translation
© 1963, 1986, 1993 The Grail

Lauda, Jerusalem, Dominum.
Lauda Deum tuum Sion.
Hosanna! Hosanna! Hosanna filio David!

1. O praise the Lord, Jerusalem!
   O Zion, sing praise to your God!

2. He has strengthened the bars of your gates,
   he has blessed the children within you.

3. He has established peace on your borders,
   he feeds you with finest wheat.

4. He sends out his word to the earth
   and swiftly runs his command.

5. He showers down snow white as wool,
   he scatters hoarfrost like ashes.

6. He hurls down hailstones like crumbs.
   The waters are frozen at his touch.

7. He sends forth his word and it melts them:
   at the breath of his mouth the waters flow.

8. He makes his word known to Jacob,
   to Israel his laws and decrees.

9. He has not dealt thus with other nations;
   he has not taught them his decrees.

412

Damian Lundy, from St Francis of Assisi
© 1981 Kevin Mayhew Ltd.

Laudato sii, O mi Signore. (x4)

1. Yes, be praised in all your creatures,
   brother sun and sister moon;
   in the stars and in the wind,
   air and fire and flowing water.

2. For our sister, mother earth,
   she who feeds us and sustains us;
   for her fruits, her grass, her flowers,
   for the mountains and the oceans.

3. Praise for those who spread forgiveness,
   those who share your peace with others,
   bearing trials and sickness bravely!
   Even sister death won't harm them.

4. For our life is but a song,
   and the reason for our singing
   is to praise you for the music;
   join the dance of your creation.

5. Praise to you, Father most holy,
   praise and thanks to you, Lord Jesus,
   praise to you, most Holy Spirit,
   life and joy of all creation!

The Italian phrase 'Laudato sii, O mi
Signore' translates as 'Praise be to you,
O my Lord'.

413

Carey Landry
©1977 North American Liturgy Resources

Lay your hands gently upon us,
let their touch render your peace,
let them bring your forgiveness and healing,
lay your hands, gently lay your hands.

1. You were sent to free the broken-hearted.
   You were sent to give sight to the blind.
   You desire to heal all our illness.
   Lay your hands, gently lay your hands.

2. Lord, we come to you through
      one another,
   Lord, we come you in all our need.
   Lord, we come to you seeking wholeness.
   Lay your hands, gently lay your hands.

414

Joseph W. Reeks

1. Leader, now on earth no longer,
   soldier of th'eternal King,
   victor in the fight for heaven,
   we thy loving praises sing.

   Great Saint George, our patron,
   help us, in the conflict be thou nigh;
   help us in that daily battle,
   where each one must win or die.

2. Praise him who in deadly battle
   never shrank from foeman's sword,
   proof against all earthly weapon,
   gave his life for Christ the Lord.

3. Who, when earthly war was over,
   fought, but not for earth's renown;
   fought, and won a nobler glory,
   won the martyr's purple crown.

4. Help us when temptation presses,
   we have still our crown to win;
   help us when our soul is weary
   fighting with the pow'rs of sin.

5. Clothe us in thy shining armour,
   place thy good sword in our hand;
   teach us how to wield it, fighting
   onward t'wards the heav'nly land.

6. Onward till, our striving over,
   on life's battlefield we fall,
   resting then, but ever ready,
   waiting for the angel's call.

415 John Henry Newman

1. Lead, kindly light,
   amid th'encircling gloom,
   lead thou me on;
   the night is dark,
   and I am far from home;
   lead thou me on.
   Keep thou my feet;
   I do not ask to see
   the distant scene;
   one step enough for me.

2. I was not ever thus,
   nor prayed that thou
   shouldst lead me on;
   I loved to choose
   and see my path; but now
   lead thou me on.
   I loved the garish day,
   and, spite of fears,
   pride ruled my will:
   remember not past years.

3. So long thy pow'r
   hath blest me, sure it still
   will lead me on,
   o'er moor and fen,

o'er crag and torrent, till
the night is gone;
and with the morn
those angel faces smile,
which I have loved long since,
and lost awhile.

416 James Edmeston

1. Lead us, heav'nly Father, lead us
   o'er the world's tempestuous sea;
   guard us, guide us, keep us, feed us,
   for we have no help but thee;
   yet possessing ev'ry blessing
   if our God our Father be.

2. Saviour, breathe forgiveness o'er us,
   all our weakness thou dost know,
   thou didst tread this earth before us,
   thou didst feel its keenest woe;
   lone and dreary, faint and weary,
   through the desert thou didst go.

3. Spirit of our God, descending,
   fill our hearts with heav'nly joy,
   love with ev'ry passion blending,
   pleasure that can never cloy;
   thus provided, pardoned, guided,
   nothing can our peace destroy.

417 Willard Jabusch
© 1998 Willard F. Jabusch

*Leave your country and your people,
leave your fam'ly and your friends.
Travel to the land I'll show you;
God will bless the ones he sends.*

1. Go, like Abraham before you,
   when he heard the Father's call,
   walking forth in faith and trusting;
   God is master of us all.

2. Sometimes God's word is demanding,
   leave security you know,
   breaking ties and bonds that hold you,
   when the voice of God says, 'Go'.

Continued overleaf

3. Take the path into the desert;
   barren seems the rock and sand.
   God will lead you through the desert
   when you follow his command.

4. Go with courage up the mountain,
   climb the narrow, rocky ledge,
   leave behind all things that hinder,
   go with only God as pledge.

418 Liturgy of St James, trans. G. Moultrie

1. Let all mortal flesh keep silence
   and with fear and trembling stand;
   ponder nothing earthly-minded,
   for with blessing in his hand
   Christ our God on earth descendeth,
   our full homage to demand.

2. King of kings, yet born of Mary,
   as of old on earth he stood,
   Lord of lords, in human vesture,
   in the body and the blood.
   He will give to all the faithful
   his own self for heav'nly food.

3. Rank on rank the host of heaven
   spreads its vanguard on the way,
   as the Light of light descendeth
   from the realms of endless day,
   that the pow'rs of hell may vanish
   as the darkness clears away.

4. At his feet the six-winged seraph;
   cherubim, with sleepless eye,
   veil their faces to the Presence,
   as with ceaseless voice they cry,
   alleluia, alleluia,
   alleluia, Lord most high.

419 Unknown

1. Let all that is within me cry: holy.
   Let all that is within me cry: holy.
   Holy, holy,
   holy is the Lamb that was slain.

2. Let all that is within me cry: mighty. *(x2)*
   Mighty, mighty,
   mighty is the Lamb that was slain.

3. Let all that is within me cry: worthy. *(x2)*
   Worthy, worthy,
   worthy is the Lamb that was slain.

4. Let all that is within me cry: blessèd. *(x2)*
   Blessèd, blessèd,
   blessèd is the Lamb that was slain.

5. Let all that is within me cry: Jesus. *(x2)*
   Jesus, Jesus,
   Jesus is the Lamb that was slain.

420 George Herbert

1. Let all the world in ev'ry corner sing,
   my God and King!
   The heav'ns are not too high,
   his praise may thither fly;
   the earth is not too low,
   his praises there may grow.
   Let all the world in ev'ry corner sing,
   my God and King!

2. Let all the world in ev'ry corner sing,
   my God and King!
   The Church with psalms must shout,
   no door can keep them out;
   but, above all, the heart
   must bear the longest part.
   Let all the world in ev'ry corner sing,
   my God and King!

421 Michael Forster
© 1995 Kevin Mayhew Ltd.

1. Let love be real, in giving and receiving,
   without the need to manage and to own;
   a haven free from posing and pretending,
   where ev'ry weakness may be safely known.
   Give me your hand,
   along the desert pathway,
   give me your love
   wherever we may go.

As God loves us,
so let us love each other:
with no demands,
just open hands and space to grow.

2. Let love be real, not grasping or confining,
   that strange embrace that holds yet sets
      us free;
   that helps us face the risk of truly living,
   and makes us brave to be what we
      might be.
   Give me your strength
   when all my words are weakness;
   give me your love
   in spite of all you know.

3. Let love be real, with no manipulation,
   no secret wish to harness or control;
   let us accept each other's incompleteness,
   and share the joy of learning to be whole.
   Give me your hope
   through dreams and disappointments;
   give me your trust
   when all my failings show.

422
Bryan Spinks, based on Psalm 140
© 1996 Kevin Mayhew Ltd.

Let our praise to you be as incense,
let us bless your holy name;
let our praise to you be as incense,
as your glory we proclaim.
May our voices join with the angels
as we praise your holy name:
holy, holy, holy is the Lord almighty,
who was, and is, and is to come.

423
Mike Anderson
© 1999 Kevin Mayhew Ltd.

Let the heavens declare,
let the mountains sing,
let the oceans roar
that Jesus lives and is our King.

Lift your hands in praise,
let your spirits soar,
let the heavens declare,
let the mountains sing,
let the oceans roar.

1. All the sins we've ever sinned
   died upon the cross with him,
   but we know he lives again:
   the vict'ry is won, the vict'ry is won,
   the vict'ry is won, the vict'ry is won.

2. Hanging on the cross for me
   Jesus died in agony.
   Blood and tears he shed for me,
   that I might have life. *(x4)*

3. In the kingdom he revealed
   broken hearts can all be healed,
   through the covenant he sealed
   with his holy blood. *(x4)*

424
Delores Dufner. © 1985 Sisters of St. Benedict.
Published by World Library Publications, a divison of
J. S. Paluch Co. Inc.

1. Let the hungry come to me,
   let the poor be fed.
   Let the thirsty come and drink,
   share my wine and bread.
   Though you have no money,
   come to me and eat.
   Drink the cup I offer,
   feed on finest wheat!

2. I myself am living bread;
   feed on me and live.
   In this cup, my blood for you;
   drink the wine I give.
   All who eat my body,
   all who drink my blood
   shall have joy for ever,
   share the life of God.

Continued overleaf

3. Here among you shall I dwell,
   making all things new.
   You shall be my very own,
   I, your God with you.
   Blest are you invited
   to my wedding feast.
   You shall live for ever,
   all your joys increased.

4. Nourished by the Word of God,
   now we eat the bread.
   With the gift of God's own life,
   hungry hearts are fed.
   Manna in the desert,
   in our darkest night!
   Food for pilgrim people,
   pledge of glory bright!

5. Many grains become one loaf,
   many grapes, the wine.
   So shall we one body be,
   who together dine.
   As the bread is broken,
   as the wine is shared:
   so must we be given,
   caring as Christ cared.

6. Risen Saviour, walk with us,
   lead us by the hand.
   Heal our blinded eyes and hearts,
   help us understand.
   Lord, make known your presence
   at this table blest.
   Stay with us for ever,
   God, our host and guest!

425 Dave Bilbrough
© 1979 Kingsway's Thankyou Music

Let there be love shared among us,
let there be love in our eyes.
May now your love sweep this nation;
cause us, O Lord, to arise.
Give us a fresh understanding,
brotherly love that is real.
Let there be love shared among us,
let there be love.

426 Traditional Zulu, trans. Helen Taylor, adapt. Tom Colvin
© Hope Publishing. Administered by CopyCare

1. Let the world in concert sing
   praises to our glorious King.*

   Alleluia, alleluia to our King!

2. Of his pow'r and glory tell;
   all his work he does right well:

3. Come, behold what he has done,
   deeds of wonder, every one:

4. O you fearful ones, draw near;
   praise our God who holds you dear:

5. Let us now in concert sing
   praises to our glorious King:*

   * *For Eastertide 'risen King' may be
   substituted.*

427 Marie Lydia Pereira
© 1999 Kevin Mayhew Ltd.

1. Let us sing your glory, Lord, alleluia,
   let us praise your name adored, alleluia.
   Joy and beauty come from you, alleluia,
   and each hour your love shines through,
   alleluia.

   Alleluia, alleluia, allelu, alleluia. (x2)

2. Leaf that quivers on the tree, alleluia,
   flowers that we delight to see, alleluia.
   Planets as they reel in space, alleluia,
   tell us of your power and grace, alleluia.

3. All creation sings your praise, alleluia,
   young and old their voices raise, alleluia.
   Children as they laugh and sing, alleluia,
   to your goodness homage bring, alleluia.

428 John Milton, based on Psalm 136

1. Let us, with a gladsome mind,
   praise the Lord, for he is kind;

   *for his mercies ay endure,
   ever faithful, ever sure.*

2. Let us blaze his name abroad,
    for of gods he is the God;

3, He, with all-commanding might,
    filled the new-made world with light;

4. He the golden-tressèd sun
    caused all day his course to run;

5. And the moon to shine at night,
    'mid her starry sisters bright;

6. All things living he doth feed,
    his full hand supplies their need;

7. Let us, with a gladsome mind,
    praise the Lord, for he is kind;

429 George William Kitchin and Michael Robert
Newbolt, alt. © *Hymns Ancient & Modern Ltd.*

Lift high the Cross,
the love of Christ proclaim
till all the world adores his sacred name!

1. Come, Christians,
    follow where our Saviour trod,
    o'er death victorious,
    Christ the Son of God.

2. Led on their way by this
    triumphant sign,
    the hosts of God in joyful
    praise combine:

3. Each new disciple
    of the Crucified
    is called to bear the seal
    of him who died:

4. Saved by the Cross
    whereon their Lord was slain,
    now Adam's children
    their lost home regain:

5. From north and south,
    from east and west they raise
    in growing harmony
    their song of praise:

6. O Lord, once lifted
    on the glorious tree,
    as thou hast promised,
    draw us unto thee:

7. Let ev'ry race
    and ev'ry language tell
    of him who saves
    from fear of death and hell:

8. From farthest regions,
    let them homage bring,
    and on his Cross
    adore their Saviour King:

9. Set up thy throne,
    that earth's despair may cease
    beneath the shadow
    of its healing peace:

10. For thy blest Cross
    which doth for all atone,
    creation's praises rise
    before thy throne:

11. So let the world
    proclaim with one accord
    the praise of our
    ever-living Lord.

430 Roc O'Connor, based on Psalm 66. © 1981, 1993,
Robert F. O'Connor, S. J. and New Dawn Music

Lift up your hearts to the Lord
in praise of his mercy!
Sing out your joy to the Lord:
his love is enduring.

1. Shout with joy to the Lord, all the earth!
    Praise the glory of his name!
    Say to God 'How wondrous your works,
    how glorious your name!'

2. Let the earth worship, singing your praise.
    Praise the glory of your name!
    Come and see the deeds of the Lord;
    come, worship his name!

Continued overleaf

3. At his touch the dry land did appear;
   paths were opened in the sea.
   Let the earth rejoice in his might,
   the might of his love.

4. Listen now, all you servants of God,
   as I tell of his great works.
   Blessed be the Lord of my life!
   His love shall endure!

431
Estelle White
© 1976 Kevin Mayhew Ltd.

1. Like a sea without a shore,
   love divine is boundless.
   Time is now and evermore,
   and his love surround us.

   Maranatha! Maranatha!
   Maranatha! Come, Lord Jesus, come!

2. So that we could all be free,
   he appeared among us.
   Blest are those who have not seen,
   yet believe his promise.

3. All our visions, all our dreams,
   are but ghostly shadows
   of the radiant clarity
   waiting at life's close.

4. Death, where is your victory?
   Death, where is your sting?
   Closer than air we breathe
   is our risen King.

   'Maranatha' is an Aramaic word meaning
   'Lord, come!' See 1 Corinthians 16:22

432
Psalm 41/42. © 1963, 1986, 1993 The Grail,
England. Used by permission of A. P. Watt Ltd.

Like as the deer
that yearns for flowing waters,
so longs my soul for God,
the living God.

1. My soul is thirsting for God,
   the God of my life;
   when can I enter and see
   the face of God?

2. These things will I remember
   as I pour out my soul:
   how I would lead the rejoicing crowd
   into the house of God.

3. Send forth your light and your truth,
   let these be my guide;
   let them bring me to your
        holy mountain,
   to the place where you dwell.

4. And I will come to the altar of God,
   the God of my joy!
   my Redeemer, I will thank you on
        the harp,
   O God, my God!

433
Luke Connaughton and Kevin Mayhew, based on
Psalm 41. © 1976 Kevin Mayhew Ltd.

1. Like the deer that yearns for water,
   O God, I long for you.
   Weeping, I have heard them taunt me:
   'What help is in your God?'

2. Gladly I would lead your people,
   rejoicing to your house.
   Trust in God, my soul, and praise him,
   and he will dry your tears.

3. Grief and pain, like roaring torrents,
   had swept my soul away.
   But his mercy is my rescue,
   I will praise him all my days.

4. Weeping, I have heard them taunt me:
   'What help is in your God?'
   Rock of strength, do not forget me,
   in you alone I trust.

5. To the Father praise and honour,
   all glory to the Son,
   honour to the Holy Spirit:
   let God be glorified.

434
Carl P. Daw Jr.
© 1989 Hope Publishing/CopyCare

1. Like the murmur of the dove's song,
   like the challenge of her flight,
   like the vigour of the wind's rush,
   like the new flame's eager might:
   come, Holy Spirit, come.

2. To the members of Christ's body,
   to the branches of the Vine,
   to the Church in faith assembled,
   to her midst as gift and sign:
   come, Holy Spirit, come.

3. With the healing of division,
   with the ceaseless voice of prayer,
   with the power to love and witness,
   with the peace beyond compare:
   come, Holy Spirit, come.

435
Aniceto Nazareth
© 1984 Kevin Mayhew Ltd.

Listen, let your heart keep seeking;
listen to his constant speaking;
listen to the Spirit calling you.
Listen to his inspiration;
listen to his invitation;
listen to the Spirit calling you.

1. He's in the sound of the thunder,
   in the whisper of the breeze.
   He's in the might of the whirlwind,
   in the roaring of the seas.

2. He's in the laughter of children,
   in the patter of the rain.
   Hear him in cries of the suff'ring,
   in their moaning and their pain.

3. He's in the noise of the city,
   in the singing of the birds.
   And in the night-time the stillness
   helps you listen to his word.

436
Mike Anderson
© 1999 Kevin Mayhew Ltd.

Listen to me, Yahweh, answer me,
poor and needy as I am.
Listen to me, Yahweh, answer me,
I rely on you.

1. Lord, I invoke you in my trouble;
   give me reason to rejoice.

2. Lord, in your goodness, please forgive me;
   listen to me, hear my plea.

3. Lord, you are merciful and faithful;
   turn to me now in my need.

4. Lord, give me strength, I am your servant;
   show me that you really care.

437
Francesca Leftley
© 1999 Kevin Mayhew Ltd.

1. Listen to my voice,
   and then turn back to me:
   I will heal your heart,
   and I will set you free.
   Oh, my dearest child,
   how much you mean to me:
   let me fill your life
   and love you tenderly.

2. Rest within my arms
   and let your fears depart,
   feel my peace and joy
   bind up your broken heart.
   I will wipe your tears
   and make you whole again:
   come to me, my child,
   and turn away from sin.

3. Take my hand, and now
   we will begin once more,
   I will walk beside you
   as I did before.
   I have never left you,
   though your eyes were dim:
   walk with me in light,
   and turn away from sin.

438
Charles Wesley, John Cennick and Martin Madan

1. Lo, he comes with clouds descending,
   once for mortal sinners slain;
   thousand thousand saints attending
   swell the triumph of his train.
   Alleluia! Alleluia! Alleluia!
   Christ appears on earth to reign.

2. Ev'ry eye shall now behold him
   robed in dreadful majesty;
   we who set at naught and sold him,
   pierced and nailed him to the tree,
   deeply grieving, deeply grieving,
       deeply grieving,
   shall the true Messiah see.

3. Those dear tokens of his passion
   still his dazzling body bears,
   cause of endless exultation
   to his ransomed worshippers:
   with what rapture, with what rapture,
       with what rapture
   gaze we on those glorious scars!

4. Yea, amen, let all adore thee,
   high on thine eternal throne;
   Saviour, take the pow'r and glory,
   claim the kingdom for thine own.
   Alleluia! Alleluia! Alleluia!
   Thou shalt reign, and thou alone.

439
Bernadette Farrell
© 1993 Bernadette Farrell/OCP

1. Longing for light, we wait in darkness.
   Longing for truth, we turn to you.
   Make us your own, your holy people,
   light for the world to see.

   Christ, be our light! Shine in our hearts.
   Shine through the darkness.
   Christ be our light!
   Shine in your Church gathered today.

2. Longing for peace, our world is troubled.
   Longing for hope, many despair.
   Your word alone has power to save us.
   Make us your living voice.

3. Longing for food, many are hungry.
   Longing for water, still many thirst.
   Make us your bread, broken for others,
   shared until all are fed.

4. Longing for shelter, many are homeless.
   Longing for warmth, many are cold.
   Make us your building, sheltering others,
   walls made of living stone.

5. Many the gifts, many the people,
   many the hearts that yearn to belong.
   Let us be servants to one another,
   making your kingdom come.

440
Jodi Page Clark
© 1976 Celebration/Kingsway's Thankyou Music

1. Look around you, can you see?
   Times are troubled, people grieve.
   See the violence, feel the hardness;
   all my people, weep with me.

   Kyrie, eleison. Christe, eleison.
   Kyrie eleison.

2. Walk among them, I'll go with you.
   Reach out to them with my hands.
   Suffer with me, and together
   we will serve them, help them stand.

3. Forgive us, Father; hear our prayer.
   We'll walk with you anywhere,
   through your suff'ring, with forgiveness,
   take your life into the world.

441
Damian Lundy
© 1982 Kevin Mayhew Ltd.

1. Look at the sky!
   The stars proclaim my glory.
   I am the Lord,
   the author of your story.
   Sing and make music,
   share my celebration!
   Spread the good news!
   Bring joy to ev'ry nation.

   I am your God, your Father and your joy.
   You are my own, my children and my joy!

2. See I am near you,
   in my own creation!
   May ev'ry moment
   bring you my salvation!
   The moon is your sister
   and the sun your brother!
   Living and fruitful
   is the earth, your mother.

3. Listen to all my
   Word is still revealing!
   Filled with my Spirit,
   you will know my healing,
   for I am near you –
   in your heart I'm living.
   You'll recognise me,
   loving and forgiving.

4. Know I am with you,
   I am all around you.
   All my attention
   and my love surround you.
   You are my children:
   Jesus is your brother.
   Find me in him,
   and him in one another.

442 St Alphonsus, trans. Edmund Vaughan

1. Look down, O mother Mary,
   from thy bright throne above;
   cast down upon thy children
   one only glance of love;
   and if a heart so tender
   with pity flows not o'er,
   then turn away, O mother,
   and look on us no more.

   Look down, O mother Mary,
   from thy bright throne above,
   cast down upon thy children
   one only glance of love.

2. See how, ungrateful sinners,
   we stand before thy Son;
   his loving heart upbraids us
   the evil we have done,

but if thou wilt appease him,
   speak for us but one word;
   for thus thou canst obtain us,
   the pardon of our Lord.

3. O Mary, dearest mother,
   if thou wouldst have us live,
   say that we are thy children,
   and Jesus will forgive.
   Our sins make us unworthy
   that title still to bear,
   but thou art still our mother;
   then show a mother's care.

4. Unfold to us thy mantle,
   there stay we without fear;
   what evil can befall us
   if, mother, thou art near?
   O kindest, dearest mother,
   thy sinful children save;
   look down on us with pity,
   who thy protection crave.

443 Sister M. Teresine

1. Lord, accept the gifts we offer
   at this Eucharistic feast,
   bread and wine to be transformed now
   through the action of thy priest.
   Take us too, Lord, and transform us,
   be thy grace in us increased.

2. May our souls be pure and spotless
   as the host of wheat so fine;
   may all stain of sin be crushed out,
   like the grape that forms the wine,
   as we, too, become partakers,
   in the sacrifice divine.

3. Take our gifts, almighty Father,
   living God, eternal, true,
   which we give through Christ our Saviour,
   pleading here for us anew.
   Grant salvation to all present,
   and our faith and love renew.

444

George Hugh Bourne

1. Lord, enthroned in heav'nly splendour,
   glorious first-born from the dead,
   you alone our strong defender
   lifting up your people's head:
   alleluia, alleluia,
   Jesus, true and living bread!

2. Prince of life, for us now living,
   by your body souls are healed;
   Prince of peace, your pardon giving,
   by your blood our peace is sealed:
   alleluia, alleluia,
   Word of God in flesh revealed.

3. Paschal Lamb! your off'ring finished,
   once for all, when you were slain;
   in its fulness undiminished
   shall for evermore remain:
   alleluia, alleluia,
   cleansing souls from ev'ry stain.

4. Great High Priest of our profession,
   through the veil you entered in,
   by your mighty intercession
   grace and mercy there to win:
   alleluia, alleluia,
   only sacrifice for sin.

5. Life-imparting heavenly Manna,
   stricken rock, with streaming side;
   heav'n and earth, with loud hosanna,
   worship you, the Lamb who died:
   alleluia, alleluia,
   ris'n, ascended, glorified!

445

Sister M. Xavier

1. Lord, for tomorrow and its needs
   I do not pray;
   keep me, my God, from stain of sin,
   just for today.

2. Let me both diligently work
   and duly pray;
   let me be kind in word and deed,
   just for today.

3. Let me no wrong or idle word
   unthinking say;
   set thou a seal upon my lips,
   just for today.

4. And if today my tide of life
   should ebb away,
   give me thy sacraments divine,
   sweet Lord, today.

5. So, for tomorrow and its needs
   I do not pray;
   but keep me, guide me, love me, Lord,
   just for today.

446

Gerard Markland, based on Ezekiel

Lord, have mercy. Lord, have mercy.
Lord, have mercy on your people. (Repeat)

1. Give me the heart of stone within you,
   and I'll give you a heart of flesh.
   Clean water I will use to cleanse all
   your wounds.
   My Spirit I give to you.

2. You'll find me near the broken-hearted:
   those crushed in spirit I will save.
   So turn to me, for my pardon is great;
   my word will heal all your wounds.

447

Patrick Appleford

1. Lord Jesus Christ, you have come to us,
   you are one with us, Mary's Son.
   Cleansing our souls from all their sin,
   pouring your love and goodness in,
   Jesus, our love for you we sing,
   living Lord.

2. Lord Jesus Christ, now and ev'ry day
   teach us how to pray, Son of God.
   You have commanded us to do
   this in remembrance, Lord, of you.
   Into our lives your pow'r breaks through,
   living Lord.

3. Lord Jesus Christ, you have come to us,
   born as one of us, Mary's Son.
   Led out to die on Calvary,
   risen from death to set us free,
   living Lord Jesus, help us see
   you are Lord.

4. Lord Jesus Christ, I would come to you,
   live my life for you, Son of God.
   All your commands I know are true,
   your many gifts will make me new,
   into my life your pow'r breaks through,
   living Lord.

448 Bishop Synesius, trans. Allen William Chatfield

1. Lord Jesus, think on me,
   and purge away my sin;
   from earth-born passions set me free,
   and make me pure within.

2. Lord Jesus, think on me,
   with care and woe opprest;
   let me thy loving servant be,
   and taste thy promised rest.

3. Lord Jesus, think on me
   amid the battle's strife;
   in all my pain and misery
   be thou my health and life.

4. Lord Jesus, think on me,
   nor let me go astray;
   through darkness and perplexity
   point thou the heav'nly way.

5. Lord Jesus, think on me,
   when flows the tempest high:
   when on doth rush the enemy,
   O Saviour, be thou nigh.

6. Lord Jesus, think on me,
   that, when the flood is past,
   I may th'eternal brightness see,
   and share thy joy at last.

449 John B. Foley, based on the Prayer of St Francis
© 1976 John B. Foley, S. J./New Dawn Music

1. Lord, make me a means of your peace.
   Where there's hatred grown,
   let me sow your love.
   Where there's inj'ry, Lord,
   let forgiveness be my sword.
   Lord, make me a means of your peace.

2. Lord, make me a means of your peace.
   Where there's doubt and fear,
   let me sow your faith.
   In this world's despair,
   give me hope in you to share.
   Lord, make me a means of your peace.

3. Lord, make me a means of your peace.
   When there's sadness here,
   let me sow your joy.
   When the darkness nears,
   may your light dispel our fears.
   Lord, make me a means of your peace.

4. Lord, grant me to seek and to share:
   less to be consoled
   than to help console,
   less be understood
   than to understand your good.
   Lord, make me a means of your peace.

5. Lord, grant me to seek and to share:
   to receive love less
   than to give love free,
   just to give in thee,
   just receiving from your tree.
   Lord, make me a means of your peace.

6. Lord, grant me to seek and to share:
   to forgive in thee,
   you've forgiven me;
   for to die in thee
   is eternal life to me.
   Lord, make me a means of your peace.

450

Jan Struther
© *Oxford University Press*

1. Lord of all hopefulness,
   Lord of all joy,
   whose trust, ever childlike,
   no cares could destroy,
   be there at our waking,
   and give us, we pray,
   your bliss in our hearts, Lord,
   at the break of the day.

2. Lord of all eagerness,
   Lord of all faith,
   whose strong hands were skilled
   at the plane and the lathe,
   be there at our labours,
   and give us, we pray,
   your strength in our hearts, Lord,
   at the noon of the day.

3. Lord of all kindliness,
   Lord of all grace,
   your hands swift to welcome,
   your arms to embrace,
   be there at our homing,
   and give us, we pray,
   your love in our hearts, Lord,
   at the eve of the day.

4. Lord of all gentleness,
   Lord of all calm,
   whose voice is contentment,
   whose presence is balm,
   be there at our sleeping,
   and give us, we pray,
   your peace in our hearts, Lord,
   at the end of the day.

451

Patrick Appleford
© *1984 Kevin Mayhew Ltd.*

1. Lord of life, you give us all our days:
   let your life fill ours with hope and praise.
   May our learning, seeking, yearning,
   lead us on to share your risen life.

2. 'Come to me, and I will give you rest.'
   Help us see your Way is richly blest;
   guide our questing, working, resting,
   till we hear you calling 'follow me'.

3. Lord, we come, encouraged by your grace,
   Lord, we come, and things fall into place;
   pilgrims ever, we endeavour,
   Lord, to follow as you bring us home.

4. Lord, may we bring all our strength and skill:
   help us to be prepared to do your will.
   Turn our living into giving
   love and service as you set us free.

5. Glory be to God for all his love;
   here may we with saints below, above,
   go rejoicing, ever voicing
   praise for such a welcome 'Come to me'.

452

Kevin Nichols
© *1976 Kevin Mayhew Ltd.*

1. Lord our God, O Lord our Father,
   Lord of love and Lord of fear,
   now we gather round your altar
   and we know your Word is near.

2. All our lives lie open to you,
   Lord of age, and Lord of youth,
   as we bring our sins and falsehoods
   to the judgement of your truth.

3. Lord of times and Lord of seasons,
   Lord of calmness, Lord of stress,
   heart that sees our secret terrors,
   Lord of strength and gentleness.

4. Lord of storms and Lord of sunsets,
   Lord of darkness, Lord of light,
   cast the shadow of your blessing
   on us gathered in your sight.

5. Lord of foes and Lord of friendships,
   Lord of laughter, Lord of tears,
   Lord of toil and Lord of Sabbath,
   Master of the hurrying years.

6. Lord of hope and Lord of hunger,
   Lord of atoms, Lord of space,
   take this world we bring before you
   to the haven of your grace.

453
Graham Kendrick
© 1987 Make Way Music

1. Lord, the light of your love is shining,
   in the midst of the darkness, shining;
   Jesus, Light of the World, shine upon us,
   set us free by the truth you now bring us.
   Shine on me, shine on me.

   Shine, Jesus, shine,
   fill this land with the Father's glory;
   blaze, Spirit, blaze,
   set our hearts on fire.
   Flow, river, flow,
   flood the nations with grace and mercy;
   send forth your word, Lord,
   and let there be light.

2. Lord, I come to your awesome presence,
   from the shadows into your radiance;
   by the blood I may enter your brightness,
   search me, try me, consume all
        my darkness.
   Shine on me, shine on me.

3. As we gaze on your kingly brightness,
   so our faces display your likeness,
   ever changing from glory to glory;
   mirrored here may our lives tell your story.
   Shine on me, shine on me.

454
Henry Williams Baker

1. Lord, thy word abideth,
   and our footsteps guideth;
   who its truth believeth
   light and joy receiveth.

2. When our foes are near us,
   then thy word doth cheer us,
   word of consolation,
   message of salvation.

3. When the storms are o'er us,
   and dark clouds before us,
   then its light directeth,
   and our way protecteth.

4. Who can tell the pleasure,
   who recount the treasure,
   by thy word imparted
   to the simple-hearted?

5. Word of mercy, giving
   succour to the living;
   word of life, supplying
   comfort to the dying.

6. O that we, discerning
   its most holy learning,
   Lord, may love and fear thee,
   evermore be near thee.

455
Marie Lydia Pereira
© 1999 Kevin Mayhew Ltd.

Lord, unite all nations in your love.
Bless us with your bounty from above.
And may all in heaven one day sing
at the banquet of their Lord and King.

1. Draw us in love, grant us your peace
   that ev'rywhere your Spirit may increase.
   Help us proclaim that all are one in you:
   Lord, unite all nations in your love.

2. Fill us with love, give us your peace,
   let grace abound and charity increase.
   From East to West may all be one in love:
   Lord, unite all nations in your love.

3. Teach us your love, teach us your peace,
   that joy may grow and happiness increase.
   Help us to work to make all nations one;
   Lord, unite all nations in your love.

456
Jean Holloway
© 1995 Kevin Mayhew Ltd.

1. Lord, we come to ask your healing,
   teach us of love;
   all unspoken shame revealing,
   teach us of love.

Tune: All thro' the night ?

Take our selfish thoughts and actions,
petty feuds, divisive factions,
hear us now to you appealing,
teach us of love.

2. Soothe away our pain and sorrow,
hold us in love;
grace we cannot buy or borrow,
hold us in love.
Though we see but dark and danger,
though we spurn both friend and stranger,
though we often dread tomorrow,
hold us in love.

3. When the bread is raised and broken,
fill us with love;
words of consecration spoken,
fill us with love.
As our grateful prayers continue,
make the faith that we have in you
more than just an empty token,
fill us with love.

4. Help us live for one another,
bind us in love;
stranger, neighbour, father, mother –
bind us in love.
All are equal at your table,
through your Spirit make us able
to embrace as sister, brother,
bind us in love.

457 Brian Foley, based on Psalm 5
© 1971 Faber Music Ltd.

1. Lord, when I wake I turn to you,
yourself my day's first thought and prayer,
your strength to help, your peace to bless,
your will to guide me ev'rywhere!

2. I live with many in our world –
their worldly eyes too blind to see –
who never think what is your will,
or why you brought our world to be!

3. Your thought for me, your loving care,
those favours I could never earn,
call for my thanks in praise and prayer,
call me to love you in return!

4. There is no blessing, Lord, from you
for those who make their will their way,
no praise for those who do not praise,
no peace for those who do not pray!

5. Make then my life a life of love,
keep me from sin in all I do,
your way to be my only way,
your will my will for love of you!

458 Claudia Frances Hernaman

1. Lord, who throughout these forty days
for us didst fast and pray,
teach us with thee to mourn our sins,
and at thy side to stay.

2. As thou with Satan didst contend
and didst the vict'ry win,
O give us strength in thee to fight,
in thee to conquer sin.

3. As thirst and hunger thou didst bear,
so teach us, gracious Lord,
to die to self, and daily live
by thy most holy word.

4. And through these days of penitence,
and through thy Passiontide,
yea, evermore, in life and death,
Lord Christ, with us abide.

459 Jeffrey Rowthorn
© 1978 Hope Publishing/CopyCare

1. Lord, you give the great commission:
'Heal the sick and preach the word.'
Lest the Church neglect its mission,
and the Gospel go unheard,
help us witness to your purpose
with renewed integrity;
with the Spirit's gifts empow'r us
for the work of ministry.

2. Lord, you call us to your service:
   'In my name baptise and teach,'
   that the world may trust your promise,
   life abundant meant for each,
   give us all new fervour,
   draw us closer in community;
   with the Spirit's gifts empower us
   for the work of ministry.

3. Lord, you make the common holy:
   'This my body, this my blood.'
   Let us all, for earth's true glory,
   daily lift life heavenward,
   asking that the world around us
   share your children's liberty;
   with the Spirit's gifts empower us
   for the work of ministry.

4. Lord, you show us love's true measure;
   'Father what they do, forgive.'
   Yet we hoard as private treasure
   all that you so freely give.
   May your care and mercy lead us
   to a just society;
   with the Spirit's gifts empow'r us
   for the work of ministry.

5. Lord, you bless with words assuring:
   'I am with you to the end.'
   Faith and hope and love restoring,
   may we serve as you intend,
   and, amid the cares that claim us,
   hold in mind eternity;
   with the Spirit's gifts empow'r us
   for the work of ministry.

460 Christina Georgina Rossetti

1. Love came down at Christmas,
   Love all lovely, Love divine;
   Love was born at Christmas,
   star and angels gave the sign.

2. Worship we the Godhead,
   Love incarnate, Love divine;
   worship we our Jesus:
   but wherewith for sacred sign?

3. Love shall be our token,
   love be yours and love be mine,
   love to God and all men,
   love for plea and gift and sign.

461 Charles Wesley

1. Love divine, all loves excelling,
   joy of heav'n, to earth come down,
   fix in us thy humble dwelling,
   all thy faithful mercies crown.

2. Jesu, thou art all compassion,
   pure unbounded love thou art;
   visit us with thy salvation,
   enter ev'ry trembling heart.

3. Breathe, O breathe thy loving Spirit
   into ev'ry troubled breast;
   let us all in thee inherit,
   let us find thy promised rest.

4. Take away the love of sinning,
   Alpha and Omega be;
   end of faith, as its beginning,
   set our hearts at liberty.

5. Come, almighty to deliver,
   let us all thy grace receive;
   suddenly return, and never,
   never more thy temples leave.

6. Thee we would be always blessing,
   serve thee as thy hosts above;
   pray, and praise thee without ceasing,
   glory in thy perfect love.

7. Finish then thy new creation,
   pure and spotless let us be;
   let us see thy great salvation
   perfectly restored in thee.

8. Changed from glory into glory,
   till in heav'n we take our place,
   till we cast our crowns before thee,
   lost in wonder, love, and praise.

462 Luke Connaughton

1. Love is his word, love is his way,
   feasting with all, fasting alone,
   living and dying, rising again,
   love only love, is his way.

   Richer than gold is the love of my Lord:
   better than splendour and wealth.

2. Love is his way, love is his mark,
   sharing his last Passover feast,
   Christ at the table, host to the twelve,
   love, only love, is his mark.

3. Love is his mark, love is his sign,
   bread for our strength, wine for our joy,
   'This is my body, this is my blood.'
   Love, only love, is his sign.

4. Love is his sign, love is his news,
   'Do this,' he said, 'lest you forget
   all my deep sorrow, all my dear blood.'
   Love, only love, is his name.

5. Love is his news, love is his name,
   we are his own, chosen and called,
   family, brethren, cousins and kin.
   Love, only love, is his name.

6. Love is his name, love is his law,
   hear his command, all who are his,
   'Love one another, I have loved you.'
   Love, only love, is his law.

7. Love is his law, love is his word:
   love of the Lord, Father and Word,
   love of the Spirit, God ever one,
   love, only love, is his word.

463 Sister Patrick Ignatius, based on 1 Corinthians 13

Love is patient, love is always kind,
love can take the roughest path
and never seem to mind.
Love is never boastful or jealous of the rest,
love is strong and faces ev'ry test.

1. If I speak with eloquence
   and make the angels stare,
   I'm a tinkling cymbal,
   if love is never there.
   If I am a prophet
   and know all things to come,
   if I have not love,
   I might as well be dumb!

2. If my faith is strong,
   then I might make the mountains move,
   feed the hungry people,
   but what does all that prove?
   I can give up all things –
   possessions come and go –
   but unless there's love
   it doesn't count, I know.

3. Love goes on for evermore
   but prophecies will pass;
   tongues will cease their wagging,
   and knowledge will not last;
   for we know so little,
   the future's very dim,
   but with faith and hope,
   our love leads us to him.

464 Michael Forster

1. Love is the only law
   for God and humankind,
   love your God with all your heart,
   your strength and soul and mind.
   Love your neighbour as yourself,
   of ev'ry creed and race,
   turn the water of endless laws
   into the wine of grace.

   Love is God's only law,
   love is God's only law;
   love is God's wisdom,
   love is God's strength,
   love of such height,
   such depth, such length,
   love is God's only law.

2. Give to the poor a voice
and help the blind to see,
feed the hungry, heal the sick
and set the captive free.
All that God requires of you
will then fall into place,
turn the water of endless laws
into the wine of grace.

3. Let love like fountains flow
and justice like a stream,
faith become reality
and hope your constant theme.
Then shall freedom, joy and peace
with righteousness embrace,
turn the water of endless laws
into the wine of grace.

465
Pamela Hayes
© 1998 Kevin Mayhew Ltd.

1. Lovely in your littleness,
longing for our lowliness,
longing for our lowliness,
searching for our meekness:
Jesus is our joy, Jesus is our joy.

2. Peace within our powerlessness,
hope within our helplessness,
hope within our helplessness,
love within our loneliness:
Jesus is our joy, Jesus is our joy.

3. Held in Mary's tenderness,
tiny hands are raised to bless,
tiny hands are raised to bless,
touching us with God's caress:
Jesus is our joy, Jesus is our joy.

4. Joy, then, in God's graciousness,
peace comes with gentleness,
peace comes with gentleness,
filling hearts with gladness:
Jesus is our joy, Jesus is our joy.

466
Jane Elizabeth Leeson

1. Loving shepherd of thy sheep,
keep me, Lord, in safety keep;
nothing can thy pow'r withstand,
none can pluck me from thy hand.

2. Loving shepherd, thou didst give
thine own life that I might live;
may I love thee day by day,
gladly thy sweet will obey.

3. Loving shepherd, ever near,
teach me still thy voice to hear;
suffer not my steps to stray
from the straight and narrow way.

4. Where thou leadest may I go,
walking in thy steps below;
then, before thy Father's throne,
Jesu, claim me for thine own.

467
From the Gospel of John

Lumen Christi, alleluia! Amen!

1. I am the <u>light</u> of the world:
everyone who follows me will have
the <u>light</u> of life.

2. You are the <u>light</u> of the world:
your light must shine in the <u>light</u> of all.

3. You will shine in the <u>world</u> like
bright stars
because you are offering it the <u>word</u>
of life.

4. The sheep that belong to me
<u>listen</u> to my voice:
I know them and they <u>follow</u> me.

5. I call you friends because I have made
<u>known</u> to you
everything I have <u>learnt</u> from my Father.

6. I am the resurrection <u>and</u> the life;
whoever lives and believes in <u>me</u>
will never die.

Continued overleaf

7. You believe, Thomas,
   because you can see me.
   Happy are those who have not seen and
   yet believe.

8. Go, make disciples of all the nations:
   I am with you always;
   yes, to the end of time.

468
Dante Alighieri, trans. Ronald Arbuthnott Knox
© Burns and Oates Ltd.

1. Maiden, yet a mother,
   daughter of thy Son,
   high beyond all other,
   lowlier is none;
   thou the consummation
   planned by God's decree,
   when our lost creation
   nobler rose in thee!

2. Thus his place preparèd,
   he who all things made
   'mid his creatures tarried,
   in thy bosom laid;
   there his love he nourished,
   warmth that gave increase
   to the root whence flourished
   our eternal peace.

3. Lady, lest our vision,
   striving heav'nward, fail,
   still let thy petition
   with thy Son prevail,
   unto whom all merit,
   pow'r and majesty
   with the Holy Spirit
   and the Father be.

469
Jack W. Hayford
© Rocksmith Music Inc./Leosong Copyright Service Ltd.

Majesty, worship his majesty;
unto Jesus be glory, honour and praise.
Majesty, kingdom authority
flow from his throne unto his own:
his anthem raise.

So exalt, lift up on high the name of Jesus;
magnify, come glorify Christ Jesus the King.
Majesty, worship his majesty,
Jesus who died, now glorified,
King of all kings.

470
Sebastian Temple, based on the Prayer of St Francis
© 1967 OCP Publications

1. Make me a channel of your peace.
   Where there is hatred, let me bring
      your love.
   Where there is injury, your pardon, Lord;
   and where there's doubt, true faith in you.

2. Make me a channel of your peace.
   Where there's despair in life, let me
      bring hope.
   Where there is darkness, only light,
   and where there's sadness, ever joy.

3. O, Master, grant that I may never seek
   so much to be consoled as to console,
   to be understood as to understand,
   to be loved as to love with all my soul.

4. Make me a channel of your peace.
   It is in pardoning that we are pardoned,
   in giving to all that we receive,
   and in dying that we're born to eternal life.

471
Graham Kendrick
© 1986 Kingsway's Thankyou Music

1. Make way, make way, for Christ the King
   in splendour arrives;
   fling wide the gates and welcome him
   into your lives.

   *Make way (make way), make way (make way),
   for the King of kings (for the King of kings);
   make way (make way), make way (make way),
   and let his kingdom in!*

2. He comes the broken hearts to heal,
   the pris'ners to free;
   the deaf shall hear, the lame shall dance,
   the blind shall see.

3. And those who mourn with heavy hearts,
   who weep and sigh,
   with laughter, joy and royal crown
   he'll beautify.

4. We call you now to worship him
   as Lord of all,
   to have no gods before him,
   their thrones must fall.

472 West Indian Spiritual
© 1999 Kevin Mayhew Ltd.

1. Mary had a baby, yes, Lord,
   Mary had a baby, yes, my Lord,
   Mary had a baby, yes, Lord,
   the people came to Bethlehem
   to see her son.

2. What did she name him, yes, Lord? *(x3)*

3. Mary named him Jesus, yes, Lord *(x3)*

4. Where was he born, yes, Lord? *(x3)*

5. Born in a stable, yes, Lord *(x3)*

6. Where did she lay him, yes, Lord? *(x3)*

7. Laid him in a manger, yes, Lord *(x3)*

473 F. W. Weatherell

1. Mary immaculate,
   star of the morning,
   chosen before
   the creation began,
   chosen to bring,
   for thy bridal adorning,
   woe to the serpent
   and rescue to man.

2. Here, in an orbit
   of shadow and sadness
   veiling thy splendour,
   thy course thou hast run;
   now thou art throned
   in all glory and gladness,
   crowned by the hand
   of thy Saviour and Son.

3. Sinners, we worship
   thy sinless perfection,
   fallen and weak,
   for thy pity we plead;
   grant us the shield
   of thy sov'reign protection,
   measure thine aid
   by the depth of our need.

4. Frail is our nature
   and strict our probation,
   watchful the foe
   that would lure us to wrong,
   succour our souls
   in the hour of temptation,
   Mary immaculate,
   tender and strong.

5. See how the wiles
   of the serpent assail us,
   see how we waver
   and flinch in the fight;
   let thine immaculate
   merit avail us,
   make of our weakness
   a proof of thy might.

6. Bend from thy throne
   at the voice of our crying;
   bend to this earth
   which thy footsteps have trod;
   stretch out thine arms
   to us living and dying,
   Mary immaculate,
   mother of God.

474 Gregory Murray
© 1999 Kevin Mayhew Ltd.

1. May you see the face of God,
   your loving Father.
   May you live in joy with him
   whose hands once made you.

   *May the light of God
   now shine on you for ever.*

Continued overleaf

2. May you rest in Christ
the Shepherd-King who feeds you.
May his peace be yours where sorrow
may not enter.

3. May the flame of love,
the Holy Spirit, warm you.
May he welcome you
to perfect love in heaven.

475

Graham Kendrick
© 1986 Kingsway's Thankyou Music

1. Meekness and majesty,
manhood and deity,
in perfect harmony, the Man who is God.
Lord of eternity dwells in humanity,
kneels in humility and washes our feet.

O what a mystery, meekness and majesty.
Bow down and worship for this is your God,
this is your God.

2. Father's pure radiance,
perfect in innocence,
yet learns obedience to death on a cross.
Suff'ring to give us life,
conqu'ring through sacrifice,
and as they crucify prays: 'Father forgive.'

3. Wisdom unsearchable,
God the invisible,
love indestructible in frailty appears.
Lord of infinity, stooping so tenderly,
lifts our humanity to the heights of
his throne.

476

Eleanor Farjeon
© David Higham Associates

1. Morning has broken like the first morning,
blackbird has spoken like the first bird.
Praise for the singing!
Praise for the morning!
Praise for them, springing
fresh from the Word!

2. Sweet the rain's new fall, sunlit from heaven,
like the first dew-fall on the first grass.
Praise for the sweetness of the wet garden,
sprung in completeness where his feet pass.

3. Mine is the sunlight! Mine is the morning
born of the one light Eden saw play!
Praise with elation, praise ev'ry morning,
God's re-creation of the new day!

477

Estelle White
© McCrimmon Publishing Co. Ltd.

1. 'Moses, I know you're the man,'
the Lord said.
'You're going to work out my plan,'
the Lord said.
'Lead all the Israelites out of slavery,
and I shall make them a wandering race
called the people of God.'

So ev'ry day we're on our way,
for we're a travelling, wandering race
called the people of God.

2. 'Don't get too set in your ways,'
the Lord said.
'Each step is only a phase,'
the Lord said.
'I'll go before you and I shall be a sign
to guide my travelling, wandering race.
You're the people of God.'

3. 'No matter what you may do,'
the Lord said,
'I shall be faithful and true,'
the Lord said.
'My love will strengthen you as you go along,
for you're my travelling, wandering race.
You're the people of God.'

4. 'Look at the birds in the air,'
the Lord said.
'They fly unhampered by care,'
the Lord said.
'You will move easier if you're trav'lling
light,
for you're a wandering, vagabond race.'
You're the people of God.'

5. 'Foxes have places to go,'
the Lord said.
'but I've no home here below,'
the Lord said.

'So if you want to be with me all
    your days,
keep up the moving and travelling on.
You're the people of God.'

478 Damian Lundy
© 1978 Kevin Mayhew Ltd.

1. Mother of God's living Word,
   glorifying Christ your Lord;
   full of joy, God's people sing,
   grateful for your mothering.

2. Virgin soil, untouched by sin,
   for God's seed to flourish in;
   watered by the Spirit's dew,
   in your womb the Saviour grew.

3. Sharing his humility,
   Bethlehem and Calvary,
   with him in his bitter pain,
   now as queen with him you reign.

4. We are God's new chosen race,
   new-born children of his grace,
   citizens of heaven who
   imitate and honour you.

5. We, God's people on our way,
   travelling by night and day,
   moving to our promised land,
   walk beside you hand in hand.

6. Christ, your Son, is always near,
   so we journey without fear,
   singing as we walk along:
   Christ our joy, and Christ our song!

7. Sing aloud to Christ with joy,
   who was once a little boy.
   Sing aloud to Mary, sing,
   grateful for her mothering.

479 Matthew Bridges

1. My God, accept my heart this day,
   and make it wholly thine,
   that I from thee no more may stray,
   no more from thee decline.

2. Before the cross of him who died,
   behold, I prostrate fall;
   let ev'ry sin be crucified,
   and Christ be all in all.

3. Anoint me with thy heav'nly grace,
   and seal me for thine own,
   that I may see thy glorious face,
   and worship at thy throne.

4. Let ev'ry thought and work and word
   to thee be ever giv'n.
   then life shall be thy service, Lord,
   and death the gate of heav'n.

5. All glory to the Father be,
   all glory to the Son,
   all glory, Holy Ghost, to thee,
   while endless ages run.

480 Philip Doddridge, alt. v 3 Michael Forster
© 1996 Kevin Mayhew Ltd.

1. My God, and is thy table spread,
   and does thy cup with love o'erflow?
   Thither be all thy children led,
   and let them all thy sweetness know.

2. Hail, sacred feast, which Jesus makes!
   Rich banquet of his flesh and blood!
   Thrice happy all, who here partake
   that sacred stream, that heav'nly food.

3. What wondrous love! What perfect grace,
   for Jesus, our exalted host,
   invites us to this special place
   who offer least and need the most.

4. O let thy table honoured be,
   and furnished well with joyful guests;
   and may each soul salvation see,
   that here its sacred pledges tastes.

481 Frederick William Faber, alt.
© Jubilate Hymns

1. My God, how wonderful you are,
   your majesty how bright;
   how beautiful your mercy-seat,
   in depths of burning light!

Continued overleaf

2. Creator from eternal years
   and everlasting Lord,
   by holy angels day and night
   unceasingly adored!

3. How wonderful, how beautiful
   the sight of you must be –
   your endless wisdom, boundless power,
   and awesome purity!

4. O how I fear you, living God,
   with deepest, tenderest fears,
   and worship you with trembling hope
   and penitential tears!

5. But I may love you too, O Lord,
   though you are all-divine,
   for you have stooped to ask of me
   this feeble love of mine.

6. Father of Jesus, love's reward,
   great King upon your throne,
   what joy to see you as you are
   and know as I am known.

482 Susan Sayers, based on Psalm 21
© 1995 Kevin Mayhew Ltd.

My God, my God,
why have you forsaken me?

1. People who see me are scornful,
   sneering at me, and tossing their heads,
   'His trust was in God, let God save him,
   come to the aid of his own special friend!'

2. Dogs have surrounded me, howling;
   criminal gangs approach and attack.
   My hands and my feet they are tearing,
   all of my bones can be easily seen.

3. They have divided my clothing,
   gambling with straws or dice for my robe.
   Please, God, do not leave me forsaken,
   hasten to help me, O God of my strength.

4. I will proclaim to my people;
   your name, O Lord,
      they worship and praise.
   All children of Jacob, give glory,
   children of Israel, come worship your God.

483 Louis Welker
© 1982 Kevin Mayhew Ltd.

My God said to me, 'Follow!'
My God said to me, 'Come!'
My God called out my name.
Here I am! Here I am to do your will!

1. To follow the Lord is to be set free;
   to follow the Lord is to know his way.

2. To live with the Lord is to live in love;
   to live with the Lord is to live in peace.

484 Robin Mark
© 1996 Daybreak Music Ltd.

1. My heart will sing to you
   because of your great love,
   a love so rich, so pure,
   a love beyond compare;
   the wilderness, the barren place,
   become a blessing
   in the warmth of your embrace.

   May my heart sing your praise for ever,
   may my voice lift your name, my God;
   may my soul know no other treasure
   than your love, than your love.

2. When earthly wisdom dims
   the light of knowing you,
   or if my search for understanding
   clouds your way,
   to you I fly, my hiding-place,
   where revelation
   is beholding face to face.

485 Francesca Leftley, based on the Good Friday
Reproaches. © 1984 Kevin Mayhew Ltd.

My people, what have I done to you?
How have I hurt you? Answer me.

1. I led you out of Egypt,
   I set you free, I set you free.
   I led you through the desert,
   and yet you turn away from me.

2. I fed you in the desert,
   I led you through the raging sea,
   I gave you saving water,
   and yet you found a cross for me.

3. I gave you a royal sceptre;
   you offered me a crown of thorns.
   I raised you as a nation;
   you mocked and treated me with scorn.

486 Psalm 22 Grail translation
© 1963, 1986, 1993 The Grail

Response 1:
My shepherd is the Lord,
nothing indeed shall I want.

Response 2:
His goodness shall follow me always
to the end of my days.

1. The Lord is my shepherd;
   there is nothing I shall want.
   Fresh and green are the pastures
   where he gives me repose.
   Near restful waters he leads me,
   to revive my drooping spirit.

2. He guides me along the right path;
   he is true to his name.
   If I should walk in the valley of darkness
   no evil would I fear.
   You are there with your crook and
       your staff;
   with these you give me comfort.

3. You have prepared a banquet for me
   in the sight of my foes.
   My head you have anointed with oil;
   my cup is overflowing.

4. Surely goodness and kindness shall
       follow me
   all the days of my life.
   In the Lord's own house shall I dwell
   for ever and ever.

5. To the Father and Son give glory,
   give glory to the Spirit.
   To God who is, who was, and who
       will be
   for ever and ever.

487 Samuel Crossman

1. My song is love unknown,
   my Saviour's love to me,
   love to the loveless shown,
   that they might lovely be.
   O who am I, that for my sake,
   my Lord should take frail flesh and die?

2. He came from his blest throne,
   salvation to bestow;
   but sin made blind, and none
   the longed-for Christ would know.
   But O, my friend, my friend indeed,
   who at my need his life did spend!

3. Sometimes they strew his way,
   and his sweet praises sing:
   resounding all the day
   hosannas to their King:
   then 'Crucify'! is all their breath,
   and for his death they thirst and cry.

4. Why what hath my Lord done?
   What makes this rage and spite?
   He made the lame to run,
   he gave the blind their sight.
   Sweet injuries! Yet they at these
   themselves displease,
       and 'gainst him rise.

5. They rise, and needs will have
   my dear Lord made away;
   a murderer they save,
   the Prince of Life they slay.
   Yet cheerful he to suff'ring goes,
   that he his foes from thence might free.

Continued overleaf

6. Here might I stay and sing,
   no story so divine;
   never was love, dear King,
   never was grief like thine.
   This is my friend in whose sweet praise
   I all my days could gladly spend.

488
Based on Luke 1:46-55, v 1 unknown, vs 2-4 Damian Lundy. © 1987 Kevin Mayhew Ltd.

1. My soul doth magnify the Lord,
   and my spirit hath rejoiced
       in God my Saviour,
   for he that is mighty hath done great things,
   and holy is his name.

   My soul doth magnify the Lord,
   my soul doth magnify the Lord,
   and my spirit hath rejoiced
   in God my Saviour,
   for he that is mighty hath done great things,
   and holy is his name.

2. From age to age he shows his love,
   and his mercy is for ever to his servants,
   for he stretches out his arm, casts down
       the mighty,
   and raises up the meek.

3. He fills the hungry with good food.
   When the rich demand their share, their
       hands are empty.
   He has kept all his promises to Israel:
   his mercy is made known.

4. To God the Father we sing praise,
   and to Jesus, whom he sent to be
       our Saviour!
   To the Spirit of God be all glory,
   for holy is his name!

489
Unknown, based on Luke 1:46-55

1. My soul is filled with joy
   as I sing to God my Saviour:
   he has looked upon his servant,
   he has visited his people.

And holy is his name
through all generations!
Everlasting is his mercy
to the people he has chosen,
and holy is his name!

2. I am lowly as a child,
   but I know from this day forward
   that my name will be remembered
   and the world will call me blessèd.

3. I proclaim the pow'r of God!
   He does marvels for his servants;
   though he scatters the proud-hearted
   and destroys the might of princes.

4. To the hungry he gives food,
   sends the rich away empty.
   In his mercy he is mindful
   of the people he has chosen.

5. In his love he now fulfills
   what he promised to our fathers.
   I will praise the Lord, my Saviour.
   Everlasting is his mercy.

490
Lucien Deiss, based on Psalm 130
© 1965 World Library Publications

My soul is longing for your peace,
near to you, my God.

1. Lord, you know that my heart is not proud
   and my eyes are not lifted from the earth.

2. Lofty thoughts have never filled my mind,
   far beyond my sight all ambitious deeds.

3. In your peace I have maintained my soul,
   I have kept my heart in your quiet peace.

4. As a child rests on a mother's knee,
   so I place my soul in your loving care.

5. Israel, put all your hope in God,
   place your trust in him, now and evermore.

491
Anne Carter, based on Luke 1:46-55
© 1988 Society of the Sacred Heart

1. My soul proclaims you, mighty God.
My spirit sings your praise.
You look on me, you lift me up,
and gladness fills my days.

2. All nations now will share my joy;
your gifts you have outpoured.
Your little one you have made great;
I magnify my God.

3. For those who love your holy name,
your mercy will not die.
Your strong right arm puts down
the proud
and lifts the lowly high.

4. You fill the hungry with good things,
the rich you send away.
The promise made to Abraham
is filled to endless day.

5. Magnificat, magnificat,
magnificat, praise God!
Praise God, praise God, praise God,
praise God,
magnificat, praise God!

492
Damian Lundy, based on a French poem
© 1978 Kevin Mayhew Ltd.

1. New daytime dawning,
breaking like the spring.
New voices singing, and new songs to sing!
Christ has come back, alleluia!
He is risen, like the springtime!
Say, what does he bring?

2. Death in the tree tops!
Jesus cried with pain,
hanging in the branches.
Now he lives again!
For the tree of death has flowered,
life has filled the furthest branches!
Sunlight follows rain.

3. The man of sorrows,
sleeping in his tomb,
the man of sorrows, he is coming home.
He is coming like the springtime.
Suddenly you'll hear him talking,
you will see him come.

4. Say, are you hungry?
Come and eat today!
Come to the table, nothing to pay!
Take your place, the meal is waiting.
Come and share the birthday party,
and the holiday.

5. Look where the garden
door is open wide!
Come to the garden,
there's no need to hide.
God has broken down the fences
and he stands with arms wide open.
Come along inside!

493
The Venerable Bede, trans. Ronald Arbuthnott Knox
© Burns and Oates Ltd.

1. New praises be given
to Christ newly crowned,
who back to his heaven
a new way hath found;
God's blessedness sharing
before us he goes,
what mansions preparing,
what endless repose!

2. His glory still praising
on thrice holy ground,
th'apostles stood gazing,
his mother around;
with hearts that beat faster,
with eyes full of love,
they watched while their
master ascended above.

3. 'No star can disclose him,'
the bright angels said;
'eternity knows him,
your conquering head;

Continued overleaf

those high habitations,
he leaves not again,
till, judging all nations,
on earth he shall reign.'

4. Thus spoke they and straightway,
where legions defend
heav'n's glittering gateway,
their Lord they attend,
and cry, looking thither,
'Your portals let down
for him who rides hither
in peace and renown.'

5. They asked, who keep sentry
in that blessèd town,
'Who thus claimeth entry,
a king of renown?'
'The Lord of all valiance,'
that herald replied,
'who Satan's battalions
laid low in their pride.'

6. Grant, Lord, that our longing
may follow thee there,
on earth who are thronging
thy temples with prayer;
and unto thee gather,
Redeemer, thine own,
where thou with thy Father
dost sit on the throne.

494 Noel and Tricia Richards

*Nothing shall separate us
from the love of God. (Repeat)*

1. God did not spare his only Son,
gave him to save us all.
Sin's price was met by Jesus' death
and heaven's mercy falls.

2. Up from the grave Jesus was raised
to sit at God's right hand;
pleading our case in heaven's courts,
forgiven we can stand.

3. Now by God's grace we have embraced
a life set free from sin;
we shall deny all that destroys
our union with him.

495 Michael Forster, based on 'Te lucis ante terminum'

1. Now as the evening shadows fall,
God our Creator, hear our call:
help us to trust your constant grace,
though darkness seems to hide your face.

2. Help us to find, in sleep's release,
bodily rest and inner peace;
so may the darkness of the night
refresh our eyes for morning light.

3. Father almighty, holy Son,
Spirit eternal, three in One,
grant us the faith that sets us free
to praise you for eternity.

496 Mike Anderson

*Now I know what love is,
now I know your Spirit is here,
living deep within me,
now I know love is real.*

1. Death could never hide your love:
your love lifts me high.

2. Darkness will not hide your love,
shining like a star.

3. What could ever quench your love,
love that changes hearts.

497

Martin Rinkart, trans. Catherine Winkworth

1. Now thank we all our God,
   with hearts and hands and voices,
   who wondrous things hath done,
   in whom his world rejoices;
   who from our mother's arms
   hath blessed us on our way
   with countless gifts of love,
   and still is ours today.

2. O may this bounteous God
   through all our life be near us,
   with ever joyful hearts
   and blessèd peace to cheer us;
   and keep us in his grace,
   and guide us when perplexed,
   and free us from all ills
   in this world and the next.

3. All praise and thanks to God
   the Father now be given,
   the Son and him who reigns
   with them in highest heaven,
   the one eternal God,
   whom earth and heav'n adore;
   for thus it was, is now,
   and shall be evermore.

498

John Macleod Campbell Crum, alt.
© 1928 Oxford University Press

1. Now the green blade riseth
   from the buried grain,
   wheat that in the dark earth
   many days has lain;
   Love lives again,
   that with the dead has been:
   Love is come again,
   like wheat that springeth green.

2. In the grave they laid him,
   Love by hatred slain,
   thinking that never
   he would wake again,
   laid in the earth
   like grain that sleeps unseen:
   Love is come again,
   like wheat that springeth green.

3. Forth he came at Easter,
   like the risen grain,
   he that for three days
   in the grave had lain;
   quick from the dead,
   my risen Lord is seen:
   Love is come again,
   like wheat that springeth green.

4. When our hearts are wintry,
   grieving or in pain,
   thy touch can call us
   back to life again;
   fields of our hearts,
   that dead and bare have been:
   Love is come again,
   like wheat that springeth green.

499

7th century Latin trans. Edward Caswell

1. Now with the fast departing light,
   maker of all, we ask of thee,
   of thy great mercy, through the night
   our guardian and defence to be.

2. Far off let idle visions fly,
   no phantom of the night molest;
   curb thou our raging enemy,
   that we in chaste repose may rest.

3. Father of mercies, hear our cry,
   hear us, O sole-begotten Son
   who, with the Holy Ghost most high,
   reignest while endless ages run.

500 St Alphonus, trans. Edmund Vaughan

1. O bread of heav'n beneath this veil
thou dost my very God conceal;
my Jesus, dearest treasure, hail;
I love thee and adoring kneel;
each loving soul by thee is fed
with thine own self in form of bread.

2. O food of life, thou who dost give
the pledge of immortality;
I live; no, 'tis not I that live;
God gives me life, God lives in me;
he feeds my soul, he guides my ways,
and ev'ry grief with joy repays.

3. O bond of love, that dost unite
the servant to his living Lord;
could I dare live, and not requite
such love – then death were meet reward:
I cannot live unless to prove
some love for such unmeasured love.

4. Beloved Lord in heav'n above,
there, Jesus, thou awaitest me;
to gaze on thee with changeless love,
yes, thus I hope, thus shall it be:
for how can he deny me heav'n
who here on earth himself hath given?

501 Possibly by John Francis Wade,
trans. Frederick Oakeley and others

1. O come, all ye faithful,
joyful and triumphant,
O come ye, O come ye to Bethlehem;
come and behold him,
born the king of angels:

O come, let us adore him,
O come let us adore him,
O come, let us adore him,
Christ the Lord.

2. God of God,
Light of Light,
lo, he abhors not the Virgin's womb;
very God, begotten not created:

3. Sing, choirs of angels,
sing in exultation,
sing, all ye citizens of heav'n above;
glory to God in the highest:

4. Yea, Lord, we greet thee,
born this happy morning,
Jesu, to thee be glory giv'n;
Word of the Father,
now in flesh appearing:

502 Frederick William Faber, alt. the Editors
© 1999 Kevin Mayhew Ltd.

1. O come and mourn with me awhile;
see, Mary calls us to her side;
O come and let us mourn with her;

Jesus our love, Jesus our love, is crucified.

2. Have we no tears to shed for him
while soldiers scoff and people sneer?
Ah, look how patiently he hangs!

3. How fast his feet and hands are nailed,
his blessèd tongue with thirst is tied;
his failing eyes are blind with blood;

4. Sev'n times he spoke, sev'n words of love,
and all three hours his silence cried
for mercy on poor human souls.

5. O break, O break, hard heart of mine:
thy weak self-love and guilty pride
his Pilate and his Judas were:

6. A broken heart, a fount of tears,
ask, and they will not be denied;
a broken heart, love's cradle is;

7. O love of God! O mortal sin!
In this dread act your strength is tried;
and victory remains with love;

503

'Great O Antiphons' 12th-13th century, trans. John Mason Neale

1. O come, O come, Emmanuel,
   and ransom captive Israel,
   that mourns in lonely exile here,
   until the Son of God appear.

   Rejoice, rejoice!
   Emmanuel shall come to thee, O Israel.

2. O come, thou rod of Jesse, free
   thine own from Satan's tyranny;
   from depths of hell thy people save,
   and give them vic'try o'er the grave.

3. O come, thou dayspring, come and cheer
   our spirits by thine advent here;
   disperse the gloomy clouds of night,
   and death's dark shadows put to flight.

4. O come, thou key of David, come
   and open wide our heav'nly home;
   make safe the way that leads on high,
   and close the path to misery.

5. O come, O come, thou Lord of might,
   who to thy tribes on Sinai's height
   in ancient times didst give the Law,
   in cloud and majesty and awe.

504

Kevin Mayhew, based on Isaiah 55:1-4
© 1984 Kevin Mayhew Ltd.

O, come to the water,
all you who are thirsty,
and drink, drink deeply.
Though you don't have a penny
and your clothes are in rags,
you'll be welcome to drink all you can.

1. Come take your choice of wine and milk:
   ev'rything here is free!
   Why spend your money on
      worthless food:
   ev'rything here is free!

2. Now, listen well and you will find
   food that will feed your soul.
   Just come to me to receive your share,
   food that will feed your soul.

3. I promise you good things to come;
   you are my chosen ones.
   I name you witnesses to my world;
   you are my chosen ones.

505

Chrysogonus Waddell, based on Isaiah 40
© Chrysogonus Waddell

1. O comfort my people
   and calm all their fear,
   and tell them the time
   of salvation draws near.
   O tell them I come
   to remove all their shame.
   Then they will forever
   give praise to my name.

2. Proclaim to the cities
   of Judah my word;
   that 'gentle yet strong
   is the hand of the Lord.
   I rescue the captives,
   my people defend,
   and bring them to justice
   and joy without end.'

3. 'All mountains and hills
   shall become as a plain,
   for vanished are mourning
   and hunger and pain.
   And never again shall
   these war against you.
   Behold I come quickly
   to make all things new.'

506

'Maintzisch Gesangbuch'
trans. Walter H. Shewring and others

1. O food of trav'llers, angels' bread,
   manna where with the blest are fed,
   come nigh, and with thy sweetness fill
   the hungry hearts that seek thee still.

Continued overleaf

2. O fount of love, O well unpriced,
   outpouring from the heart of Christ,
   give us to drink of very thee,
   and all we pray shall answered be.

3. O Jesus Christ, we pray to thee
   that this thy presence which we see,
   though now in form of bread concealed,
   to us may be in heav'n revealed.

507 Michael Forster
© 1997 Kevin Mayhew Ltd.

O fountain of life and infinite grace,
unaltered by time, unhindered by space.
Immortal well-spring of holiness and peace;
eternal, infinite love without cease.

1. Preserve and keep me all my days,
   in good intent and faithful ways.
   And lead me to such holiness
   as mortal pray'rs cannot express.

2. Lord, lead me out and guide me in.
   Protect me both from fear and sin.
   Enfold me in your constant love,
   with grace abundant from above.

3. Be there to guide me when I speak.
   To strengthen when my love is weak:
   be there to calm my final breath,
   and light the way to life through death.

508 Aurelius Clemens Prudentius,
trans. John Mason Neale, alt.

1. Of the Father's love begotten,
   ere the worlds began to be,
   he is Alpha and Omega,
   he the source, the ending he,
   of the things that are, and have been,
   and that future years shall see,
   evermore and evermore.

2. At his word they were created;
   he commanded; it was done:
   heav'n and earth and depths of ocean
   in their threefold order one;

all that grows beneath the shining
of the light of moon and sun,
evermore and evermore.

3. O that birth for ever blessèd,
   when the Virgin, full of grace,
   by the Holy Ghost conceiving,
   bore the Saviour of our race,
   and the babe, the world's Redeemer,
   first revealed his sacred face,
   evermore and evermore.

4. O ye heights of heav'n, adore him;
   angel hosts, his praises sing;
   pow'rs, dominions, bow before him,
   and extol our God and King:
   let no tongue on earth be silent,
   ev'ry voice in concert ring,
   evermore and evermore.

5. This is he whom seers and sages
   sang of old with one accord;
   whom the writings of the prophets
   promised in their faithful word;
   now he shines, the long-expected;
   let our songs declare his worth,
   evermore and evermore.

6. Christ, to thee, with God the Father,
   and, O Holy Ghost, to thee,
   hymn and chant and high thanksgiving,
   and unwearied praises be;
   honour, glory, and dominion,
   and eternal victory,
   evermore and evermore.

509 St. Thomas Aquinas,
trans. John Mason Neale, alt.

1. Of the glorious body telling,
   O my tongue, its myst'ries sing,
   and the blood, all price excelling,
   which the world's eternal King.
   in a noble womb once dwelling,
   shed for this world's ransoming.

2. Giv'n for us, for us descending,
   of a virgin to proceed,
   he with us in converse blending,
   scattered he the gospel seed,
   till his sojourn drew to ending,
   which he closed in wondrous deed.

3. At the last great supper lying,
   circled by his brethren's band,
   meekly with the law complying,
   first he finished its command.
   Then, immortal food supplying,
   gave himself with his own hand.

4. Word made flesh, by word is making
   very bread his flesh to be;
   we, in wine, Christ's blood partaking,
   and if senses fail to see,
   faith alone the true heart waking,
   to behold the mystery.

5. Therefore, we before him bending,
   this great sacrament revere;
   types and shadows have their ending,
   for the newer rite is here;
   faith our outward sense befriending,
   makes the inward vision clear.

6. Glory let us give, and blessing,
   to the Father and the Son,
   honour, might and praise addressing,
   while eternal ages run;
   ever too his love confessing,
   who from both, with both is one.

510 Michael Perry
© Mrs B. Perry/Jubilate Hymns

1. O God beyond all praising,
   we worship you today,
   and sing the love amazing
   that songs cannot repay;
   for we can only wonder
   at ev'ry gift you send,

at blessings without number
and mercies without end:
we lift our hearts before you
and wait upon your word,
we honour and adore you,
our great and mighty Lord.

2. Then hear, O gracious Saviour,
   accept the love we bring,
   that we who know your favour
   may serve you as our King;
   and whether our tomorrows
   be filled with good or ill,
   we'll triumph through our sorrows
   and rise to bless you still:
   to marvel at your beauty
   and glory in your ways,
   and make a joyful duty
   our sacrifice of praise.

511 St Thomas Aquinas, trans. Edward Caswall

1. O Godhead hid, devoutly I adore thee,
   who truly art within the forms before me;
   to thee my heart I bow with bended knee,
   as failing quite in contemplating thee.

2. Sight, touch and taste in thee are
         each deceived,
   the ear alone most safely is believed:
   I believe all the Son of God has spoken;
   than Truth's own word there is not
         truer token.

3. God only on the cross lay hid from view;
   but here lies hid at once the manhood too;
   and I, in both professing my belief,
   make the same prayer as the repentant thief.

4. Thy wounds, as Thomas saw, I do not see;
   yet thee confess my Lord and God to be;
   make me believe thee ever more and more,
   in thee my hope, in thee my love to store.

Continued overleaf

5. O thou memorial of our Lord's own dying!
   O bread that living art and vivifying!
   Make ever thou my soul on thee to live;
   ever a taste of heav'nly sweetness give.

6. O loving Pelican! O Jesus, Lord!
   Unclean I am, but cleanse me in thy blood,
   of which single drop, for sinners spilt,
   is ransom for a world's entire guilt.

7. Jesus, whom for the present veiled I see,
   what I so thirst for, O, vouchsafe to me;
   that I may see thy countenance unfolding,
   and may be blest in thy glory in beholding.

512 Gilbert Keith Chesterton
© Copyright control

1. O God of earth and altar,
   bow down and hear our cry,
   our earthly rulers falter,
   our people drift and die;
   the walls of gold entomb us,
   the swords of scorn divide,
   take not thy thunder from us,
   but take away our pride.

2. From all that terror teaches,
   from lies of tongue and pen,
   from all the easy speeches
   that comfort cruel men,
   from sale and profanation
   of honour and the sword,
   from sleep and from damnation,
   deliver us, good Lord!

3. Tie in a living tether
   the prince and priest and thrall,
   bind all our lives together,
   smite us and save us all;
   in ire and exultation
   aflame with faith and free,
   lift up a living nation,
   a single sword to thee.

513 Michael Forster
© 1996 Kevin Mayhew Ltd.

1. O God of grace we thank you
   for that most blessèd tree,
   from which the Saviour fashioned
   salvation full and free.
   Your story of redemption
   is proudly carved in wood,
   since in the Ark you rescued
   a remnant from the flood.

2. The bush that lit the desert –
   'though burned, yet not consumed –
   became the seed of promise
   from which salvation bloomed.
   The light of life eternal
   still shines with hope and joy,
   from him whom hell's inferno
   could burn but not destroy.

3. The staff which Moses carried,
   as shepherd of your choice,
   is lifted high to rally
   the sheep who know your voice.
   From farthest bounds, you call us,
   as people of the cross,
   to find eternal value
   in your most bitter loss.

4. Christ is the vine eternal,
   producing wholesome fruit;
   the rod that brings salvation,
   the branch from Jesse's root.
   In crib and crucifixion,
   in boats upon the sea,
   the Saviour's earthly journey
   is shadowed by the tree.

5. This tree of life gives knowledge
   of love that conquers all,
   the fruits of goodness ripen,
   and evil's strongholds fall.
   It sprang from this creation
   of which we all are made,
   and where, by sign and symbol,
   your purpose is displayed.

6. The log which, in the desert,
   made bitter water sweet,
   transforms the foulest hatred,
   and renders hope complete;
   for in its awesome presence
   all earthly glory pales;
   the Carpenter is reigning,
   enthroned on wood and nails.

514 Isaac Watts, alt.

1. O God, our help in ages past,
   our hope for years to come,
   our shelter from the stormy blast,
   and our eternal home.

2. Beneath the shadow of thy throne,
   thy saints have dwelt secure;
   sufficient is thine arm alone,
   and our defence is sure.

3. Before the hills in order stood,
   or earth received her frame,
   from everlasting thou art God,
   to endless years the same.

4. A thousand ages in thy sight
   are like an evening gone;
   short as the watch that ends the night
   before the rising sun.

5. Time, like an ever-rolling stream,
   will bear us all away;
   we fade and vanish, as a dream
   dies at the op'ning day.

6. O God, our help in ages past,
   our hope for years to come,
   be thou our guard while troubles last,
   and our eternal home.

515 Frances M. Kelly, based on Psalm 54
© 1999 Kevin Mayhew Ltd.

1. O God, please listen to my cry,
   and give me answer.
   I am afraid of what the future
   holds for me, O Lord.

Let me hide, Lord,
in the shadow of your wings. (Repeat)

2. If only I had wings to fly
   I would escape, Lord:
   I'd fly as far as I could go
   to find some peace of mind.

3. I feel defeated by life's trials
   and disappointments.
   My days and nights are spent in fear,
   with no one I can trust.

4. But all of this I can survive
   if you are with me:
   my life is here, my life is now,
   and I must carry on.

5. Within the shadow of your wings
   I find my refuge.
   You are the only one I have;
   I count on you, O Lord.

516 Anthony Nye, alt.
© The Trustees for Roman Catholic Purposes Registered

1. O God, we give ourselves today
   with this pure host to thee,
   the self-same gift which thy dear Son
   gave once on Calvary.

2. Entire and whole, our life and love
   with heart and soul and mind,
   for all our errors, faults and needs,
   thy Church and humankind.

3. With humble and with contrite heart
   this bread and wine we give
   because thy Son once gave himself
   and died that we might live.

4. Though lowly now, soon by thy word
   these offered gifts will be
   the very body of our Lord,
   his soul and deity.

Continued overleaf

5. His very body, offered up,
   a gift beyond all price,
   he gives to us, that we may give,
   in loving sacrifice.

6. O Lord, who took our human life,
   as water mixed with wine,
   grant through this sacrifice that we
   may share thy life divine.

517 Anthony Nye

1. O God, your people gather,
   obedient to your word,
   around your holy altar
   to praise your name, O Lord.
   For all your loving kindness
   our grateful hearts we raise;
   but pardon first the blindness
   of all our sinful ways.

2. You are our loving Father,
   you are our holiest Lord,
   but we have sinned against you,
   by thought and deed and word.
   Before the court of heaven
   we stand and humbly pray
   our sins may be forgiven,
   our faults be washed away.

3. Though sinful, we implore you
   to turn and make us live,
   that so we may adore you,
   and our due off'ring give,
   and may the prayers and voices
   of your glad people rise,
   as your whole Church rejoices
   in this great sacrifice.

518 Traditional Baptist hymn

1. O healing river, send down your waters,
   send down your water upon this land.
   O healing river, send down your waters
   and wash the blood from off the sand.

2. This land is parching, this land is burning,
   no seed is growing in the barren ground.
   O healing river, send down your waters,
   O healing river, send your waters down.

3. Let the seed of freedom awake
       and flourish,
   let the deep roots nourish, let the tall
       stalks rise.
   O healing river, send down your waters,
   O healing river, from out of the skies.

519 Maurice F. Bell, alt. © Oxford University Press
    From the 'English Hymnal'

1. O holy Lord, by all adored,
   our trespasses confessing,
   to thee this day thy children pray,
   our holy faith professing!
   Accept, O King, the gifts we bring,
   our songs of praise, the prayers we raise,
   and grant us, Lord, thy blessing.

2. To God on high be thanks and praise,
   who deigns our bond to sever;
   his care shall guide us all our days,
   and harm shall reach us never;
   on him we rest with faith assured
   of all that live he is the Lord,
   for ever and for ever.

520 Traditional

O, how good is the Lord! (x3)
I never will forget what he has done for me.

1. He gives us salvation,
   how good is the Lord. *(x3)*
   I never will forget
   what he has done for me.

2. He gives us his Spirit . . .

3. He gives us healing . . .

4. He gives us his body . . .

5. He gives us his freedom . . .

6. He gives us each other . . .

7. He gives us his glory . . .

521 Edward Caswall

1. O Jesus Christ, remember,
   when thou shalt come again
   upon the clouds of heaven,
   with all thy shining train;
   when ev'ry eye shall see
   thee in deity revealed,
   who now upon this altar
   in silence art concealed.

2. Remember then, O Saviour,
   I supplicate of thee,
   that here I bowed before thee
   upon my bended knee;
   that here I owned thy presence,
   and did not thee deny,
   and glorified thy greatness
   though hid from human eye.

3. Accept, divine Redeemer,
   the homage of my praise;
   be thou the light and honour
   and glory of my days.
   Be thou my consolation
   when death is drawing nigh;
   be thou my only treasure
   through all eternity.

522 John E. Bode

1. O Jesus, I have promised
   to serve thee to the end;
   be thou for ever near me,
   my Master and my friend:
   I shall not fear the battle
   if thou art by my side,
   nor wander from the pathway
   if thou wilt be my guide.

2. O let me feel thee near me;
   the world is ever near;
   I see the sights that dazzle,
   the tempting sounds I hear;
   my foes are ever near me,
   around me and within;
   but, Jesus, draw thou nearer,
   and shield my soul from sin.

3. O let me hear thee speaking
   in accents clear and still,
   above the storms of passion,
   the murmurs of self-will;
   O speak to reassure me,
   to hasten or control;
   O speak and make me listen,
   thou guardian of my soul.

4. O Jesus, thou hast promised,
   to all who follow thee,
   that where thou art in glory
   there shall thy servant be;
   and, Jesus, I have promised
   to serve thee to the end:
   O give me grace to follow,
   my Master and my friend.

5. O let me see thy foot-marks,
   and in them plant mine own;
   my hope to follow duly
   is in thy strength alone:
   O guide me, call me, draw me,
   uphold me to the end;
   and then in heav'n receive me,
   my Saviour and my friend.

523 Gregory Murray. © *Estate of Gregory Murray* Used by permission of The Trustees of Downside Abbey

1. O King of might and splendour,
   creator most adored,
   this sacrifice we render
   to thee as sov'reign Lord.
   May these our gifts be pleasing
   unto thy majesty,
   mankind from sin releasing
   who have offended thee.

2. Thy body thou hast given,
   thy blood thou hast outpoured,
   that sin might be forgiven,
   O Jesus, loving Lord.
   As now with love most tender,
   thy death we celebrate,
   our lives in self-surrender
   to thee we consecrate.

524 Estelle White
© 1976 Kevin Mayhew Ltd.

1. O lady, full of God's own grace,
   whose caring hands the child embraced,
   who listened to the Spirit's word,
   believed and trusted in the Lord.

   O virgin fair, star of the sea,
   my dearest mother, pray for me. (Repeat)

2. O lady, who felt daily joy
   in caring for the holy boy,
   whose home was plain and shorn
         of wealth,
   yet was enriched by God's own breath.

3. O lady, who bore living's pain
   but still believed that love would reign,
   who on a hill watched Jesus die,
   as on the cross they raised him high.

4. O lady, who, on Easter day,
   had all your sorrow wiped away
   as God the Father's will was done
   when from death's hold he freed your Son.

525 John Foley, based on Isaiah 55:1, 2 and Matthew
11:28-30. © 1978 John B. Foley, S. J. and New Dawn
Music

1. O let all who thirst,
   let them come to the water.
   And let all who have nothing,
   let them come to the Lord:
   without money, without price.
   Why should you pay the price,
   except for the Lord?

2. And let all who seek,
   let them come to the water.
   And let all who have nothing,
   let them come to the Lord:
   without money, without strife.
   Why should you spend your life,
   except for the Lord?

3. And let all who toil,
   let them come to the water.
   And let all who are weary,
   let them come to the Lord:
   all who labour, without rest.
   How can your soul find rest,
   except for the Lord?

4. And let all the poor,
   let them come to the water.
   Bring the ones who are laden,
   bring them all to the Lord:
   bring the children without might.
   Easy the load and light:
   oh come to the Lord.

526 Philip Brooks, alt.

1. O little town of Bethlehem,
   how still we see thee lie!
   Above thy deep and dreamless sleep
   the silent stars go by.
   Yet in thy dark streets shineth
   the everlasting light;
   the hopes and fears of all the years
   are met in thee tonight.

2. O morning stars, together
   proclaim the holy birth,
   and praises sing to God the King,
   and peace upon the earth.
   For Christ is born of Mary;
   and, gathered all above,
   while mortals sleep, the angels keep
   their watch of wond'ring love;

3. How silently, how silently,
the wondrous gift is giv'n!
So God imparts to human hearts
the blessings of his heav'n.
No ear may hear his coming;
but in this world of sin,
where meek souls will receive him still,
the dear Christ enters in.

4. O holy child of Bethlehem,
descend to us, we pray;
cast out our sin, and enter in,
be born in us today.
We hear the Christmas angels
the great glad tidings tell:
O come to us, abide with us,
our Lord Emmanuel.

527 Virginia Vissing
© 1974, 1998 Sisters of St Mary of Namur

O living water, refresh my soul.
O living water, refresh my soul.
Spirit of joy, Lord of creation
Spirit of hope, Spirit of peace.

1. Spirit of God. Spirit of God.

2. O set us free. O set us free.

3. Come, pray in us. Come, pray in us.

528 Lucien Deiss, based on Psalm 102:17-18 and Psalm
78:9. © 1965 World Library Publications, a division of
J. S. Paluch Co. Inc.

O Lord, be not mindful
of our guilt and our sins;
O Lord do not judge us
for our faults and offences.
May your merciful love be upon us.

1. Help your people, Lord,
O God our Saviour,
deliver us for the glory of your name!

2. Pardon us, O Lord,
all our sins,
deliver us for the glory of your name!

3. Praise to you, O Lord,
through all ages without end,
deliver us for the glory of your name!

529 Karl Boberg, trans. Stuart K. Hine. © 1953 Stuart K.
Hine. Administered by Kingsway's Thankyou Music

1. O Lord, my God,
when I in awesome wonder
consider all the works
thy hand has made,
I see the stars,
I hear the rolling thunder,
thy pow'r throughout
the universe displayed.

Then sings my soul,
my Saviour God, to thee:
how great thou art, how great thou art.
Then sings my soul,
my Saviour God, to thee;
how great thou art, how great thou art.

2. When through the woods
and forest glades I wander
and hear the birds sing
sweetly in the trees;
when I look down
from lofty mountain grandeur,
and hear the brook,
and feel the gentle breeze.

3. And when I think that God,
his Son not sparing,
sent him to die,
I scarce can take it in
that on the cross,
my burden gladly bearing,
he bled and died
to take away my sin.

Continued overleaf

4. When Christ shall come
with shout of acclamation
and take me home,
what joy shall fill my heart;
when I shall bow
in humble adoration,
and there proclaim:
my God, how great thou art.

530
Graham Kendrick
© 1986 Kingsway's Thankyou Music

O Lord, your tenderness,
melting all my bitterness,
O Lord, I receive your love.
O Lord, your loveliness,
changing all my ugliness,
O Lord, I receive your love.
O Lord I receive your love.
O Lord I receive your love.

531
Damian Lundy
© 1978 Kevin Mayhew Ltd.

1. O Mary, when our God chose you
to bring his only Son to birth,
a new creation made in you
gave joy to all the earth.

2. When he was born on Christmas night
and music made the rafters ring,
the stars were dancing with delight;
now all God's children sing.

3. One winter's night, a heap of straw
becomes a place where ages meet,
when kings come knocking at the door
and kneeling at your feet.

4. In you, our God confounds the strong
and makes the crippled dance with joy;
and to our barren world belong
his mother and her boy.

5. In empty streets and broken hearts
you call to mind what he has done;
where all his loving kindness starts
in sending you a Son.

6. And, Mary, while we stand with you,
may once again his Spirit come,
and all his people follow you
to reach our Father's home.

532
St Alphonsus, trans. Edmund Vaughan

1. O Mother blest, whom God bestows
on sinners and on just,
what joy, what hope thou givest those
who in thy mercy trust.

   Thou art clement, thou art chaste,
   Mary, thou art fair;
   of all mothers sweetest, best,
   none with thee compare.

2. O heav'nly mother, maiden sweet!
It never yet was told
that suppliant sinner left thy feet
unpitied, unconsoled.

3. O mother pitiful and mild,
cease not to pray for me;
for I do love thee as a child
and sigh for love of thee.

4. O mother blest, for me obtain,
ungrateful though I be,
to love that God who first could deign
to show such love for me.

533
Estelle White, based on Psalm 130
© 1976, 1997 Kevin Mayhew Ltd.

1. O my Lord, within my heart
pride will have no home,
ev'ry talent that I have
comes from you alone.

   And like a child at rest
   close to its mother's breast,
   safe in your arms
   my soul is calmed.

2. Lord, my eyes do not look high
nor my thoughts take wings,
I can find such treasures
in ordinary things.

3. Great affairs are not for me,
   deeds beyond my scope.
   In the simple things I do
   I find joy and hope.

534

Damian Lundy, based on the Good Friday 'Reproaches'. © 1978 Kevin Mayhew Ltd.

O my people, what have I done to you?
How have I hurt you? Answer me.

1. I led you out of Egypt;
   from slavery I set you free.
   I brought you into a land of promise;
   you have prepared a cross for me.

2. I led you as a shepherd,
   I brought you safely through the sea,
   fed you with manna in the desert;
   you have prepared a cross for me.

3. I fought for you in battles,
   I won you strength and victory,
   gave you a royal crown and sceptre;
   you have prepared a cross for me.

4. I planted you, my vineyard,
   and cared for you most tenderly,
   looked for abundant fruit,
       and found none –
   only the cross you made for me.

5. Then listen to my pleading,
   and do not turn away from me.
   You are my people: will you reject me?
   For you I suffer bitterly.

535

George Bennard. © The Rodeheaver Co./ Word Music. Administered by CopyCare

1. On a hill far away
   stood an old rugged cross,
   the emblem of suff'ring and shame;
   and I loved that old cross
   where the dearest and best
   for a world of lost sinners was slain.

So I'll cherish the old rugged cross,
till my trophies at last I lay down;
I will cling to the old rugged cross
and exchange it some day for a crown.

2. O that old rugged cross,
   so despised by the world,
   has a wondrous attraction for me:
   for the dear Lamb of God
   left his glory above
   to bear it to dark Calvary.

3. In the old rugged cross,
   stained with blood so divine,
   a wondrous beauty I see.
   For 'twas on that old cross
   Jesus suffered and died
   to pardon and sanctify me.

4. To the old rugged cross
   I will ever be true,
   its shame and reproach gladly bear.
   Then he'll call me some day
   to my home far away;
   there his glory for ever I'll share.

536

Cecil Frances Alexander, alt.

1. Once in royal David's city
   stood a lowly cattle shed,
   where a mother laid her baby
   in a manger for his bed;
   Mary was that mother mild,
   Jesus Christ her little child.

2. He came down to earth from heaven,
   who is God and Lord of all,
   and his shelter was a stable,
   and his cradle was a stall;
   with the needy, poor and lowly,
   lived on earth our Saviour holy.

Continued overleaf

3. For he is our childhood's pattern,
   day by day like us he grew;
   he was little, weak and helpless,
   tears and smiles like us he knew;
   and he feeleth for our sadness,
   and he shareth in our gladness.

4. And our eyes at last shall see him
   through his own redeeming love,
   for that child so dear and gentle
   is our Lord in heav'n above;
   and he leads his children on
   to the place where he is gone.

537 Traditional English carol

1. On Christmas night all Christians sing,
   to hear the news the angels bring,
   on Christmas night all Christians sing,
   to hear the news the angels bring.
   new of great joy, news of great mirth,
   news of our merciful King's birth.

2. Then why should we on earth be so sad,
   since our Redeemer made us glad,
   then why should we on earth be so sad,
   since our Redeemer made us glad,
   when from our sin he set us free,
   all for to gain our liberty?

3. When sin departs before his grace,
   then life and health come in its place,
   when sin departs before his grace,
   then life and health come in its place,
   angels and earth with joy may sing,
   all for to see the new-born King.

4. All out of darkness we have light,
   which made the angels sing this night:
   All out of darkness we have light,
   which made the angels sing this night:
   'Glory to God and peace to men,
   now and for evermore. Amen.'

538 John Foley, based on 1 Cor. 10:16, 17; 12:4, Gal. 3:28; Didaché 9
© 1978 John B. Foley, S. J. and New Dawn Music

One bread, one body, one Lord of all,
one cup of blessing which we bless:
and we, though many, throughout the earth,
we are one body in this one Lord.

1. Gentile or Jew,
   servant or free,
   woman or man, no more.

2. Many the gifts,
   many the works,
   one in the Lord of all.

3. Grain for the fields,
   scattered and grown,
   gathered to one, for all.

539 Damian Lundy
© 1978 Kevin Mayhew Ltd.

1. One cold night in spring the wind
      blew strong;
   then the darkness had its hour.
   A man was eating with his friends,
   for he knew his death was near.

2. And he broke a wheaten loaf to share,
   for his friends a last goodbye.
   'My body is the bread I break.
   O, my heart will break and die.'

3. Then he poured good wine into a cup,
   blessed it gently, passed it round.
   'This cup is brimming with my blood.
   Soon the drops will stain the ground.'

4. See a dying man with arms outstretched
   at the setting of the sun,
   he stretches healing hands to you.
   Will you take them for your own?

5. Soon a man will come with arms
      outstretched
   at the rising of the sun.
   His wounded hands will set you free
   if you take them for your own.

540

Gerard Markland
© 1998 Kevin Mayhew Ltd.

One Father who's giving me life,
one Saviour who's conquered my fears,
one Spirit changing my heart,
O my God, I rejoice in you.

1. Creator Lord, almighty Father,
   what God is this who carves my name
   upon his hand?

2. Lord Jesus, now enthroned in glory,
   what God is this who gives his life
   to set me free?

3. O loving breath of God almighty,
   what God is this who through
         my weakness
   sings his praise?

541

Charles Coffin, trans. John Chandler, alt.

1. On Jordan's bank the Baptist's cry
   announces that the Lord is nigh;
   awake, and hearken, for he brings
   glad tidings of the King of kings.

2. Then cleansed be ev'ry breast from sin;
   make straight the way for God within;
   prepare we in our hearts a home,
   where such a mighty guest may come.

3. For thou art our salvation, Lord,
   our refuge and our great reward;
   without thy grace we waste away,
   like flow'rs that wither and decay.

4. To heal the sick stretch out thine hand,
   and bid the fallen sinner stand;
   shine forth and let thy light restore
   earth's own true loveliness once more.

5. All praise, eternal Son, to thee
   whose advent doth thy people free,
   whom with the Father we adore
   and Holy Ghost for evermore.

542

Marie Lydia Pereira
© 1999 Kevin Mayhew Ltd.

On this day of joy, on this day of hope,
we come to you in love, O Lord,
on this day of joy, on this day of hope,
we come to you in love.

1. With this bread and wine we come
   to this eucharistic feast.
   On this day of joy, on this day of hope,
   we come to you in love.

2. Bread to be your body, Lord,
   wine to be your saving blood;
   on this day of joy, on this day of hope,
   we come to you in love.

543

Marie Lydia Pereira
© 1976 Kevin Mayhew Ltd.

1. On this house your blessing, Lord,
   on this house your grace bestow.
   On this house your blessing, Lord,
   may it come and never go.
   Bringing peace and joy and happiness,
   bringing love that knows no end.
   On this house your blessing, Lord,
   on this house your blessing send.

2. On this house your loving, Lord,
   may it overflow each day.
   On this house your loving, Lord,
   may it come and with us stay.
   Drawing us in love and unity
   by the love received from you.
   On this house your loving, Lord,
   may it come each day anew.

3. On this house your giving, Lord,
   may it turn and ever flow.
   On this house your giving, Lord,
   on this house your wealth bestow.
   Filling all our hopes and wishes, Lord,
   in the way you know is best.
   On this house your giving, Lord,
   may it come and with us rest.

Continued overleaf

4. On this house your calling, Lord,
   may it come to us each day.
   On this house your calling, Lord,
   may it come to lead the way.
   Filling us with nobler yearnings, Lord,
   calling us to live in you.
   On this house your calling, Lord,
   may it come each day anew.

544 Michael Forster
© 1996 Kevin Mayhew Ltd.

1. Onward, Christian pilgrims,
   Christ will be our light;
   see, the heav'nly vision
   breaks upon our sight!
   Out of death's enslavement
   Christ has set us free,
   on then to salvation,
   hope and liberty.

   Onward, Christian pilgrims,
   Christ will be our light;
   see, the heav'nly vision
   breaks upon our sight!

2. Onward, Christian pilgrims,
   up the rocky way,
   where the dying Saviour
   bids us watch and pray.
   Through the darkened valley
   walk with those who mourn,
   share the pain and anger,
   share the promised dawn!

3. Onward, Christian pilgrims,
   in the early dawn;
   death's great seal is broken,
   life and hope reborn!
   Faith in resurrection
   strengthens pilgrim's hearts,
   ev'ry load is lightened,
   ev'ry fear departs.

4. Onward, Christian pilgrims,
   hearts and voices raise,
   till the whole creation
   echoes perfect praise;
   swords are turned to ploughshares,
   pride and envy cease,
   truth embrace justice,
   hope resolves in peace.

545 Robert Cull
© 1976 Maranatha! Music/CopyCare

Open our eyes, Lord, we want to see Jesus,
to reach out and touch him
and say that we love him;
open our ears, Lord, and help us to listen;
O, open our eyes, Lord,
we want to see Jesus!

546 Willard F. Jabusch
© 1988 Willard F. Jabusch

1. Open your ears, O Christian people,
   open your ears and hear Good News!
   Open your hearts, O royal priesthood,
   God has come to you!

   God has spoken to his people, alleluia,
   and his words are words of wisdom,
   alleluia.

2. Israel comes to greet the Saviour,
   Judah is glad to see his day.
   From east and west the peoples travel,
   he will show the way.

3. All who have ears to hear his message,
   all who have ears then let them hear.
   All who would learn the way of wisdom,
   let them hear God's words.

547 Dorothy F. Gurney
© Copyright control

1. O perfect love,
   all human thought transcending,
   lowly we kneel
   in prayer before thy throne,

that theirs may be
the love which knows no ending,
whom thou for evermore
dost join in one.

2. O perfect life,
be thou their full assurance
of tender charity
and steadfast faith,
of patient hope
and quiet, brave endurance,
with childlike trust that fears
not pain nor death.

3. Grant them the joy
which brightens earthly sorrow,
grant them the peace
which calms all earthly strife;
and to life's day
the glorious unknown morrow
that dawns upon
eternal love and life.

548 Henry Williams Baker, based on Psalms 148 and 150, alt.

1. O praise ye the Lord!
praise him in the height;
rejoice in his word, ye angels of light;
ye heavens, adore him,
by whom ye were made,
and worship before him,
in brightness arrayed.

2. O praise ye the Lord!
praise him upon earth,
in tuneful accord, all you of new birth;
praise him who hath brought you
his grace from above,
praise him who hath taught you
to sing of his love.

3. O praise ye the Lord!
all things that give sound;
each jubilant chord re-echo around;
loud organs his glory
forth tell in deep tone,
and, sweet harp, the story
of what he hath done.

4. O praise ye the Lord!
thanksgiving and song
to him be outpoured all ages along:
for love in creation,
for heaven restored,
for grace of salvation,
O praise ye the Lord!

549 Frederick William Faber

1. O purest of creatures!
Sweet mother, sweet maid;
the one spotless womb
wherein Jesus was laid.
Dark night hath come
down on us, mother, and we
look out for thy shining,
sweet star of the sea.

2. Earth gave him one lodging;
'twas deep in thy breast,
and God found a home where
the sinner finds rest;
his home and his hiding-place,
both were in thee;
he was won by thy shining,
sweet star of the sea.

3. O, blissful and calm
was the wonderful rest
that thou gavest thy God
in thy virginal breast;
for the heaven he left
he found heaven in thee,
and he shone in thy shining,
sweet star of the sea.

550 James Quinn
© *Geoffrey Chapman, an imprint of Cassell plc.*

1. O Queen of heav'n,
to you the angels sing,
the Maiden Mother
of their Lord and King.
O woman,
raised above the stars,
receive the homage of your children,
sinless Eve.

Continued overleaf

2. O full of grace,
   in grace your womb did bear
   Emmanuel,
   King David's promised heir.
   O Eastern Gate,
   whom God had made his own,
   by you, God's glory came
   to Zion's throne.

3. O Burning Bush,
   you gave the world its light,
   when Christ, your Son,
   was born on Christmas night.
   O Mary Queen,
   who bore God's holy one,
   for us your children,
   pray to God your Son.

4. In this thy sacred passion
   O, that some share had I!
   O, may thy Cross's fashion
   o'erlook me when I die!
   For these dear pains that rack thee
   a sinner's thanks receive;
   O, lest in death I lack thee,
   a sinner's care relieve.

5. Since death must be my ending,
   in that drear hour of need,
   my friendless cause befriending,
   Lord, to my rescue speed;
   thyself, dear Jesus, trace me
   that passage to the grave,
   and from thy cross embrace me
   with arms outstretched to save.

551
Paul Gerhardt, trans. Ronald Arbuthnott Knox
© Burns and Oates Ltd.

1. O sacred head ill-used,
   by reed and bramble scarred,
   that idle blows have bruised,
   and mocking lips have marred,
   how dimmed that eye so tender,
   how wan those cheeks appear,
   how overcast the splendour
   that angel hosts revere!

2. What marvel if thou languish,
   vigour and virtue fled,
   wasted and spent with anguish,
   and pale as are the dead?
   O by thy foes' derision,
   that death endured for me,
   grant that thy open vision
   a sinner's eyes may see.

3. Good Shepherd, spent with loving,
   look on me, who have strayed,
   oft by those lips unmoving
   with milk and honey stayed;
   spurn not a sinner's crying
   nor from thy love outcast,
   but rest thy head in dying
   on these frail arms at last.

552
Paul Gerhardt, trans. Robert Bridges
© Oxford University Press

1. O sacred head sore wounded,
   defiled and put to scorn;
   O kingly head surrounded
   with mocking crown of thorn:
   what sorrow mars thy grandeur?
   Can death thy bloom de-flower?
   O countenance whose splendour
   the hosts of heav'n adore.

2. Thy beauty, long-desirèd,
   hath vanished from our sight;
   thy pow'r is all expirèd,
   and quenched the light of light.
   Ah me, for whom thou diest,
   hide not so far thy grace:
   show me, O love most highest,
   the brightness of thy face.

3. I pray thee, Jesus, own me,
   me, shepherd good, for thine;
   who to thy fold hast won me,
   and fed with truth divine.
   Me guilty, me refuse not,
   incline thy face to me,
   this comfort that I lose not,
   on earth to comfort thee.

4. In thy most bitter passion
   my heart to share doth cry,
   with thee for my salvation
   upon the cross to die.
   Ah, keep my heart thus movèd,
   to stand thy cross beneath,
   to mourn thee, well-belovèd,
   yet thank thee for thy death.

5. My days are few, O fail not,
   with thine immortal power,
   to hold me that I quail not
   in death's most fearful hour:
   that I may fight befriended,
   and see in my last strife
   to me thine arms extended
   upon the cross of life.

553 Francis Stanfield

1. O Sacred Heart,
   our home lies deep in thee;
   on earth thou art an exile's rest,
   in heav'n the glory of the blest,
   O Sacred Heart.

2. O Sacred Heart,
   thou fount of contrite tears;
   where'er those living waters flow,
   new life to sinners they bestow,
   O Sacred Heart.

3. O Sacred Heart,
   our trust is all in thee,
   for though earth's night be dark and
        drear,
   thou breathest rest where thou art near,
   O Sacred Heart.

4. O Sacred Heart,
   lead exiled children home,
   where we may ever rest near thee,
   in peace and joy eternally,
   O Sacred Heart.

554

Jean-Paul Lécot, based on Matthew 2:11; Romans 6:8; Wisdom 8:1, trans. W. R. Lawrence.
© 1988 Kevin Mayhew Ltd.

O sing a new song
giving praise to the Lord,
alleluia, alleluia, alleluia!

1. People of God, be glad and rejoice,
   your Saviour comes; harken his voice!

2. He who will save the world from its stain
   comes from the clouds, gentle as rain.

3. This is the day the Saviour was born;
   God's love and peace shine in this dawn.

4. Mother of God, we honour your worth;
   you gave us Christ to ransom earth.

5. This Child you see is Saviour and Lord,
   God's Son made Man, by kings adored.

6. Glory to Christ who brought us his light;
   coming from God, he gives us sight.

7. As we have died with Christ unto sin,
   so we now share new life with him.

8. God's Spirit fills the earth with his love,
   makes all things new, draws them above.

9. Spirit of God, come dwell in our hearts;
   kindle the fire your love imparts.

10. To Father, Son and Spirit be giv'n
    eternal praise, here and in heav'n.

555

Michael Forster
1999 Kevin Mayhew Ltd.

1. O suff'ring Jesus, what were your offences,
   except to live on earth without defences?
   Why was this holy life that you presented
   so much resented?

2. The challenge of perfection made
        us tremble –
   a love we knew we never could resemble –
   and so you bore the sins of all creation
   for our salvation.

Continued overleaf

3. Those sins were ours – how grudgingly
we own them!
We treat them lightly, pardon and
condone them.
Yet, through the pain, your love shines
out, revealing
judgement and healing.

4. O suff'ring Christ, still found in
every nation,
you bear the pain and hope of all creation.
Love reigns triumphant, sin and
death defeated;
all is completed.

556 Susan Sayers, based on Psalm 94
© 1995 Kevin Mayhew Ltd.

O that today you would listen to his voice,
'Harden not your hearts.'

1. Come let us joyfully sing to the Lord,
saluting the rock who preserves us.
Let us approach him to offer him thanks,
with songs let us welcome our God.

2. Let us come in, let us kneel and adore,
in rev'rence for God who has made us.
We are his people, the sheep of his flock,
we graze in the pastures of God.

3. Out in the desert they hardened
their hearts,
at Massah they tested their Saviour,
O that today you would listen to him,
and open your hearts to his love.

557 Estelle White
© McCrimmon Publishing Co. Ltd.

1. O, the love of my Lord is the essence
of all that I love here on earth.
All the beauty I see he has given to me,
and his giving is gentle as silence.

2. Ev'ry day, ev'ry hour, ev'ry moment
have been blessed by the strength of
his love.

At the turn of each tide he is there at
my side,
and his touch is as gentle as silence.

3. There've been times when I've turned
from his presence,
and I've walked other paths, other ways;
but I've called on his name in the dark of
my shame,
and his mercy was gentle as silence.

558 Damian Lundy, based on Jeremiah 1
© 1978 Kevin Mayhew Ltd.

O the word of my Lord,
deep within my being,
O the word of my Lord,
you have filled my mind.

1. Before I formed you in the womb,
I knew you through and through,
I chose you to be mine.
Before you left your mother's side,
I called to you, my child, to be my sign.

2. I know that you are very young,
but I will make you strong,
I'll fill you with my word;
and you will travel through the land,
fulfilling my command which you
have heard.

3. And ev'rywhere you are to go
my hand will follow you;
you will not be alone.
In all the danger that you fear
you'll find me very near, your words
my own.

4. With all my strength you will be filled:
you will destroy and build,
for that is my design.
You will create and overthrow,
reap harvests I will sow, your word is mine.

559
William Harry Turton, based on John 17
© Copyright control

1. O thou, who at thy Eucharist didst pray
   that all thy Church might be for
      ever one,
   grant us at ev'ry eucharist to say,
   with longing heart and soul,
      'Thy will be done.'
   O may we all one bread, one body be,
   through this blest sacrament of unity.

2. For all thy Church, O Lord, we intercede;
   make thou our sad divisions soon
      to cease;
   draw us the nearer each to each,
      we plead,
   by drawing all to thee, O Prince of Peace:
   thus may we all one bread, one body be,
   through this blest sacrament of unity.

3. We pray thee too for wand'rers from
      thy fold;
   O bring them back, good Shepherd of
      the sheep,
   back to the faith which saints believed
      of old,
   back to the Church which still that faith
      doth keep;
   soon may we all one bread, one body be,
   through this blest sacrament of unity.

4. So, Lord, at length when sacraments
      shall cease,
   may we be one with all thy Church above,
   one with thy saints in one unbroken peace,
   one with thy saints in one unbounded love;
   more blessèd still, in peace and love to be
   one with the Trinity in unity.

560
v 1 unknown, vs 2-5 Sandra Joan Billington
© 1976 Kevin Mayhew Ltd.

1. Our God loves us,
   his love will never end.
   He rests within our hearts
   for our God loves us.

2. His gentle hand
   he stretches over us.
   Though storm-clouds threaten the day,
   he will set us free.

3. He comes to us
   in sharing bread and wine.
   He brings us life that will reach
   past the end of time.

4. Our God loves us,
   his faithful love endures,
   and we will live like his child
   held in love secure.

5. The joys of love
   as off'rings now we bring.
   The pains of love will be lost
   in the praise we sing.

561
Damian Lundy
© 1982 Kevin Mayhew Ltd.

1. Our God sent his Son long ago,
   and he came to bring joy to us all.
   For the Lord wants his children
   to know he loves them.

   So sing the good news to the poor
   and the young!
   Praise the Lord for his Word!
   Sharing the gospel with all those in need,
   become the good news you have heard!

2. But how will the good news be heard?
   When we answer the call of the Lord,
   when we live so our faith
   can be shared with others.

3. From the Spirit of God comes our call,
   bringing pow'r to be joyful and free,
   to be brothers and sisters
   to all; to love them.

4. Praise and glory to God for his Word,
   always living in those who believe,
   still made flesh in our lives
   to be shared with others.

562 Aniceto Nazareth, based on Scripture
© 1984 Kevin Mayhew Ltd.

Our hearts were made for you, Lord,
our hearts were made for you;
they'll never find, never find, never find rest
until they find their rest in you.

1. When you call me I will answer,
   when you seek me you will find.
   I will lead you back from exile,
   and reveal to you my mind.

2. I will take you from the nations,
   and will bring you to your land.
   From your idols I will cleanse you
   and you'll cherish my command.

3. I will put my law within you,
   I will write it on your heart;
   I will be your God and Saviour,
   you, my people set apart.

563 Michael Forster, based on Philippians 2:6-11
© 1997 Kevin Mayhew Ltd.

1. Our Saviour, Christ, of Godly nature
   and equal in the Father's eyes,
   refused to clutch his rightful glory
   the way a miser grasps the prize.

2. Of all his heav'nly glory emptied,
   his very self he freely gave,
   to clothe himself in human nature
   and wear the mantle of a slave.

3. Immortal God for us made mortal,
   the God-breathed Word drew
       human breath,
   then gave up even that to save us,
   obedient to the very death.

4. From death to life did God exalt him,
   to heaven's joy and earth's acclaim;
   on him, and him alone, bestowing
   the Name above all other names.

5. That at the glorious Name of Jesus
   all nations shall acclaim his worth,
   and every knee shall bow before him
   above, below and on the earth.

6. Let every tongue in earth and heaven
   proclaim that Jesus Christ is Lord,
   who shows the glory of the Father,
   our God for evermore adored.

564 Francesca Leftley
© 1985, 1994 Francesca Leftley

Ours were the sufferings he bore,
ours were the sorrows he carried.
He bears a punishment
that brings us peace,
and through his wounds we are healed.

1. Come, Lord, and heal us;
   O Lamb of God, O Lamb of God.
   Come, Lord, and heal us;
   O Lamb of God, O Lamb of God.

2. Come, Lord, and heal us;
   you died for us, you died for us.
   Come, Lord, and heal us;
   you died for us, you died for us.

3. Come, Lord, and heal us;
   grant us your peace, grant us your peace.
   Come, Lord, and heal us;
   grant us your peace, grant us your peace.

565 Christopher Walker
©1989 Christopher Walker. Published by OCP

Out of darkness God has called us,
claimed by Christ as God's own people.
Holy nation, royal priesthood,
walking in God's marv'lous light.

1. Let us take the words you give,
   strong and faithful words to live,
   words that in our hearts are sown,
   words that bind us as your own.

2. Let us take the Christ you give,
   Broken Body Christ we live,
   Christ, the risen from the tomb,
   Christ, who calls us as your own.

3. Let us take the love you give,
   that the way of love we live,
   love to bring your people home,
   love to make us all your own.

566

Damian Lundy, based on the 'O' Antiphons
© 1987, 1996 Kevin Mayhew Ltd.

1. O Wisdom, source of harmony,
   the Word of God who made the world,
   sustaining life and liberty,
   come, living Lord, and set us free.

2. O sov'reign Lord who long ago
   led Israel to liberty,
   come once again! On earth below
   your pow'r and loving kindness show.

3. O Root of Jesse, hope for all
   who long to see a new life grow,
   come, raise your people when we fall,
   come, flower among us when we call.

4. Oh shine on us, dear Morning Star!
   Your radiant light be over all,
   for death is banished where you are.
   Come, shine in darkness from afar!

5. O David's key, your people wait
   to know your faithfulness and care.
   Come, save us from our gloomy state!
   Oh come and open heaven's gate!

6. O King of ev'ry nation, come
   and bring the joy for which we wait.
   Lord, to the earth you made us from
   come once again and be at home.

7. Emmanuel, God with us, Lord,
   the ancient Word dispelling gloom,
   in human flesh the living Word,
   fulfil the promise we have heard.

8. Lord Jesus, come again, we pray,
   come, live with us! Lord, with us stay!
   Take all our shame and fear away.
   Come, Lord! Be born again today.

567

Michael Forster, based on 'Creator alme siderum'
7th century. © 1977, 1999 Kevin Mayhew Ltd.

1. O Word, in uncreated light,
   who brought to birth the starry height;
   incarnate Saviour of us all,
   hear us, God's people, when we call.

2. Attentive to our helpless cry
   as mortals, so afraid to die,
   you took our flesh in truth and grace
   to save the fallen human race.

3. When earth was in its crisis' hour,
   you came in love's redeeming pow'r,
   with life and grace to burst the tomb,
   unsealing first the Virgin's womb.

4. Now to the glory of your Name
   let praise be sung and due acclaim;
   let all on earth and all above
   declare you Lord of life and love.

5. Prepare us, Lord and Judge, we pray
   to face you on the final day;
   and keep us in this present hour
   from yielding to temptation's pow'r.

6. To God the Father, God the Son,
   and God the Spirit, Three in One,
   all glory, praise and honour be,
   from age to age eternally.

568

Robert Grant, based on Psalm 103

1. O worship the King
   all glorious above;
   O gratefully sing
   his pow'r and his love:
   our shield and defender,
   the Ancient of Days,
   pavilioned in splendour,
   and girded with praise.

Continued overleaf

2. O tell of his might,
   O sing of his grace,
   whose robe is the light,
   whose canopy space;
   his chariots of wrath
   the deep thunder-clouds form,
   and dark in his path
   on the wings of the storm.

3. This earth, with its store
   of wonders untold,
   almighty, thy pow'r
   hath founded of old:
   hath stablished it fast
   by a changeless decree,
   and round it hath cast,
   like a mantle, the sea.

4. Thy bountiful care
   what tongue can recite?
   It breathes in the air,
   it shines in the light;
   it streams from the hills,
   it descends to the plain,
   and sweetly distils
   in the dew and the rain.

5. Frail children of dust,
   and feeble as frail,
   in thee do we trust,
   nor find thee to fail;
   thy mercies how tender,
   how firm to the end!
   Our maker, defender,
   redeemer, and friend.

6. O measureless might,
   ineffable love,
   while angels delight
   to hymn thee above,
   thy humbler creation,
   though feeble their lays,
   with true adoration
   shall sing to thy praise.

569 John Samuel Bewley Monsell

1. O worship the Lord
   in the beauty of holiness;
   bow down before him,
   his glory proclaim;
   with gold of obedience
   and incense of lowliness,
   kneel and adore him:
   the Lord is his name.

2. Low at his feet lay
   thy burden of carefulness:
   high on his heart
   he will bear it for thee,
   comfort thy sorrows,
   and answer thy prayerfulness,
   guiding thy steps
   as may best for thee be.

3. Fear not to enter
   his courts in the slenderness
   of the poor wealth
   thou wouldst reckon as thine:
   truth in its beauty,
   and love in its tenderness,
   these are the off'rings
   to lay on his shrine.

4. These, though we bring them
   in trembling and fearfulness,
   he will accept
   for the name that is dear;
   mornings of joy give
   for evenings of tearfulness,
   trust for our trembling
   and hope for our fear.

570 St Thomas Aquinas

1. Pange lingua gloriosi,
   Corporis Mysterium,
   Sanguinisque pretiosi
   quem in mundi pretium,
   fructus ventris generosi
   Rex effudit gentium.

2. Nobis datus, nobis natus
   ex intacta Virgine;
   et in mundo conversatus,
   sparso verbi semine,
   sui moras incolatus
   miro clausit ordine.

3. In supremæ nocte coenæ
   recumbens cum fratribus,
   observata lege plene
   cibis in legalibus:
   cibum turbæ duodenæ
   se dat suis manibus.

4. Verbum caro, panem verum,
   verbo carnem efficit:
   fitque sanguis Christi merum;
   et si sensus deficit,
   ad firmandum cor sincerum
   sola fides sufficit.

5. Tantum ergo Sacramentum
   veneremur cernui:
   et antiquum documentum
   novo cedat ritui;
   præstet fides supplementum
   sensuum defectui.

6. Genitori, genitoque
   laus, et jubilatio,
   salus, honor, virtus quoque
   sit et benedictio;
   procedenti ab utroque
   compar sit laudatio. Amen.

571
Peter Madden
© 1976 Kevin Mayhew Ltd.

Peace I leave with you,
peace I give to you;
not as the world gives peace,
do I give.
Take and pass it on,
on to ev'ryone;
thus the world will know,
you are my friends.

572
v 1-4 unknown, v 5 the Editors
© 1999 Kevin Mayhew Ltd.

1. Peace is flowing like a river,
   flowing out through you and me,
   spreading out into the desert,
   setting all the captives free.

   (This refrain is not always sung.)
   Let it flow through me,
   let it flow through me,
   let the mighty peace of God
   flow out through me. (Repeat)

2. Love is flowing like a river,
   flowing out through you and me,
   spreading out into the desert,
   setting all the captives free.

3. Joy is flowing like a river,
   flowing out through you and me,
   spreading out into the desert,
   setting all the captives free.

4. Hope is flowing like a river,
   flowing out through you and me,
   spreading out into the desert,
   setting all the captives free.

5. Christ brings peace to all creation,
   flowing out through you and me,
   love, joy, hope and true salvation,
   setting all the captives free.

573
John Glynn
© 1976 Kevin Mayhew Ltd.

1. Peace is the gift of heaven to earth,
   softly enfolding our fears.
   Peace is the gift of Christ to the world,
   given for us:
   he is the Lamb who bore
   the pain of peace.

2. Peace is the gift of Christ to his Church,
   wound of the lance of his love.
   Love is the pain he suffered for all,
   offered to us:
   O, to accept the wound
   that brings us peace!

Continued overleaf

3. Joy is the gift the Spirit imparts,
born of the heavens and earth.
We are his children, children of joy,
people of God:
he is our Lord, our peace,
our love, our joy!

574 Kevin Mayhew
© 1976 Kevin Mayhew Ltd.

1. Peace, perfect peace
is the gift of Christ our Lord.
Peace, perfect peace,
is the gift of Christ our Lord.
Thus says the Lord,
will the world know my friends.
Peace, perfect peace,
is the gift of Christ our Lord.

2. Love, perfect love . . .

3. Faith, perfect faith . . .

4. Hope, perfect hope . . .

5. Joy, perfect joy . . .

575 Unknown

1. Praise him, praise him,
praise him in the morning,
praise him in the noontime.
Praise him, praise him,
praise him when the sun goes down.

2. Love him, love him, . . .

3. Trust him, trust him, . . .

4. Serve him, serve him, . . .

5. Jesus, Jesus, . . .

576 Henry Francis Lyte

1. Praise, my soul, the King of heaven!
To his feet thy tribute bring;
ransomed, healed, restored, forgiven,
who like me his praise should sing?
Praise him! Praise him!
Praise him! Praise him!
Praise the everlasting King!

2. Praise him for his grace and favour
to our fathers in distress;
praise him still the same as ever,
slow to chide and swift to bless.
Praise him! Praise him!
Praise him! Praise him!
Glorious in his faithfulness!

3. Father-like, he tends and spares us;
well our feeble frame he knows;
in his hands he gently bears us,
rescues us from all our foes.
Praise him! Praise him!
Praise him! Praise him!
Widely as his mercy flows!

4. Angels, help us to adore him;
ye behold him face to face;
sun and moon, bow down before him,
dwellers all in time and space.
Praise him! Praise him!
Praise him! Praise him!
Praise with us the God of grace!

577 Mike Anderson, based on Psalm 46
© 1999 Kevin Mayhew Ltd.

Praise the Lord, all of you peoples,
praise the Lord, shout for joy!
Praise the Lord, sing him a new song,
praise the Lord and bless his name.

1. Clap your hands, now, all of you nations.
shout for joy, acclaim the Lord.

2. He goes up to shouts which acclaim him,
he goes up to trumpet blast.

3. Let the music sound for the Lord, now;
let your chords resound in praise.

4. He is King of all the nations;
honour him by singing psalms.

578 Frances M. Kelly, based on Psalm 150
© 1984 Kevin Mayhew Ltd.

Praise the Lord in his holy house,
in the firmament of his majesty.
Praise the Lord! Praise the Lord!

1. Praise the Lord in his holy house,
   in the firmament of his majesty.
   Praise him, for all his pow'rful works.
   Praise him, he is truly great.

2. Praise him with your resounding horns,
   praise him with your lutes,
       your guitars and harps.
   Praise with dancing and tambourines,
   tune your strings and play your flute!

3. Praise with cymbals and pounding drums,
   praise him, brass and woodwind,
       let choirs rejoice.
   Alleluia, alleluia!
   All living, sing praise to God!

579 vs 1 and 2 from 'Foundling Hospital Collection'
vs 3 Edward Osler

1. Praise the Lord, ye heav'ns, adore him!
   Praise him, angels, in the height;
   sun and moon, rejoice before him,
   praise him, all ye stars and light.
   Praise the Lord, for he hath spoken;
   worlds his mighty voice obeyed:
   laws, which never shall be broken,
   for their guidance he hath made.

2. Praise the Lord, for he is glorious:
   never shall his promise fail.
   God hath made his saints victorious;
   sin and death shall not prevail.
   Praise the God of our salvation,
   hosts on high, his pow'r proclaim;
   heav'n and earth and all creation,
   laud and magnify his name!

3. Worship, honour, glory, blessing,
   Lord, we offer to thy name;
   young and old, thy praise expressing,
   join their Saviour to proclaim.
   As the saints in heav'n adore thee,
   we would bow before thy throne;
   as thine angels serve before thee,
   so on earth thy will be done.

580 Michael Forster
© 1999 Kevin Mayhew Ltd.

1. Praise to God for saints and martyrs
   inspiration to us all;
   in the presence of our Saviour,
   their example we recall:
   lives of holy contemplation,
   sacrifice or simple love,
   witnesses to truth and justice,
   honoured here and crowned above.

2. How we long to share their story,
   faithful in response to grace,
   signs of God's eternal presence
   in the realm of time and space.
   Now, their pilgrimage completed,
   cross of Christ their only boast,
   they unite their own rejoicing
   with the great angelic host.

3. Saints and martyrs, now in glory,
   robed before your Saviour's face,
   let us join your intercession
   for God's holy human race.
   Let us join with you in singing
   Mary's liberation song,
   till a just and free creation sings,
   with the angelic throng:

4. Praise and honour to the Father,
   adoration to the Son,
   with the all-embracing Spirit
   wholly Three and holy One.
   All the universe, united
   in complete diversity,
   sings as one your endless praises,
   ever blessèd Trinity!

581 Unknown

1. Praise to God in the highest!
   Bless us, O Father! *Praise to you!*

2. Guide and prosper the nations,
   rulers and peoples. *Praise to you!*

3. May the truth in its beauty
   flourish triumphant. *Praise to you!*

4. May the mills bring us bread
   for food and for giving. *Praise to you!*

5. May the good be obeyed
   and evils be conquered. *Praise to you!*

6. Give us laughter and set all
   your people rejoicing. *Praise to you!*

7. Peace on earth and good will
   ever among us. *Praise to you!*

582 John Henry Newman

1. Praise to the Holiest in the height,
   and in the depth be praise;
   in all his words most wonderful,
   most sure in all his ways.

2. O loving wisdom of our God!
   when all was sin and shame,
   a second Adam to the fight,
   and to the rescue came.

3. O wisest love! that flesh and blood,
   which did in Adam fail,
   should strive afresh against the foe,
   should strive and should prevail.

4. And that a higher gift than grace
   should flesh and blood refine,
   God's presence and his very self,
   and essence all-divine.

5. And in the garden secretly,
   and on the cross on high,
   should teach his brethren, and inspire
   to suffer and to die.

6. Praise to the Holiest in the height,
   and in the depth be praise;
   in all his words most wonderful,
   most sure in all his ways.

583 Joachim Neander, trans. Catherine Winkworth, alt.

1. Praise to the Lord,
   the Almighty, the King of creation!
   O my soul, praise him,
   for he is your health and salvation.
   All you who hear,
   now to his altar draw near;
   join in profound adoration.

2. Praise to the Lord,
   let us offer our gifts at his altar;
   let not our sins and transgressions
   now cause us to falter.
   Christ, the High Priest,
   bids us all join in his feast;
   victims with him on the altar.

3. Praise to the Lord,
   O, let all that is in us adore him!
   All that has life and breath,
   come now in praise before him.
   Let the 'Amen'
   sound from his people again,
   now as we worship before him.

584 Joachim Neander, trans. Catherine Winkworth

For Ecumenical occasions

1. Praise to the Lord,
   the Almighty, the King of creation!
   O my soul, praise him,
   for he is thy health and salvation.
   All ye who hear,
   now to his temple draw near;
   joining in glad adoration.

2. Praise to the Lord,
who o'er all things so wondrously reigneth,
shieldeth thee gently from harm,
or when fainting sustaineth:
hast thou not seen
how thy heart's wishes have been
granted in what he ordaineth?

3. Praise to the Lord,
who doth prosper thy work and defend thee,
surely his goodness and mercy
shall daily attend thee:
ponder anew
what the Almighty can do,
if to the end he befriend thee.

4. Praise to the Lord,
O let all that is in us adore him!
All that hath life and breath,
come now with praises before him.
Let the 'Amen'
sound from his people again,
gladly for ay we adore him.

585 Bernadette Farrell. © 1986 Bernadette Farrell
Published by OCP Publications

*Praise to you, O Christ, our Saviour,
Word of the Father, calling us to life;
Son of God who leads us to freedom:
glory to you, Lord Jesus Christ!*

1. You are the Word
who calls us out of darkness;
you are the Word
who leads us into light;
you are the Word
who brings us through the desert:
glory to you, Lord Jesus Christ!

2. You are the one
whom prophets hoped and longed for;
you are the one
who speaks to us today;
you are the one
who leads us to our future:
glory to you, Lord Jesus Christ!

3. You are the Word
who calls us to be servants;
you are the Word
whose only law is love;
you are the Word-made-flesh
who lives among us:
glory to you, Lord Jesus Christ!

4. You are the Word
who binds us and unites us;
you are the Word
who calls us to be one;
you are the Word
who teaches us forgiveness:
glory to you, Lord Jesus Christ!

586 Frederick Oakley and others

1. Praise we our God with joy
and gladness never-ending;
angels and saints with us
their grateful voices blending.
He is our Father dear,
o'er filled with parent's love;
mercies unsought, unknown,
he showers from above.

2. He is our shepherd true;
with watchful care unsleeping,
on us, his erring sheep,
an eye of pity keeping;
he with a mighty arm
the bonds of sin doth break,
and to our burdened hearts
in words of peace doth speak.

3. Graces in copious stream
from that pure fount are welling,
where, in our heart of hearts,
our God hath set his dwelling.
His word our lantern is;
his peace our comfort still;
his sweetness all our rest;
our law, our life, his will.

587

Luke Connaughton
© McCrimmon Publishing Co. Ltd.

1. Reap me the earth as a harvest to God,
   gather and bring it again,
   all that is his, to the Maker of all.
   Lift it and offer it high.

   Bring bread, bring wine,
   give glory to the Lord;
   whose is the earth's but God's,
   whose is the praise but his?

2. Go with your song and your music
      with joy,
   go to the altar of God.
   Carry your offerings, fruits of the earth,
   work of your labouring hands.

3. Gladness and pity and passion and pain,
   all that is mortal in man,
   lay all before him, return him his gift.
   God, to whom all shall go home.

588

Unknown 12th century

Regina cæli, lætare, alleluia,
quia quem meruisti portare, alleluia.
resurrexit sicut dixit, alleluia,
Ora pro nobis Deum, alleluia.

589

Michael Forster
© 1997 Kevin Mayhew Ltd.

1. Rejoice, all heaven'ly pow'rs,
   O choirs of angels sing!
   and let the universe with alleluias ring!
   For Jesus lives in glory bright,
   and endless light to us he gives.

2. Rejoice, O shining earth,
   in glorious hope reborn,
   and praise the Light who wrought
   the first creation's dawn.
   Redeemed and free, in Christ we rise,
   and darkness dies eternally.

3. Rejoice, O Mother church;
   on you the Saviour shines;
   then let the vaults resound
   with joy and peace divine!
   His truth proclaim, and loud and long,
   in glorious song, exalt his name.

4. The people who have walked
   in terror through the night,
   from shades of death released,
   have seen a glorious light.
   God's word is sure, and he will bless
   with righteousness the humble poor.

5. O God of hope and love,
   who lit the desert way,
   and led from slav'ry's night
   to liberation's day:
   still go before, till we rejoice,
   with heart and voice, on Canaan's shore.

6. We light these gentle flames
   to be our pledge and sign;
   we share the risen life
   of Christ, the light divine.
   Throughout the earth, oppression's night
   shall flee the light of human worth.

7. Arise, O Morning Star,
   O Sun who never sets,
   and bring these humble flames
   to greater glory yet.
   Let all adore, in glorious strains,
   the Christ who reigns for evermore.

590

Based on Philippians 4:4

Rejoice in the Lord always and again
I say rejoice. *(Repeat)*
Rejoice, rejoice and again I say rejoice.
(Repeat)

591

Charles Wesley

1. Rejoice the Lord is King!
   Your Lord and King adore;
   mortals, give thanks and sing,
   and triumph evermore.

Lift up your heart, lift up your voice;
rejoice, again I say, rejoice.

2. Jesus the Saviour reigns,
   the God of truth and love;
   when he had purged our stains,
   he took his seat above.

3. His kingdom cannot fail;
   he rules o'er earth and heav'n;
   the keys of death and hell
   are to our Jesus giv'n.

4. He sits at God's right hand
   till all his foes submit,
   and bow to his command,
   and fall beneath his feet.

592 Psalm 24. © 1963, 1986, 1993 The Grail, England. Used by permission of A. P. Watt

Remember, remember your mercy Lord.
Remember, remember your mercy Lord.
Hear your people's prayer as they call to you;
remember, remember your mercy Lord.

1. Lord, make me know your ways.
   Lord, teach me your paths.
   Make we walk in your truth,
       and teach me:
   for you are God my Saviour.

2. Remember your mercy, Lord,
   and the love you have shown from of old.
   Do not remember the sins of my youth.
   In your love remember me,
   in your love remember me,
   because of your goodness, O Lord.

3. The Lord is good and upright.
   He shows the path to all who stray,
   he guides the humble in the right path;
   he teaches his way to the poor.

593 Henry Hart Milman, alt.

1. Ride on, ride on in majesty!
   Hark all the tribes hosanna cry;
   thy humble beast pursues his road
   with palms and scattered garments
       strowed.

2. Ride on, ride on in majesty!
   In lowly pomp ride on to die;
   O Christ, thy triumphs now begin
   o'er captive death and conquered sin.

3. Ride on, ride on in majesty!
   The wingèd squadrons of the sky
   look down with sad and wond'ring eyes
   to see th'approaching sacrifice.

4. Ride on, ride on in majesty!
   Thy last and fiercest strife is nigh;
   the Father, on his sapphire throne,
   awaits his own appointed Son.

5. Ride on, ride on in majesty!
   in lowly pomp ride on to die;
   bow thy meek head to mortal pain,
   then take, O God, thy pow'r, and reign.

594 Aniceto Nazareth, based on the Canticle of Daniel © 1984 Kevin Mayhew Ltd.

Ring out your joy, give glory to God.
Lift up your hearts and sing.
Let all creation tell of his name.
Praise him for evermore!

1. Blessed are you, God of creation;
   glory and praise for evermore!
   Blest be your holy, glorious, great name;
   Glory and praise for evermore!

2. Blest in the temple of your glory;
   glory and praise for evermore!
   Blessèd, enthroned over your kingdom;
   glory and praise for evermore!

3. Blest, you who know the deeps
       and highest;
   glory and praise for evermore!
   Blest in the firmament of heaven;
   glory and praise for evermore!

4. All things the Lord has made,
       now bless him;
   glory and praise for evermore!
   Angels and saints, now bless and praise
       him;
   glory and praise for evermore!

595

Sydney Carter
© 1964 Stainer & Bell Ltd.

1. Said Judas to Mary,
   'Now what will you do
   with your ointment so rich and so rare?'
   'I'll pour it all over the feet of the Lord,
   and I'll wipe it away with my hair,' she said,
   'I'll wipe it away with my hair.'

2. 'Oh Mary, oh Mary,
   oh think of the poor,
   this ointment, it could have been sold,
   and think of the blankets and think of
      the bread
   you could buy with the silver and gold,'
      he said,
   'you could buy with silver and gold.'

3. 'Tomorrow, tomorrow,
   I'll think of the poor,
   tomorrow,' she said, 'not today;
   for dearer than all of the poor in the world
   is my love who is going away,' she said,
   'my love who is going away.'

4. Said Jesus to Mary,
   'Your love is so deep,
   today you may do as you will.
   Tomorrow you say I am going away,
   but my body I leave with you still,'
      he said,
   'my body I leave with you still.'

5. 'The poor of the world
   are my body,' he said,
   'to the end of the world they shall be.
   The bread and the blankets you give to
      the poor
   you'll find you have given to me,' he said,
   'you'll find you have given to me.

6. 'My body will hang
   on the cross of the world,
   tomorrow,' he said, 'and today,
   and Martha and Mary will find me again
   and wash all my sorrow away,' he said,
   'and wash all my sorrow away.'

596

James Quinn, based on Revelation 19: 1,2, 5-9
© Geoffrey Chapman, an imprint of Cassell plc

1. Salvation is God's and glory and pow'r,
   his judgements are true,
      his judgements are just!

All kingship is yours, all glory, all pow'r!

2. Give praise to our God,
      you servants of God,
   both little and great, revering his name!

3. The Lord is now King, the Ruler of all;
   give glory to him, in him take your joy!

4. The wedding day dawns
      for Lamb and for Bride;
   in beauty adorned, she waits for the Lamb.

5. The grace of the Lamb
      has robed her in white;
   in glory she shines, fit Bride for the Lamb.

6. How happy are those invited to share
   the Supper prepared
      for Bridegroom and Bride!

597

Hermann the Lame

Salve, Regina, mater misericordiæ;
vita, dulcedo, et spes nostra, salve.
Ad te clamamus, exules filii hevæ.
Ad te suspiramus, gementes et fientes
in hac lacrimarum valle.
Eia ergo, advocata nostra,
illos tuos misericordes oculos ad nos
      converte.
Et Jesum, benedictum fructum ventris tui,
nobis post hoc exilium ostende.
O clemens, O pia, O dulcis Virgo Maria.

598

The Office of Night Prayer

Save us, O Lord, while we are awake,
and guard us while we sleep,
that awake we may watch with Christ,
and asleep we may rest in peace,
in Jesus' name, in Jesus' name.

599 Luke 2:29-32, trans. The Grail. © 1963, 1986, 1993 the Grail. Used by permission of A. P. Watt Ltd.

Save us, O Lord, while we're awake.
Guard us, O Lord, when we're asleep
that we may watch with Christ
and rest in peace,
that we may watch with Christ
and rest in peace.

1. At last, all-powerful Master,
   you give leave to your servant
   to go in peace according to your promise.

2. For my eyes have seen your salvation
   which you have prepared for all nations.

3. The light to enlighten the Gentiles
   and give glory to Israel, your people.

4. Give glory to the Father almighty,
   to his Son, Jesus Christ, the Lord.

5. To the Spirit who dwells in our hearts,
   both now and for ever. Amen.

600 Bob Dufford
© 1981 Robert J. Dufford, SJ. and New Dawn Music

Save us, O Lord, carry us back.
Rouse your power and come.
Rescue your people, show us your face.
Bring us back.

1. O Shepherd of Israel, hear us;
   return and we shall be saved.
   Arise, O Lord; hear our cries, O Lord.
   Bring us back!

2. How long will you hide from your people?
   We long to see your face.
   Give ear to us, draw near to us,
   Lord God of hosts!

3. Turn again, care for your vine,
   protect what your right hand has planted.
   Your vineyards are trampled, uprooted
      and burned.
   Come to us, Father of might!

601 Edward Caswall

1. See, amid the winter's snow,
   born for us on earth below,
   see, the tender Lamb appears,
   promised from eternal years.

   Hail, thou ever-blessèd morn,
   hail, redemption's happy dawn!
   Sing through all Jerusalem,
   Christ is born in Bethlehem.

2. Lo, within a manger lies
   he who built the starry skies;
   he, who, throned in heights sublime,
   sits amid the cherubim.

3. Say, ye holy shepherds, say,
   what your joyful news today?
   Wherefore have ye left your sheep
   on the lonely mountain steep?

4. 'As we watched at dead of night,
   lo, we saw a wondrous light;
   angels, singing peace on earth,
   told us of the Saviour's birth.'

5. Sacred infant, all divine,
   what a tender love was thine,
   thus to come from highest bliss,
   down to such a world as this!

6. Virgin mother, Mary, blest,
   by the joys that fill thy breast,
   pray for us, that we may prove
   worthy of the Saviour's love.

602 Brian Foley
© 1971 Faber Music Ltd., from 'New Catholic Hymnal'

1. See, Christ was wounded for our sake,
   and bruised and beaten for our sin,
   so by his suff'rings we are healed,
   for God has laid our guilt on him.

2. Look on his face, come close to him –
   see, you will find no beauty there;
   despised, rejected, who can tell
   the grief and sorrow he must bear?

Continued overleaf

3. Like sheep that stray we leave God's path,
   to choose our own and not his will;
   like lamb to slaughter he has gone,
   obedient to his Father's will.

4. Cast out to die by those he loved,
   reviled by those he died to save,
   see how sin's pride has sought his death,
   see how sin's hate has made his grave.

5. For on his shoulders God has laid
   the weight of sin that we should bear;
   so by his passion we have peace,
   through his obedience and his prayer.

603
Michael Perry
© 1965 Mrs B. Perry/Jubilate Hymns

1. See him lying on a bed of straw:
   a draughty stable with an open door.
   Mary cradling the babe she bore:
   the Prince of Glory is his name.

   O now carry me to Bethlehem
   to see the Lord of Love again:
   just as poor as was the stable then,
   the Prince of Glory when he came!

2. Star of silver, sweep across the skies,
   show where Jesus in the manger lies;
   shepherds, swiftly from your stupor rise
   to see the Saviour of the world!

3. Angels, sing again the song you sang,
   sing the glory of God's gracious plan;
   sing that Bethl'em's little baby can
   be the saviour of us all.

4. Mine are riches, from your poverty;
   from your innocence, eternity;
   mine, forgiveness by your death for me,
   child of sorrow for my joy.

604
v 1 Karen Lafferty, vs 2 and 3 unknown,
based on Matthew 6:33, 7:7
© 1972 Maranatha! Music/CopyCare

1. Seek ye first the kingdom of God,
   and his righteousness,
   and all these things shall be added
       unto you;
   allelu, alleluia.

Alleluia, alleluia,
alleluia, allelu, alleluia.

2. You shall not live by bread alone,
   but by every word
   that proceeds from the mouth of God;
   allelu, alleluia.

3. Ask and it shall be given unto you,
   seek and ye shall find;
   knock, and it shall be opened unto you;
   allelua, alleluia.

605
Michael Forster
© 1993 Kevin Mayhew Ltd.

1. See the holy table,
   spread for our healing;
   hear the invitation
   to share in bread and wine.
   Catch the scent of goodness,
   taste and touch salvation;
   all mortal senses
   tell of love divine!

2. As the bread is broken,
   Christ is remembered;
   as the wine is flowing,
   his passion we recall;
   as redemption's story
   opens up before us,
   hope is triumphant,
   Christ is all in all.

3. Tell again the story,
   wonder of wonders:
   Christ, by grace eternal,
   transforms the simplest food!
   Sign of hope and glory,
   life in all its fullness,
   God's whole creation
   ransomed and renewed!

606

1. See us, Lord, about your altar;
   though so many, we are one;
   many souls by love united
   in the heart of Christ your Son.

2. Hear our prayers, O loving Father,
   hear in them your Son, our Lord;
   hear him speak our love and worship,
   as we sing with one accord.

3. Once were seen the blood and water;
   now he seems but bread and wine;
   then in human form he suffered,
   now his form is but a sign.

4. Wheat and grape contain the meaning;
   food and drink he is to all;
   one in him, we kneel adoring,
   gathered by his loving call.

5. Hear us yet; so much is needful
   in our frail, disordered life;
   stay with us and tend our weakness
   till that day of no more strife.

6. Members of his mystic body,
   now we know our prayer is heard,
   heard by you, because your children
   have received th'eternal Word.

607

See, your Saviour comes. (x2)

1. Desolate cities, desolate homes,
   desolate lives on the streets,
     angry and restless.
   When will you know the things
   that would make for your peace?

2. Father of mercy, hear as we cry
   for all who live in this place;
   show here your glory, come satisfy
   your longing that all should be saved.

3. Where lives are broken, let there be hope,
   where there's division bring peace;
   where there's oppression, judge and reprove,
   and rescue the crushed and the weak.

4. Lord, let your glory dwell in this land,
   in mercy restore us again:
   pour out salvation, grant us your peace,
   and strengthen the things that remain.

608

Send forth, send forth your Spirit, O Lord,
to renew, renew the face of the earth,
send your Spirit to renew the earth.

1. Send the Spirit of wisdom
   and understanding,
   the Spirit of right judgement and courage,
   send the Spirit of knowledge and reverence,
   send your Spirit to renew us all.

2. Send your Spirit upon us
   as helper and guide,
   may he fill us with wonder and awe.
   Seal us, O Lord, with your holy gift,
   send your Spirit to renew our lives.

609

Send forth your Spirit, O Lord,
that the face of the earth be renewed.

1. O my soul, arise and bless the Lord God.
   Say to him: 'My God, how great you are.
   You are clothed with majesty and splendour,
   and light is the garment you wear.'

2. 'You have built your palaces on the waters.
   Like the winds, the angels do your word,
   you have set the earth on its foundations,
   so firm, to be shaken no more.'

Continued overleaf

3. 'All your creatures look to you for comfort;
   from your open hand they have their fill,
   you send forth your Spirit and revive them,
   the face of the earth you renew.'

4. While I live, I sing the Lord God's praises;
   I will thank the author of these marvels.
   Praise to God, the Father, Son and Spirit
   both now and for ever. Amen.

610 Michael Forster, based on Psalm 104
© 1997 Kevin Mayhew Ltd.

Send forth your Spirit, Lord,
renew the face of the earth. (Repeat)

1. Bless the Lord, O my soul,
   O Lord God, how great you are;
   you are clothed in honour and glory,
   you set the world on its foundations.

2. Lord, how great are your works,
   in wisdom you made them all;
   all the earth is full of your creatures,
   your hand always open to feed them.

3. May your wisdom endure,
   rejoice in your works, O Lord.
   I will sing for ever and ever,
   in praise of my God and my King.

611 Traditional South African, collected and translated by
Anders Nyberg. © 1990 WGRG, Iona Community.
From 'Freedom is coming' (Wild Goose Publications 1990)

1. Send me, Lord.

   Send me, Jesus. Send me, Jesus.
   Send me, Jesus. Send me, Lord.

1. Lead me, Lord.

   Lead me, Jesus . . .

1. Fill me, Lord.

   Fill me, Jesus . . .

   or

   Thuma mina.

   Thuma mina, thuma mina,
   thuma mina, Somandla. Thuma dla.

612 Sandra Joan Billington
© 1976 Kevin Mayhew Ltd.

Shalom, my friend, shalom,
my friend, shalom, shalom.
The peace of Christ I give you today,
shalom, shalom.

613 John L. Bell and Graham Maule
© 1988 WGRG, Iona Community. From 'Enemy of
Apathy' (Wild Goose Publications 1988)

1. She sits like a bird,
   brooding on the waters,
   hov'ring on the chaos
   of the world's first day;
   she sighs and she sings,
   mothering creation,
   waiting to give birth
   to all the Word will say.

2. She wings over earth,
   resting where she wishes,
   lighting close at hand
   or soaring through the skies;
   she nests in the womb,
   welcoming each wonder,
   nourishing potential
   hidden to our eyes.

3. She dances in fire,
   startling her spectators,
   walking tongues of ecstasy
   where dumbness reigned;
   she weans and inspires
   all whose hearts are open,
   nor can she be captured,
   silenced or restrained.

4. For she is the Spirit,
   one with God in essence,
   gifted by the Saviour
   in eternal love;
   she is the key
   opening the scriptures,
   enemy of apathy
   and heav'nly dove.

614
Joseph Mohr, trans. John Freeman Young

1. Silent night, holy night.
   All is calm, all is bright,
   round yon virgin mother and child;
   holy infant, so tender and mild,
   sleep in heavenly peace,
   sleep in heavenly peace.

2. Silent night, holy night.
   Shepherds quake at the sight,
   glories stream from heaven afar,
   heav'nly hosts sing alleluia:
   Christ, the Saviour is born,
   Christ, the Saviour is born.

3. Silent night, holy night.
   Son of God, love's pure light,
   radiant beams from thy holy face,
   with the dawn of redeeming grace:
   Jesus, Lord, at thy birth,
   Jesus, Lord, at thy birth.

615
James Quinn, based on Psalm 99
© 1969 Geoffrey Chapman, an imprint of Cassell plc

1. Sing, all creation,
   sing to God in gladness!
   Joyously serve him,
   singing hymns of homage!
   Chanting his praises,
   come before his presence!
   Praise the Almighty.

2. Know that our God
   is Lord of all the ages!
   He is our maker;
   we are all his creatures,
   people he fashioned,
   sheep he leads to pasture!
   Praise the Almighty!

3. Enter his Temple,
   ringing out his praises!
   Sing in thanksgiving
   as you come before him!
   Blessing his bounty,
   glorify his greatness!
   Praise the Almighty!

4. Great in his goodness
   is the Lord we worship;
   steadfast his kindness,
   love that knows no ending!
   Faithful his word is,
   changeless, everlasting!
   Praise the Almighty!

616
Dan Schutte, based on Psalm 97
© 1972, 1974, Daniel L. Schutte/New Dawn Music

Sing a new song unto the Lord,
let your song be sung from mountains high.
Sing a new song unto the Lord,
singing alleluia.

1. All God's people dance for joy,
   O come before the Lord,
   and play for him on glad tambourines,
   and let your trumpet sound.

2. Rise, O children, from your sleep,
   your Saviour now has come,
   and he has turned your sorrow to joy,
   and filled your soul with song.

3. Glad my soul, for I have seen
   the glory of the Lord.
   The trumpet sounds, the dead shall
     be raised.
   I know my Saviour lives.

617
Linda Stassen
© 1974 Linda Stassen/New Song Creations

Sing hallelujah to the Lord.
Sing hallelujah to the Lord.
Sing hallelujah, sing hallelujah,
sing hallelujah to the Lord.

618
Michael Forster
© 1997 Kevin Mayhew Ltd.

Sing, holy mother, bringing hope to birth,
with the poor and humble
sing of human worth.

1. Blessed are you among women,
full of mysterious grace;
holding the hopes of creation
in your maternal embrace.

2. Stand with the lost and the lonely,
those whom the vain world denies,
join with the weak and the foolish,
humbling the strong and the wise!

3. Sing of the values of heaven,
shame our respectable pride!
Sing to the spurned and the fearful,
tell them no longer to hide!

619
Mike Anderson
© 1999 Kevin Mayhew Ltd.

Sing it in the valleys,
shout it from the mountain tops,
Jesus came to save us,
and his saving never stops.
He is King of kings,
and new life he brings,
sing it in the valleys,
shout it from the mountain tops,
Oh, shout it from the mountain tops.

1. Jesus, you are by my side,
you take all my fears.
If I only come to you,
you will heal the pain of years.

2. You have not deserted me,
though I go astray.
Jesus, take me in your arms,
help me walk with you today.

3. Jesus, you are living now,
Jesus, I believe.
Jesus, take me, heart and soul,
yours alone I want to be.

620
Michael Cockett
© 1976 Kevin Mayhew Ltd.

Sing, my soul. Sing, my soul.
Sing, my soul of his mercy. (Repeat)

1. The Lord is good to me.
His light will shine on me.
When city lights would blind my eyes.
He hears my silent call.
His hands help when I fall.
His gentle voice stills my sighs.

2. The Lord is good to me.
His word will set me free
when men would tie me to the ground.
He mocks my foolish ways
with love that never fails.
When I'm most lost then I'm found.

3. The Lord is good to me.
I hear him speak to me.
His voice is in the rain that falls.
He whispers in the air
of his unending care.
If I will hear, then he calls.

621
Venantius Fortunatus, trans. from 'The Three Days'

1. Sing, my tongue, the song of triumph,
tell the story far and wide;
tell of dread and final battle,
sing of Saviour crucified;
how upon the cross a victim
vanquishing in death he died.

2. He endured the nails, the spitting,
vinegar and spear and reed;
from that holy body broken
blood and water forth proceed;
earth and stars and sky and ocean
by that flood from stain are freed.

3. Faithful Cross, above all other,
one and only noble tree,
none in foliage, none in blossom,
none in fruit your peer may be;
sweet the wood and sweet the iron
and your load, most sweet is he.

4. Bend your boughs, O Tree of glory!
all your rigid branches, bend!
For a while the ancient temper
that your birth bestowed, suspend;
and the King of earth and heaven
gently on your bosom tend.

622 Anonymous

1. Sing of Mary, pure and lowly,
virgin mother undefiled.
Sing of God's own Son most holy,
who became her little child.
Fairest child of fairest mother,
God, the Lord, who came to earth,
Word made flesh, our very brother,
takes our nature by his birth.

2. Sing of Jesus, son of Mary,
in the home of Nazareth.
Toil and labour cannot weary
love enduring unto death.
Constant was the love he gave her,
though he went forth from her side,
forth to preach and heal and suffer,
till on Calvary he died.

3. Glory be to God the Father,
glory be to God the Son,
glory be to God the Spirit,
glory to the Three in One.
From the heart of blessèd Mary,
from all saints the song ascends,
and the Church the strain re-echoes
unto earth's remotest ends.

623 Sebastian Temple
© 1971 OCP Publications

1. Sing praises to the living God,
glory, alleluia.
Come, adore the living God,
glory, alleluia.

Though sun and moon may pass away
his words will ever stay.
His power is for evermore,
glory, alleluia.
Glory to the Trinity,
The undivided Unity,
the Father, Son and Spirit one,
from whom all life and greatness come.

2. And to the living God we sing,
glory, alleluia.
Let our love and praises ring,
glory, alleluia.
To all of us he always gives
his mercy and his love.
So praise him now for evermore,
glory, alleluia.

3. And to the God who cannot die,
glory, alleluia.
To the living God we cry,
glory, alleluia.
He promised to be with us and
he lives in ev'ryone.
We love him now for evermore,
glory, alleluia.

624 Michael Forster
© 1993 Kevin Mayhew Ltd.

1. Sing the gospel of salvation,
tell it out to all the earth;
to the ones so long excluded,
speak of hope and human worth.
All the darkness of injustice
cannot dim salvation's light,
for the outcast and exploited
count as worthy in God's sight.

2. Christ, the one eternal Shepherd,
calls creation to rejoice,
and the victims of oppression
thrill to hear salvation's voice.
All who recognise the Saviour
take their place within the fold,
there, in perfect truth and freedom,
life's eternal joys to hold.

Continued overleaf

3. See, the host that none can number
gathers in from ev'ry side,
once the victims of injustice,
now redeemed and glorified.
Fear and weeping here are ended,
hunger and oppression cease.
Now the Lamb becomes the Shepherd!
Now begins the reign of peace!

625 John Foley, based on Psalm 96
© 1970, 1974 John B. Foley, S.J. and New Dawn Music

Sing to the Lord, alleluia,
sing to the Lord.

1. Bless his name, announce his salvation,
day after day, alleluia.

2. Give to him, you fam'lies of peoples,
glory and praise, alleluia.

3. Great is he and worthy of praises,
day after day, alleluia.

4. He it is who gave us the heavens,
glory to God, alleluia.

5. Tell his glories, tell all the nations,
day after day, alleluia.

6. Bring your gifts and enter his temple
worship the Lord, alleluia.

626 Bob Dufford, based on Psalm 117
© 1975 Robert J. Dufford and New Dawn Music

Sing to the mountains, sing to the sea,
raise your voices, lift your hearts.
This is the day the Lord has made,
let all the earth rejoice.

1. I will give thanks to you, my Lord,
you have answered my plea;
you have saved my soul from death,
you are my strength and my song.

2. Holy, holy, holy Lord,
heaven and earth are full of your glory.

3. This is the day that the Lord has made,
let us be glad and rejoice.
He has turned all death to life,
sing of the glory of God.

627 Edward Caswall

1. Sleep, holy babe,
upon thy mother's breast;
great Lord of earth and sea and sky,
how sweet it is to see thee lie
in such a place of rest.

2. Sleep, holy babe,
thine angels watch around,
all bending low, with folded wings,
before th'incarnate King of kings,
in reverent awe profound.

3. Sleep, holy babe,
while I with Mary gaze
in joy upon thy face awhile,
upon the loving infant smile,
which there divinely plays.

4. Sleep, holy babe,
ah, take thy brief repose;
too quickly will thy slumbers break,
and thou to lengthened pains awake,
that death alone shall close.

5. O lady blest,
sweet virgin, hear my cry;
forgive the wrong that I have done
to thee, in causing thy dear Son
upon the cross to die.

628 Ascribed to John XXII, trans. unknown

1. Soul of my Saviour,
sanctify my breast;
Body of Christ,
be thou my saving guest;
Blood of my Saviour,
bathe me in thy tide,
wash me with water
flowing from thy side.

2. Strength and protection
   may thy passion be;
   O blessèd Jesus,
   hear and answer me;
   deep in thy wounds, Lord,
   hide and shelter me;
   so shall I never,
   never part from thee.

3. Guard and defend me
   from the foe malign;
   in death's dread moments
   make me only thine;
   call me, and bid me
   come to thee on high,
   when I may praise thee
   with thy saints for aye.

629
Noel Donnelly
© Noel Donnelly

1. Spirit hov'ring o'er the waters,
   when the world from chaos began,
   living Spirit, re-create us!
   Come, restore our hearts with life.

   Veni, veni, Sancte Spiritus.

2. Spirit speaking through the prophets
   when they cried for justice and peace,
   living Spirit, come renew us,
   fill the earth with peace and love.

3. Spirit hov'ring o'er the virgin,
   Word and flesh are mothered in her,
   living Spirit, breath of Yahweh,
   bring the Word to life in us.

4. Spirit breathed on John and Mary
   as they stood here under the cross,
   living Spirit, strengthen, comfort,
   guide, unite your church today.

5. Spirit hov'ring o'er apostles,
   wind and fire of Pentecost Day,
   living Spirit, now confirm us,
   come inspire us, come, we pray.

630
Daniel Iverson. © 1963 Birdwing Music/EMI
Christian Music Publishing. Administered by CopyCare

1. Spirit of the living God, fall afresh on me.
   Spirit of the living God, fall afresh on me.
   Melt me, mould me, fill me, use me.
   Spirit of the living God, fall afresh on me.

2. Spirit of the living God, fall afresh on us.
   Spirit of the living God, fall afresh on us.
   Melt us, mould us, fill us, use us.
   Spirit of the living God, fall afresh on us.

*When appropriate a third verse may be added,
singing 'on them', for example, before
Confirmation, or at a service for the sick.*

631
Noel Donnelly, based on the Roman Missal
© 1986 Kevin Mayhew Ltd.

*Springs of water, bless the Lord!
Praise be God for evermore!*

1. With this gift of water, Lord,
   you have given us a sign,
   our baptismal sacrament.

2. At the wat'ry dawn of all,
   order out of chaos came,
   when your Spirit hovered there.

3. With the waters of the flood
   you renewed baptismal sign.
   Sin gave way to spring of life.

4. Through the waters of the sea
   you led Israel, set her free,
   image of your baptised Church.

5. In the Jordan waters, John
   saw your Son baptised and sealed
   with your Spirit resting there.

6. Blood and water from his side,
   symbols of his life outpoured,
   as he hung upon the cross.

7. Then the risen Lord proclaimed:
   'Go and teach, baptising all.
   I will always be with you!'

632

'Ave Maris Stella', 9th century, trans. Ralph Wright
© Ralph Wright, OSB

1. Star of sea and ocean,
   gateway to God's haven,
   mother of our Maker,
   hear our pray'r, O Maiden.

2. Welcoming the Ave
   of God's simple greeting,
   you have borne a Saviour,
   far beyond all dreaming.

3. Loose the bonds that hold us
   bound in sin's own blindness
   that with eyes now opened
   God's own light may guide us.

4. Show yourself our mother;
   he will hear your pleading
   whom your womb has sheltered
   and whose hand brings healing.

5. Gentlest of all virgins,
   that our love be faithful
   keep us from all evil
   gentle, strong and grateful.

6. Guard us through life's dangers,
   never turn and leave us.
   May our hope find harbour
   in the calm of Jesus.

7. Sing to God our Father
   through the Son who saves us,
   joyful in the Spirit,
   everlasting praises.

633 Spiritual

Steal away, steal away,
steal away to Jesus.
Steal away, steal away home.
I ain't got long to stay here.

1. My Lord, he calls me,
   he calls me by the thunder.
   The trumpet sounds within my soul;
   I ain't got long to stay here.

2. Green trees are bending,
   the sinner stands a-trembling.
   The trumpet sounds within my soul;
   I ain't got long to stay here.

3. My Lord, he calls me,
   he calls me by the lightning.
   The trumpet sounds within my soul;
   I ain't got long to stay here.

634 Sister Marie Josephine

1. Sweet heart of Jesus,
   fount of love and mercy,
   today we come,
   thy blessing to implore;
   O touch our hearts,
   so cold and so ungrateful,
   and make them, Lord,
   thine own for evermore.

   Sweet heart of Jesus, we implore,
   O make us love thee more and more.

2. Sweet heart of Jesus,
   make us know and love thee,
   unfold to us
   the treasures of thy grace;
   that so our hearts,
   from things of earth uplifted,
   may long alone
   to gaze upon thy face.

3. Sweet heart of Jesus,
   make us pure and gentle,
   and teach us how
   to do thy blessèd will;
   to follow close
   the print of thy dear footsteps,
   and when we fall
   – sweet heart, O love us still.

4. Sweet heart of Jesus,
   bless all hearts that love thee,
   and may thine own heart
   ever blessèd be;

bless us, dear Lord,
and bless the friends we cherish,
and keep us true
to Mary and to thee.

635 Francis Stanfield

1. Sweet sacrament divine,
hid in thy earthly home,
lo, round thy lowly shrine,
with suppliant hearts we come;
Jesus, to thee our voice we raise,
in songs of love and heartfelt praise,
sweet sacrament divine,
sweet sacrament divine.

2. Sweet sacrament of peace,
dear home of ev'ry heart,
where restless yearnings cease,
and sorrows all depart,
there in thine ear all trustfully
we tell our tale of misery,
sweet sacrament of peace,
sweet sacrament of peace.

3. Sweet sacrament of rest,
Ark from the ocean's roar,
within thy shelter blest
soon may we reach the shore;
save us, for still the tempest raves,
save, lest we sink beneath the waves,
sweet sacrament of rest,
sweet sacrament of rest.

4. Sweet sacrament divine,
earth's light and jubilee,
in thy far depths doth shine
thy Godhead's majesty;
sweet light, so shine on us, we pray,
that earthly joys may fade away,
sweet sacrament divine,
sweet sacrament divine.

636 Frederick William Faber

1. Sweet Saviour, bless us ere we go,
thy word into our minds instil;
and make our lukewarm hearts to glow
with lowly love and fervent will.

Through life's long day
and death's dark night,
O gentle Jesus, be our light.

2. The day is done; its hours have run,
and thou hast taken count of all
the scanty triumphs grace has won,
the broken vow, the frequent fall.

3. Grant us, dear Lord, from evil ways,
true absolution and release;
and bless us more than in past days
with purity and inward peace.

4. Do more than pardon; give us joy,
sweet fear and sober liberty,
and loving hearts without alloy,
that only long to be like thee.

5. Labour is sweet, for thou hast toiled,
and care is light, for thou hast cared;
let not our works with self be soiled,
nor in unsimple ways ensnared.

6. For all we love – the poor, the sad,
the sinful – unto thee we call;
O let thy mercy make us glad,
thou art our Jesus and our all.

637 Christine McCann
© 1999 Kevin Mayhew Ltd.

Take and bless our gifts, (x3)
take and bless them, Lord. (Repeat)

1. Blessed are you, Lord, God of all creation.
Through your goodness
we offer you this bread,
which earth has giv'n
and human hands have made.
It will become for us the bread of life.

2. Blessed are you, Lord, God of all creation.
Through your goodness
we offer you this wine,
fruit of the vine
and work of human hands.
It will become for us the wine of life.

Continued overleaf

3. Blessed are you, Lord, God of all creation.
Through your goodness
we offer you our lives.
Accept, make holy
all we try to do,
offered in praise and glory of your name.

638 Francesca Leftley
© 1984 Kevin Mayhew Ltd.

1. Take me, Lord, use my life
in the way you wish to do.
Fill me, Lord, touch my heart
till it always thinks of you.
Take me now, as I am,
this is all I can offer.

Here today I, the clay,
will be moulded by my Lord.

2. Lord, I pray that each day
I will listen to your will.
Many times I have failed
but I know you love me still.
Teach me now, guide me,
Lord, keep me close to you always.

3. I am weak, fill me now
with your strength and set me free.
Make me whole, fashion me
so that you will live in me.
Hold me now in your hands,
form me now with your Spirit.

639 Sebastian Temple
© 1967 OCP Publications

1. Take my hands
and make them as your own,
and use them for your kingdom
here on earth.
consecrate them to your care,
anoint them for your service where
you may need your gospel to be sown.

2. Take my hands,
they speak now for my heart,
and by their actions
they will show their love.

Guard them on their daily course,
be their strength and guiding force
to ever serve the Trinity above.

3. Take my hands,
I give them to you, Lord.
Prepare them for
the service of your name.
Open them to human need
and by their love they'll sow your seed
so all may know the love and hope you give.

640 v 1 and 3 Margaret Rizza, v 2 unknown
© 1998 Kevin Mayhew Ltd.

1. Take my hands, Lord,
to share in your labours,
take my eyes, Lord, to see your needs,
let me hear the voice of lonely people,
let my love, Lord, bring riches to the poor.

2. Give me someone to feed
when I'm hungry,
when I'm thirsty give water for their thirst.
When I stand in need of tenderness,
give me someone to hold who longs
for love.

3. Keep my heart
ever open to others,
may my time, Lord, be spent with those
in need;
may I tend to those who need your care.
Take my life, Lord, and make it
truly yours.

641 Joe Wise
© 1966 GIA Publications Inc.

Take our bread, we ask you,
take our hearts, we love you,
take our lives, O Father,
we are yours, we are yours.

1. Yours as we stand at the table you set,
yours as we eat the bread
our hearts can't forget.
We are the signs of your life with us yet;
we are yours, we are yours.

2. Your holy people stand washed in
   your blood,
   Spirit-filled, yet hungry,
   we await your food.
   Poor though we are, we have brought
   ourselves to you:
   we are yours, we are yours.

642
Aniceto Nazareth, based on Scripture
© 1984 Kevin Mayhew Ltd.

Take this and eat it, for this is my body.
Take this and drink it, for this is my blood.

1. Taste and see that the Lord is
   all goodness.
   Happy those who take refuge in him.

2. 'Come to me, you who are heavy laden;
   take my yoke, for my burden is light.'

3. When you eat and you drink at
   this table,
   Jesus' death you proclaim, till he comes.

4. Eat, you poor, and be filled, you afflicted.
   Those who seek him, give praise to
   the Lord.

5. Come, be filled as you sit at my table;
   quench your thirst as you drink of
   my wine.

6. You who eat, break your bread with
   the hungry;
   you who drink of his Spirit, give praise.

7. Beautiful is the place of your dwelling;
   how my soul longs for you, O my God.

8. See how good and delightful that brethren
   share this meal to bring true unity.

9. You commanded the heavens to open,
   raining manna upon Israel.

10. This, indeed, is the bread come
    from heaven;
    those who eat it will never know death.

643
Hubert J. Richards, based on Psalm 33
© 1996 Kevin Mayhew Ltd.

Taste and see the goodness of the Lord,
the goodness of the Lord.

1. I sing God's praises all my days,
   his name is always on my lips;
   he is my one and only boast,
   the pride and joy of all the poor.

2. So come with me to sing his praise,
   together let us praise his name.
   I seek the Lord, he answers me,
   rescues me from all my fears.

3. The Lord is quick to heed the poor
   and liberate them from their chains.
   The Lord is close to broken hearts,
   he rescues slaves and sets them free.

644
Timothy Dudley-Smith, based on Luke 1:46-55
© 1961 Timothy Dudley-Smith. From 'Enlarged Songs
of Praise'

1. Tell out, my soul, the greatness of the Lord:
   unnumbered blessings, give my
   spirit voice;
   tender to me the promise of his word;
   in God my Saviour shall my heart rejoice.

2. Tell out, my soul, the greatness of
   his name:
   make known his might, the deeds his
   arm has done;
   his mercy sure, from age to age the same;
   his holy name, the Lord, the mighty one.

3. Tell out, my soul, the greatness of
   his might:
   pow'rs and dominions lay their glory by;
   proud hearts and stubborn wills are put
   to flight,
   the hungry fed, the humble lifted high.

4. Tell out, my soul, the glories of his word:
   firm is his promise, and his mercy sure.
   Tell out, my soul, the greatness of
   the Lord
   to children's children and for evermore.

645
Jean Holloway
© 1994 Kevin Mayhew Ltd.

Thanks for the fellowship found at this meal,
thanks for a day refreshed;
thanks to the Lord for his presence we feel,
thanks for the food he blessed.
Joyfully sing praise to the Lord,
praise to the risen Son,
alleluia, ever adored,
pray that his will be done.
As he was known in the breaking of bread,
now is he known again,
and by his hand have the hungry been fed,
thanks be to Christ. Amen!

646
Sabine Baring-Gould

1. The angel Gabriel from heaven came,
   his wings as drifted snow, his eyes
       as flame.
   'All hail,' said he,
   'thou lowly maiden, Mary,
   most highly favoured lady.' Gloria!

2. 'For known a blessèd Mother thou
       shalt be.
   All generations laud and honour thee.
   Thy Son shall be Emmanuel,
   by seers foretold,
   most highly favoured lady.' Gloria!

3. Then gentle Mary meekly bowed
       her head.
   'To me be as it pleaseth God,' she said.
   'My soul shall laud and magnify
   his holy name.'
   Most highly favoured lady! Gloria!

4. Of her, Emmanuel, the Christ, was born
   in Bethlehem, all on a Christmas morn;
   and Christian folk throughout
   the world will ever say:
   'Most highly favoured lady.' Gloria!

647
Samuel John Stone

1. The Church's one foundation
   is Jesus Christ, her Lord;
   she is his new creation,
   by water and the word;
   from heav'n he came and sought her
   to be his holy bride,
   with his own blood he bought her,
   and for her life he died.

2. Elect from ev'ry nation,
   yet one o'er all the earth,
   her charter of salvation,
   one Lord, one faith, one birth;
   one holy name she blesses,
   partakes one holy food,
   and to one hope she presses,
   with ev'ry grace endued.

3. 'Mid toil and tribulation,
   and tumult of her war,
   she waits the consummation
   of peace for evermore;
   till with the vision glorious
   her longing eyes are blest,
   and the great Church victorious
   shall be the Church at rest.

4. Yet she on earth hath union
   with God the Three in One,
   and mystic sweet communion
   with those whose rest is won:
   O happy ones and holy! Lord,
   give us grace that we
   like them, the meek and lowly,
   on high may dwell with thee.

648
Charles Coffin, trans. Robert Campbell and others

1. The coming of our God
   our thoughts must now employ;
   then let us meet him on the road
   with songs of holy joy.

2. The co-eternal Son,
   a maiden's offspring see;
   a servant's form Christ putteth on,
   to set his people free.

3. Daughter of Zion, rise
   to greet thine infant king,
   nor let thy stubborn heart despise
   the pardon he doth bring.

4. In glory from his throne
   again will Christ descend,
   and summon all that are his own
   to joys that never end.

5. Let deeds of darkness fly
   before th'approaching morn,
   for unto sin 'tis ours to die,
   and serve the virgin-born.

6. Our joyful praises sing
   to Christ, that set us free;
   like tribute to the Father bring
   and, Holy Ghost, to thee.

649 St John of Damascus, trans. John Mason Neale

1. The day of resurrection!
   Earth, tell it out abroad;
   the passover of gladness,
   the passover of God!
   From death to life eternal,
   from earth unto the sky,
   our Christ hath brought us over
   with hymns of victory.

2. Our hearts be pure from evil,
   that we may see aright
   the Lord in rays eternal
   of resurrection-light;
   and list'ning to his accents,
   may hear so calm and plain
   his own 'All hail' and, hearing,
   may raise the victor strain.

3. Now let the heav'ns be joyful,
   and earth her song begin,
   the round world keep high triumph,
   and all that is therein;
   let all things, seen and unseen,
   their notes of gladness blend,
   for Christ the Lord hath risen,
   our joy that hath no end.

650 John Ellerton

1. The day thou gavest, Lord, is ended:
   the darkness falls at thy behest;
   to thee our morning hymns ascended;
   thy praise shall sanctify our rest.

2. We thank thee that thy Church unsleeping,
   while earth rolls onward into light,
   through all the world her watch
       is keeping,
   and rests not now by day or night.

3. As o'er each continent and island
   the dawn leads on another day,
   the voice of prayer is never silent,
   nor dies the strain of praise away.

4. The sun that bids us rest is waking
   our brethren 'neath the western sky,
   and hour by hour fresh lips are making
   thy wondrous doings heard on high.

5. So be it, Lord; thy throne shall never,
   like earth's proud empires, pass away;
   thy kingdom stands, and grows for ever,
   till all thy creatures own thy sway.

651 From William Sandys' 'Christmas Carols, Ancient and Modern', alt.

1. The first Nowell the angel did say
   was to certain poor shepherds in fields as
       they lay:
   in fields where they lay keeping their sheep,
   on a cold winter's night that was so deep.

Continued overleaf

Nowell, Nowell, Nowell, Nowell,
born is the King of Israel!

2. They lookèd up and saw a star,
   shining in the east, beyond them far,
   and to the earth it gave great light,
   and so it continued both day and night.

3. And by the light of that same star,
   three wise men came from country far;
   to seek for a king was their intent,
   and to follow the star wherever it went.

4. This star drew nigh to the north-west,
   o'er Bethlehem it took its rest,
   and there it did both stop and stay
   right over the place where Jesus lay.

5. Then entered in those wise men three,
   full rev'rently upon their knee,
   and offered there in his presence,
   their gold and myrrh and frankincense.

6. Then let us all with one accord
   sing praises to our heav'nly Lord,
   who with the Father we adore
   and Spirit blest for evermore.

652 Thomas Kelly

1. The head that once was crowned
      with thorns
   is crowned with glory now:
   a royal diadem adorns
   the mighty victor's brow.

2. The highest place that heav'n affords
   is his, is his by right.
   The King of kings and Lord of lords,
   and heav'ns eternal light.

3. The joy of all who dwell above,
   the joy of all below,
   to whom he manifests his love,
   and grants his name to know.

4. To them the cross, with all its shame,
   with all its grace is giv'n;
   their name an everlasting name,
   their joy the joy of heav'n.

5. They suffer with their Lord below,
   they reign with him above,
   their profit and their joy to know
   the myst'ry of his love.

6. The cross he bore is life and health,
   though shame and death to him;
   his people's hope, his people's wealth,
   their everlasting theme.

653 Traditional

1. The holly and the ivy,
   when they are both full grown,
   of all the trees that are in the wood
   the holly bears the crown.

   The rising of the sun
   and the running of the deer,
   the playing of the merry organ,
   sweet singing in the choir.

2. The holly bears a blossom,
   white as the lily flower,
   and Mary bore sweet Jesus Christ
   to be our sweet Saviour.

3. The holly bears a berry,
   as red as any blood,
   and Mary bore sweet Jesus Christ
   to do poor sinners good.

4. The holly bears a prickle,
   as sharp as any thorn,
   and Mary bore sweet Jesus Christ
   on Christmas day in the morn.

5. The holly bears a bark,
   as bitter as any gall,
   and Mary bore sweet Jesus Christ
   to redeem us all.

6. The holly and the ivy,
   when they are both full grown,
   of all the trees that are in the wood
   the holly bears the crown.

654
Mike Anderson, based on Matthew 5:3-10
© 1999 Kevin Mayhew Ltd.

The kingdom of heaven,
the kingdom of heaven is yours.
A new world in Jesus
a new world in Jesus is yours.

1. Blessed are you in sorrow and grief,
   for you shall all be consoled;
   blessed are you, the gentle of heart,
   you shall inherit the earth.

2. Blessed are you who hunger for right,
   for you shall be satisfied;
   blessed are you the merciful ones,
   for you shall be pardoned too.

3. Blessed are you whose hearts are pure,
   your eyes shall gaze on the Lord;
   blessed are you who strive after peace,
   the Lord will call you his own.

4. Blessed are you who suffer for right,
   the heav'nly kingdom is yours;
   blessed are you who suffer for me,
   for you shall reap your reward.

655
Willard F. Jabusch
© 1998 Willard F. Jabusch

The King of glory comes,
the nation rejoices,
open the gates before him,
lift up your voices.

1. Who is the King of glory,
   how shall we call him?
   He is Emmanuel,
   the promised of ages.

2. In all of Galilee,
   in city and village,
   he goes among his people,
   curing their illness.

3. Sing then of David's Son,
   our Saviour and brother;
   in all of Galilee
   was never another.

4. He gave his life for us,
   the pledge of salvation.
   He took upon himself
   the sins of the nation.

5. He conquered sin and death;
   he truly has risen;
   and he will share with us
   his heavenly vision.

656
Henry Williams Baker, based on Psalm 22

1. The King of love my shepherd is,
   whose goodness faileth never;
   I nothing lack if I am his
   and he is mine for ever.

2. Where streams of living water flow
   my ransomed soul he leadeth,
   and where the verdant pastures grow
   with food celestial feedeth.

3. Perverse and foolish oft I strayed,
   but yet in love he sought me,
   and on his shoulder gently laid,
   and home, rejoicing, brought me.

4. In death's dark vale I fear no ill
   with thee, dear Lord, beside me;
   thy rod and staff my comfort still,
   thy cross before to guide me.

5. Thou spread'st a table in my sight,
   thy unction grace bestoweth:
   and O what transport of delight
   from thy pure chalice floweth!

Continued overleaf

6. And so through all the length of days
   thy goodness faileth never;
   good Shepherd, may I sing thy praise
   within thy house for ever.

657

Donald Fishel
© 1973 The Word of God Music/CopyCare

*The light of Christ
has come into he world.* (Repeat)

1. We must all be born again
   to see the kingdom of God.
   The water and the Spirit bring
   new life in God's love.

2. God gave up his only Son
   out of love for the world,
   so that all who believe in him
   will live for ever.

3. The light of God has come to us
   so that we might have salvation;
   from the darkness of our sins we walk
   into glory with Christ Jesus.

658

John Foley, based on Psalm 33
© 1978, 1991, John B. Foley, SJ, and New Dawn Music.

*The Lord hears the cry of the poor.
Blessed be the Lord.*

1. I will bless the Lord at all times,
   his praise ever in my mouth.
   Let my soul glory in the Lord,
   for he hears the cry of the poor.

2. Let the lowly hear and be glad:
   the Lord listens to their pleas;
   and to hearts broken he is near,
   for he hears the cry of the poor.

3. Ev'ry spirit crushed he will save;
   will be ransom for their lives;
   will be safe shelter for their fears,
   for he hears the cry of the poor.

4. We proclaim the greatness of God,
   his praise ever in our mouth;
   ev'ry face brightened in his light,
   for he hears the cry of the poor.

659

Jean-Paul Lécot, trans. W. R. Lawrence
© 1988 Kevin Mayhew Ltd.

1. The Lord is alive! Alleluia!
   He dwells in our midst! Alleluia!
   Give praise to his name
   throughout all the world!
   Alleluia! Alleluia!

2. He brings us great joy! Alleluia!
   He fills us with hope! Alleluia!
   He comes as our food,
   he gives us our life!
   Alleluia! Alleluia!

3. So let us rejoice! Alleluia!
   Give praise to the Lord! Alleluia!
   He showed us his love,
   by him we are saved!
   Alleluia! Alleluia!

4. The Lord is alive! Alleluia!
   So let us proclaim, alleluia,
   the Good News of Christ
   throughout all the world!
   Alleluia! Alleluia!

5. Christ Jesus has died! Alleluia!
   Christ Jesus is ris'n! Alleluia!
   Christ Jesus will come
   again as the Lord!
   Alleluia! Alleluia!

6. Sing praises to God, alleluia,
   who reigns without end! Alleluia!
   The Father, the Son,
   and Spirit – all One!
   Alleluia! Alleluia!

660

Michael Joncas, based on Psalm 27
© GIA Publications Inc.

The Lord is my life, the Lord is my strength,
the Lord is my light and my salvation.
The Lord is my hope, the Lord is my song,
the Lord is my light and my salvation.

1. The Lord is my light and my salvation;
   whom shall I fear?
   The Lord is the refuge of my life;
   of whom should I be afraid?

2. One thing I ask of the Lord,
   only one thing I seek:
   to live in the presence of the Lord,
   to dwell in the house of my God.

3. I believe I shall see the Lord's goodness
   in the land where the living dwell.
   Wait for the Lord and be brave;
   yes, wait for the living God!

661

Psalm 22 from 'The Scottish Psalter'

1. The Lord's my shepherd, I'll not want.
   He makes me down to lie
   in pastures green.
   He leadeth me the quiet waters by.

2. My soul he doth restore again,
   and me to walk doth make
   within the paths of righteousness,
   e'en for his own name's sake.

3. Yea, though I walk in death's dark vale,
   yet will I fear no ill.
   For thou art with me, and thy rod
   and staff me comfort still.

4. My table thou hast furnishèd
   in presence of my foes,
   my head thou dost with oil anoint,
   and my cup overflows.

5. Goodness and mercy all my life
   shall surely follow me.
   And in God's house for evermore
   my dwelling-place shall be.

662

Carey Landry. © 1971 Carey Landry and North
American Liturgy Resources (NALR)

1. The love I have for you, my Lord,
   is only a shadow of your love for me;
   only a shadow of your love for me;
   your deep abiding love.

2. My own belief in you, my Lord,
   is only a shadow of your faith in me;
   only a shadow of your faith in me;
   your deep and lasting faith.

3. My life is in your hands;
   my life is in your hands.
   My love for you will grow, my God.
   Your light in me will shine.

4. The dream I have today, my Lord,
   is only a shadow of your dreams for me;
   only a shadow of all that will be;
   if I but follow you.

5. The joy I feel today, my Lord,
   is only a shadow of your joys for me;
   only a shadow of your joys for me;
   when we meet face to face.

6. *Repeat verse 3*

663

Sebastian Temple, alt.
© 1967 OCP Publications

1. The Mass is ended, all go in peace.
   We must diminish, and Christ increase.
   We take him with us where-e'er we go,
   that through our actions
   his life may show.

2. We witness his love to ev'ryone
   by our communion with Christ the Son.
   We take the Mass to where people are
   that Christ may shine forth,
   their Morning Star.

Continued overleaf

3. Thanks to the Father who shows the way.
His life within us throughout each day.
Let all our living and loving be
to praise and honour
the Trinity.

4. *Repeat verse 1*

664
John Ylvisaker
© 1991 John C. Ylvisaker

1. The night was dark and filled
    with gloom.
(Come and see. Come and see.)
They hid within a secret room.
(Come and see. Come and see.)
Now Thomas had not seen the Lord,
(Come and see. Come and see.)
he doubted ev'ry single word.
(Come and see. Come and see.)

I believe this is Jesus.
(Come and see. Come and see.)
Oh, I believe this is Jesus.
(Come and see. Come and see.)

2. Then suddenly the Lord appeared
(Come and see. Come and see.)
to see his friends and calm their fears.
(Come and see. Come and see.)
'Now Thomas,' he said, 'see my hand,'
(Come and see. Come and see.)
'it happened just as God had planned.'

3. 'Well,' Thomas said, 'my God, my Lord.
(Come and see. Come and see.)
'Now I believe the living Word.'
(Come and see. Come and see.)
Go tell the people far and wide,
(Come and see. Come and see.)
'twas for their sins that Jesus died.

665
John Morrison, based on Isaiah 9:2-7

1. The race that long in darkness pined
has seen a glorious light:
the people dwell in day,
who dwelt in death's surrounding night.

2. To hail thy rise, thou better sun,
the gath'ring nations come,
joyous as when the reapers bear
the harvest treasures home.

3. To us a child of hope is born,
to us a Son is giv'n;
him shall the tribes of earth obey,
him all the hosts of heav'n.

4. His name shall be the Prince of Peace
for evermore adored,
the Wonderful, the Counsellor,
the great and mighty Lord.

5. His pow'r increasing still shall spread,
his reign no end shall know;
justice shall guard his throne above,
and peace abound below.

666
Cecil Frances Alexander, alt.

1. There is a green hill far away,
outside a city wall,
where the dear Lord was crucified
who died to save us all.

2. We may not know, we cannot tell
what pains he had to bear,
but we believe it was for us
he hung and suffered there.

3. He died that we might be forgiv'n,
he died to make us good;
that we might go at last to heav'n,
saved by his precious blood.

4. There was no other good enough
to pay the price of sin;
he only could unlock the gate
of heav'n, and let us in.

5. O, dearly, dearly has he loved,
and we must love him too,
and trust in his redeeming blood,
and try his works to do.

667
v 1 unknown, vs 2-5 Robert B. Kelly, from Scripture
© 1999 Kevin Mayhew Ltd.

1. There is a river
   that flows from God above;
   there is a fountain
   that's filled with his great love.

   Come to the waters, there is a great supply;
   there is a river that never shall run dry.

2. Wash me with water,
   and then I shall be clean;
   white as the new snow,
   if you remove my sin.

3. Plunged in the water,
   the tomb of our rebirth,
   so may we rise up
   to share in Christ's new life.

4. All who are thirsty,
   now hear God as he calls;
   come to the Lord's side,
   his life pours out for all.

5. Safe in the new Ark,
   the Church of Christ our Lord,
   praise God for water,
   his sign to save the world.

668
Venantius Fortunatus, trans. John Mason Neale and others

1. The royal banners forward go,
   the cross shines forth in mystic glow,
   where he in flesh, our flesh who made,
   our sentence bore, our ransom paid.

2. There whilst he hung, his sacred side
   by soldier's spear was opened wide,
   to cleanse us in the precious flood
   of water mingled with his blood.

3. Fulfilled is now what David told
   in true prophetic song of old,
   how God the heathen's king should be;
   for God is reigning from the tree.

4. O tree of glory, tree most fair,
   ordained those holy limbs to bear,
   how bright in purple robe it stood,
   the purple of a Saviour's blood!

5. Upon its arms, like balance true,
   he weighed the price for sinners due,
   the price which none but he could pay:
   and spoiled the spoiler of his prey.

6. To thee, eternal Three in One,
   let homage meet by all be done,
   as by the cross thou dost restore,
   so rule and guide us evermore.

669
Michael Forster, based on Isaiah 35
© 1993 Kevin Mayhew Ltd.

1. The Saviour will come,
   resplendent in joy;
   the lame and the sick
   new strength will enjoy.
   The desert, rejoicing,
   shall burst into flower,
   the deaf and the speechless
   will sing in that hour!

2. The Saviour will come,
   like rain on the earth,
   to harvest at last
   his crop of great worth.
   In patience await him,
   with firmness of mind;
   both mercy and judgement
   his people will find.

3. The Saviour will come,
   his truth we shall see:
   where lepers are cleansed
   and captives set free.
   No finely clad princeling
   in palace of gold,
   but Christ with his people,
   O wonder untold!

670 James Quinn
© Geoffrey Chapman, an imprint of Cassell plc

The seed is Christ's, the harvest his:
may we be stored within God's barn.
The sea is Christ's, the fish are his:
may we be caught within God's net.
From birth to age, from age to death,
enfold us, Christ, within your arms.
Until the end, the great re-birth,
Christ be our joy in paradise.

671 Michael Forster
© 1993 Kevin Mayhew Ltd.

1. The sign of hope, creation's joy,
   is born of purest beauty:
   the virgin's womb, now glorified,
   where grace unites with duty.

2. Emmanuel shall be his name,
   a title pure and holy,
   for God with us will truly be
   among the poor and lowly.

3. Where love divine concurs with trust
   to share redemption's story,
   Emmanuel in hope is born,
   and earth exults in glory.

4. Now we, by grace and duty called,
   proclaim to ev'ry nation
   the Sign of hope which Mary bore,
   and promise of salvation.

672 Damian Lundy
© 1978 Kevin Mayhew Ltd.

1. The Spirit lives to set us free,
   walk, walk in the light.
   He binds us all in unity,
   walk, walk in the light.

   Walk in the light (x3)
   walk in the light of the Lord.

2. Jesus promised life to all,
   walk, walk in the light.
   The dead were wakened by his call,
   walk, walk in the light.

3. He died in pain on Calvary,
   walk, walk in the light,
   to save the lost like you and me,
   walk, walk in the light.

4. We know his death was not the end,
   walk, walk in the light.
   He gave his Spirit to be our friend,
   walk, walk in the light.

5. By Jesus' love our wounds are healed,
   walk, walk in the light.
   The Father's kindness is revealed,
   walk, walk in the light.

6. The Spirit lives in you and me,
   walk, walk in the light.
   His light will shine for all to see,
   walk, walk in the light.

673 Luke 4:18, Isaiah 61:1-2

The Spirit of the Lord is now upon me
to heal the broken heart
and set the captives free,
to open prison doors
and make the blind to see.
The Spirit of the Lord is now on me.

674 Robert B. Kelly
© 1999 Kevin Mayhew Ltd.

1. The table's set, Lord, your people gathered;
   around this table each finds their place.
   Sign of the kingdom, the greatest gath'ring,
   around Christ Jesus each has their place.

2. At this same table in other places,
   so many people here in Christ's name.
   Those gone before us, who will succeed us,
   one single table throughout all time.

3. One Lord inviting, one Church
        responding;
   one single bread and one cup of wine.
   May what we do here change and
        transform us,
   one single presence, Christ through
        all time.

675

Michael Forster
© 1993 Kevin Mayhew Ltd.

1. The temple of the living God
   is built of living stones,
   a holy people, called to live
   by light of Christ alone.
   With special joy we celebrate
   the word the psalmist said:
   'The stone the builders cast aside
   is now the corner's head!'

2. The temple of the living God
   is set secure above,
   where Christ invites the world to share
   his perfect reign of love.
   And we who seek the Father's face
   are summoned to obey,
   and follow where he goes before,
   the Life, the Truth, the Way.

3. The temple of the living God
   upon the earth must grow,
   and those of ev'ry race and class
   his true compassion know.
   The widow and the fatherless
   receive a special care,
   till all creation, just and free,
   his perfect peace will share.

676

Traditional West Indian

1. The Virgin Mary had a baby boy,
   the Virgin Mary had a baby boy,
   the Virgin Mary had a baby boy,
   and they said that his name was Jesus.

   He came from the glory,
   he came from the glorious kingdom.
   He came from the glory,
   he came from the glorious kingdom.
   O yes, believer. O yes, believer.
   He came from the glory,
   he came from the glorious kingdom.

2. The angels sang when the baby
   was born, *(x3)*
   and proclaimed him the Saviour Jesus.

3. The wise men saw where the baby
   was born, *(x3)*
   and they saw that his name was Jesus.

677

Luke Connaughton
© McCrimmon Publishing Co. Ltd

1. The wandering flock of Israel
   is scattered and far from home and hope;
   the shepherd alone with crook and staff,
   can find them and lead and keep
   them safe.

   He made and upheld us, granted grace;
   his smile is our peace, his word our hope.

2. I walk on the heights, I climb and cling,
   the terrors beneath, the ice aloft.
   I look for his tracks, await his hand
   to help and to hold, to guide and save.

3. I thirst for his word as grass in drought,
   dry, brittle and barren, parched and brown;
   no shower can fall, no sap rise green
   no hope, if the Lord should send no rain.

4. Creator of all, your craftsman's care
   with fashioning hand caressed our clay;
   this vine is the work your hands
   have wrought,
   your love is the sun, our soil of growth.

678

Edmond Louis Budry, trans. Richard Birch Hoyle
© Copyright control

1. Thine be the glory,
   risen, conqu'ring Son,
   endless is the vict'ry
   thou o'er death hast won;
   angels in bright raiment
   rolled the stone away,
   kept the folded grave-clothes
   where thy body lay.

Continued overleaf

Thine be the glory, risen, conqu'ring Son,
endless is the vict'ry thou o'er death has won.

2. Lo! Jesus meets us,
   risen from the tomb;
   lovingly he greets us,
   scatters fear and gloom.
   Let the Church with gladness
   hymns of triumph sing,
   for her Lord now liveth;
   death hath lost its sting.

3. No more we doubt thee,
   glorious Prince of Life!
   Life is naught without thee:
   aid us in our strife.
   Make us more than conqu'rors
   through thy deathless love.
   Bring us safe through Jordan
   to thy home above.

679
Graham Kendrick
© 1988 Make Way Music

1. This Child, secretly comes in the night,
   O this Child, hiding a heavenly light,
   O this Child, coming to us like a stranger,
   this heavenly Child.

   This Child, heaven come down now
   to be with us here,
   heavenly love and mercy appear,
   softly in awe and wonder come near
   to this heavenly Child.

2. This Child, rising on us like the sun,
   O this Child, given to light everyone,
   O this Child, guiding our feet on
      the pathway
   to peace on earth.

3. This Child, raising the humble and poor,
   O this Child, making the proud ones
      to fall;
   O this Child, filling the hungry with
      good things,
   this heavenly Child.

680
Ascribed to St. Patrick, adapted by James Quinn
© Geoffrey Chapman, an imprint of Cassell plc

1. This day God gives me
   strength of high heaven,
   sun and moon shining, flame in
      my hearth,
   flashing of lighting, wind in its swiftness,
   deeps of the ocean, firmness of earth.

2. This day God sends me
   strength to sustain me,
   might to uphold me, wisdom as guide.
   Your eyes are watchful, your ears are
      list'ning,
   your lips are speaking, friend at my side.

3. God's way is my way,
   God's shield is round me,
   God's host defends me, saving from ill.
   Angel of heaven, drive from me always
   all that would harm me, stand by me still.

4. Rising, I thank you,
   mighty and strong One,
   King of creation, giver of rest,
   firmly confessing Threeness of persons,
   Oneness of Godhead, Trinity blest.

681
vs 1 & 2 Jimmy Owens; vs 3-5 Damian Lundy
© 1978 Bud John Songs/EMI Christian Music
Publishing/CopyCare

1. This is my body, broken for you,
   bringing you wholeness, making you free.
   Take it and eat it, and when you do,
   do it in love for me.

2. This is my blood, poured out for you,
   bringing forgiveness, making you free.
   Take it and drink it, and when you do,
   do it in love for me.

3. Back to my Father soon I shall go.
   Do not forget me; then you will see
   I am still with you, and you will know
   you're very close to me.

4. Filled with my Spirit, how you will grow!
   You are my branches; I am the tree.
   If you are faithful, others will know
   you are alive in me.

5. Love one another; I have loved you,
   and I have shown you how to be free;
   serve one another, and when you do,
   do it in love for me.

682 James Quinn
© Geoffrey Chapman, an imprint of Cassell plc

1. This is my will, my one command,
   that love should dwell among you all.
   This is my will that you should love
   as I have shown that I love you.

2. No greater love can be than this:
   to choose to die to save one's friends.
   You are my friends if you obey
   all I command that you should do.

3. I call you now no longer slaves;
   no slave knows all his master does.
   I call you friends, for all I hear
   my Father say, you hear from me.

4. You chose not me, but I chose you,
   that you should go and bear much fruit.
   I called you out that you in me
   should bear much fruit that will abide.

5. All that you ask my Father dear
   for my name's sake you shall receive.
   This is my will, my one command,
   that love should dwell in each, in all.

683 From the Renewal of Baptismal Promises

This is our faith,
this is our faith in Christ Jesus our Lord
which we are proud to confess.

684 Les Garrett
© 1967 Scripture in Song/Integrity Music/
Kingsway's Thankyou Music

1. This is the day, this is the day
   that the Lord has made,
   that the Lord has made;
   we will rejoice, we will rejoice
   and be glad in it, and be glad in it.
   This is the day that the Lord has made;
   we will rejoice and be glad in it.
   This is the day, this is the day
   that the Lord has made.

2. This is the day, this is the day
   when he rose again,
   when he rose again;
   we will rejoice, we will rejoice
   and be glad in it, and be glad in it.
   This is the day when he rose again;
   we will rejoice and be glad in it.
   This is the day, this is the day
   when he rose again.

3. This is the day, this is the day
   when the Spirit came,
   when the Spirit came;
   we will rejoice, we will rejoice
   and be glad in it, and be glad in it.
   This is the day when the Spirit came;
   we will rejoice and be glad in it.
   This is the day, this is the day
   when the Spirit came.

685 Edward Caswall

1. This is the image of the queen
   who reigns in bliss above;
   of her who is the hope of men,
   whom men and angels love.
   Most holy Mary, at thy feet
   I bend a suppliant knee;
   in this thy own sweet month of May,
   do thou remember me.

Continued overleaf

2. The homage offered at the feet
of Mary's image here
to Mary's self at once ascends
above the starry sphere.
Most holy Mary, at thy feet
I bend a suppliant knee;
in all my joy, in all my pain,
do thou remember me.

3. How fair soever be the form
which here your eyes behold,
its beauty is by Mary's self
excelled a thousandfold.
Most holy Mary, at thy feet
I bend a suppliant knee;
in my temptations, each and all,
do thou remember me.

686 George Ratcliffe Woodward
© Copyright control

1. This joyful Eastertide,
away with sin and sorrow.
My love, the Crucified,
hath sprung to life this morrow.

Had Christ, that once was slain,
ne'er burst his three-day prison,
our faith had been in vain:
but now hath Christ arisen,
arisen, arisen, arisen.

2. My flesh in hope shall rest,
and for a season slumber;
till trump from east to west
shall wake the dead in number.

3. Death's flood hath lost its chill,
since Jesus crossed the river:
lover of souls, from ill
my passing soul deliver.

687 Damian Lundy, based on Ephesians 3:14-21
© 1978 Kevin Mayhew Ltd.

This, then, is my prayer,
falling on my knees before God
who is Father and source of all life.

May he in his love,
through the Spirit of Christ,
give you pow'r to grow strong
in your innermost self.

1. May Christ live in your hearts
and may your lives, rooted in love,
grow strong in him.

2. May you, with all the saints,
grow in the pow'r to understand
how he loves you.

3. O how can I explain
in all its depth and all its scope
his love, God's love!

The chorus is not sung after verse 3.

4. For his love is so full,
it is beyond all we can dream:
his love, in Christ!

5. And so, glory to him
working in us, who can do more
than we can pray!

688 Dan Schutte, based on Isaiah
© 1975 Daniel L. Schutte and New Dawn Music

Though the mountains may fall
and the hills turn to dust,
yet the love of the Lord will stand
as a shelter for all who will call on his name.
Sing the praise and the glory of God.

1. Could the Lord ever leave you?
Could the Lord forget his love?
Though the mother forsake her child,
he will not abandon you.

2. Should you turn and forsake him,
he will gently call your name.
Should you wander away from him,
he will always take you back.

3. Go to him when you're weary;
   he will give you eagle's wings.
   You will run, you will never tire,
   for your God will be your strength.

4. As he swore to your fathers,
   when the flood destroyed the land,
   he will never forsake you;
   he will swear to you again.

689 John Marriott

1. Thou, whose almighty word
   chaos and darkness heard,
   and took their flight;
   hear us, we humbly pray,
   and where the gospel day
   sheds not its glorious ray,
   let there be light.

2. Thou, who didst come to bring
   on thy redeeming wing,
   healing and sight,
   health to the sick in mind,
   sight to the inly blind,
   O now to humankind
   let there be light.

3. Spirit of truth and love,
   life-giving, holy Dove,
   speed forth thy flight;
   move on the water's face,
   bearing the lamp of grace,
   and in earth's darkest place
   let there be light.

4. Holy and blessèd Three,
   glorious Trinity,
   Wisdom, Love, Might;
   boundless as ocean's tide
   rolling in fullest pride,
   through the earth far and wide
   let there be light.

690 Edward Hayes Plumptre, alt.

1. Thy hand, O God, has guided
   thy flock, from age to age;
   the wondrous tale is written,
   full clear, on ev'ry page;
   our forebears owned thy goodness,
   and we their deeds record;
   and both of this bear witness:
   one Church, one Faith, one Lord.

2. Thy heralds brought glad tidings
   to greatest, as to least;
   they bade them rise, and hasten
   to share the great King's feast;
   and this was all their teaching,
   in ev'ry deed and word,
   to all alike proclaiming:
   one Church, one Faith, one Lord.

3. Through many a day of darkness,
   through many a scene of strife,
   the faithful few fought bravely
   to guard the nation's life.
   Their gospel of redemption,
   sin pardoned, hope restored,
   was all in this enfolded:
   one Church, one Faith, one Lord.

4. And we, shall we be faithless?
   Shall hearts fail, hands hang down?
   Shall we evade the conflict,
   and cast away our crown?
   Not so: in God's deep counsels
   some better thing is stored:
   we will maintain, unflinching,
   one Church, one Faith, one Lord.

5. Thy mercy will not fail us,
   nor leave thy work undone;
   with thy right hand to help us,
   the vict'ry shall be won;
   and then by all creation,
   thy name shall be adored.
   And this shall be their anthem:
   One Church, one Faith, one Lord.

691

Noel Richards
© 1991 Kingsway's Thankyou Music

1. To be in your presence,
   to sit at your feet,
   where your love surrounds me
   and makes me complete.

   This is my desire, O Lord, this is my desire,
   this is my desire, O Lord, this is my desire.

2. To rest in your presence,
   not rushing away,
   to cherish each moment,
   here I would stay.

692

From 'Catholicum Hymnologium',
trans. Edward Caswall

1. To Christ, the Prince of peace,
   and Son of God most high,
   the Father of the world to come,
   sing we with holy joy.

2. Deep in his heart for us
   the wound of love he bore;
   that love wherewith he still inflames
   the hearts that him adore.

3. O Jesu, victim blest,
   what else but love divine
   could thee constrain to open thus
   that sacred heart of thine?

4. O fount of endless life,
   O spring of water clear,
   O flame celestial, cleansing all
   who unto thee draw near!

5. Hide us in thy dear heart,
   for thither we do fly;
   where seek thy grace through life, in death
   thine immortality.

6. Praise to the Father be,
   and sole-begotten Son;
   praise, holy Paraclete, to thee,
   while endless ages run.

693

Aloys Schlör, trans. A. J. Christie, alt.

1. To Jesus' heart, all burning
   with fervent love for men,
   my heart with fondest yearning
   shall raise its joyful strain.

   While ages course along,
   blest be with loudest song
   the sacred heart of Jesus
   by ev'ry heart and tongue,
   the sacred heart of Jesus
   by ev'ry heart and tongue.

2. O heart, for me on fire
   with love that none can speak,
   my yet untold desire
   God gives me for thy sake.

3. Too true, I have forsaken
   thy love for wilful sin;
   yet now let me be taken
   back by thy grace again.

4. As thou art meek and lowly,
   and ever pure of heart,
   so may my heart be wholly
   of thine the counterpart.

5. When life away is flying,
   and earth's false glare is done,
   still, Sacred Heart, in dying,
   I'll say I'm all thine own.

694

Susan Sayers, based on Psalm 24
© 1996 Kevin Mayhew Ltd.

To you, O Lord, I lift up my soul,
I lift up my soul.

1. Teach me, Lord, your holy ways
   and help me learn your paths.
   Guide my footsteps in your truth,
   my Saviour and my God.

2. Good and upright is the Lord
   who guides the wand'rer back,
   leads the humble in this path
   and shows the poor his ways.

3. Faithfulness and love abound
   for all who keep his word;
   those who love him have a friend
   whose promise is made clear.

695 Julian Wiener
© 1999 Kevin Mayhew Ltd.

To your altar we bring you
these gifts of bread and wine.
Take, Lord, receive,
make them holy and divine.
They're our joys and our hopes,
all our failures and our strife.
Take, Lord, and make these gifts
our food of life.

1. Take and bless these gifts we offer;
   make them pleasing to you, O Lord.

2. Take these gifts and make them holy
   by the pow'r of your Holy Spirit.

3. They'll become the body and blood
   of your Son, Jesus Christ, our Lord.

696 John B. Foley
© 1975 John B. Foley, S. J. and New Dawn Music

Turn to me, O turn and be saved,
says the Lord, for I am God;
there is no other, none beside me.
I call your name.

1. I am he that comforts you;
   who are you to be afraid
   of flesh that fades,
   is made like the grass of the field,
   soon to wither.

2. Listen to me, my people,
   give ear to me, my nation:
   a law will go forth from me,
   and my justice for a light
   to the people.

3. Lift up your ryes to the heavens,
   and look at the earth down below.
   The heavens will vanish like smoke,
   and the earth will wear out
   like a garment.

697 Bernadette Farrell, based on Scripture
© 1983 Bernadette Farrell/OCP Publications

Unless a grain of wheat shall fall
upon the ground and die,
it remains but a single grain with no life.

1. If we have died with him,
   then we shall live with him;
   if we hold firm we shall reign with him.

2. If anyone serves me,
   then they must follow me;
   where-ever I am my servants will be.

3. Make your home in me
   as I make mine in you;
   those who remain in me bear much fruit.

4. If you remain in me
   and my word lives in you;
   then you will be my disciples.

5. Those who love me
   are loved by my Father;
   we shall be with them and dwell in them.

6. Peace I leave with you,
   my peace I give to you;
   peace which the world cannot give is
       my gift.

698 15th century, trans. Percy Dearmer, alt.
© Oxford University Press

1. Unto us a boy is born!
   King of all creation;
   came he to a world forlorn,
   the Lord of ev'ry nation,
   the Lord of ev'ry nation.

2. Cradled in a stall was he,
   watched by cows and asses;
   but the very beasts could see
   that he the world surpasses,
   that he the world surpasses.

Continued overleaf

3. Then the fearful Herod cried,
   'Pow'r is mine in Jewry!'
   So the blameless children died
   the victims of his fury,
   the victims of his fury.

4. Now may Mary's Son, who came
   long ago to love us,
   lead us all with hearts aflame
   unto the joys above us,
   unto the joys above us.

5. Omega and Alpha he!
   Let the organ thunder,
   while the choir with peals of glee
   shall rend the air asunder,
   shall rend the air asunder.

699 M. F. C. Wilson, alt.
© Copyright control

1. Upon thy table, Lord, we place
   these symbols of our work and thine,
   life's food won only by thy grace,
   who giv'st to all the bread and wine.

2. Within these simple things there lie
   the height and depth of human life,
   the thought of all, our tears and toil,
   our hopes and fears, our joy and strife.

3. Accept them, Lord; from thee they come:
   we take them humbly at thy hand.
   These gifts of thine for higher use
   we offer, as thou dost command.

700 Unknown

1. Vaster far than any ocean,
   deeper than the deepest sea
   is the love of Christ my Saviour,
   reaching through eternity.

2. But my sins are truly many,
   is God's grace so vast, so deep?
   Yes, there's grace o'er sin abounding,
   grace to pardon, grace to keep.

3. Can he quench my thirst for ever?
   Will his Spirit strength impart?
   Yes, he gives me living water,
   springing up within my heart.

701 Ascribed to Rabanus Maurus

1. Veni, Creator Spiritus,
   mentes tuorum visita,
   imple superna gratia,
   quæ tu creasti pectora. Amen

2. Qui diceris Paraclitus,
   Altissimi donum Dei,
   fons vivus, ignis, caritas,
   et spiritalis unctio.

3. Tu septiformis munere,
   digitus paternæ dexteræ,
   tu rite promissum Patris,
   sermone ditans guttura.

4. Accende lumen sensibus,
   infunde amorem cordibus,
   infirma nostri corporis
   virtute firmans perpeti.

5. Hostem repellas longius,
   pacemque dones protinus:
   ductore sic te prævio,
   vitemus omne noxium.

6. Per te sciamus da Patrem,
   noscamus atque Filium,
   teque utriusque Spiritum
   credamus omni tempore.

7. Deo Patri sit gloria,
   et Filio, qui a mortuis
   surrexit, ac Paraclito,
   in sæculorum sæcula. Amen.

702 Ascribed to Stephen Langton

1. Veni, Sancte Spiritus,
   et emitte cælitus
   lucis tuæ radium.

2. Veni, pater pauperum,
   veni, dator munerum,
   veni, lumen cordium.

3. Consolator optime,
   dulcis hospes animæ,
   dulce refrigerium.

4. In labore requies,
   in æstu temperies,
   in fletu solatium.

5. O lux beatissima
   reple cordis intima
   tuorum fidelium.

6. Sine tuo numine,
   nihil est in homine,
   nihil est innoxium.

7. Lava quod est sordidum,
   riga quod est aridum,
   sana quod est saucium.

8. Flecte quod est rigidum,
   fove quod est frigidum,
   rege quod est devium.

9. Da tuis fidelibus,
   in te confidentibus,
   sacrum septenarium.

10. Da virtutis meritum,
    da salutis exitum,
    da perenne gaudium. Amen. Alleluia.

703 11th century, attributed to Wipo

1. Victimae Paschali laudes
   immolent Christiani.

2. Agnus redemit oves:
   Christus innocens Patri
   reconciliavit peccatores.

3. Mors et vita duello conflixere mirando:
   dux vitae mortuus, regnat vivus.

4. Dic nobis, Maria, quid vidisti in via?

5. Sepulchrum Christi viventis,
   et gloriam vidi resurgentis:

6. Angelicos testes, sudarium, et vestes.

7. Surrexit Christus spes mea:
   praecedet suos in Galilaeam.

8. Scimus Christum surrexisse
   a mortuis vere:
   tu nobis, victor Rex, miserere.
   Amen. Alleluia.

704 Michael Forster
© 1993 Kevin Mayhew Ltd.

1. Waken, O sleeper, wake and rise,
   salvation's day is near,
   and let the dawn of light and truth
   dispel the night of fear.

2. Let us prepare to face the day
   of judgement and of grace,
   to live as people of the light,
   and perfect truth embrace.

3. Watch then and pray, we cannot know
   the moment or the hour,
   when Christ, unheralded, will come
   with life-renewing power.

4. Then shall the nations gather round
   to learn his ways of peace,
   when spears to pruning-hooks are turned
   and all our conflicts cease.

705 Marie Lydia Pereira
© 1984 Kevin Mayhew Ltd.

Wake up, O people, the Lord is very near!
Wake up, and stand for the Lord. (Repeat)

1. Your saving Lord is near. Wake up!
   His glory will appear. Wake up!
   Your hour of grace is nearer than it
      ever was.

2. The night of sin has passed. Wake up!
   The light is near at last. Wake up!
   The day star, Christ, the Son of God, will
      soon appear.

3. To live in love and peace. Wake up!
   To let all quarrels cease. Wake up!
   To live that all you do may stand the
      light of day.

Continued overleaf

4. That Christ may be your shield.
   Wake up!
   That death to life may yield. Wake up!
   That heaven's gate be opened wide again
   for you.

706
Estelle White
© 1976 Kevin Mayhew Ltd.

Walk with me, O my Lord,
through the darkest night and brightest day.
Be at my side, O Lord,
hold my hand and guide me on my way.

1. Sometimes the road seems long,
   my energy is spent.
   Then, Lord, I think of you
   and I am given strength.

2. Stones often bar my path
   and there are times I fall,
   but you are always there
   to help me when I call.

3. Just as you calmed the wind
   and walked upon the sea,
   conquer, my living Lord,
   the storms that threaten me.

4. Help me to pierce the mists
   that cloud my heart and mind,
   so that I shall not fear
   the steepest mountain-side.

5. As once you healed the lame
   and gave sight to the blind,
   help me when I'm downcast
   to hold my head up high.

707
Unknown

1. We are gathering together unto him.
   We are gathering together unto him.
   Unto him shall the gath'ring of
      the people be,
   we are gathering together unto him.

2. We are offering together unto him . . .

3. We are singing together unto him . . .

4. We are praying together unto him . . .

708
Graham Kendrick
© 1990 Make Way Music

1. We are his children, the fruit of
      his suff'ring,
   saved and redeemed by his blood;
   called to be holy, a light to the nations:
   clothed with his pow'r, filled with his love.

   Go forth in his name,
   proclaiming, 'Jesus reigns!'
   Now is the time for the church to arise
   and proclaim him
   'Jesus, Saviour, Redeemer and Lord.'

2. Countless the souls that are stumbling
      in darkness,
   why do we sleep in the light?
   Jesus commands us to go make disciples,
   this is our case, this is our fight.

3. Listen, the wind of the Spirit is blowing,
   the end of the age is so near;
   powers in the earth and the heavens
      are shaking,
   Jesus our Lord soon shall appear!

709
Susan Sayers, based on Psalm 99
© 1995 Kevin Mayhew Ltd.

We are his people, the sheep of his flock,
his people, the sheep of his flock.

1. Shout with gladness to God
   all the earth, joyfully obey him.
   Come and gather before him now,
   singing songs of gladness.

2. Understand that the Lord is our God;
   he it is who made us.
   We his people belong to him,
   he our loving shepherd.

3. O how faithful and good is the Lord,
   loving us for ever;
   rich in mercy and faithfulness,
   true through all the ages.

710 Traditional South African, trans. Anders Nyberg
© 1990 Wild Goose Publications

We are marching in the light of God. *(x4)*

We are marching,
Oo-ooh! We are marching in the light
   of God. *(Repeat)*

711 Carey Landry
© 1976 North American Liturgy Resources (NALR)

We behold the splendour of God
shining on the face of Jesus.
We behold the splendour of God
shining on the face of the Son.

1. And O how his beauty transforms us,
   the wonder of Presence abiding.
   Transparent hearts give reflection
   of Tabor's light within,
   of Tabor's light within.

2. Jesus, Lord of glory,
   Jesus beloved Son.
   O how good to be with you;
   how good to share your light,
   how good to share your light.

712 Michael Forster
© 1992 Kevin Mayhew Ltd.

1. We believe in one almighty
   God and Father of us all,
   maker of the earth and heaven,
   holding worlds and stars in thrall.
   All things seen and all things unseen
   come to being at his call.

2. We believe in one Redeemer,
   Christ, the Father's only Son.
   Timelessly in love begotten,
   through him all God's work is done.
   Light from Light and God
      from Godhead,
   with the Father's Being, one.

3. All for us and our salvation,
   Christ his glory set aside,
   by the Holy Spirit's power,
   and the womb of virgin bride;
   suffered under Pilate's sentence,
   for our sake was crucified.

4. He has burst the grave asunder,
   rising as the prophets said;
   seated in the Father's presence,
   he is our exalted head.
   He will come again with glory,
   judge the living and the dead.

5. We acclaim the Holy Spirit,
   of all life the source and Lord;
   with the Son and Father worshipped,
   ever honoured and adored;
   speaking through the holy prophets,
   pow'r of sacrament and word.

6. Holy Church, and universal,
   apostolic company!
   In one sacrament forgiven,
   signed by water, his to be.
   In the resurrection body
   we shall share eternity.

713 The Iona Community
© 1989 WGRG/Iona Community

1. We cannot measure how you heal
   or answer ev'ry suff'rer's prayer,
   yet we believe your grace responds
   where faith and doubt unite to care.
   Your hands, though bloodied on the cross,
   survive to hold and heal and warm,
   to carry all through death to life
   and cradle children yet unborn.

Continued overleaf

2. The pain that will not go away,
    the guilt that clings from things
        long past,
    the fear of what the future holds,
    are present as if meant to last.
    But present too is love which tends
    the hurt we never hoped to find,
    the private agonies inside,
    the memories that haunt the mind.

3. So some have come who need your help
    and some have come to make amends,
    as hands which shaped and saved
        the world
    are present in the touch of friends.
    Lord, let your Spirit meet us here
    to mend the body, mind and soul,
    to disentangle peace from pain
    and make your broken people whole.

714 Michael Forster
© 1993 Kevin Mayhew Ltd.

1. We celebrate the new creation,
    to God, in Christ, now reconciled,
    and recognise our full salvation
    in him whom people once reviled.

2. In token of our liberation,
    within God's presence now we stand,
    to share the banquet of salvation,
    the harvest of the promised land.

3. The news of reconciliation
    is now entrusted to our care;
    so spread the word throughout creation,
    the feast is here for all to share.

4. Begin the joyful celebration:
    the lost return, the dead arise,
    to see the light of exultation
    which shines from God's forgiving eyes.

715 Willard F. Jabusch
© 1998 Willard F. Jabusch

1. We celebrate this festive day
    with pray'r and joyful song.
    Our Father's house is home to us,
    we know that we belong.

The bread is broken, wine is poured,
a feast to lift us up!
Then thank the Lord who gives himself
as food and saving cup!

2. The door is open, enter in,
    and take your place by right.
    For you've been chosen as his guest
    to share his love and light.

3. We come together as the twelve
    came to the Upper Room.
    Our host is Jesus Christ the Lord,
    now risen from the tomb.

4. Who travels needs both food and drink
    to help them on their way.
    Refreshed and strong we'll journey on
    and face another day.

5. Who shares this meal receives the Lord
    who lives, though he was dead.
    So death can hold no terrors now
    for those who eat his bread.

716 Michael Forster, based on the speech by Martin
Luther King Jr. © 1997 Kevin Mayhew Ltd.

1. We have a dream:
    this nation will arise,
    and truly live
    according to its creed,
    that all are equal
    in their maker's eyes,
    and none shall suffer
    through another's greed.

2. We have a dream
    that one day we shall see
    a world of justice,
    truth and equity,
    where children of the slaves
    and of the free
    will share the banquet
    of community.

3. We have a dream
of deserts brought to flow'r,
once made infertile
by oppression's heat,
when love and truth
shall end oppressive pow'r,
and streams of righteousness
and justice meet.

4. We have a dream:
our children shall be free
from judgements based on
colour or on race;
free to become
whatever they may be,
of their own choosing
in the light of grace.

5. We have a dream
that truth will overcome
the fear and anger
of our present day;
that black and white
will share a common home,
and hand in hand
will walk the pilgrim way.

6. We have a dream:
each valley will be raised,
and ev'ry moutain,
ev'ry hill brought down;
then shall creation
echo perfect praise,
and share God's glory
under freedom's crown!

717 John Foley, based on 2 Cor. 4 and 1 Cor. 1
© 1975 John B. Foley, S.J. and New Dawn Music

We hold a treasure, not made of gold,
in earthen vessels, wealth untold;
one treasure only: the Lord, the Christ,
in earthen vessels.

1. Light has shone in our darkness;
God has shone in our heart,
with the light of the glory
of Jesus, the Lord.

2. He has chosen the lowly,
who are small in this world;
in his weakness is glory,
in Jesus the Lord.

718 Matthias Claudius,
trans. Jane Montgomery Campbell

1. We plough the fields and scatter
the good seed on the land,
but it is fed and watered
by God's almighty hand:
he sends the snow in winter,
the warmth to swell the grain,
the breezes and the sunshine,
and soft, refreshing rain.

All good gifts around us
are sent from heav'n above;
then thank the Lord, O thank the Lord,
for all his love.

2. He only is the maker
of all things near and far;
he paints the wayside flower,
he lights the evening star;
he fills the earth with beauty,
by him the birds are fed;
much more to us, his children,
he gives our daily bread.

3. We thank thee then, O Father,
for all things bright and good:
the seed-time and the harvest,
our life, our health, our food.
Accept the gifts we offer
for all thy love imparts,
and, what thou most desirest,
our humble, thankful hearts.

719 Spiritual, alt.

1. Were you there
when they crucified my Lord? *(Repeat)*
O, sometimes it causes me to
tremble, tremble, tremble.
Were you there
when they crucified my Lord?

Continued overleaf

2. Were you there
   when they nailed him to a tree? . . .

3. Were you there
   when they pierced him in the side? . . .

4. Were you there
   when they laid him in the tomb? . . .

5. Were you there
   when he rose to glorious life? . . .

720 Paul Inwood
© 1988 Paul Inwood

We shall draw water joyfully,
singing joyfully, singing joyfully;
we shall draw water joyfully
from the well-springs of salvation.

1. Truly God is our salvation;
   we trust, we shall not fear.
   For the Lord is our strength,
   the Lord is our song;
   he became our Saviour.

2. Give thanks, O give thanks to the Lord;
   give praise to his holy name!
   Make his mighty deeds known
   to all of the nations;
   proclaim his greatness.

3. Sing a psalm, sing a psalm to the Lord
   for he has done glorious deeds.
   Make known his works to all of the earth;
   people of Zion, sing for joy,
   for great in your midst,
   great in your midst
   is the Holy One of Israel.

721 Pierre-Marie Hoog and Robert B. Kelly
© Rev Pierre-Marie Hoog, S.J.

Advent 1

We shall stay awake
and pray at all times,
ready to welcome Christ,
the Prince of Justice.
We shall set aside
all fears and worries,
ready to welcome Christ,
the Prince of Peace.

Advent 2

We shall set our sights
on what is righteous,
ready to welcome Christ,
the Prince of Justice.
We shall smooth the path,
prepare the Lord's way,
ready to welcome Christ,
the Prince of Peace.

Advent 3

We shall plunge into
the saving water,
ready to welcome Christ,
the Prince of Justice.
We shall be reborn
and rise to new life,
ready to welcome Christ,
the Prince of Peace.

Advent 4

We shall hold with faith
to what God promised,
ready to welcome Christ,
the Prince of Justice.
We shall be
attentive to his Spirit,
ready to welcome Christ,
the Prince of Peace.

722 John Henry Hopkins, alt.

1. We three kings of Orient are;
   bearing gifts we traverse afar;
   field and fountain, moor and mountain,
   following yonder star.

   O star of wonder, star of night,
   star with royal beauty bright,
   westward leading still proceeding,
   guide us to thy perfect light.

2. Born a King on Bethlehem plain,
   gold I bring, to crown him again,
   King for ever, ceasing never,
   over us all to reign.

3. Frankincense to offer have I,
   incense owns a Deity nigh,
   prayer and praising, gladly raising,
   worship him, God most high.

4. Myrrh is mine, its bitter perfume
   breathes a life of gathering gloom;
   sorrowing, sighing, bleeding, dying,
   sealed in the stone-cold tomb.

5. Glorious now behold him arise,
   King and God and sacrifice;
   alleluia, alleluia,
   earth to heav'n replies.

723 William Chatterton Dix

1. What child is this who, laid to rest,
   on Mary's lap is sleeping?
   Whom angels greet with anthems sweet,
   while shepherds watch are keeping?
   This, this is Christ the King,
   whom shepherds guard and angels sing:
   come, greet the infant Lord,
   the babe, the Son of Mary!

2. Why lies he in such mean estate,
   where ox and ass are feeding?
   Good Christians, fear: for sinners here
   the silent Word is pleading.
   Nails, spear, shall pierce him through,
   the cross be borne for me, for you;
   hail, hail the Word made flesh,
   the babe, the Son of Mary!

3. So bring him incense, gold and myrrh,
   come rich and poor, to own him.
   The King of kings salvation brings,
   let loving hearts enthrone him.
   Raise, raise the song on high,
   the Virgin sings her lullaby:
   joy, joy for Christ is born,
   the babe the Son of Mary!

724 Delores Dufner

1. What feast of love is offered here,
   what banquet come from heaven?
   What food of everlasting life,
   what gracious gift is given?
   This, this is Christ the King,
   the bread come down from heaven.
   O taste and see and sing!
   How sweet the manna given!

2. What light of truth is offered here,
   what covenant from heaven?
   What hope of everlasting life,
   what wondrous word is given?
   This, this is Christ the King,
   the Sun come down from heaven.
   O see, and list'ning, sing!
   The Word of God is given!

3. What wine of love is offered here,
   what crimson drink from heaven?
   What stream of everlasting life,
   what precious blood is given?
   This, this is Christ the King,
   the sweetest wine of heaven.
   O taste and see and sing!
   The Son of God is given!

725 Graham Kendrick

1. What kind of greatness can this be,
   that chose to be made small?
   Exchanging untold majesty
   for a world so pitiful.
   That God should come as one of us,
   I'll never understand.
   The more I hear the story told,
   the more amazed I am.

   O what else can I do
   but kneel and worship you,
   and come just as I am,
   my whole life an offering.

Continued overleaf

2. The One in whom we live and move
   in swaddling cloths lies bound.
   The voice that cried, 'Let there be light',
   asleep without a sound.
   The One who strode among the stars,
   and called each one by name,
   lies helpless in a mother's arms
   and must learn to walk again.

3. What greater love could he have shown
   to shamed humanity,
   yet human pride hates to believe
   in such deep humility.
   But nations now may see his grace
   and know that he is near,
   when his meek heart, his words, his works
   are incarnate in us here.

726 Willard F. Jabusch
© 1998 Willard F. Jabusch

Whatsoever you do
to the least of my people,
that you do unto me.

1. When I was hungry you gave me to eat.
   When I was thirsty you gave me to drink.
   Now enter into the home of my Father.

2. When I was homeless you opened
      your door.
   When I was naked you gave me your coat.
   Now enter into the home of my Father.

3. When I was weary you helped me
      find rest.
   When I was anxious you calmed all
      my fears.
   Now enter into the home of my Father.

4. When in a prison you came to my cell.
   When on a sick-bed you cared for
      my needs.
   Now enter into the home of my Father.

5. When I was aged you bothered to smile.
   When I was restless you listened
      and cared.
   Now enter into the home of my Father.

6. When I was laughed at you stood by
      my side.
   When I was happy you shared in my joy.
   Now enter into the home of my Father.

727 E. M. Barrett

1. When Christ our Lord to Andrew cried:
   'Come, thou and follow me,'
   the fisher left his net beside
   the Sea of Galilee.
   To teach the truth his Master taught,
   to tread the path he trod was all his will,
   and thus he brought
   un-numbered souls to God.

2. When Andrew's hour had come, and he
   was doomed like Christ to die,
   he kissed his cross exultingly,
   and this his loving cry:
   'O noble cross! O precious wood!
   I long have yearned for thee;
   uplift me to my only good
   who died on thee for me.'

3. Saint Andrew, now in bliss above,
   thy fervent prayers renew
   that Scotland yet again may love
   the faith, entire and true;
   that I the cross allotted me
   may bear with patient love!
   'Twill lift me, as it lifted thee,
   to reign with Christ above.

728 Delores Dufner
© 1984, 1988, 1996 Delores Dufner OSB

1. When from bondage we are summoned
   out of darkness into light,
   we must go in hope and patience,
   walk by faith and not by sight.

Let us throw off all that hinders;
let us run the race to win!
Let us hasten to our homeland
and, rejoicing, enter in.

2. When our God names us a people,
Jesus leads us by the hand
through a lonely, barren desert,
to a great and glorious land.

3. Through all stages of the journey
Christ is with us, night and day,
with compassion for our weakness
ev'ry step along the way.

4. We must not lose sight of Jesus
who accepted pain and loss;
who, for joy of love unmeasured,
dared embrace the shameful cross.

5. See the prize our God has promised:
endless life with Christ the Lord.
Now we fix our eyes on Jesus
walk by faith in Jesus' word.

729 Keri Jones and David Matthew
© 1978 Word's Spirit of Praise Music/CopyCare

When I feel the touch
of your hand upon my life,
it causes me to sing a song
that I love you, Lord.
So from deep within
my spirit singeth unto thee,
you are my King,
you are my God,
and I love you, Lord.

730 Sydney Carter
© 1965 Stainer & Bell Ltd.

1. When I needed a neighbour,
were you there, were you there?
When I needed a neighbour,
were you there?

And the creed and the colour
and the name won't matter,
were you there?

2. I was hungry and thirsty,
were you there, were you there?
I was hungry and thirsty,
were you there?

3. I was cold, I was naked,
were you there, were you there?
I was cold, I was naked,
were you there?

4. When I needed a shelter,
were you there, were you there?
When I needed a shelter,
were you there?

5. When I needed a healer,
were you there, were you there?
When I needed a healer,
were you there?

6. Wherever you travel,
I'll be there, I'll be there,
wherever you travel,
I'll be there.

731 Isaac Watts

1. When I survey the wondrous cross
on which the Prince of Glory died,
my richest gain I count but loss,
and pour contempt on all my pride.

2. Forbid it, Lord, that I should boast,
save in the death of Christ, my God:
all the vain things that charm me most,
I sacrifice them to his blood.

3. See from his head, his hands, his feet,
sorrow and love flow mingling down:
did e'er such love and sorrow meet,
or thorns compose so rich a crown?

4. Were the whole realm of nature mine,
that were an off'ring far too small;
love so amazing, so divine,
demands my soul, my life, my all.

732
Didier Rimaud, trans. Margaret Foley and Robert B. Kelly. © Editions Musicales STUDIO SM

1. When the time came to stretch out
      his arms,
   and to lay down his life for his friends,
   God's only Son, in breaking the bread,
   gave his own flesh as food for us all;
   gave his own flesh as food for us all.

2. This is my flesh, O take it and eat.
   This is my blood, O take it and drink,
   and to proclaim my death for you all,
   this must you do until I return,
   this must you do until I return.

3. Hunger and thirst no longer we fear,
   Christ's holy flesh becomes now our food.
   And when we raise his chalice to drink,
   joy overflows, our hope is renewed,
   joy overflows, our hope is renewed.

4. O bread of life, O banner divine,
   sign of the love that makes us all one;
   we who now share this gift from above,
   surely have seen the goodness of God,
   surely have seen the goodness of God.

5. Through Jesus Christ, the perfect
      high Priest,
   and in the Spirit, source of our peace,
   for this great feast which you
      have prepared,
   Father above, O praised be your name,
   Father above, O praised be your name.

733
John Glynn
© 1976 Kevin Mayhew Ltd.

Where are you bound, Mary, Mary,
where are you bound, Mother of God?

1. Beauty is a dove
   sitting on a sunlit bough,
   beauty is a pray'r
   without the need of words.
   Words are more than sounds
   falling off an empty tongue:
   let it be according to his word.

2. Mary heard the word
   spoken in her inmost heart.
   Mary bore the Word
   and held him in her arms.
   Sorrow she has known,
   seeing him upon the cross:
   greater joy to see him rise again.

3. Where are we all bound,
   carrying the Word of God?
   Time and place are ours
   to make his glory known.
   Mary bore him first,
   we will tell the whole wide world:
   let it be according to his word.

734
Based on 'Ubi Caritas'
© 1966 Bishops' Conference of England and Wales

Where is love and loving kindness,
God is there.

1. The love of Christ has gathered us
   together in one:
   let us then rejoice and be glad in him.

2. Let us fear and love the living God;
   Let us love each other in the depths of
   our hearts.

3. Therefore when we are together
   let us take heed not to be divided in mind.

4. Let there be an end to
   bitterness and quarrels,
   an end to strife, and in our midst
   be Christ our God.

5. And in company with the blessed,
   may we see
   your face in glory, Christ our God:
   pure and unbounded joy
   for ever and ever. Amen.

735
Jean-Paul Lécot, based on 'Ubi Caritas', trans. W. R. Lawrence. © 1988 Kevin Mayhew Ltd.

Where love and charity endure,
God dwells therein.

1. The love of Christ has bound us all
   into one fold;
   let us rejoice and render thanks
   for his great love.

2. Let us revere and love
   the ever-living God,
   and by our love for one another
   prove that love.

3. It is together in one Body
   that we live:
   make sure that we do not divide it
   by our deeds.

4. May conflicts, quarrels, bitterness
   all disappear;
   let Jesus Christ be ever-present
   in our midst.

5. In heav'n amid the saints may
   we behold you, Lord,
   and there before the Father's throne
   your love enjoy.

6. Thus may we have unending
   happiness and joy
   in heav'n with God through endless
   ages evermore.

736
Michael Forster
© 1993 Kevin Mayhew Ltd.

1. Where the love of Christ unites us,
   there God is found.
   When we meet as love invites us,
   there God is found.
   Let us come with jubilation
   to the God of our salvation;
   love enlivens all creation;
   there God is found.

2. Where we meet without division,
   there God is found,
   free from anger and derision,
   there God is found.
   Let all bitter feuds be ended,
   strife resolved and foes befriended,
   pride and fear by love transcended;
   there God is found.

3. Where the blessèd live for ever,
   there God is found;
   bonds of love no pain can sever,
   there God is found.
   Christ in glory, we implore you,
   let us with the saints adore you,
   love resplendent flows before you;
   there God is found.

737
Michael Forster, based on 'Ubi Caritas'
© 1998 Kevin Mayhew Ltd.

1. Where true love is found with charity,
   God is present there.
   Christ's own love has called us,
   gathered us together.
   Let us come with songs
   of hope and jubilation,
   worship and adore him,
   God of our salvation,
   loving one another,
   loving one another.

2. Where true love is found with charity,
   God is present there.
   As his holy people,
   gathering together,
   let us be united,
   strife and discord ending.
   Christ, our God, among us,
   ev'ry fear transcending,
   known in one another,
   known in one another.

3. Where true love is found with charity,
   God is present there.
   With saints and martyrs,
   one in faith together,
   let us see your glory,
   Christ our great salvation,
   sharing in the great
   eternal celebration,
   there with one another,
   there with one another.

738 Hubert J. Richards, based on 'Ubi Caritas', Matthew 5:23, 1 John 4:16, Psalm 21:2
© 1997 Kevin Mayhew Ltd.

1. Where true love is present,
   God is present there.
   When we meet together
   let all quarrels cease.

   Leave your gift,
   and make peace with each other. (Repeat)

2. God is loving kindness;
   those who love like him
   live in God most truly,
   and he lives in them.

3. Let us put behind us
   bitterness and strife,
   recognising Jesus
   present in our midst.

739 Nahum Tate

1. While shepherds watched their flocks
      by night,
   all seated on the ground,
   the angel of the Lord came down,
   and glory shone around.

2. 'Fear not,' said he, (for mighty dread
   had seized their troubled mind)
   'glad tidings of great joy I bring
   to you and all mankind.'

3. 'To you in David's town this day
   is born of David's line
   a Saviour, who is Christ the Lord;
   and this shall be the sign:'

4. 'The heav'nly babe you there shall find
   to human view displayed,
   all meanly wrapped in swathing bands,
   and in a manger laid.'

5. Thus spake the seraph, and forthwith
   appeared a shining throng
   of angels praising God, who thus
   addressed their joyful song:

6. 'All glory be to God on high,
   and on the earth be peace,
   goodwill henceforth from heav'n to all
   begin and never cease.'

740 John L. Bell and Graham Maule
© 1987 WGRG, Iona Community

1. Will you come and follow me
   if I but call your name?
   Will you go where you don't know,
   and never be the same?
   Will you let my love be shown,
   will you let my name be known,
   will you let my life be grown
   in you, and you in me?

2. Will you leave yourself behind
   if I but call your name?
   Will you care for cruel and kind,
   and never be the same?
   Will you risk the hostile stare
   should your life attract or scare,
   will you let me answer prayer
   in you, and you in me?

3. Will you let the blinded see
   if I but call your name?
   Will you set the pris'ners free,
   and never be the same?
   Will you kiss the leper clean
   and do such as this unseen,
   and admit to what I mean
   in you, and you in me?

4. Will you love the 'you' you hide
   if I but call your name?
   Will you quell the fear inside,
   and never be the same?
   Will you use the faith you've found
   to reshape the world around
   through my sight and touch and sound
   in you, and you in me?

5. Lord, your summons echoes true
   when you but call my name.
   Let me turn and follow you,
   and never be the same.

In your company I'll go
where your love and footsteps show.
Thus I'll move and live and grow
in you, and you in me.

741
Susan Sayers, based on Psalm 129
© 1995 Kevin Mayhew Ltd.

With the Lord there is mercy,
with the Lord there is mercy
and fullness of redemption.

1. From the deep I call to you,
   hear me, O God.
   Give attention to my cry
   and hear my pleading words.

2. If you only saw our guilt,
   Lord, who would live?
   But forgiveness flows from you,
   and so we praise your name.

3. How my soul awaits the Lord!
   In him I trust.
   Longingly I wait for him
   as watchers for the dawn.

4. Since our great forgiving God
   comes to redeem,
   all his people will be saved
   from all their sin and shame.

742
Huub Oosterhuis, based on Psalm 72
© Burns & Oates Ltd.

With you, O God, my highest good,
with you I am secure.

1. With you, I am always with you, my God,
   you hold me tight, your hand in mine.

2. All things come to their fulfilment in you;
   you lead me on in your great love.

3. Heaven, what is that if you are not there?
   And here on earth you are my joy.

4. And when life on earth has come to
      an end,
   then I will be with you, my God.

743
Virginia Vissing
© 1974, 1998, Sisters of St Mary of Namur

1. Word made flesh, Son of God.
   Come, Lord Jesus, come again. (x2)

2. Lord and Saviour, Son of God.

3. Prince of Peace, Son of God.

4. Alleluia, Son of God.

5. Bread of Life, Son of God.

6. Light of the World, Son of God.

7. Jesus Christ, Son of God.

744
Dan Schutte, based on Psalm 138
© 1971, 1974, Daniel L. Schutte

Yahweh, I know you are near,
standing always at my side.
You guard me from the foe
and you lead me in ways everlasting.

1. Lord, you have searched my heart,
   and you know when I sit and when
      I stand,
   for your hand is upon me,
   protecting me from death,
   keeping me from harm.

2. Where can I run from your love?
   If I climb to the heavens you are there.
   If I fly to the sunrise
   or sail beyond the sea,
   still I'd find you there.

3. You know my heart and its ways,
   you who formed me before I was born,
   in the secret of darkness,
   before I saw the sun
   in my mother's womb.

4. Marv'llous to me are your works;
   how profound are your thoughts,
      my Lord!
   Even if I could count them,
   they number as the stars,
   you would still be there.

745

Gregory Norbet, based on Isaiah 12. © 1972 The Benedictine Foundation of the State of Vermont, Inc.

Yahweh is the God of my salvation:
I trust in him and have no fear.
I sing of the joy which his love gives to me,
and I draw deeply from the springs of his
great kindness.

1. Open our eyes
   to the wonder of this moment,
   the beginning of
   another day.

2. Be with us, Lord,
   as we break through with each other,
   to find the truth and beauty
   of each friend.

3. When ev'ning comes,
   and our day of toil is over,
   give us rest, O Lord,
   in the joy of many friends.

4. Take us beyond
   the vision of this day
   to the deep and wide ways
   of your infinite love and life.

746

St Fulbert of Chartres, trans. Robert Campbell

1. Ye choirs of new Jerusalem,
   your sweetest notes employ,
   the Paschal victory to hymn
   in strains of holy joy.

2. For Judah's Lion burst his chains,
   and crushed the serpent's head;
   and brought with him,
       from death's domain,
   the long-imprisoned dead.

3. From hell's devouring jaws the prey
   alone our leader bore;
   his ransomed hosts pursue their way
   where he hath gone before.

4. Triumphant in his glory now
   his sceptre ruleth all;
   earth, heav'n and hell before him bow
   and at his footstool fall.

5. While joyful thus his praise we sing,
   his mercy we implore,
   into his palace bright to bring,
   and keep us evermore.

6. All glory to the Father be,
   all glory to the Son,
   all glory, Holy Ghost, to thee,
   while endless ages run.

747

Jean Tisserand, trans. Edward Caswall

Alleluia, alleluia, alleluia.

1. Ye sons and daughters of the Lord,
   the King of glory, King adored,
   this day himself from death restored.
   Alleluia.

2. All in the early morning grey
   went holy women on their way
   to see the tomb where Jesus lay.
   Alleluia.

3. Then straightway one in white they see,
   who saith, 'Ye seek the Lord; but he
   is ris'n, and gone to Galilee.'
   Alleluia.

4. That self-same night, while out of fear
   the doors were shut, their Lord most dear
   to his apostles did appear.
   Alleluia.

5. But Thomas, when of this he heard,
   was doubtful of his brethren's word;
   wherefore again there comes the Lord.
   Alleluia.

6. 'Thomas, behold my side,' saith he;
   'my hands, my feet, my body see,
   and doubt not, but believe in me.'
   Alleluia.

7. When Thomas saw that wounded side,
   the truth no longer he denied:
   'Thou art my Lord and God!' he cried.
   Alleluia.

8. Now let us praise the Lord most high,
and strive his name to magnify
on this great day, through earth and sky.
Alleluia.

748

Mark Altrogge
© 1987 People of Destiny International/CopyCare

You are beautiful beyond description,
too marvellous for words,
too wonderful for comprehension,
like nothing ever seen or heard.
Who can grasp your infinite wisdom?
Who can fathom the depth of your love?
You are beautiful beyond description,
majesty, enthroned above.

And I stand, I stand in awe of you.
I stand, I stand in awe of you.
Holy God, to whom all praise is due,
I stand in awe of you.

749

Marty Haugen
© 1986 GIA Publications Inc.

1. You are salt for the earth, O people:
   salt for the kingdom of God!
   Share the flavour of life, O people:
   life in the kingdom of God.

   Bring forth the kingdom of mercy,
   Bring forth the kingdom of peace;
   Bring forth the kingdom of justice,
   Bring forth the city of God!

2. You are a light on the hill, O people:
   light for the city of God!
   Shine so holy and bright, O people:
   shine for the kingdom of God!

3. You are a seed of the Word, O people:
   bring forth the kingdom of God!
   Seeds of mercy and seeds of justice,
   grow in the kingdom of God!

4. We are a blest and a pilgrim people:
   bound for the kingdom of God!
   Love our journey and love our homeland:
   love is the kingdom of God!

750

Mavis Ford
© 1978 Word's Spirit of Praise Music/CopyCare

You are the King of Glory,
you are the Prince of Peace,
you are the Lord of heav'n and earth,
you're the Son of righteousness.
Angels bow down before you,
worship and adore, for
you have the words of eternal life,
you are Jesus Christ the Lord.
Hosanna to the Son of David!
Hosanna to the King of kings!
Glory in the highest heaven,
for Jesus the Messiah reigns.

751

Margaret Rizza
© 1998 Kevin Mayhew Ltd.

1. You are the light that is ever bright,
   you fill my heart, giving life;
   you give the work
   I endeavour to do,
   meaning and purpose
   are blessings from you.

   O hold me, enfold me in your love.

2. You are the beauty that fills my soul,
   you, by your wound, make me whole.
   You paid the price
   to redeem me from death;
   yours is the love that
   sustains my ev'ry breath.

3. You still the storms and the fear of night,
   you turn despair to delight.
   You feel the anguish,
   and share in my tears,
   you give the hope from
   the depth of my fears.

4. You are the word full of life and truth,
   you guide my feet since my youth;
   you are my refuge,
   my firm cornerstone,
   you I will worship
   and honour alone.

Continued overleaf

5. You have restored me and pardoned sin,
   you give me strength from within.
   You called me forth,
   and my life you made new.
   Love is the binding
   that holds me to you.

6. You are the Way, you are Truth and Life,
   you keep me safe in the strife.
   You give me the love
   I cannot comprehend,
   you guide the way
   to a life without end.

752 Gregory Murray, based on Luke 2:29-32
© 1999 Kevin Mayhew Ltd.

1. You give, Lord, the sign to your servant
   to go in your peace;
   your promise of old has been honoured,
   your word is fulfilled.

   May God give his grace in our waking
   and watch as we sleep;
   may Christ be our friend in the daylight,
   our peace through the night.

2. At last I have seen your salvation,
   your gift to the world:
   the light of the Gentiles,
   the glory in Israel's midst.

3. Give thanks to the Father of mercies,
   give thanks to his Son,
   give thanks to the joy-giving Spirit,
   give thanks to one God.

753 Carey Landry, from the Rite of Baptism.
© 1976 North American Liturgy Resources (NALR)

You have been baptised in Christ.
You have been baptised in Christ.
It is he that you have put on.
It is he that you have put on.
You are washed in this water
You are washed in this water
have hope of eternal life.
have hope of eternal life.

1. God the Father has freed you
   and given you a new birth,
   and to be a member of his holy people
   he now anoints you with oil.

2. You are a new creation.
   In Christ you have been clothed.
   See in this garment the outward sign
   of your dignity in him.

3. Receive the light of Christ;
   keep it burning brightly.
   Always walk as a child of the light,
   with his flame alive in your heart.

754 Lynn DeShazo and Martin J. Nystrom
© 1990 Integrity's Hosanna! Music/Kingsway's Thankyou Music

You have called us out of darkness,
out of darkness into your glorious light.
You have saved us from the darkness,
we rejoice in your power and might.

1. We are a chosen race,
   a royal priesthood by your grace.
   We are a holy nation
   set apart for you.

2. We are to take your light
   to ev'ry nation, tongue and tribe,
   so they may see your glory
   shining through our lives.

755 Susan Sayers, based on Psalm 18
© 1995 Kevin Mayhew Ltd.

You have the message of eternal life,
O Lord.

1. How lovely is the law of God,
   so righteous and so just;
   live out this way, the way of love
   in all you say and do.

2. This law alone can soothe the soul,
   give peace and inner joy;
   like solid ground that we may trust,
   and light to travel by.

3. As worldly values shift and slide
   the love of God holds fast,
   and though our world will pass away
   his faithfulness remains.

756

Mike Anderson
© 1999 Kevin Mayhew Ltd.

Your love's greater (greater),
greater than the greatest mountain,
your love's deeper (deeper),
deeper than the deepest sea;
a love that never dies,
a love that reaches deep inside,
more wondrous than all the universe.

1. You made the heavens, the earth and sea;
   your power is awesome,
   and you still love me.

2. Your ways are righteous, your laws are just,
   love is your promise,
   and in you I trust.

3. Your love is healing, your love endures;
   my life is changed, Lord,
   now I know I'm yours.

757

Bob Dufford, based on Isaiah 43:2-3, Luke 6:20
© 1975, 1978 Robert J. Dufford, S.J. and New Dawn
Music

1. You shall cross the barren desert,
   but you shall not die of thirst.
   You shall wander far in safety
   though you do not know the way.
   You shall speak your words in foreign
   lands and they will understand.
   You shall see the face of God and live.

   Be not afraid.
   I go before you always.
   Come follow me, and I will give you rest.

2. If you pass through raging waters in the
   sea, you shall not drown.
   If you walk amid the burning flames, you
   shall not be harmed.
   If you stand before the pow'r of hell and
   death is at your side,
   know that I am with you through it all.

3. Blessed are the poor, for the kingdom
   shall be theirs.
   Blest are you that weep and mourn, for
   one day you shall laugh.
   And if wicked men insult and hate you
   all because of me,
   blessed, blessed are you!

758

Steffi Geiser Rubin and Stuart Dauermann
© 1975 Lillenas Publishing Co./CopyCare

You shall go out with joy
and be led forth with peace,
and the mountains and the hills
shall break forth before you.
There'll be shouts of joy
and the trees of the field shall clap,
shall clap their hands.
And the trees of the field
shall clap their hands,
and the trees of the field
shall clap their hands,
and the trees of the field
shall clap their hands,
and you'll go out with joy.

759

Michael Joncas, based on Psalm 90
© 1979, 1991 New Dawn Music

1. You who dwell in the shelter of
       the Lord,
   who abide in his shadow for life,
   say to the Lord: 'My refuge,
   my rock in whom I trust!'

   And he will raise you upon eagle's wings,
   bear you on the breath of dawn,
   make you to shine like the sun,
   and hold you in the palm of his hand.

2. The snare of the fowler will never
       capture you,
   and famine will bring you no fear.
   Under his wings your refuge,
   his faithfulness your shield.

3. You need not fear the terror of the night,
   nor the arrow that flies by day;
   though thousands fall about you,
   near you it shall not come.

4. For to his angels he's given a command
   to guard you in all of your ways;
   upon their hands they will bear you up,
   lest you dash your foot against a stone.

LITURGICAL

HYMNS OLD & NEW

CHILDREN'S HYMNS AND SONGS

760
Carey Landry
© 1979 Carey Landry/NALR

1. A butterfly, *a butterfly,*
   an Easter egg, *an Easter egg,*
   a fountain flowing in the park,
   a fountain flowing in the park.

   These are signs of new life;
      the life of Jesus the Lord.
   And we sing to him, alleluia!
   We give to him our praise!
   We sing to him alleluia!
   Glory be to him! *Glory be to him!*
   Glory be to Jesus the Lord!

2. A helping hand, *a helping hand,*
   a happy smile, *a happy smile,*
   a heart so full of hope and joy,
   a heart so full of hope and joy.

3. A cup of wine, *a cup of wine,*
   a loaf of bread, *a loaf of bread,*
   now blest and broken for us all,
   now blest and broken for us all.

761
Traditional

1. All in an Easter garden,
   before the break of day,
   an angel came from heaven
   and rolled the stone away.
   When Jesus' friends came seeking,
   with myrrh and spices rare,
   they found the angels at the door,
   but Jesus was not there.

2. All in an Easter garden,
   where water lilies bloom,
   the angels gave their message
   beside an empty tomb:

'The Lord is here no longer,
come, see where once he lay;
the Lord of life is ris'n indeed,
for this is Easter day.'

762
Doug Marks-Smirchirch
© Right on the Mark Music/Copyright control

All of my heart, all of my soul,
all of my mind, all of my strength.
(Repeat)
With everything within me
I want to praise you, Lord.
I want to love you with all that I am,
and bring joy to your heart.

Last time:
Let me bring joy to your heart all of
my life.

763
Susan Sayers
© 1986 Kevin Mayhew Ltd.

All of the people on the mountain,
all of the people in the valley,
all of the people in the villages and the town,
say to each other on the way,
'Bring all your friends and don't delay,
Jesus of Nazareth is coming here today.'

1. Jesus, Jesus, when we are with you,
   it's strange, and yet it's true,
   we start to feel that there is
   more to life than living as we do.
   It's richer and more satisfying
   than we ever knew.

2. Jesus, Jesus, healing as you go,
   your loving seems to flow
   like water from a fountain,
   and as we are touched we want to grow
   in love towards each other –
   just because you love us so!

3. Jesus, Jesus, we have come to see
   that you must really be
   the Son of God our Father.
   We've been with you and we all agree
   that only in your service
   can the world be truly free.

764

Michael Cockett
© McCrimmon Publishing Co Ltd.

All the nations of the earth,
praise the Lord who brings to birth
the greatest star, the smallest flow'r.
Alleluia.

1. Let the heavens praise the Lord, alleluia.
   Moon and stars, praise the Lord, alleluia.

2. Snow-capped mountains, praise the
     Lord, alleluia.
   Rolling hills, praise the Lord, alleluia.

3. Deep sea water, praise the Lord, alleluia.
   Gentle rain, praise the Lord, alleluia.

4. Roaring lion, praise the Lord, alleluia.
   Singing birds, praise the Lord, alleluia.

5. Earthly monarchs, praise the Lord,
     alleluia.
   Young and old, praise the Lord, alleluia.

765 Unknown

And ev'ryone beneath the vine and fig tree
shall live in peace and have no fear.
And ev'ryone beneath the vine and fig tree
shall live in peace and have no fear.
And into plough shares turn their swords,
nations shall learn war no more.
And into plough shares turn their swords,
nations shall learn war no more.

766 18th century

1. As Jacob with travel
   was weary one day,
   at night on a stone
   for a pillow he lay;
   he saw in a vision
   a ladder so high
   that its foot was on earth
   and its top in the sky:

Alleluia to Jesus who died on the tree,
and has raised up a ladder of mercy for me,
and has raised up a ladder of mercy for me.

2. This ladder is long,
   it is strong and well-made,
   has stood hundreds of years
   and is not yet decayed;
   many millions have climbed it
   and reached Zion's hill,
   and thousands by faith
   are climbing it still:

3. Come let us ascend!
   all may climb it who will;
   for the angels of Jacob
   are guarding it still:
   and remember, each step
   that by faith we pass o'er,
   some prophet or martyr
   has trod it before:

4. And when we arrive
   at the haven of rest
   we shall hear the glad words,
   'Come up hither, ye blest,
   here are regions of light,
   here are mansions of bliss.'
   O who would not climb
   such a ladder as this?

767

Alan J. Price
© 1990 Daybreak Music Ltd.

1. Be the centre of my life, Lord Jesus,
   be the centre of my life, I pray;
   be my Saviour to forgive me,
   be my friend to be with me,
   be the centre of my life today!

2. Let the power of your presence,
     Lord Jesus,
   from the centre of my life shine through;
   oh, let ev'rybody know it,
   I really want to show it,
   that the centre of my life is you!

768 Susan Sayers
© 1986 Kevin Mayhew Ltd.

1. Caterpillar, caterpillar,
munching, munching,
ate through a leaf or two,
for caterpillar, caterpillar,
munching, munching,
didn't have a lot to do.
But the leaves were very tasty,
and there seemed a lot to spare,
so caterpillar, caterpillar, went on
munching, munching ev'rywhere.

2. Caterpillar, caterpillar,
feeling sleepy,
fixed up a silken bed.
Then caterpillar, caterpillar
climbed inside
and covered up his sleepy head.
In the dark he slept and rested
as the days and nights went by,
till on a sunny morning when the
silk bed burst, he was a butterfly!

3. Butterfly, oh butterfly,
a flitt'ring, flutt'ring;
oh what a sight so see.
And as the lovely butterfly
was flutt'ring by,
I heard him sing a song to me:
'Oh I never knew God could do
such a wondrous thing for me;
for he took me as a caterpillar
and he made a butterfly of me.'

769 Eddie Espinosa
© 1982 Mercy/Vineyard Publishing/
Music Services/CopyCare

Change my heart, O God,
make it ever true,
change my heart, O God,
may I be like you.

You are the potter,
I am the clay,
mould me and make me,
this is what I pray.

770 Estelle White
© 1977 Kevin Mayhew Ltd.

1. 'Cheep!' said the sparrow
on the chimney top,
'All my feathers are known to God.'
'Caw!' said the rook in a tree so tall,
'I know that God gladly made us all.'

2. 'Coo!' said the gentle one,
the grey-blue dove,
'I can tell you that God is love.'
High up above sang the lark in flight,
'I know the Lord is my heart's delight.'

3. 'Chirp!' said the robin
with his breast so red,
'I don't want to work at all, yet I'm fed.'
'Whoo!' called the owl in a leafy wood,
'Our God is wonderful, wise and good.'

771 Estelle White
© 1976 Kevin Mayhew Ltd.

Christ is our King,
let the whole world rejoice!
May all the nations sing out with one voice!
Light of the world,
you have helped us to see that
we are one people and
one day we all shall be free!

1. He came to open the eyes of the blind,
letting the sunlight pour into their minds.
Vision is waiting for those who
have hope.
He is the light of the world.

2. He came to speak tender words to
the poor,
he is the gateway and he is the door.
Riches are waiting for all those who hope.
He is the light of the world.

Continued overleaf

3. He came to open the doors of the goal;
   he came to help the downtrodden
      and frail.
   Freedom is waiting for all those
      who hope.
   He is the light of the world.

4. He came to open the lips of the mute,
   letting them speak out with courage
      and truth.
   His words are uttered by all those
      who hope.
   He is the light of the world.

5. He came to heal all the crippled
      and lame,
   sickness took flight at the sound of
      his name.
   Vigour is waiting for all those who hope.
   He is the light of the world.

6. He came to love everyone on this earth
   and through his Spirit he
      promised rebirth.
   New life is waiting for all those
      who hope.
   He is the light of the world.

772 Jimmy Owens. © 1972 Bud John Songs/EMI Christian Music Publishing

Clap your hands, all you people.
Shout to our God with a voice of triumph.
Clap your hands, all you people.
Shout to our God with a voice of praise!
Hosanna, hosanna.
Shout to our God with a voice of triumph.
Praise him, praise him.
Shout to our God with a voice of praise!

773 Jean Holloway © 1997 Kevin Mahyew Ltd.

1. Clap your hands and sing this song,
   all together,
   tap your feet and sing along,
   all together.

2. Raise your hands up in the air,
   God can reach you anywhere.

3. Fold your arms across your chest,
   in the arms of God you're blessed.

4. Close your eyes and shut them tight,
   God will keep you in his sight.

5. Now sing softly, whisper low,
   God will hear you even so.

6. Sing out loud and strong and clear,
   so that ev'ryone can hear.

7. Sing with harmony and joy,
   God loves ev'ry girl and boy.

774 Unknown

1. Come and praise the Lord our King,
   alleluia,
   come and praise the Lord our King.
   alleluia!

2. Christ was born in Bethlehem,
   Son of God and Son of Man.

3. He grew up an earthly child,
   in the world, but undefiled.

4. He who died at Calvary,
   rose again triumphantly.

5. He will cleanse us from our sin,
   if we live by faith in him.

775 Unknown

1. Come, God's children, praise the Lord,
   alleluia.
   He's our God, and we are his, *alleluia!*

2. Come to him with songs of praise,
   songs of praise, rejoice in him.

3. For the Lord is a mighty God,
   he is King of all the world.

4. In his hands are valleys deep,
   in his hands are mountain peaks.

5. In his hands are all the seas,
   and the lands which he has made.

6. Praise the Father, praise the Son,
   praise the Spirit, the Holy One.

776 Unknown

1. Come into his presence, singing,
   'Alleluia.' *(x3)*

2. Come into his presence, singing,
   'Jesus is Lord.' *(x3)*

3. Come into his presence, singing,
   'Glory to God.' *(x3)*

777 Katherine K. Davis, Henry V. Onorati and Harry Simeone. © *1941 EMI Mills Music Inc./Delaware Music Corp.*

1. Come, they told me,
   pah-rum-pum-pum-pum!
   our new-born King to see,
   pah-rum-pum-pum-pum!
   Our finest gifts we bring,
   pah-rum-pum-pum-pum!
   to lay before the King,
   pah-rum-pum-pum-pum!
   Rum-pum-pum-pum!
   Rum-pum-pum-pum!
   So, to honour him,
   pah-rum-pum-pum-pum!
   when we come.

2. Baby Jesus,
   pah-rum-pum-pum-pum!
   I am a poor child too,
   pah-rum-pum-pum-pum!
   I have no gift to bring,
   pah-rum-pum-pum-pum!
   that's fit to give a King,
   pah-rum-pum-pum-pum!
   Rum-pum-pum-pum!
   Rum-pum-pum-pum!
   Shall I play for you,
   pah-rum-pum-pum-pum!
   on my drum?

3. Mary nodded,
   pah-rum-pum-pum-pum!
   The ox and lamb kept time,
   pah-rum-pum-pum-pum!
   I played my drum for him,
   pah-rum-pum-pum-pum!
   I played my best for him,
   pah-rum-pum-pum-pum!
   Rum-pum-pum-pum!
   Rum-pum-pum-pum!
   Then he smiled at me,
   pah-rum-pum-pum-pum!
   me and my drum.

778 Unknown

Dear child divine, sweet brother mine,
be with me all the day,
and when the light has turned to night
be with me still, I pray.
Where'er I be, come down to me
and never go away.

779 Sebastian Temple © *Copyright control*

Do not worry over what to eat,
what to wear or put upon your feet;
trust and pray, go do your best today,
then leave it in the hands of the Lord,
leave it in the hands of the Lord.

1. The lilies of the field,
   they do not spin or weave,
   yet Solomon was not arrayed
   like one of these.
   The birds of the air;
   they do not sow or reap,
   but God tends to them
   like a shepherd tends his sheep.

Continued overleaf

2. The Lord will guide you
in his hidden way,
show you what to do
and tell you what to say.
When you pray for rain,
go build a dam to store
ev'ry drop of water
you have asked him for.

3. The Lord knows all your needs
before you ask.
Only trust in him
for he will do the task
of bringing in your life
whatever you must know.
He'll lead you through the darkness
wherever you must go.

780
Karen Lafferty
© 1981 Maranatha! Music/CopyCare

Don't build your house on the sandy land,
don't build it too near the shore.
Well, it might look kind of nice,
but you'll have to build it twice,
oh, you'll have to build your house
once more.

You'd better build your house upon a rock,
make a good foundation on a solid spot.
Oh, the storms may come and go
but the peace of God you will know.

781
Bev Gammon
© 1988 Kingsway's Thankyou Music

Do what you know is right.
Do what you know is right.
Do what you know is good.
Do what is good.
If no one else does it, don't be afraid.
Jesus says, 'I am with you always'.

782
Michael Forster
© 1997 Kevin Mayhew Ltd.

Each of us is a living stone,
no one needs to stand alone,
joined to other living stones,
we're building the temple of God.

1. We're building, we're building
the temple of God on earth,
but it needs no walls or steeple,
for we're making a house of greater worth,
we're building it with people!

2. The stone that, the stone that
the builders once cast aside
has been made the firm foundation,
and the carpenter who was crucified
now offers us salvation.

783
Peter Watcyn-Jones
© 1978 Kevin Mayhew Ltd.

1. Ev'ry bird, ev'ry tree
helps me know, helps me see,
helps me feel
God is love and love's around.
From each river painted blue
to the early morning dew
this is love, God is love, love's around.

2. Ev'ry prayer, ev'ry song
makes me feel I belong
to a world filled
with love that's all around.
From each daybreak to each night,
out of darkness comes the light,
this is love, God is love, love's around.

3. Ev'ry mountain, ev'ry stream,
ev'ry flower, ev'ry dream
comes from God,
God is love and love's around.
From the ever-changing sky
to a new-born baby's cry,
this is love, God is love, love's around.

784

Robin Mann
© 1986 Kevin Mayhew Ltd.

Father welcomes all his children
to his fam'ly through his Son.
Father giving his salvation,
life for ever has been won.

1. Little children, come to me,
   for my kingdom is of these.
   Love and new life have I to give,
   pardon for your sin.

2. In the water, in the word,
   in his promise, be assured:
   all who believe and are baptised
   shall be born again.

3. Let us daily die to sin;
   let us daily rise with him –
   walk in the love of Christ our Lord,
   live in the peace of God.

785

Susan Sayers
© 1986 Kevin Mayhew Ltd.

1. Fishes of the ocean
   and the birds of the air,
   they all declare
   the wonderful works of God
   who has created ev'rything ev'rywhere;
   let the whole earth sing of his love!

2. Apples in the orchard
   and the corn in the field,
   the plants all yield
   their fruit in due season,
   so the generosity of God is revealed;
   let the whole earth sing of his love!

3. Energy and colour
   from the sun with its light,
   the moon by night;
   the patterns of the stars
   all winking in the darkness on a frosty
     cold night;
   let the whole earth sing of his love!

4. Muddy hippopotamus
   and dainty gazelle,
   the mice as well,
   are all of his making,
   furry ones and hairy ones and some with
     a shell;
   let the whole earth sing of his love!

5. All that we can hear
   and ev'rything we can see,
   including me,
   we all of us spring from God
   who cares for ev'rybody unendingly;
   let the whole earth sing of his love!

786

Graham Jeffery
© 1983 Kevin Mayhew Ltd.

1. Forward in faith, forward in Christ,
   we are travelling onward;
   forward in faith, forward in Christ,
   we are trav'ling on.

   Onward, onward, we are trav'ling on,
   onward, onward, we are trav'ling on.

2. Jesus is Lord, Jesus is Lord,
   we are travelling onward;
   Jesus is Lord, Jesus is Lord,
   we are trav'ling on.

3. He is our King, he is our King,
   we are travelling onward;
   he is our King, he is our King,
   we are trav'ling on.

787

David Morstad
© Copyright control

Friends, all gather here in a circle.
It has no beginning and it has no end.
Face to face, we all have a place
in God's own circle of friends.
Hey there, *(name)*!
How do you do?
Who's that friend sitting close to you?
Thank the Lord, for *(name)* has a place
in the circle, too.
Take a look around.
Find someone near.

Continued overleaf

Take him/her by the hand,
say, 'Glad you're here.'
We're together and when we've gone,
God's love, like a circle,
rolls on and on and on.

788
Estelle White
© 1976 Kevin Mayhew Ltd.

1. Give me peace, O Lord, I pray
   in my work and in my play;
   and inside my heart and mind,
   Lord, give me peace.

2. Give peace to the world, I pray
   let all quarrels cease today.
   May we spread your light and love:
   Lord, give us peace.

789
Caroline Somerville. © The Central Board of Finance
of the Church of England

1. God almighty set a rainbow
   arching in the sky above,
   and his people understand it
   as a signal of his love.

   Thank you, Father, thank you, Father,
   thank you, Father, for your care,
   for your warm and loving kindness
   to your people ev'rywhere.

2. Clouds will gather, storms come
        streaming
   on the darkened earth below –
   too much sunshine makes a desert,
   without rain no seed can grow.

3. Through the stormcloud shines your
        rainbow,
   through the dark earth springs the wheat.
   In the future waits your harvest
   and the food for all to eat.

4. God almighty, you have promised
   after rain the sun will show;
   bless the seeds and bless the harvest.
   Give us grace to help us grow.

790
Miriam Thérèse Winter
© 1965 Medical Mission Sisters

1. God gives his people strength.
   If we believe in his way
   he's swift to repay
   all those who bear the burden of the day.
   God gives his people strength.

2. God gives his people hope.
   If we but trust in his word
   our prayers are always heard.
   He warmly welcomes anyone who's erred.
   God gives his people hope.

3. God gives his people love.
   If we but open wide our heart
   he's sure to do his part.
   He's always the first to make a start.
   God gives his people love.

4. God gives his people peace.
   When sorrow fills us to the brim
   and courage grows dim
   he lays to rest our restlessness in him.
   God gives his people peace.

791
Kathleen Middleton
© 1986 Kevin Mayhew Ltd.

1. God our Father gave us life,
   he keeps us in his care;
   help us care for others too:
   Lord, hear our prayer;
   Lord, hear our prayer.

2. When we're frightened, hurt or tired,
   there's always someone there.
   Make us thankful for their love:
   Lord, hear our prayer;
   Lord, hear our prayer.

3. All God's children need his love,
   a love that we can share.
   So, we pray for everyone:
   Lord, hear our prayer;
   Lord, hear our prayer.

792
Michael Forster
© 1997 Kevin Mayhew Ltd.

1. God sends a rainbow after the rain,
   colours of hope gleaming through pain;
   bright arcs of red and indigo light,
   making creation hopeful and bright.

   Colours of hope dance in the sun,
   while it yet rains the hope has begun;
   colours of hope shine through the rain,
   colours of love, nothing is vain.

2. When we are lonely, when we're afraid,
   though it seems dark, rainbows are made;
   even when life itself has to end,
   God is our rainbow, God is our friend.

3. Where people suffer pain or despair,
   God can be seen in those who care;
   even where war and hatred abound,
   rainbows of hope are still to be found.

4. People themselves like rainbows are made,
   colours of hope in us displayed;
   old ones and young ones, women
      and men,
   all can be part of love's great 'Amen'!

793
Michael Forster
© 1997 Kevin Mayhew Ltd.

1. God turned darkness into light,
   separated day from night,
   looked upon it with delight,
   and declared that it was good.

   God was pleased with ev'rything, (x3)
   and declared that it was good.

2. God divided land and sea,
   filled the world with plants and trees,
   all so beautiful to see,
   and declared that it was good.

3. God made animals galore,
   fishes, birds and dinosaurs,
   heard the splashes, songs and roars,
   and declared that it was good.

4. God made people last of all,
   black and white, and short and tall,
   male and female, large and small,
   and declared that it was good.

794
Michael Forster
© 1993 Kevin Mayhew Ltd.

1. Goliath was big and Goliath was strong,
   his sword was sharp and his spear
      was long;
   he bragged and boasted but he was wrong:
   biggest isn't always best!

   Biggest isn't always best!
   Biggest isn't always best!
   God told David, 'Don't be afraid,
   biggest isn't always best!'

2. A shepherd boy had a stone and sling;
   he won the battle and pleased the King!
   Then all the people begain to sing:
   'Biggest isn't always best!'

3. So creatures made in a smaller size,
   like tiny sparrows and butterflies,
   are greater than we may realise:
   biggest isn't always best!

795
Luke 1:28

Hail, Mary, full of grace,
the Lord is with thee.
Blessed art thou among women,
and blessed is the fruit
of thy womb, Jesus.
Holy Mary, mother of God,
pray for us sinners,
now and at the hour of our death.
Amen.

796
Unknown

Hallulu, hallelu, hallelu, hallelujah;
we'll praise the Lord! *(Repeat)*
We'll praise the Lord, hallelujah! *(x3)*
We'll praise the Lord!

797

Christian Strover
© Christian Strover/Jubilate Hymns

1. Have you heard the raindrops
drumming on the rooftops?
Have you heard the raindrops
dripping on the ground?
Have you heard the raindrops
splashing in the streams
and running to the rivers all around?

   There's water, water of life,
   Jesus gives us the water of life;
   there's water, water of life,
   Jesus gives us the water of life.

2. There's a busy worker
digging in the desert,
digging with a spade that
flashes in the sun;
soon there will be water
rising in the well-shaft,
spilling from the bucket as it comes.

3. Nobody can live
who hasn't any water,
when the land is dry,
then nothing much grows;
Jesus gives us life if we drink
the living water,
sing it so that everybody knows.

798

Unknown

He is the King of kings,
he is the Lord of lords,
his name is Jesus, Jesus, Jesus, Jesus
O, he is the King.

799

Orien Johnson. © 1982 Fred Bock Music
Company/Kingsway's Thankyou Music

Hey, now, ev'rybody sing,
ev'rybody sing to the Lord our God!
Hey, now, ev'rybody sing,
ev'rybody sing to the Lord our God!
Ev'rybody join in a song of praise,
come and sing along with me!
Glory, alleluia, glory, alleluia,
I'm so glad I'm free!

Hey, now, ev'rybody sing,
ev'rybody sing to the Lord our God!
Hey, now, ev'rybody sing,
ev'rybody sing to the Lord our God!
Ev'rybody sing, ev'rybody sing,
ev'rybody sing to the Lord our God!
Ev'rybody sing, ev'rybody sing,
ev'rybody sing to the Lord our God!
Ev'rybody sing!

800

Brian Howard. © 1975 Mission Hills Music.
Administered by CopyCare

1. If I were a butterfly,
I'd thank you Lord, for giving me wings,
and if I were a robin in a tree,
I'd thank you, Lord, that I could sing,
and if I were a fish in the sea,
I'd wiggle my tail and I'd giggle with glee,
but I just thank you, Father,
for making me 'me'.

   For you gave me a heart,
   and you gave me a smile,
   you gave me Jesus
   and you made me your child,
   and I just thank you, Father,
   for making me 'me'.

2. If I were an elephant,
I'd thank you, Lord, by raising my trunk,
and if I were a kangaroo,
you know I'd hop right up to you,
and if I were an octopus,
I'd thank you, Lord, for my fine looks,
but I just thank you, Father,
for making me 'me'.

3. If I were a wiggly worm,
I'd thank you, Lord, that I could squirm,
and if I were a billy goat,
I'd thank you, Lord, for my strong throat,
and if I were a fuzzy wuzzy bear,
I'd thank you, Lord, for my fuzzy
wuzzy hair,
but I just thank you, Father,
for making me 'me'.

801

Estelle White
© 1978 Kevin Mayhew Ltd.

1. I give my hands to do your work
and, Jesus Lord, I give them willingly.
I give my feet to go your way
and ev'ry step I shall take cheerfully,

O, the joy of the Lord is my strength,
my strength!
O, the joy of the Lord is my help, my help!
For the pow'r of his Spirit is in my soul
and the joy of the Lord is my strength.

2. I give my eyes to see the world
and ev'ryone, in just the way you do.
I give my tongue to speak your words,
to spread your name and freedom-
giving truth.

3. I give my mind in every way
so that each thought I have will come
from you.
I give my spirit to you, Lord,
and every day my prayer will spring anew.

4. I give my heart that you may love
in me your Father and the human race.
I give myself that you may grow
in me and make my life a song of praise.

802

Michael Forster
© 1993 Kevin Mayhew Ltd.

1. I'm black, I'm white, I'm short, I'm tall,
I'm all the human race.
I'm young, I'm old, I'm large, I'm small,
and Jesus knows my face.

The love of God is free to ev'ryone,
free to ev'ryone, free to ev'ryone.
The love of God is free, oh yes!
That's what the gospel says.

2. I'm rich, I'm poor, I'm pleased, I'm sad,
I'm ev'ryone you see.
I'm quick, I'm slow, I'm good, I'm bad,
I know that God loves me.

3. So tall and thin, and short and wide,
and any shade of face,
I'm one of those for whom Christ died,
part of the human race.

803

Gerard Fitzpatrick
© 1986 Kevin Mayhew Ltd.

1. In the upper room, Jesus and his friends
met to celebrate their final supper.
Jesus took a bowl, knelt to wash their feet,
told them:
'You must do for others as I do for you.'

2. Peter was annoyed: 'This will never do!
You, as Master, should not play
the servant!'
Jesus took a towel, knelt to dry their feet,
told them:
'You must do for others as I do for you.'

804

Alan J. Price
© 1992 Daybreak Music Ltd.

Isn't it good to be together,
being with friends old and new?
Isn't it good?
The Bible tells us Jesus our Lord is here too!
Isn't it good to be together,
being with friends old and new?
Isn't it good?
The Bible tells us Jesus our Lord is here too!

He's here!
By his Spirit he's with us. He's here!
His promise is true. He's here!
Though we can't see him, he's here
for me and you. *(Repeat)*

805
Spiritual

It's me, it's me, it's me, O Lord,
standing in the need of prayer. (Repeat)

1. Not my brother or my sister,
   but it's me, O Lord,
   standing in the need of prayer. *(Repeat)*

2. Not my mother or my father . . .

3. Not the stranger or my neighbour . . .

806
Spiritual

1. I've got peace like a river,
   I've got peace like a river,
   I've got peace like a river in my soul.

2. I've got joy like a fountain . . .

3. I've got love like an ocean . . .

807
Ian Smale
©1985 Kingsway's Thankyou Music

I will wave my hands
in praise and adoration, *(x3)*
praise and adoration to the living God.
For he's given me hands
that just love clapping:
one, two, one, two, three;
and he's given me a voice
that just loves shouting,
'Hallelujah!'
He's given me feet that just love dancing:
one, two, one, two, three;
and he's put me in a being
that has no trouble seeing
that whatever I am feeling
he is worthy to be praised.

808
Michael Forster
© 1993 Kevin Mayhew Ltd.

Jesus had all kinds of friends,
so the gospel stories say.
Jesus had all kinds of friends,
and there's room for us today.

1. Some were happy, some were sad,
   some were good and some were bad,
   some were short and some were tall,
   Jesus said he loved them all.

2. Some were humble, some were proud,
   some were quiet, some were loud,
   some were fit and some were lame,
   Jesus loved them all the same.

3. Some were healthy, some were sick,
   some were slow and some were quick,
   some were clever, some were not,
   Jesus said he loved the lot!

809
Gill Hutchinson
© 1992 Sea Dream Music

Jesus is greater than the greatest heroes.
Jesus is closer than the closest friends.
He came from heaven and he died to
save us,
to show us love that never ends.
(Repeat)
Son of God, and the Lord of glory,
he's the light, follow in his way.
He's the truth that we can believe in,
and he's the life, he's living today.
(Repeat)

810
Graham Kendrick
© 1986 Kingsway's Thankyou Music

1. Jesus put this song into our hearts, *(x2)*
   it's a song of joy no one can take away.
   Jesus put this song into our hearts.

2. Jesus taught us how to live in
   harmony, *(x2)*
   diff'rent faces, diff'rent races, he made
   us one.
   Jesus taught us how to live in harmony.

3. Jesus turned our sorrow into dancing, *(x2)*
   changed our tears of sadness into rivers
   of joy.
   Jesus turned our sorrow into a dance.

811
Michael Forster
© 1997 Kevin Mayhew Ltd.

1. Jesus went away to the desert, praying,
   listened for his Father's voice.
   Then he heard the voice
   of the tempter saying,
   'Why not make the easy choice?'

   Ain't list'nin' to no temptation,
   ain't fallin' for no persuasion,
   ain't gonna turn away from salvation,
   I'm a waitin' on the word of the Lord.

2. 'There's an easy way if you'd only
        choose it,
   you can turn the stones to bread!
   What's the good of pow'r
   if you don't abuse it?
   Gotta keep youself well fed!'

3. 'What about a stunt to attract attention,
   showing off your special pow'r?
   You'd get more applause
   than I'd care to mention
   jumping from the Temple tow'r!'

4. 'Ev'rything you want will be right there
        for you,
   listen to the words I say!
   Nobody who matters
   will dare ignore you;
   my way is the easy way.'

812
Greg Leavers
© 1990 Greg Leavers

Jesus will never, ever,
no not ever, never, ever change.
He will always, always,
that's for all days,
always be the same;
so as Son of God and King of kings
he will for ever reign.
Yesterday, today, for ever,
Jesus is the same.
Yesterday, today, for ever,
Jesus is the same.

813
David Hind
© 1992 Kingsway's Thankyou Music

Jesus, you love me more than I can know.
Jesus, you love me more than words can say.
I'm special, I'm planned;
I'm born with a future, I'm in your hands.
I'm forgiven, I've been changed;
loved by my Father who knows me by name.
I'm loved by my Father who knows me
by name.

814
Marie Lydia Pereira
© 1976 Kevin Mayhew Ltd.

1. Joseph was an honest man,
   he was an honest man.
   He pleased the Lord in all his ways
   because he was an honest man;
   and God said: 'I am choosing you,
   because you are an honest man,
   to care for the one who'll bear my Son,
   because you are an honest man.'

2. Joseph was a faithful man,
   he was a faithful man.
   He kept the trust the Lord had given
   because he was a faithful man.
   He cared for Mary and her Son,
   because he was a faithful man,
   through days of pain and days of fun,
   because he was a faithful man.

3. Joseph was a working man,
   he was a working man.
   He laboured as a carpenter
   because he was a working man.
   And daily at his work he'd be
   because he was a working man,
   no idler or a shirker he,
   because he was a working man.

4. Joseph was a praying man,
   he was a praying man.
   He walked with God each single day
   because he was a praying man.
   In joy or pain he'd turn to him,
   because he was a praying man,
   if fear did rage or hope grew dim,
   because he was a praying man.

Continued overleaf

5. Joseph was an honest man,
   he was an honest man.
   His blameless life won its reward
   because he was an honest man.
   The Lord was pleased and called
      him home,
   because he was an honest man,
   with him to rest, no more to roam,
   because he was an honest man.

6. Joseph is a helping man,
   he is a helping man.
   He rescues those who turn to him
   because he is a helping man.
   So go to Joseph in your need,
   because he is a helping man,
   you'll see him work with speed
      and power,
   because he is a helping man.

815 Spiritual

1. Kum ba yah, my Lord, kum ba yah. *(x3)*
   O Lord, kum ba yah.

2. Someone's crying, Lord,
      kum ba yah, *(x3)*
   O Lord, kum ba yah.

3. Someone's singing, Lord,
      kum ba yah, *(x3)*
   O Lord, kum ba yah.

4. Someone's praying, Lord,
      kum ba yah, *(x3)*
   O Lord, kum ba yah.

816 Susan Sayers
© 1984 Kevin Mayhew Ltd.

1. Let the mountains dance and sing!
   let the trees all sway and swing!
   All creation praise its King! Alleluia!

2. Let the water sing its song!
   And the pow'rful wind so strong
   whistle as it blows along! Alleluia!

3. Let the blossom all break out
   in a huge unspoken shout,
   just to show that God's about! Alleluia!

817 Michael Forster
© 1993 Kevin Mayhew Ltd.

1. Life for the poor was hard and tough,
   Jesus said, 'That's not good enough;
   life should be great and here's the sign:
   I'll turn the water into wine.'

   Jesus turned the water into wine, (x3)
   and the people saw that life was good.

2. Life is a thing to be enjoyed,
   not to be wasted or destroyed.
   Laughter is part of God's design;
   let's turn the water into wine!

3. Go to the lonely and the sad,
   give them the news to make them glad,
   helping the light of hope to shine,
   turning the water into wine!

818 Eric Boswell. © 1959 Warner Chappell Music Ltd.

1. Little donkey, little donkey,
   on the dusty road,
   got to keep on plodding onwards
   with your precious load.
   Been a long time, little donkey,
   through the winter's night;
   don't give up now, little donkey,
   Bethlehem's in sight.

   Ring out those bells tonight,
   Bethlehem, Bethlehem,
   follow that star tonight,
   Bethlehem, Bethlehem.
   Little donkey, little donkey,
   had a heavy day,
   little donkey, carry Mary safely on her way.

2. Little donkey, little donkey,
   on the dusty road,
   ther are wise men, waiting for a
   sign to bring them here.
   Do not falter, little donkey,
   there's a star ahead;
   it will guide you, little donkey,
   to a cattle shed.

819 Christopher Massey
© 1999 Kevin Mayhew Ltd.

1. Little Jesus, sleep away, in the hay,
   while we worship, watch and pray.
   We will gather at the manger,
   worship this amazing stranger:
   little Jesus born on earth,
   sign of grace and human worth.

2. Little Jesus, sleep away, while you may;
   pain is for another day.
   While you sleep, we will not wake you,
   when you cry we'll not forsake you.
   Little Jesus, sleep away,
   we will worship you today.

820 Ian D. Craig
© 1994 Daybreak Music Ltd.

1. Lord of the future, Lord of the past,
   Lord of our lives, we adore you.
   Lord of forever, Lord of our hearts,
   we give all praise to you.

2. Lord of tomorrow, Lord of today,
   Lord over all, you are worthy.
   Lord of creation, Lord of all truth,
   we give all praise to you.

821 Ian Smale
© 1989 Kingsway's Thankyou Music

Lord, we've come to worship you,
Lord, we've come to praise;
Lord, we've come to worship you
in oh so many ways.

Some of us shout and some of us sing,
and some of us whisper the praise we bring,
but Lord, we all are gathering
to give to you our praise.

822 Alan J. Price
© 1992 Daybreak Music Ltd.

*Lord, you've promised, through your Son,
you'll forgive the wrongs we've done;
we confess them, every one,
please, dear Lord, forgive us.*

1. Things we've done and things we've said,
   we regret the hurt they spread.
   Lord, we're sorry. Lord, we're sorry.

2. Sinful and unkind thoughts too,
   all of these are known to you.
   Lord, we're sorry. Lord, we're sorry.

3. And the things we've left undone,
   words and deeds we should have done.
   Lord, we're sorry. Lord, we're sorry.

Last refrain:
*Lord, you've promised, through your Son,
you'll forgive the wrong we've done;
we receive your pardon,
Lord, as you forgive us.*

823 Ian Smale
© 1989 Glorie Music/Kingsway's Thankyou Music

1. My mouth was made for worship,
   my hands were made to raise,
   my feet were made for dancing,
   my life is one of praise to Jesus.
   And all God's people said: Amen,
   hallelujah, amen, praise and glory,
   amen, amen, amen, amen.
   Wo, wo, wo, wo.

2. My heart was made for loving,
   my mind to know God's ways,
   my body was made a temple,
   my life is one of praise to Jesus.
   And all God's people said: Amen,
   hallelujah, amen, praise and glory,
   amen, amen, amen, amen.
   Wo, wo, wo, wo, wo.

824

John Hardwick
© 1993 Daybreak Music Ltd.

1. Nobody's a nobody,
   believe me 'cause it's true.
   Nobody's a nobody,
   especially not you.
   Nobody's a nobody,
   and God wants us to see
   that ev'rybody's somebody,
   and that means even me.

2. I'm no cartoon, I'm human,
   I have feelings, treat me right.
   I'm not a super hero
   with super strength and might.
   I'm not a mega pop star
   or super athlete,
   but did you know I'm special,
   in fact I'm quite unique!

3. *Repeat verse 1*

825

Marie Lydia Pereira
© 1998 Kevin Mayhew Ltd.

1. Now the Mass is ended, Lord,
   now it's time to go,
   but we will not leave alone,
   we will take you too.
   In our work, in our play,
   all throughout our busy day,
   we will not be left alone,
   we'll live this day with you.

2. Through this Mass we have received
   blessing, grace and pow'r
   loving truly as you did,
   loving hour by hour,
   to be kind, to be true,
   just like you in all we do.
   Stay with us, we ask you, Lord,
   and help us stay with you.

826

Graham Kendrick
© 1998 Make Way Music

1. O come and join the dance
   that all began so long ago,
   when Christ the Lord
   was born in Bethelehem.
   Through all the years of darkness
   still the dance goes on and on,
   oh, take my hand
   and come and join the song.

   Rejoice! Rejoice! Rejoice! Rejoice!
   O lift your voice and sing,
   and open up your heart to welcome him.
   Rejoice! Rejoice! Rejoice! Rejoice
   and welcome now your King,
   for Christ the Lord was born in Bethlehem.

2. Come shed your heavy load
   and dance your worries away,
   for Christ the Lord was
   born in Bethlehem.
   He came to break the pow'r of sin
   and turn your night to day,
   oh, take my hand
   and come and join the song.

3. Let laughter ring and angels sing
   and joy be all around,
   for Christ the Lord
   was born in Bethlehem.
   and if you seek with all your heart
   he surely can be found,
   oh, take my hand
   and come and join the song.

827

Joanne Pond
© 1980 Kingsway's Thankyou Music

O give thanks to the Lord,
all you his people,
O give thanks to the Lord,
for he is good.
Let us praise, let us thank,
let us celebrate and dance,
O give thanks to the Lord,
for he is good.

828

Patrick Appleford
© 1965 Josef Weinberger Ltd.

1. O Lord, all the world belongs to you,
   and you are always making all things new.
   What is wrong you forgive,
   and the new life you give
   is what's turning the world upside down.

2. The world's only loving to its friends,
   but you have brought us love that
        never ends;
   loving enemies too,
   and this loving with you
   is what's turning the world upside down.

3. This world lives divided and apart.
   You draw us all together and we start,
   in your body, to see
   that in a fellowship we
   can be turning the world upside down.

4. The world wants the wealth to live
        in state,
   but you show us a new way to be great:
   like a servant you came,
   and if we do the same,
   we'll be turning the world upside down.

5. O Lord, all the world belongs to you,
   and you are always making all things new.
   Send your Spirit on all
   in your Church, whom you call
   to be turning the world upside down.

829

Michael Forster
© 1993 Kevin Mayhew Ltd.

One hundred and fifty-three! (x2)
The number of all the fish in the sea:
one hundred and fifty-three!

1. We'd fished all the night for nothing,
   but Jesus said, 'Try once more.'
   So we doubtfully tried on the other side,
   and found there were fish galore!

2. We got all the fish to the shore,
   we wondered how many there'd be,
   So we started to count,
   and what an amount:
   one hundred and fifty-three!

3. Now here was a wonderful sight
   we'd never expected to see;
   and the net didn't break,
   it was able to take
   the hundred and fifty-three!

4. So whether you're rich or you're poor,
   whatever your race or your sect,
   be you black, white or brown,
   Jesus wants you around,
   there's plenty of room in the net!

830

Unknown

Our God is so great,
so strong and so mighty,
there's nothing that he cannot do.
(Repeat)
The rivers are his,
the mountains are his,
the stars are his handiwork too.
Our God is so great,
so strong and so mighty,
there's nothing that he cannot do.

831

Michael Forster
© 1993 Kevin Mayhew Ltd.

Out to the great wide world we go! (3)
and we sing of the love of Jesus.

1. Go and tell our neighbours,
   go and tell our friends,
   Jesus gives his people
   love that never ends. So:

2. People sad and lonely,
   wond'ring how to cope;
   let's find ways of showing
   Jesus gives us hope. So:

832 Traditional

1. O when the saints go marching in,
   O when the saints go marching in,
   I want to be in that number
   when the saints go marching in.
2. O when they crown him Lord of all . . .
3. O when all knees bow at his name . . .
4. O when they sing the Saviour's praise . . .
5. O when the saints go marching in . . .

833 Unknown, based on Acts 3

Peter and John went to pray,
they met a lame man on the way.
He asked for alms
and held out his palms
and this is what Peter did say:
'Silver and gold have I none,
but such as I have I give thee,
in the name of Jesus Christ of Nazareth,
rise up and walk!'
He went walking and leaping
and praising God,
walking and leaping and praising God.
'In the name of Jesus Christ of Nazareth,
rise up and walk.'

834 Unknown

Praise and thanksgiving let ev'ryone bring
unto our Father for ev'ry good thing!
All together joyfully sing.

835 Michael Forster
© 1997 Kevin Mayhew Ltd.

1. Praise God in his holy place!
   He's the God of time and space.
   Praise him, all the human race!
   Let ev'rything praise our God!
2. Praise him with the ol' wood block!
   Let it swing and let it rock,
   praising God around the clock!
   Let ev'rything praise our God!

3. Praise him with the big bass drum,
   if you've got guitars, then strum!
   Now let's make those rafters hum!
   Let ev'rything praise our God!
4. Praise him with the chime bars' chime,
   tell the bells it's party time,
   help those singers find a rhyme!
   Let ev'rything praise our God!
5. Violin or xylophone,
   trumpets with their awesome tone;
   bowed or beaten, bashed or blown,
   let ev'rything praise our God!
6. Cymbals, triangles and things,
   if it crashes, howls or rings,
   ev'rybody shout and sing!
   Let ev'rything praise our God!

836 Estelle White
© 1983 Kevin Mayhew Ltd.

1. Put your trust in the man
   who tamed the sea,
   put your trust in the man
   who calmed the waves,
   put your trust in the Lord Jesus,
   it is he who rescues and saves.
2. Put your trust in the man
   who cured the blind,
   put your trust in the man
   who helped the lame,
   put your trust in the Lord Jesus,
   there is healing strength in his name.
3. Put your trust in the man
   who died for you,
   put your trust in the man
   who conquered fear,
   put your trust in the Lord Jesus,
   for he rose from death and he's near.
4. Put your trust in the man
   who understands,
   put your trust in the man
   who is your friend,
   put your trust in the Lord Jesus,
   who will give you life without end.

837

Unknown, based on Genesis 6:4

Rise and shine,
and give God his glory, glory, (x3)
children of the Lord.

1. The Lord said to Noah,
   'There's gonna be a floody, floody.'
   Lord said to Noah,
   'There's gonna be a floody, floody,'
   Get those children out of the muddy,
       muddy,
   children of the Lord.'

2. So Noah, he built him,
   he built him an arky, arky,
   Noah, he built him,
   he built him an arky, arky,
   built it out of hickory barky, barky,
   children of the Lord.

3. The animals, they came on,
   they came on, by twosies, twosies,
   animals, they came on, they came on,
   by twosies, twosies,
   elephants and kangaroosies, roosies,
   children of the Lord.

4. It rained and poured
   for forty daysies, daysies,
   rained and poured
   for forty daysies, daysies,
   nearly drove those animals
       crazies, crazies,
   children of the Lord.

5. The sun came out
   and dried up the landy, landy,
   sun came out
   and dried up the landy, landy,
   ev'rything was fine and dandy, dandy,
   children of the Lord.

6. If you get to heaven
   before I do-sies, do-sies,
   you get to heaven
   before I do-sies, do-sies,
   tell those angels I'm coming
       too-sies, too-sies,
   children of the Lord.

838

Carey Landry
© 1976 North American Liturgy Resources

1. Sing a simple song unto the Lord,
   sing a simple song unto the Lord,
   sing it with your heart,
   sing it with your soul,
   sing a simple song unto the Lord.

   O Lord, I love you,
   O Lord, I see.
   O Lord, I love you,
   I see that you love me.

2. Say a simple prayer unto the Lord,
   say a simple prayer unto the Lord,
   say it with your heart,
   say it with your soul,
   say a simple prayer unto the Lord.

3. Give a simple gift unto the Lord,
   give a simple gift unto the Lord,
   give it with your heart,
   give it with your soul,
   give a simple gift unto the Lord.

839

W. L. Wallace
© 1997 Kevin Mayhew Ltd.

1. Sing praise to God,
   sing praise to God for life,
   for beauty, hope and love,
   for tenderness and grace.
   Sing praise to God,
   sing praise to God for life,
   with all of earth,
   sing and praise all God's life.

2. Lift up your eyes
   to see the works of God,
   in ev'ry blade of grass,
   in ev'ry human face.
   Lift up your eyes
   to see the works of God,
   through all of life,
   in all time and all space.

3. Open your ears
   to hear the cries of pain
   arising from the poor
   and all who are oppressed.
   Open your mind
   and use your wits to find
   who are the cause
   of this world's unjust ways.

4. Reach out your hands
   to share the wealth God gave
   with those who are oppressed,
   and those who feel alone.
   Reach out your hands
   and gently touch with Christ
   each frozen heart
   which has said 'No' to love.

5. Open our hearts
   to love the world with Christ,
   each person in this world,
   each creature of this earth.
   Open our hearts
   to love the ones who hate,
   and in their hearts
   find a part of ourselves.

6. Live life with love,
   for love encircles all;
   it casts out all our fears,
   it fills the heart with joy.
   Live life with love,
   for love transforms our life,
   as we praise God with our eyes,
   hands and hearts.

840 Gill Hutchinson
© 1994 Sea Dream Music

Step by step, on and on,
we will walk with Jesus till the journey's done.
Step by step, day by day,
because Jesus is the living way.

1. He's the one to follow,
   in his footsteps we will tread.
   Don't worry about tomorrow,
   Jesus knows the way ahead. Oh,

2. He will never leave us,
   and his love he'll always show,
   so wherever Jesus leads us,
   that's the way we want to go. Oh,

841 Diane Davis Andrew, adapted by Geoffrey Marshall-
Taylor. © 1971 Celebration/Kingsway's Thankyou Music

1. Thank you, Lord, for this new day, *(x3)*
   right where we are.

   Alleluia, praise the Lord, (x3)
   right where we are.

2. Thank you, Lord, for food to eat, *(x3)*
   right where we are.

3. Thank you, Lord, for clothes to wear, *(x3)*
   right where we are.

4. Thank you, Lord, for all your gifts, *(x3)*
   right where we are.

842 John Gowans. © Salvationist Publishing & Supplies.
Administered by CopyCare

1. There are hundreds of sparrows,
   thousands, millions,
   they're two a penny, far too many there
   must be;
   there are hundreds and thousands,
   millions of sparrows,
   but God knows ev'ry one, and God
   knows me.

2. There are hundreds of flowers,
   thousands, millions,
   and flowers fair the meadows wear for all
   to see;
   there are hundreds and thousands,
   millions of flowers,
   but God knows ev'ry one, and God
   knows me.

3. There are hundreds of planets,
   thousands, millions,
   way out in space each has a place by
   God's decree;
   there are hundreds and thousands,
   millions of planets,
   but God knows ev'ry one, and God
   knows me.

4. There are hundreds of children,
   thousands, millions,
   and yet their names are written on God's
   memory;
   there are hundreds and thousands,
   millions of children,
   but God knows ev'ry one, and God
   knows me.

843

Michael Forster
© 1997 Kevin Mayhew Ltd.

There's a great big world out there.
  Let's go! (x3)
Celebrate the love of God!

1. We've sung about the love of God,
   now it's time to let it show.
   If we don't act as though it's true,
   how on earth will people know?

2. We've brought to God our prayers
      and hymns,
   now it's time to live his life,
   to sow a little love and peace
   in the place of selfish strife.

3. We've listened to the word of God,
   now it's time to live it out,
   to show by ev'rything we do
   what the gospel is about.

844

Michael Forster
© 1993 Kevin Mayhew Ltd.

There's a rainbow in the sky,
and it's okay! (x3)
It's a sign that God is good.

1. Forty days and nights afloat,
   all cooped up on Noah's boat!
   Now the rain is almost done;
   wake up world, here comes the sun!

2. Now we've got another start,
   ev'ryone can play a part:
   make the world a better place,
   put a smile on ev'ry face!

3. Sometimes, still, the world is bad,
   people hungry, people sad.
   Jesus wants us all to care,
   showing people ev'rywhere:

845

Christina Wilde
© 1997 Kevin Mayhew Ltd.

There was one, there were two,
there were three friends of Jesus,
there were four, there were five,
there were six friends of Jesus,
there were sev'n there were eight,
there were nine friends of Jesus,
ten friends of Jesus in the band.

1. Bells are going to ring in praise of Jesus,
   praise of Jesus, praise of Jesus,
   bells are going to ring in praise of Jesus,
   praising Jesus the Lord.

2. Drums are going to boom in praise
      of Jesus,
   praise of Jesus, praise of Jesus,
   drums are going to boom in praise
      of Jesus,
   praising Jesus the Lord.

3. Tambourines will shake in praise of Jesus,
   praise of Jesus, praise of Jesus,
   tambourines will shake in praise of Jesus,
   praising Jesus the Lord.

4. Trumpets will resound in praise of Jesus,
   praise of Jesus, praise of Jesus,
   trumpets will resound in praise of Jesus,
   praising Jesus the Lord.

Continued overleaf

Verses can be added ad lib, for example:

Clarinets will swing, in praise of Jesus . . .

Play recorders, too . . .

Triangles will ting . . .

Fiddles will be scraped . . .

Let guitars be strummed . . .

Chime bars will be chimed . . .

Glockenspiels will play . . .

Vibraphones will throb . . .

Trombones slide about . . .

846 Michael Forster
© 1993 Kevin Mayhew Ltd.

1. The voice from the bush said:
Moses, look snappy,
have I got a job for you!
I've looked around
and I'm not very happy.
Here is what you have to do:

   Lead my people to freedom! (3)
   Got to go to the Promised Land!

2. The people of God
were suff'ring and dying,
sick and tired of slavery.
All God could hear
was the sound of their crying;
Moses had to set them free.

3. We know that the world
is still full of sorrow,
people need to be set free.
We've got to give them
a better tomorrow,
so God says to you and me:

847 Unknown

1. The wise man built his house
upon the rock, *(x3)*
and the rain came tumbling down.

And the rain came down
and the floods came up, *(x3)*
and the house on the rock stood firm.

2. The foolish man built his house
upon the sand, *(x3)*
and the rain came tumbling down.
And the rain came down
and the floods came up, *(x3)*
and the house on the sand fell flat.

848 Michael Forster
© 1997 Kevin Mayhew Ltd.

The world is full of smelly feet,
weary from the dusty street.
The world is full of smelly feet,
we'll wash them for each other.

1. Jesus said to his disciples,
'Wash those weary toes!
Do it in a cheerful fashion,
never hold your nose!'

2. People on a dusty journey
need a place to rest;
Jesus says, 'You say you love me,
this will be the test!'

3. We're his friends, we recognise him
in the folk we meet;
smart or scruffy, we'll still love him,
wash his smelly feet!

849 Traditional

This little light of mine,
I'm gonna let it shine, (x3)
let it shine, let it shine, let it shine.

1. The light that shines is the light of love,
lights the darkness from above,
it shines on me and it shines on you,
and shows what the power of love can do.
I'm gonna shine my light both far
     and near,
I'm gonna shine my light both bright
     and clear.
Where there's a dark corner in this land,
I'm gonna let my little light shine.

2. On Monday he gave me the gift of love,
   Tuesday peace came from above.
   On Wednesday he told me to have
       more faith,
   on Thursday he gave me a little
       more grace.
   On Friday he told me to watch and pray,
   on Saturday he told me just what to say,
   on Sunday he gave me the power divine
   to let my little light shine.

850 Ian Smale
© 1984 Kingsway's Thankyou Music

We will praise, we will praise,
we will praise the Lord,
we will praise the Lord because he is good.
We will praise, we will praise,
we will praise the Lord
because his love is everlasting.

Bring on the trumpets and harps,
let's hear the cymbals ring,
then in harmony lift our voices
and sing, sing.

851 David Palmer
© 1976 Kevin Mayhew Ltd.

1. When is he coming, when,
   O when is he coming, the Redeemer?
   When will we see him, when,
   O when will we see him, the Redeemer?

   Come, O come,
   from your kingdom up there,
   from your kingdom up there above!
   Come, O come to your people on earth,
   to your people on earth bring love!
   Emmanuel! Emmanuel! Emmanuel!

2. Long years awaiting,
   many years here awaiting the Redeemer!
   Ready to greet him,
   always ready to meet him, the Redeemer!

3. Spare us from evil,
   from the clutches of evil, O Redeemer!
   Though we are sinners
   we have known your forgiveness,
       O Redeemer!

852 Unknown

1. When the Spirit of the Lord
   is within my heart
   I will sing as David sang. *(Repeat)*
   I will sing, I will sing,
   I will sing as David sang. *(Repeat)*

2. When the Spirit of the Lord
   is within my heart
   I will clap as David clapped . . .

3. When the Spirit of the Lord
   is within my heart
   I will dance as David danced . . .

4. When the Spirit of the Lord
   is within my heart
   I will praise as David praised . . .

853 Anne Conlon
© 1996 Josef Weinberger Ltd.

1. When your Father made the world,
   before that world was old,
   in his eye what he had made
   was lovely to behold.
   Help your people to care for your world.

   The world is a garden you made,
   and you are the one who planted the seed,
   the world is a garden you made,
   a life for our food, life for our joy,
   life we could kill with our selfish greed.

2. All the world that he had made,
   the seas, the rocks, the air,
   all the creatures and the plants
   he gave into our care.
   Help your people to care for your world.

Continued overleaf

3. When you walked in Galilee,
   you said your Father knows
   when each tiny sparrow dies,
   each fragile lily grows.
   Help your people to care for your world.

4. And the children of the earth,
   like sheep within your fold,
   should have food enough to eat,
   and shelter from the cold.
   Help your people to care for your world.

854 Paul Booth
© Paul Booth/CopyCare

1. Who put the colours in the rainbow?
   Who put the salt into the sea?
   Who put the cold into the snowflake?
   Who made you and me?
   Who put the hump upon the camel?
   Who put the neck on the giraffe?
   Who put the tail upon the monkey?
   Who made hyenas laugh?
   Who made whales and snails and quails?
   Who made hogs and dogs and frogs?
   Who made bats and cats and rats?
   Who made ev'rything?

2. Who put the gold into the sunshine?
   Who put the sparkle in the stars?
   Who put the silver in the moonlight?
   Who made Earth and Mars?
   Who put the scent into the roses?
   Who taught the honey-bee to dance?
   Who put the tree inside the acorn?
   It surely can't be chance!
   Who made seas and leaves and trees?
   Who made snow and winds that blow?
   Who made streams and rivers flow?
   God made all of these!

855 Unknown

Yesterday, today, forever,
Jesus is the same;
all may change, but Jesus never,
glory to his name!
Glory to his name! Glory to his name!
All may change, but Jesus never,
glory to his name!

856 Traditional

1. You've got to move
   when the Spirit says move,
   you've got to move
   when the Spirit says move,
   'cause when the Spirit says move,
   you've got to move when the Spirit,
   move when the Spirit says move.

2. You've got to sing
   when the Spirit says sing . . .

3. You've got to clap
   when the Spirit says clap . . .

4. You've got to shout
   when the Spirit says shout . . .

5. You've got to move
   when the Spirit says move . . .

857 Unknown

Zacchaeus was a very little man,
and a very little man was he.
He climbed up into a sycamore tree,
for the Saviour he wanted to see.
And when the Saviour passed that way,
he looked into the tree and said,
'Now Zacchaeus, you come down,
for I'm, coming to your house for tea.'

858

Sue McClellan, John Paculabo and Keith Ryecroft
© 1972 Kingsway's Thankyou Music

Zip bam boo, zama lama la boo,
there's freedom in Jesus Christ. (Repeat)
Though we hung him on a cross
till he died in pain,
three days later he's alive again.
Zip bam boo, zama lama la boo,
there's freedom in Jesus Christ.

1. This Jesus was a working man
   who shouted 'Yes' to life,
   but didn't choose to settle down,
   or take himself a wife.
   To live for God he made his task,
   'Who is this man?' the people ask.
   Zip bam boo, zama lama la boo,
   there's freedom in Jesus Christ.

2. He'd come to share good news from God
   and show that he is Lord.
   He made folk whole who trusted him
   and took him at his word.
   He fought oppression, loved the poor,
   gave the people hope once more.
   Zip bam boo, zama lama la boo,
   there's freedom in Jesus Christ.

3. 'He's mad! He claims to be God's Son
   and give new life to men!
   Let's kill this Christ, once and for all,
   no trouble from him then!'
   'It's death then, Jesus, the cross for you!'
   Said, 'Man, that's what I came to do!'
   Zip bam boo, zama lama la boo,
   there's freedom in Jesus Christ.

LiTURGiCAL
HYMNS OLD & NEW

CHANTS

859
Taizé Community
© Ateliers et Presses de Taizé

Adoramus te, Domine

1. With the angels and archangels:
2. With the patriarchs and prophets:
3. With the Virgin Mary, mother of God:
4. With the apostles and evangelists:
5. With all the martyrs of Christ:
6. With all who witness to the Gospel of the Lord:
7. With all your people of the Church throughout the world.

860
Traditional

Adoramus te, Domine Deus.

Translation: We adore you, O Lord God.

861
From the Roman Missal

Benedictus qui venit
in nomine Domini. *(x2)*
Hosanna, hosanna,
hosanna in excelsis.

862
Taizé Community, from Psalm 102
© Ateliers et Presses de Taizé

*Bless the Lord, my soul,
and bless God's holy name.
Bless the Lord, my soul,
who leads me into life.*

1. It is God who forgives all your guilt,
who heals ev'ry one of your ills,
who redeems your life from the grave,
who crowns you with love and
compassion.

2. The Lord is compassion and love,
the Lord is patient and rich in mercy.
God does not treat us according to our sins
nor repay us according to our faults.

3. As a father has compassion on
his children,
the Lord has mercy on those who
revere him;
for God knows of what we are made,
and remembers that we are dust.

863
David Adam. © SPCK, Holy Trinity Church

Calm me, Lord, as you calmed the storm;
still me, Lord, keep me from harm.
Let all the tumult within me cease;
enfold me, Lord, in your peace.

Last time:
Lord enfold me in your peace.

864
Psalm 117
© 1981 Ateliers et Presses de Taizé

Confitemini Domino quoniam bonus.
Confitemini Domino. Alleluia!

*Translation: Give thanks to the Lord for he
is good*

865
Taizé Community, based on Scripture
© Ateliers et Presses de Taizé

*Eat this bread, drink this cup,
come to him and never be hungry.
Eat this bread, drink this cup,
trust in him and you will not thirst.*

1. Christ is the Bread of Life,
the true bread sent from the Father.

2. Your ancestors ate manna in the desert,
but this is the bread come down
from heaven.

3. Eat his flesh, and drink his blood,
and Christ will raise you up on the last day.

Continued overleaf

4. Anyone who eats this bread
   will live for ever.

5. If we believe and eat this bread
   we will have eternal life.

866 Traditional

Exaudi nos, Domine;
donna nobis pacem tuam.

*Translation: Hear us, O Lord, give us
your peace.*

867 Kevin Mayhew, based on the Aaronic Blessing, Numbers 6: 24-26

Holy God,
we place ourselves into your hands.
Bless us and care for us,
be gracious and loving to us;
look kindly upon us, and give us peace.

868 Taizé Community
© Ateliers et Presses de Taizé

In the Lord I'll be ever thankful,
in the Lord, I will rejoice!
Look to God, do not be afraid;
lift up your voices: the Lord is near,
lift up your voices: the Lord is near.

869 Margaret Rizza
© 1998 Kevin Mayhew Ltd.

In the Lord is my joy and salvation,
he gives light to all his creation.
In the Lord is my joy and salvation,
he gives peace and true consolation.
In the Lord is my salvation.
In the Lord is my salvation.

870 Taizé Community, based on Scripture
© Ateliers et Presses de Taizé

Jesus, remember me
when you come into your kingdom.

871 From Psalm 32
© Ateliers et Presses de Taizé

Jubilate Deo, Jubilate Deo, alleluia.

Translation: Rejoice in God.

872 Traditional
© Ateliers et Presses de Taizé

Jubilate Deo omnis terra.
Servite Domino in lætitia.
Alleluia, alleluia, in lætitia.
Alleluia, alleluia, in lætitia.

*Translation: Rejoice in God, all the earth.
Serve the Lord with gladness.*

873 John L. Bell and Graham Maul
© WGRG, Iona Community

Kindle a flame to lighten the dark
and take all fear away.

874 Taizé Community, based on Scripture
© Ateliers et Presses de Taizé

*Laudate Dominum,
laudate Dominum,
omnes gentes, alleluia.* (Repeat)

or

*Sing praise and bless the Lord,
sing praise and bless the Lord,
peoples, nations, alleluia.* (Repeat)

1. Praise the Lord, all you nations,
   praise God all you peoples.
   Alleluia.
   Strong is God's love and mercy,
   always faithful for ever. Alleluia

2. Alleluia, alleluia.
   Let ev'rything living give praise to
   the Lord.
   Alleluia, alleluia.
   Let ev'rything living give praise to
   the Lord.

875

From Psalm 116
© Ateliers et Presses de Taizé

Laudate omnes gentes,
laudate Dominum. *(Repeat)*

or

Sing praises, all you peoples,
sing praises to the Lord.

876

Colin Mawby
© 1991 Kevin Mayhew Ltd.

Lord of creation,
may your will be done.
Lord of creation,
may your will be done.

877

Luke 1:46

Magnificat, magnificat
anima mea Dominum. *(Repeat)*

Translation: My soul praises and magnifies
the Lord

878

Gaelic Blessing, adapted by Margaret Rizza
© 1998 Kevin Mayhew Ltd.

May the Lord bless you,
may the Lord protect you and guide you,
may his strength uphold you,
his light shine upon you,
his peace surround you,
his love enfold you.

Last time:
May the Lord bless you,
the Lord bless you,
the Lord bless you.

879

Psalm 88
© Ateliers et Presses de Taizé

Misericordias Domini
in aeternum cantabo.

Translation: I will sing for ever of the mercy
of the Lord.

1. From age to age, through all generations,
   my mouth shall proclaim your truth, O
   Lord.

2. Who, O God, who in the universe can
   compare with you?

3. Blest be the Lord for ever, throughout
   eternity. Amen! Amen!

880

St. Teresa of Avila
© Ateliers et Presses de Taizé

Nada te turbe,
nada te espante.
Quien a Dios tiene nada le falta.
Nada te turbe,
nada te espante.
Solo Dios basta.

or

Nothing can trouble,
nothing can frighten.
Those who seek God shall never go wanting.
Nothing can trouble,
nothing can frighten.
God alone fills us.

881

© The Grail, England

O Christe, Domine Jesu!

Translation: O Christ, Lord Jesus.

1. The Lord is my shepherd;
   there is nothing I shall want.
   Fresh and green are the pastures
   where he gives me repose.
   Near restful waters he leads me,
   to revive my drooping spirit.
   He guides me along the right path;
   he is true to his name.
   If I should walk in the valley of darkness
   no evil would I fear.

Continued overleaf

2. You are there with your rod and staff;
with these you give me comfort.
You have prepared a banquet for me
in the sight of my foes.
My head you have anointed with oil;
my cup is overflowing.
Surely goodness and kindness shall follow me
all the days of my life.
In the Lord's own house shall I dwell
for ever and ever.

882 Taizé Community
© Ateliers et Presses de Taizé

O Lord, hear my prayer.
O Lord, hear my prayer:
when I call answer me.
O Lord, hear my prayer.
O Lord, hear my prayer.
Come and listen to me.

883 Psalm 130
© The Grail. Used by permission of A.P. Watt Ltd.

O Lord, my heart is not proud,
nor haughty my eyes.
I have not gone after things too great,
nor marvels beyond me.
Truly I have set my soul in silence and peace;
at rest, as a child in its mother's arms,
so is my soul.

884 Traditional

O Sacrament most holy,
O Sacrament divine,
all praise and all thanksgiving
be ev'ry moment thine.

885 Taizé Community
© Ateliers et Presses de Taizé

Ostende nobis Domine,
misericordiam tuam.
Amen! Amen! Maranatha! Maranatha!

*Translation: Lord, show us your mercy.
Amen! Come soon!*

886 Traditional

Sanctum nomen Domini
magnificat anima mea. *(Repeat)*

Last time:
Sanctum, sanctum nomen Domini.

*Translation: My soul magnifies the holy
name of the Lord*

887 v 1 Pamela Hayes; v 2 Margaret Rizza
© 1998 Kevin Mayhew Ltd.

Silent, surrendered, calm and still,
open to the word of God.
Heart humbled to his will,
offered is the servant of God.

*Come, Holy Spirit, bring us light,
teach us, heal us, give us life.
Come, Lord, O let our hearts
flow with love and all that is true.

* for use at Pentecost

888 Taizé Community, from Matthew 26
© Ateliers et Presses de Taizé

*Stay here and keep watch with me;
the hour has come.
Stay here and keep watch with me;
watch and pray.*

1. My heart is nearly broken with sorrow.
Remain here, remain here and stay awake
with me.

2. Father, if it is possible let this cup pass
me by.

3. Father, if this cannot pass me by without
my drinking it,
then your will be done.

889
Matthew 26:36-42
© Ateliers et Presses de Taizé

Stay with me, remain here with me,
watch and pray, watch and pray.

1. Stay here and keep watch with me.
   Watch and pray, watch and pray!

2. Watch and pray not to give way to
   temptation.

3. The Spirit is eager, but the flesh is weak.

4. My heart is nearly broken with sorrow.
   Remain here with me, stay awake
   and pray.

5. Father, if it is possible let this cup pass
   me by.

6. Father, if this cannot pass me by without
   my drinking it, your will be done.

890
From Daniel 3
© Ateliers et Presses de Taizé

Surrexit Christus, alleluia!
Cantate Domino, alleluia!

Translation: Christ is risen. Sing to the Lord.

1. All you heavens, bless the Lord.
   Stars of the heavens, bless the Lord.

2. Sun and moon, bless the Lord.
   And you, night and day, bless the Lord.

3. Frost and cold, bless the Lord.
   Ice and snow, bless the Lord.

4. Fire and heat, bless the Lord.
   And you, light and darkness,
   bless the Lord.

5. Spirits and souls of the just,
   bless the Lord.
   Saints and the humble hearted,
   bless the Lord.

891
From Psalm 26

The Lord is my light, in him I trust. *(x2)*
The Lord is my light, in him I trust,
in him I trust.

892
Taizé Community
© Ateliers et Presses de Taizé

The Lord is my song, the Lord is my praise:
all my hope comes from God.
The Lord is my song, the Lord is my praise:
God the well-spring of life.

893
Taizé Community
© Ateliers et Presses de Taizé

Ubi caritas et amor.
Ubi caritas Deus ibi est.

Translation: Where there is charity and
love, there is God.

1. Your love, O Jesus Christ,
   has gathered us together.

2. May your love, O Jesus Christ,
   be foremost in our lives.

3. Let us love one another
   as God has loved us.

4. Let us be one in love together
   in the one bread of Christ.

5. The love of God in Jesus Christ
   bears eternal joy.

6. The love of God in Jesus Christ
   will never have an end.

894
Stephen Langton

Veni, lumen cordium.
Veni, Sancte Spiritus.

Translation: Come, light of our hearts.
Come, Holy Spirit, come.

895

Veni, veni,
veni, Sancte Spiritus.

Translation: Come, Holy Spirit

896

Stephen Langton, trans. Edward Caswall,
alt. Christopher Walker

Veni, Sancte Spiritus. (x4)

1. Holy Spirit, Lord of light,
   radiance give from celestial height.
   Come, thou Father of the poor,
   come now with treasures that endure:
   Light of all who live.

2. Thou, of all consolers, the best.
   Thou the soul's delightful guest;
   refreshing peace bestow.
   Thou, in toil, my comfort sweet;
   thou, coolness in the heat.
   Thou, my solace in time of woe.

3. Light immortal, light divine;
   fire of love, our hearts refine,
   our inmost being fill.
   Take thy grace away and
   nothing pure in us will stay,
   all our good is turned to ill.

4. Heal our wounds, our strength renew,
   on our dryness pour thy dew;
   wash guilt away,
   bend the stubborn heart,
   melt the frozen, warm the chill
   and guide the steps that go astray.

5. Sevenfold gifts on us be pleased to pour,
   who thee confess and thee adore;
   bring us thy comfort when we die;
   give us life with thee on high;
   give us joys, give us joys, that never end.

897

Taizé Community, based on Scripture
© Ateliers et Presses de Taizé

Wait for the Lord, whose day is near.
Wait for the Lord: keep watch take heart!

1. Prepare the way for the Lord.
   Make a straight path for God.
   Prepare the way for the Lord.

2. Rejoice in the Lord always: God is at hand.
   Joy and gladness for all who seek the Lord.

3. The glory of the Lord shall be revealed.
   All the earth will see the Lord.

4. I waited for the Lord. God heard my cry.

5. Our eyes are fixed on the Lord our God.

6. Seek first the kingdom of God.
   Seek and you shall find.

7. O Lord show us your way.
   Guide us in your truth.

898

Taizé Community
© Ateliers et Presses de Taizé

Within our darkest night,
you kindle the fire that never dies away,
that never dies away. *(Repeat)*

899

Margaret Rizza
© 1998 Kevin Mayhew Ltd.

You are the centre, you are my life,
you are the centre, O Lord, of my life.
Come, Lord, and heal me, Lord of my life,
come, Lord, and teach me, Lord of my life.
You are the centre, Lord, of my life.
Give me your Spirit and teach me your ways,
give me your peace, Lord, and set me free. *
You are the centre, Lord, of my life.

* *Second time:*
You are the centre, you are my life,
you are the centre, O Lord, of my life.

RESPONSORIAL PSALMS

900 1st Advent (A)
Psalm 121:1-2, 4-5, 6-9. Ry cf. v.1

I re-joiced when I heard them say:

'Let us go to God's house.'

1. I rejoiced when I heard them say:
   'Let us go to God's house.'
   And now our feet are standing
   within your gates, O Jerusalem.

2. It is there that the tribes go up,
   the tribes of the Lord.
   For Israel's law it is,
   there to praise the Lord's name.

3. For the peace of Jerusalem pray:
   'Peace be to your homes!
   May peace reign in your walls,
   in your palaces, peace!'

4. For love of my brethren and friends
   I say: 'Peace upon you!'
   For love of the house of the Lord
   I will ask for your good.

Gospel Acclamation Psalm 84:8

Alleluia. Let us see, O Lord, your mercy
and give us your saving help. Alleluia.

901 1st Advent (B)
Psalm 79:2-3, 15-16, 18-19. Ry v.4

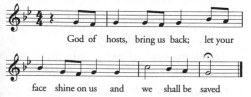

God of hosts, bring us back; let your

face shine on us and we shall be saved

1. O Shepherd of Israel, hear us,
   shine forth from your cherubim throne.
   O Lord, rouse up your might,
   O Lord, come to our help.

2. God of hosts, turn again, we implore,
   look down from heaven and see.
   Visit this vine and protect it,
   the vine your right hand has planted.

3. May your hand be on the one you have
   chosen,
   the one you have given your strength.
   And we shall never forsake you again:
   give us life that we may call upon your
   name.

Gospel Acclamation Psalm 84:8

Alleluia. Let us see, O Lord, your mercy
and give us your saving help. Alleluia.

902 1st Advent (C)
Psalm 24:4-5, 8-9, 10, 14. Ry v.1

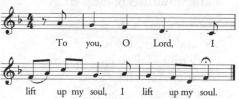

To you, O Lord, I

lift up my soul, I lift up my soul.

1. Lord, make me know your ways.
   Lord, teach me your paths.
   Make me walk in your truth, and teach me:
   for you are God my saviour.

2. The Lord is good and upright.
   He shows the path to those who stray,
   he guides the humble in the right path;
   he teaches his way to the poor.

3. His ways are faithfulness and love
   for those who keep his covenant and will.
   The Lord's friendship is for those who
   revere him;
   to them he reveals his covenant.

Gospel Acclamation Psalm 84:8

Alleluia. Let us see, O Lord, your mercy
and give us your saving help. Alleluia.

903
2nd Advent (A)
Psalm 71:1-2, 7-8, 12-13, 17. R℟ cf. v.7

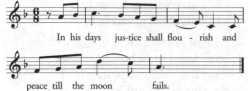

In his days jus-tice shall flou - rish and peace till the moon fails.

1. O God, give your judgement to the king,
   to a king's son your justice,
   that he may judge your people in justice
   and your poor in right judgement.

2. In his days justice shall flourish
   and peace till the moon fails.
   He shall rule from sea to sea,
   from the Great River to earth's bounds.

3. For he shall save the poor when they cry
   and the needy who are helpless.
   He will have pity on the weak
   and save the lives of the poor.

4. May his name be blest for ever
   and endure like the sun.
   Every tribe shall be blest in him,
   all nations bless his name.

Gospel Acclamation Luke 3:4, 6

Alleluia. Prepare a way for the Lord and
make his paths straight, and all mankind
shall see the salvation of our God. Alleluia.

904
2nd Advent (B)
Psalm 84:9-14. R℟ v.8

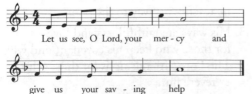

Let us see, O Lord, your mer - cy and
give us your sav - ing help

1. I will hear what the Lord God has to say,
   a voice that speaks of peace.
   His help is near for those who fear him
   and his glory will dwell in our land.

2. Mercy and faithfulness have met;
   justice and peace have embraced.
   Faithfulness shall spring from the earth
   and justice look down from heaven.

3. The Lord will make us prosper
   and our earth shall yield its fruit.
   Justice shall march before him
   and peace shall follow his steps.

Gospel Acclamation Luke 3:4, 6

Alleluia. Prepare a way for the Lord and
make his paths straight, and all mankind
shall see the salvation of our God. Alleluia.

905
2nd Advent (C)
Psalm 125. R℟ v.3

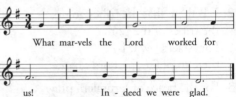

What mar-vels the Lord worked for us!
In - deed we were glad.

1. When the Lord delivered Zion from
      bondage,
   it seemed like a dream.
   Then was our mouth filled with laughter,
   on our lips there were songs.

2. The heathens themselves said:
   'What marvels
   the Lord worked for them!'
   What marvels the Lord worked for us!
   Indeed we were glad.

3. Deliver us, O Lord, from our bondage
   as streams in dry land.
   Those who are sowing in tears
   will sing when they reap.

4. They go out, they go out, full of tears
   carrying seed for the sowing:
   they come back, they come back,
      full of song,
   carrying their sheaves.

Gospel Acclamation Luke 3:4, 6

Alleluia. Prepare a way for the Lord and make <u>his</u> paths straight, and all mankind shall see the salvation <u>of</u> our God. Alleluia.

906 3rd Advent (A)
Psalm 145:6-10. R℣ cf. Isaiah 35:4

Come, Lord, and save us,

come, Lord, and save us.

1. It is the Lord who keeps <u>faith</u> for ever, who is just to those who <u>are</u> oppressed. It is he who gives bread <u>to</u> the hungry, the Lord, who sets pri<u>son</u>ers free.

2. It is the Lord who gives sight <u>to</u> the blind, who raises up those who <u>are</u> bowed down, the Lord, who pro<u>tects</u> the stranger and upholds the wi<u>dow</u> and orphan.

3. It is the Lord who <u>loves</u> the just but thwarts the path <u>of</u> the wicked. the Lord will <u>reign</u> for ever, Zion's God, from <u>age</u> to age.

Gospel Acclamation Isaiah 61:1 (Luke 4:18)

Alleluia. The spirit of the Lord has been <u>given</u> to me. He has sent me to bring good news <u>to</u> the poor. Alleluia.

907 3rd Advent (B)
Luke 1:46-50, 53-54. R℣ Isaiah 61:10

My soul re - joi - ces in my God.

1. My soul glor<u>ifies</u> the Lord, my spirit rejoices in <u>God</u>, my Saviour He looks on his servant <u>in</u> her nothingness; henceforth all ages will <u>call</u> me blessed.

2. The Almighty works mar<u>vels</u> for me. Holy <u>is</u> his name! His mercy is from <u>age</u> to age, on <u>those</u> who fear him.

3. He fills the star<u>ving</u> with good things, sends the rich <u>away</u> empty. He protects Isra<u>el</u>, his servant, remembe<u>ring</u> his mercy.

Gospel Acclamation Isaiah 61:1 (Luke 4:18)

Alleluia. The spirit of the Lord has been <u>given</u> to me. He has sent me to bring good news <u>to</u> the poor. Alleluia.

908 3rd Advent (C)
Isaiah 12:2-6. R℣ v.6

Sing and shout for joy for

great in your midst is the

Ho - ly One of Is - ra - el.

1. Truly, God is <u>my</u> salvation, I trust, I <u>shall</u> not fear. For the Lord is my <u>strength</u>, my song, he be<u>came</u> my saviour.

2. Give thanks <u>to</u> the Lord, give praise <u>to</u> his name! Make his mighty deeds known <u>to</u> the peoples! Declare the greatness <u>of</u> his name.

3. Sing a psalm to the Lord for he has done glor<u>ious</u> deeds, make them known to <u>all</u> the earth! People of Zion, sing and <u>shout</u> for joy for great in your midst is the Holy <u>One</u> of Israel.

Gospel Acclamation Isaiah 61:1 (Luke 4:18)

Alleluia. The spirit of the Lord has been <u>given</u> to me. He has sent me to bring good news <u>to</u> the poor. Alleluia.

909 4th Advent (A)
Psalm 23:1-6. R℣ cf. vv. 7, 10

Let the Lord en - ter, let the Lord en - ter!

He is the king of glo - ry.

1. The Lord's is the earth <u>and</u> its fullness,
   the world and <u>all</u> its peoples.
   It is he who set it <u>on</u> the seas;
   on the waters he <u>made</u> it firm.

2. Who shall climb the mountain <u>of</u> the
   Lord?
   Who shall stand in his <u>holy</u> place?
   Those with clean hands <u>and</u> pure heart,
   who desire not <u>worthless</u> things.

3. They shall receive blessings <u>from</u> the
   Lord
   and reward from the <u>God</u> who saves them.
   Such are the <u>ones</u> who seek him,
   seek the face of the <u>God</u> of Jacob.

Gospel Acclamation Matthew 1:23

Alleluia. The virgin will conceive and
give birth <u>to</u> a son and they will call him
Emmanuel, a name which means 'God-
is-with-us'. Alleluia.

910 4th Advent (B)
Psalm 88:2-5, 27, 29. R℣ cf. v.2

I will sing for e-ver of your love, O Lord.

1. I will sing for ever of your <u>love</u>, O Lord;
   through all ages my mouth will <u>proclaim</u>
   your truth.
   Of this I am sure, that your love <u>lasts</u> for
   ever,
   that your truth is firmly established <u>as</u> the
   heavens.

2. 'I have made a covenant <u>with</u> my chosen
   one;
   I have sworn to <u>David</u> my servant:
   I will establish your <u>dynasty</u> for ever
   and set up your throne <u>through</u> all ages.'

3. He will say to me: 'You <u>are</u> my father,
   my God, the <u>rock</u> who saves me.'
   I will keep my love <u>for</u> him always;
   for him my covenant <u>shall</u> endure.

Gospel Acclamation Luke 1:38

Alleluia. I am the handmaid <u>of</u> the Lord:
let what you have <u>said</u> be done to me.
Alleluia.

911 4th Advent (C)
Psalm 79:2-3, 15-16, 18-19. R℣ v.4

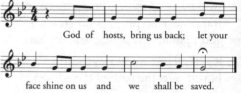

God of hosts, bring us back; let your
face shine on us and we shall be saved.

1. O shepherd of <u>Israel</u>, hear us,
   shine forth from your <u>cherubim</u> throne.
   O Lord, rouse <u>up</u> your might,
   O Lord, come <u>to</u> our help.

2. God of hosts, turn again, <u>we</u> implore,
   look down from <u>heaven</u> and see.
   Visit this vine <u>and</u> protect it,
   the vine your right <u>hand</u> has planted.

3. May your hand be on the one <u>you</u> have
   chosen,
   the one you have <u>given</u> your strength,
   and we shall never forsake <u>you</u> again:
   give us life that we may call <u>upon</u> your
   name.

Gospel Acclamation Luke 1:38

Alleluia. I am the handmaid <u>of</u> the Lord:
let what you have <u>said</u> be done to me.
Alleluia.

912 The Nativity of Our Lord – Midnight Mass (A, B, C)

Psalm 95:1-3, 11-13. R/ Luke 2:11

To-day a sa - viour has been born to us; he is Christ the Lord.

1. O sing a new song to the Lord,
   sing to the Lord all the earth.
   O sing to the Lord, bless his name.
   Proclaim his help day by day,
   tell among the nations his glory
   and his wonders among all the peoples.

2. Let the heavens rejoice and earth be glad,
   let the sea and all within it thunder praise,
   let the land and all it bears rejoice,
   all the trees of the wood shout for joy
   at the presence of the Lord for he comes,
   he comes to rule the earth.

Gospel Acclamation Luke 2:10-11

Alleluia. I bring you news of great joy:
today a saviour has been born to us,
Christ the Lord. Alleluia.

913 The Nativity of Our Lord – Mass during the Day (A, B, C)

Psalm 97:1-6. R/ v.3

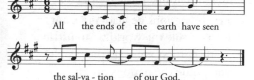

All the ends of the earth have seen the sal-va - tion of our God.

1. Sing a new song to the Lord
   for he has worked wonders.
   His right hand and his holy arm
   have brought salvation.

2. The Lord has made known his salvation;
   has shown his justice to the nations.
   He has remembered his truth and love
   for the house of Israel.

3. All the ends of the earth have seen
   the salvation of our God.
   Shout to the Lord all the earth,
   ring out your joy.

4. Sing psalms to the Lord with the harp,
   with the sound of music.
   With trumpets and the sound of the horn
   acclaim the King, the Lord.

Gospel Acclamation

Alleluia. Come, you nations, worship the
Lord, for today a great light has shone
down upon the earth. Alleluia.

914 The Holy Family (A, B, C)

Psalm 127:1-5. R/ cf. v.1

O bless - ed are those who fear the Lord, who fear the Lord.

1. O blessed are those who fear the Lord
   and walk in his ways!
   By the labour of your hands you shall eat.
   You will be happy and prosper.

2. Your wife like a fruitful vine
   in the heart of your house;
   your children like shoots of the olive,
   around your table.

3. Indeed thus shall be blessed
   the man who fears the Lord.
   May the Lord bless you from Zion
   all the days of your life!

Gospel Acclamation Colossians 3:15, 16

Alleluia. May the peace of Christ reign in
your hearts; let the message of Christ find
a home within you. Alleluia.

915 The Holy Family (B ad lib)
Psalm 104:1-6, 8-9. R∤ vv. 7, 8

He, the Lord, is our God. He re-
mem - bers his co-ven-ant for e - ver.

1. Give thanks to the Lord, tell his name,
make known his deeds among the peoples.
O sing to him, sing his praise;
tell all his wonderful works!

2. Be proud of his holy name,
let the hearts that seek the Lord rejoice.
Consider the Lord and his strength;
constantly seek his face.

3. Remember the wonders he has done,
his miracles, the judgements he spoke.
O children of Abraham, his servant,
O sons of the Jacob he chose.

4. He remembers his covenant for ever,
his promise for a thousand generations,
the covenant he made with Abraham,
the oath he swore to Isaac.

Gospel Acclamation Hebrews 1:1-2

Alleluia. At various times in the past
and in various different ways, God spoke
to our ancestors through the prophets;
but in our own time, the last days, he has
spoken to us through his Son. Alleluia.

916 The Holy Family (C ad lib)
Psalm 83:2-3, 5-6, 9-10. R∤ v.5

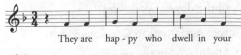

They are hap - py who dwell in your

house, O Lord.

1. How lovely is your dwelling place,
Lord God of hosts.
My soul is longing and yearning,
is yearning for the courts of the Lord.

2. They are happy, who dwell in your house,
for ever singing your praise.
They are happy, whose strength is in you;
they walk with ever growing strength.

3. O Lord, God of hosts, hear my prayer,
give ear, O God of Jacob.
Turn your eyes, O God, our shield,
look on the face of your anointed.

Gospel Acclamation cf. Acts 16:14

Alleluia. Open our heart, O Lord,
to accept the words of your Son. Alleluia.

917 Solemnity of Mary,
Mother of God (A, B, C)
Psalm 66:2-3, 5, 6, 8. R∤ v.2

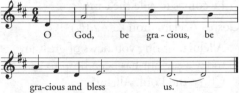

O God, be gra - cious, be
gra-cious and bless us.

1. God, be gracious and bless us
and let your face shed its light upon us.
So will your ways be known upon earth
and all nations learn your saving help.

2. Let the nations be glad and exult
for you rule the world with justice.
With fairness you rule the peoples,
you guide the nations on earth.

3. Let the peoples praise you, O God;
let all the peoples praise you.
May God still give us his blessing
till the ends of the earth revere him.

Gospel Acclamation Hebrews 1:1-2

Alleluia. At various times in the past
and in various different ways, God spoke
to our ancestors through the prophets;

but in our own time, the last days, he has spoken to us through his Son. Alleluia.

918 Second after Christmas (A, B, C)
Psalm 147:12-15, 19-20. R℟ John 1:14

The Word was made flesh, and lived a - mong us.

1. O praise the Lord, Jerusalem!
   Zion, praise your God!
   He has strengthened the bars of your gates,
   he has blessed the children within you.

2. He established peace on your borders,
   he feeds you with finest wheat.
   He sends out his word to the earth
   and swiftly runs his command.

3. He makes his word known to Jacob,
   to Israel his laws and decrees.
   He has not dealt thus with other nations;
   he has not taught them his decrees.

Gospel Acclamation cf. 1 Timothy 3:16

Alleluia. Glory be to you, O Christ, proclaimed to the pagans; Glory be to you, O Christ, believed in by the world. Alleluia.

919 The Epiphany of the Lord
(A, B, C)
Psalm 71:1-2, 7-8, 10-13. R℟ cf. v.11

All na - tions shall fall pro-strate be - fore you, O Lord.

1. O God, give your judgement to the king,
   to a king's son your justice,
   that he may judge your people in justice
   and your poor in right judgement.

2. In his days justice shall flourish
   and peace till the moon fails.
   He shall rule from sea to sea,
   from the Great River to earth's bounds.

3. The kings of Tarshish and the sea coasts
   shall pay him tribute.
   The kings of Sheba and Seba shall bring
   him gifts.
   Before him all kings shall fall prostrate,
   all nations shall serve him.

4. For he shall save the poor when they cry
   and the needy who are helpless.
   He will have pity on the weak
   and save the lives of the poor.

Gospel Acclamation Matthew 2:2

Alleluia. We saw his star as it rose and have come to pay homage to the Lord. Alleluia.

920 The Baptism of the Lord (A)
Psalm 28:1-4, 9-10. R℟ v.11

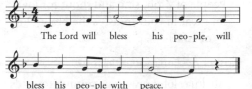

The Lord will bless his peo-ple, will bless his peo-ple with peace.

1. O give the Lord you children of God,
   give the Lord glory and power;
   give the Lord the glory of his name.
   Adore the Lord in his holy court.

2. The Lord's voice resounding on the waters,
   the Lord on the immensity of waters;
   the voice of the Lord, full of power,
   the voice of the Lord, full of splendour.

3. The God of glory thunders.
   In his temple they all cry: 'Glory!'
   The Lord sat enthroned over the flood;
   the Lord sits as king for ever.

Gospel Acclamation cf. Mark 9:8

Alleluia. The heavens opened and the Father's voice resounded: 'This is my Son, the Beloved. Listen to him.' Alleluia.

921 The Baptism of the Lord (B ad lib)
Isaiah 12:2-6. R℣ v.6

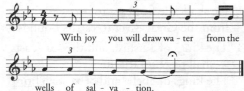

With joy you will draw wa-ter from the
wells of sal-va-tion.

1. Truly, God is my salvation
   I trust, I shall not fear.
   For the Lord is my strength, my song,
   he became my saviour.

2. Give thanks to the Lord,
   give praise to his name!
   Make his mighty deeds known to the
       peoples!
   Declare the greatness of his name.

3. Sing a psalm to the Lord for he has done
       glorious deeds,
   make them known to all the earth!
   People of Zion, sing and shout for joy
   for great in your midst is the Holy One
       of Israel.

Gospel Acclamation cf. John 1:29

Alleluia. John saw Jesus coming towards
him, and said: This is the Lamb of God
who takes away the sin of the world.
Alleluia.

922 The Baptism of the Lord (C ad lib)
Psalm 103:1-2, 3-4, 24-25, 27-30. R℣ v.1

Bless the Lord, my soul! Lord
God, how great you are.

1. Lord God, how great you are,
   clothed in majesty and glory,
   wrapped in light as in a robe!
   You stretch out the heavens like a tent.

2. The earth is full of your riches.
   There is the sea, vast and wide,
   with its moving swarms past counting,
   living things great and small.

3. All of these look to you
   to give them their food in due season.
   You give it, they gather it up:
   you open your hand, they have their fill.

4. You take back your spirit, they die,
   returning to the dust from which they
       came.
   You send forth your spirit, they are created;
   and you renew the face of the earth.

Gospel Acclamation cf. Luke 3:16

Alleluia. Someone is coming, said John,
someone greater than I. He will baptise
you with the Holy Spirit and with fire.
Alleluia.

923 Ash Wednesday (A, B, C)
Psalm 50:3-6, 12-14, 17. R℣ v.3

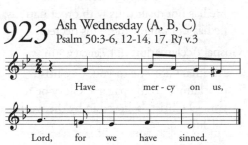

Have mer-cy on us,
Lord, for we have sinned.

1. Have mercy on me, God, in your kindness.
   In your compassion blot out my offence.
   O wash me more and more from my guilt
   and cleanse me from my sin.

2. My offences truly I know them;
   my sin is always before me.
   Against you, you alone, have I sinned;
   what is evil in your sight I have done.

3. A pure heart create for me, O God,
   put a steadfast spirit within me.
   Do not cast me away from your presence,
   nor deprive me of your holy spirit.

4. Give me again the joy of your help;
   with a spirit of fervour sustain me.
   O Lord, open my lips
   and my mouth shall declare your praise.

Gospel Acclamation Psalm 50:12,14

   A pure heart create for me, O God, and
   give me again the joy of your help.

or cf. Psalm 94:8

   Harden not your hearts today,
   but listen to the voice of the Lord.

924 1st Lent (A)
Psalm 50:3-6, 12-14, 17. R℣ cf. v.3

1. Have mercy on me, God, in your
   kindness.
   In your compassion blot out my offence.
   O wash me more and more from my guilt
   and cleanse me from my sin.

2. My offences truly I know them;
   my sin is always before me.
   Against you, you alone, have I sinned;
   what is evil in your sight I have done.

3. A pure heart create for me, O God,
   put a steadfast spirit within me.
   Do not cast me away from your presence,
   nor deprive me of your holy spirit.

4. Give me again the joy of your help;
   with a spirit of fervour sustain me.
   O Lord, open my lips
   and my mouth shall declare your praise.

Gospel Acclamation Matthew 4:4

   Man does not live on bread alone, but on
   every word that comes from the mouth
   of God.

925 1st Lent (B)
Psalm 24:4-9. R℣ cf. v.10

1. Lord, make me know your ways.
   Lord, teach me your paths.
   Make me walk in your truth, and teach me:
   for you are God my saviour.

2. Remember your mercy, Lord,
   and the love you have shown from of old.
   In your love remember me,
   because of your goodness, O Lord.

3. The Lord is good and upright.
   He shows the path to those who stray,
   he guides the humble in the right path;
   he teaches his way to the poor.

Gospel Acclamation Matthew 4:4

   Man does not live on bread alone, but on
   every word that comes from the mouth
   of God.

926 1st Lent (C)
Psalm 90:1-2, 10-15. R℣ v.15

1. He who dwells in the shelter of the Most
   High
   and abides in the shade of the Almighty,
   says to the Lord: 'My refuge,
   my stronghold, my God in whom I trust!'

2. Upon you no evil shall fall,
   no plague approach where you dwell.
   For you has he commanded his angels,
   to keep you in all your ways.

Continued overleaf

3. They shall bear you up<u>on</u> their hands
   lest you strike your foot a<u>gainst</u> a stone.
   On the lion and the viper <u>you</u> will tread
   and trample the young lion <u>and</u> the
   dragon.

4. His love he set on me, so <u>I</u> will rescue him;
   protect him for he <u>knows</u> my name.
   When he calls I shall answer: '<u>I</u> am with
   you.'
   I will save him in distress and <u>give</u> him
   glory.

Gospel Acclamation Matthew 4:4

Man does not live on <u>bread</u> alone, but on
every word that comes from the <u>mouth</u>
of God.

927 2nd Lent (A)
Psalm 32:4-5, 18-20, 22. R℣ v.22

May your love be up - on us,   O Lord,
as we place all   our hope in   you.

1. The word of the <u>Lord</u> is faithful
   and all his works <u>to</u> be trusted.
   The Lord loves jus<u>tice</u> and right
   and fills the earth <u>with</u> his love.

2. The Lord looks on those <u>who</u> revere him,
   on those who hope <u>in</u> his love,
   to rescue their <u>souls</u> from death,
   to keep them a<u>live</u> in famine.

3. Our soul is waiting <u>for</u> the Lord.
   The Lord is our help <u>and</u> our shield.
   May your love be upon <u>us</u>, O Lord,
   as we place all our <u>hope</u> in you.

Gospel Acclamation Matthew 17:5

From the bright cloud the Father's <u>voice</u>
was heard: 'This is my Son, the Beloved.
<u>Lis</u>ten to him.'

928 2nd Lent (B)
Psalm 115:10, 15-19. R℣ Psalm 114:9

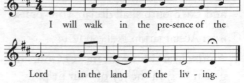

I will walk   in the pre-sence of the
Lord   in the land   of the   liv - ing.

1. I trusted, even <u>when</u> I said:
   'I am sore<u>ly</u> afflicted.'
   O precious in the eyes <u>of</u> the Lord
   is the death <u>of</u> his faithful.

2. Your servant, Lord, your ser<u>vant</u> am I;
   you have loo<u>sened</u> my bonds.
   A thanksgiving sacri<u>fice</u> I make:
   I will call on <u>the</u> Lord's name.

3. My vows to the Lord I <u>will</u> fulfil
   before <u>all</u> his people,
   in the courts of the house <u>of</u> the Lord,
   in your midst, <u>O</u> Jerusalem.

Gospel Acclamation Matthew 17:5

From the bright cloud the Father's <u>voice</u>
was heard: 'This is my Son, the Beloved.
<u>Lis</u>ten to him.'

929 2nd Lent (C)
Psalm 26:1, 7-9, 13-14. R℣ v.1

The   Lord   is my   light
and   my   help.

1. The Lord is my light <u>and</u> my help;
   whom <u>shall</u> I fear?
   The Lord is the stronghold <u>of</u> my life;
   before whom <u>shall</u> I shrink?

2. O Lord, hear my voice <u>when</u> I call;
   have mer<u>cy</u> and answer.
   Of you my <u>heart</u> has spoken:
   '<u>Seek</u> his face.'

3. It is your face, O Lord, that I seek;
hide not your face.
Dismiss not your servant in anger;
you have been my help.

4. I am sure I shall see the Lord's goodness
in the land of the living.
Hope in him, hold firm and take heart.
Hope in the Lord!

Gospel Acclamation Matthew 17:5

From the bright cloud the Father's voice
was heard: 'This is my Son, the Beloved.
Listen to him.'

930 3rd Lent (A)
Psalm 94:1-2, 6-9. R℣ v.8

O that to-day you would lis-ten to his
voice: 'Har-den not your hearts.'

1. Come, ring out our joy to the Lord;
hail the rock who saves us.
Let us come before him, giving thanks,
with songs let us hail the Lord.

2. Come in; let us bow and bend low;
let us kneel before the God who made us
for he is our God, and we the people
who belong to his pasture,
the flock that is led by his hand.

3. O that today you would listen to his voice!
'Harden not your hearts as at Meribah,
as on that day at Massah in the desert,
when your fathers put me to the test;
when they tried me, though they saw my
work.'

Gospel Acclamation cf. John 4:42, 15

Lord, you are really the saviour of the world;
give me the living water, so that I may
never get thirsty.

931 3rd Lent (B)
Psalm 18:8-11. R℣ John 6:68

You have the mes-sage of e-
ter-nal life, O Lord.

1. The law of the Lord is perfect,
it revives the soul.
The rule of the Lord is to be trusted,
it gives wisdom to the simple.

2. The precepts of the Lord are right,
they gladden the heart.
The command of the Lord is clear,
it gives light to the eyes.

3. The fear of the Lord is holy,
abiding for ever.
The decrees of the Lord are truth
and all of them just.

4. They are more to be desired than gold,
than the purest of gold
and sweeter are they than honey,
than honey from the comb.

Gospel Acclamation John 11:25-26

I am the resurrection and the life, says the
Lord, whoever believes in me will never die.

932 3rd Lent (C)
Psalm 102:1-4, 6-8, 11. R℣ v.8

The Lord is com-pas-sion and love, the
Lord is com-pas-sion and love.

1. My soul, give thanks to the Lord,
all my being, bless his holy name.
My soul give thanks to the Lord
and never forget all his blessings.

Continued overleaf

2. It is he who forgives <u>all</u> your guilt,
   who heals every one <u>of</u> your ills,
   who redeems your life <u>from</u> the grave,
   who crowns you with love <u>and</u> compassion.

3. The Lord does <u>deeds</u> of justice,
   gives judgement for all who <u>are</u> oppressed.
   He made known his <u>ways</u> to Moses
   and his deeds to Is<u>ra</u>el's sons.

4. The Lord is compa<u>ssion</u> and love,
   slow to anger and <u>rich</u> in mercy,
   for as the heavens are high a<u>bove</u> the earth
   so strong is his love for <u>those</u> who fear him.

Gospel Acclamation Matthew 4:17

Repent, <u>says</u> the Lord, for the kingdom
of heaven is <u>close</u> at hand.

4. You have prepared a ban<u>quet</u> for me
   in the sight <u>of</u> my foes.
   My head you have anoin<u>ted</u> with oil;
   my cup is <u>over</u>flowing.

5. Surely goodness and kind<u>ness</u> shall
       follow me
   all the days <u>of</u> my life.
   In the Lord's own house <u>shall</u> I dwell
   for <u>ev</u>er and ever.

   Note: Verse 3 may be omitted.

Gospel Acclamation John 8:12

I am the light of the world, <u>says</u> the Lord;
anyone who follows me will have the
<u>light</u> of life.

933 4th Lent (A)
Psalm 22. R℣ v.1

The Lord is my shep-herd; there is

no-thing I shall want, the Lord is my

shep-herd; there is no-thing I shall want.

1. The Lord <u>is</u> my shepherd;
   there is nothing <u>I</u> shall want.
   Fresh and green <u>are</u> the pastures
   where he gives <u>me</u> repose.

2. Near restful wa<u>ters</u> he leads me,
   to revive my <u>drooping</u> spirit.
   He guides me along <u>the</u> right path;
   he is true <u>to</u> his name.

3. If I should walk in the val<u>ley</u> of darkness
   no evil <u>would</u> I fear.
   You are there with your crook <u>and</u> your
       staff;
   with these you <u>give</u> me comfort.

934 4th Lent (B)
Psalm 136. R℣ v.6

O let my tongue cleave to my

mouth if I re-mem-ber you not!

1. By the rivers of Babylon there we <u>sat</u> and
       wept,
   remember<u>ing</u> Zion;
   on the pop<u>lars</u> that grew there
   we hung <u>up</u> our harps.

2. For it was there that they asked us our
       cap<u>tors</u>, for songs,
   our oppress<u>ors</u>, for joy.
   'Sing to <u>us</u>,' they said,
   'one of <u>Zi</u>on's songs.'

3. O how could we sing the song <u>of</u> the Lord
   on a<u>li</u>en soil?
   If I forget <u>you</u>, Jerusalem,
   let my <u>right</u> hand wither!

4. O let my tongue cleave <u>to</u> my mouth
   if I remem<u>ber</u> you not,
   if I prize <u>not</u> Jerusalem
   above <u>all</u> my joys!

Gospel Acclamation John 3:16

God loved the world so much that he
gave his only Son; everyone who believes
in him has eternal life.

935 4th Lent (C)
Psalm 33:2-7. R℣ v.9

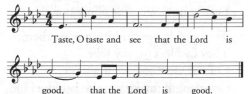

Taste, O taste and see that the Lord is
good, that the Lord is good.

1. I will bless the Lord at all times,
his praise always on my lips;
in the Lord my soul shall make its boast.
The humble shall hear and be glad.

2. Glorify the Lord with me.
Together let us praise his name.
I sought the Lord and he answered me;
from all my terrors he set me free.

3. Look towards him and be radiant;
let your faces not be abashed.
This poor man called; the Lord heard him
and rescued him from all his distress.

Gospel Acclamation Luke 15:18

I will leave this place and go to my father
and say: 'Father, I have sinned against
heaven and against you.'

936 5th Lent (A)
Psalm 129. R℣ v.7

With the Lord there is mer - cy and
full - ness of re - demp - tion.

1. Out of the depths I cry to you, O Lord,
Lord, hear my voice!
O let your ears be attentive
to the voice of my pleading.

2. If you, O Lord, should mark our guilt,
Lord, who would survive?
But with you is found forgiveness:
for this we revere you.

3. My soul is waiting for the Lord,
I count on his word.
My soul is longing for the Lord
more than watchman for daybreak.

4. Because with the Lord there is mercy
and fullness of redemption,
Israel indeed he will redeem
from all its iniquity.

Gospel Acclamation John 11:25, 26

I am the resurrection and the life, says
the Lord; whoever believes in me will
never die.

937 5th Lent (B)
Psalm 50:3-4, 12-15. R℣ v.12

A pure heart cre-ate for
me, for me, O God.

1. Have mercy on me, God, in your
kindness.
In your compassion blot out my offence.
O wash me more and more from my guilt
and cleanse me from my sin.

2. A pure heart create for me, O God,
put a steadfast spirit within me.
Do not cast me away from your presence,
nor deprive me of your holy spirit.

3. Give me again the joy of your help;
with a spirit of fervour sustain me,
that I may teach transgressors your ways
and sinners may return to you.

Gospel Acclamation John 12:26

If a man serves me, says the Lord, he
must follow me, wherever I am, my
servant will be there too.

938 5th Lent (C)
Psalm 125. R℣ v.3

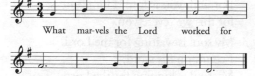

What mar-vels the Lord worked for us! In - deed we were glad.

1. When the Lord delivered Zion from
   bondage,
   it seemed like a dream.
   then was our mouth filled with laughter,
   on our lips there were songs.

2. The heathens themselves said: 'What
   marvels
   the Lord worked for them!'
   What marvels the Lord worked for us!
   Indeed we were glad.

3. Deliver us, O Lord, from our bondage
   as streams in dry land.
   Those who are sowing in tears
   will sing when they reap.

4. They go out, they go out, full of tears,
   carrying seed for the sowing;
   they come back, they come back, full of
   song,
   carrying their sheaves.

Gospel Acclamation Amos 5:14

Seek good and not evil so that you may
live, and that the Lord God of hosts may
really be with you.

939 Passion Sunday (A, B, C)
Psalm 21:8-9, 17-20, 23-24. R℣ v.2

My God, my God, why have you for - sa - ken me?

1. All who see me deride me,
   they curl their lips, they toss their heads.
   'He trusted in the Lord, let him save him;
   let him release him if this is his friend.'

2. Many dogs have surrounded me,
   a band of the wicked beset me.
   They tear holes in my hands and my feet
   I can count every one of my bones.

3. They divide my clothing among them.
   They cast lots for my robe.
   O Lord, do not leave me alone,
   my strength, make haste to help me!

4. I will tell of your name to my brethren
   and praise you where they are assembled.
   'You who fear the Lord give him praise;
   all sons of Jacob, give him glory.'

Gospel Acclamation Philippians 2:8-9

Christ was humbler yet, even to
accepting death, death on a cross.
But God raised him high and gave him
the name which is above all names.

940 Holy Thursday – Evening Mass of
the Lord's Supper (A, B, C)
Ps 115:12-13, 15-18. R℣ cf. 1 Cor 10:16

The bless- ing cup that we bless is a com-mu- nion with the blood of Christ.

1. How can I repay the Lord
   for his goodness to me?
   The cup of salvation I will raise;
   I will call on the Lord's name.

2. O precious in the eyes of the Lord
   is the death of his faithful.
   Your servant, Lord, your servant am I;
   you have loosened my bonds.

3. A thanksgiving sacrifice I make:
I will call on the Lord's name.
My vows to the Lord I will fulfil
before all his people.

Gospel Acclamation John 13:34

I give you a new commandment: love
one another just as I have loved you, says
the Lord.

Gospel Acclamation Philippians 2:8-9

Christ was humbler yet, even to
accepting death, death on a cross.
But God raised him high and gave him
the name which is above all names.

941 Good Friday – Celebration of the Lord's Passion (A, B, C)
Ps 30:2, 6, 12-13, 15-17, 25. R/ Lk 23:46

Father, into your
hands I com-mend my spi-rit.

1. In you, O Lord, I take refuge,
let me never be put to shame.
In your justice, set me free.
It is you who will redeem me, Lord.

2. In the face of all my foes
I am a reproach,
an object of scorn to my neighbours
and of fear to my friends.

3. Those who see me in the street
run far away from me.
I am like the dead, forgotten by all,
like a thing thrown away.

4. But as for me, I trust in you, Lord,
I say: 'You are my God.'
My life is in your hands, deliver me
from the hands of those who hate me.

5. Let your face shine on your servant.
Save me in your love.
Be strong, let your heart take courage,
all who hope in the Lord.

942 Easter Sunday – The Easter Vigil (A, B, C)

After the first Reading
Psalm 103:1-2, 5-6, 10, 12-14, 24, 35. R/ cf. v.30

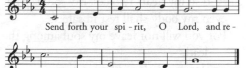

Send forth your spi-rit, O Lord, and renew the face of the earth.

1. Bless the Lord, my soul!
Lord God, how great you are,
clothed in majesty and glory,
wrapped in light as in a robe!

2. You founded the earth on its base,
to stand firm from age to age.
You wrapped it with the ocean like a cloak:
the waters stood higher than the
mountains.

3. You make springs gush forth in the valleys:
they flow in between the hills.
On their banks dwell the birds of heaven;
from the branches they sing their song.

4. From your dwelling you water the hills;
earth drinks its fill of your gift.
You make the grass grow for the cattle
and the plants to serve our needs.

5. How many are your works, O Lord!
In wisdom you have made them all.
The earth is full of your riches.
Bless the Lord, my soul!

Continued overleaf

After the second Reading
Psalm 15:5, 8-11. R℟ v.1

Pre - serve me, God, I take
ref - uge in you.

1. O Lord, it is you who are my por<u>tion</u>
   and cup;
   it is you yourself who <u>are</u> my prize.
   I keep the Lord ever <u>in</u> my sight:
   since he is at my right hand, I <u>shall</u> stand
   firm.

2. And so my heart rejoices, my <u>soul</u> is glad;
   even my body shall <u>rest</u> in safety.
   For you will not leave my soul a<u>mong</u> the
   dead,
   nor let your beloved <u>know</u> decay.

3. O Lord, <u>you</u> will show me
   the <u>path</u> of life,
   the fullness of joy <u>in</u> your presence,
   at your right hand happi<u>ness</u> for ever.

After the third Reading
Exodus 15:1-6, 17-18. R℟ v.1

I will sing to the Lord,
glo - ri - ous his tri - umph!

1. I will sing to the Lord, glor<u>ious</u> his
   triumph!
   Horse and rider he has thrown in<u>to</u> the
   sea!
   The Lord is my strength, my song, <u>my</u>
   salvation.
   This is my God and <u>I</u> extol him,
   my father's God and I <u>give</u> him praise.

2. The Lord <u>is</u> a warrior!
   The Lord <u>is</u> his name.
   The chariots of Pharaoh he hurled in<u>to</u>
   the sea,
   the flower of his army is drowned <u>in</u> the
   sea.
   The deeps hide them; they sank <u>like</u> a
   stone.

3. Your right hand, Lord, glorious <u>in</u> its
   power,
   your right hand, Lord, has shat<u>tered</u> the
   enemy.
   In the greatness of your glory you
   <u>crushed</u> the foe.
   You will lead your people and plant them
   <u>on</u> your mountain,
   the sanctuary, Lord, which your <u>hands</u>
   have made.
   The Lord will reign for e<u>ver</u> and ever.

After the fourth Reading
Psalm 29:2, 4-6, 11-13. R℟ v.2

I will praise you, Lord,
you have res - cued me.

1. I will praise you, Lord, <u>you</u> have rescued
   me
   and have not let my enemies rejoice <u>over</u>
   me.
   O Lord, you have raised my soul <u>from</u>
   the dead,
   restored me to life from those who sink
   in<u>to</u> the grave.

2. Sing psalms to the Lord, <u>you</u> who love
   him,
   give thanks to his <u>holy</u> name.
   His anger lasts but a moment; his fa<u>vour</u>
   through life.
   At night there are tears, but joy <u>comes</u>
   with dawn.

3. The Lord listened <u>and</u> had pity.
   The Lord came <u>to</u> my help.
   For me you have changed my mourning
      <u>in</u>to dancing,
   O Lord my God, I will thank <u>you</u> for ever.

After the fifth Reading
Isaiah 12:2-6. R℟ v.3

With joy you will draw wa-ter from the wells of sal-va-tion.

1. Truly God is <u>my</u> salvation,
   I trust, I <u>shall</u> not fear.
   For the Lord is my <u>strength</u>, my song,
   he be<u>came</u> my saviour.

2. Give thanks <u>to</u> the Lord,
   give praise <u>to</u> his name!
   Make his mighty deeds known <u>to</u> the
      peoples,
   declare the greatness <u>of</u> his name.

3. Sing a psalm to the Lord for he has done
      glo<u>ri</u>ous deeds,
   make them known to <u>all</u> the earth!
   People of Zion, sing and <u>shout</u> for joy
   for great in your midst is the Holy <u>One</u>
      of Israel.

After the sixth Reading
Psalm 18:8-11. R℟ John 6:69

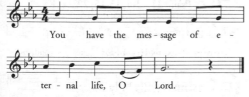

You have the mes-sage of e-ter-nal life, O Lord.

1. The law of the <u>Lord</u> is perfect,
   it re<u>vives</u> the soul.
   The rule of the Lord is <u>to</u> be trusted,
   it gives wisdom <u>to</u> the simple.

2. The precepts of the <u>Lord</u> are right,
   they glad<u>den</u> the heart.
   The command of the <u>Lord</u> is clear,
   it gives light <u>to</u> the eyes.

3. The fear of the <u>Lord</u> is holy,
   ab<u>id</u>ing for ever.
   The decrees of the <u>Lord</u> are truth
   and all <u>of</u> them just.

4. They are more to be de<u>sired</u> than gold,
   than the pu<u>rest</u> of gold
   and sweeter are <u>they</u> than honey,
   than honey <u>from</u> the comb.

After the seventh Reading
Psalm 41:3, 5. 42:3, 4. R℟ 41:2

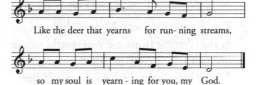

Like the deer that yearns for run-ning streams, so my soul is yearn-ing for you, my God.

1. My soul is thir<u>sting</u> for God,
   the God <u>of</u> my life;
   when can I en<u>ter</u> and see
   the <u>face</u> of God?

2. These things will I remember as I pour
      <u>out</u> my soul:
   how I would lead the rejoicing crowd
      into the <u>house</u> of God,
   amid cries of gladness <u>and</u> thanksgiving,
   the throng <u>wild</u> with joy.

3. O send forth your light <u>and</u> your truth;
   let these <u>be</u> my guide.
   Let them bring me to your <u>holy</u> mountain
   to the place <u>where</u> you dwell.

4. And I will come to the al<u>tar</u> of God,
   the God <u>of</u> my joy.
   My redeemer, I will thank you <u>on</u> the harp,
   O <u>God</u>, my God.

Continued overleaf

If a Baptism takes place, the Psalm which follows the fifth Reading is used, or the one that follows here.

Psalm 50:12-15, 18, 19. R℣ v.12

A pure heart cre-ate for me, for me, O God.

1. A pure heart create for <u>me</u>, O God,
   put a steadfast spi<u>rit</u> within me.
   Do not cast me away <u>from</u> your presence,
   nor deprive me of your <u>ho</u>ly spirit.

2. Give me again the joy <u>of</u> your help;
   with a spirit of fer<u>vour</u> sustain me,
   that I may teach transgres<u>sors</u> your ways
   and sinners may re<u>turn</u> to you.

3. For in sacrifice you take <u>no</u> delight,
   burnt offering from me you <u>would</u> refuse,
   my sacrifice, a <u>con</u>trite spirit.
   A humbled, contrite heart you <u>will</u> not
   spurn.

943 Easter Sunday – The Mass of Easter Night (A, B, C)
Psalm 117:1-2, 16-17, 22-23

Al - le - lu - ia, al - le - lu - ia,

al - le - lu - ia.

1. Give thanks to the Lord for <u>he</u> is good,
   for his love <u>has</u> no end.
   Let the family of Is<u>rael</u> say:
   'His love <u>has</u> no end.'

2. The Lord's right <u>hand</u> has triumphed;
   his right hand <u>raised</u> me up.
   I shall not die, <u>I</u> shall live
   and re<u>count</u> his deeds.

3. The stone which the buil<u>ders</u> rejected
   has be<u>come</u> the corner stone.
   This is the work <u>of</u> the Lord,
   a marvel <u>in</u> our eyes.

944 Easter Sunday – Mass of the Day (A, B, C)
Psalm 117:1-2, 16-17, 22-23. R℣ v.24

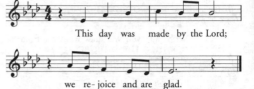

This day was made by the Lord; we re-joice and are glad.

1. Give thanks to the Lord for <u>he</u> is good,
   for his love <u>has</u> no end.
   Let the family of Is<u>rael</u> say:
   'His love <u>has</u> no end.'

2. The Lord's right <u>hand</u> has triumphed;
   his right hand <u>raised</u> me up.
   I shall not die, <u>I</u> shall live
   and re<u>count</u> his deeds.

3. The stone which the buil<u>ders</u> rejected
   has be<u>come</u> the corner stone.
   This is the work <u>of</u> the Lord,
   a marvel <u>in</u> our eyes.

Gospel Acclamation 1 Corinthians 5:7-8

Alleluia. Christ, our passover, <u>has</u> been sacrificed; let us celebrate the feast then, <u>in</u> the Lord. Alleluia.

945 2nd Easter (A)
Psalm 117:2-4, 13-15, 22-24. R℣ v.1

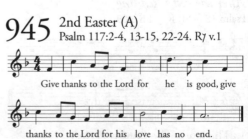

Give thanks to the Lord for he is good, give thanks to the Lord for his love has no end.

1. Let the sons of Is<u>rael</u> say:
   'His love <u>has</u> no end.'
   Let the sons of <u>Aaron</u> say:

'His love has no end.'
Let those who fear the Lord say:
'His love has no end.'

2. I was thrust down, thrust down and
      falling
   but the Lord was my helper.
   The Lord is my strength and my song:
   he was my saviour.
   There are shouts of joy and victory
   in the tents of the just.

3. The stone which the builders rejected
   has become the corner stone.
   This is the work of the Lord,
   a marvel in our eyes.
   This day was made by the Lord;
   we rejoice and are glad.

Gospel Acclamation John 20:29

   Alleluia. Jesus said: 'You believe because
   you can see me. Happy are those who
   have not seen and yet believe.' Alleluia.

946 2nd Easter (B)
Psalm 117:2-4, 15-18, 22-24. Ry v.1

Give thanks to the Lord for   he is good, give

thanks to the Lord for his love has no end.

1. Let the sons of Israel say:
   'His love has no end.'
   Let the sons of Aaron say:
   'His love has no end.'
   Let those who fear the Lord say:
   'His love has no end.'

2. The Lord's right hand has triumphed;
   his right hand raised me up.
   I shall not die, I shall live
   and recount his deeds.
   I was punished, I was punished by the
      Lord,
   but not doomed to die.

3. The stone which the builders rejected
   has become the corner stone.
   This is the work of the Lord,
   a marvel in our eyes.
   This day was made by the Lord;
   we rejoice and are glad.

Gospel Acclamation John 20:29

   Alleluia. Jesus said: 'You believe because you
   can see me. Happy are those who have not
   seen and yet believe.' Alleluia.

947 2nd Easter (C)
Psalm 117:2-4, 22-27. Ry v.1

Give thanks to the Lord for   he is good, give

thanks to the Lord for his love has no end.

1. Let the sons of Israel say:
   'His love has no end.'
   Let the sons of Aaron say:
   'His love has no end.'
   Let those who fear the Lord say:
   'His love has no end.'

2. The stone which the builders rejected
   has become the corner stone.
   This is the work of the Lord,
   a marvel in our eyes.
   This day was made by the Lord;
   we rejoice and are glad.

3. O Lord, grant us salvation;
   O Lord, grant success.
   Blessed in the name of the Lord
   is he who comes.
   We bless you from the house of the Lord;
   the Lord God is our light.

Gospel Acclamation John 20:29

   Alleluia. Jesus said: 'You believe because
   you can see me. Happy are those who
   have not seen and yet believe.' Alleluia.

948 3rd Easter (A)
Psalm 15:1-2, 5, 7-11. R℣ v.11

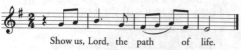

Show us, Lord, the path of life.

1. Preserve me, God, I take refuge in you.
   I say to the Lord: 'You are my God.
   O Lord, it is you who are my portion
       and cup;
   it is you yourself who are my prize.'

2. I will bless the Lord who gives me counsel,
   who even at night directs my heart.
   I keep the Lord ever in my sight:
   since he is at my right hand, I shall stand
       firm.

3. And so my heart rejoices, my soul is glad;
   even my body shall rest in safety.
   For you will not leave my soul among the
       dead,
   nor let your beloved know decay.

4. O Lord, you will show me
   the path of life,
   the fullness of joy in your presence,
   at your right hand happiness for ever.

Gospel Acclamation cf. Luke 24:32

   Alleluia. Lord Jesus, explain the scriptures
   to us. Make our hearts burn within us as
   you talk to us. Alleluia.

949 3rd Easter (B)
Psalm 4:2, 4, 7, 9. R℣ v.7

Lift up the light of your
face on us, O Lord.

1. When I call, answer me, O God of justice;
   from anguish you release me, have mercy
       and hear me!
   It is the Lord who grants favours to those
   whom he loves;
   the Lord hears me whenever I call him.

2. 'What can bring us happiness?' many say.
   Lift up the light of your face on us,
       O Lord.
   I will lie down in peace and sleep comes
       at once,
   for you alone, Lord, make me dwell in
       safety.

Gospel Acclamation cf. Luke 24:32

   Alleluia. Lord Jesus, explain the scriptures
   to us. Make our hearts burn within us as
   you talk to us. Alleluia.

950 3rd Easter (C)
Psalm 29:2, 4-6, 11-13. R℣ v.2

I will praise you, Lord,
you have res - cued me.

1. I will praise you, Lord, you have rescued
       me
   and have not let my enemies rejoice over
       me.
   O Lord, you have raised my soul from
       the dead,
   restored me to life from those who sink
   into the grave.

2. Sing psalms to the Lord, you who love
       him,
   give thanks to his holy name.
   His anger lasts but a moment; his favour
       through life.
   At night there are tears, but joy comes
   with dawn.

3. The Lord listened and had pity.
   The Lord came to my help.
   For me you have changed my mourning
   into dancing;
   O Lord my God, I will thank you for
   ever.

Gospel Acclamation cf. Luke 24:32

Alleluia. Lord Jesus, explain the scriptures to us. Make our hearts burn within us as you talk to us. Alleluia.

Gospel Acclamation John 10:14

Alleluia. I am the good shepherd, says the Lord; I know my own sheep and my own know me. Alleluia.

951 4th Easter (A)
Psalm 22:1-6. R℣ v.1

The Lord is my shep-herd; there is no-thing I shall want, the Lord is my shep-herd; there is no-thing I shall want.

952 4th Easter (B)
Ps 117:1, 8-9, 21-23, 26, 28-29. R℣ v.22

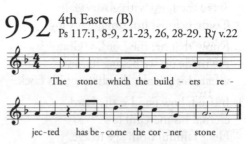

The stone which the build-ers re-jec-ted has be-come the cor-ner stone

1. The Lord is my shepherd;
   there is nothing I shall want.
   Fresh and green are the pastures
   where he gives me repose.

2. Near restful waters he leads me
   to revive my drooping spirit.
   He guides me along the right path;
   he is true to his name.

3. If I should walk in the valley of darkness
   no evil would I fear.
   You are there with your crook and your staff;
   with these you give me comfort.

4. You have prepared a banquet for me
   in the sight of my foes.
   My head you have anointed with oil;
   my cup is overflowing.

5. Surely goodness and kindness shall follow me
   all the days of my life.
   In the Lord's own house shall I dwell
   for ever and ever.

Note: verse 3 may be omitted.

1. Give thanks to the Lord for he is good,
   for his love has no end.
   It is better to take refuge in the Lord
   than to trust in mortals;
   it is better to take refuge in the Lord
   than to trust in rulers.

2. I will thank you for you have given answer
   and you are my saviour.
   The stone which the builders rejected
   has become the corner stone.
   This is the work of the Lord,
   a marvel in our eyes.

3. Blessed in the name of the Lord is he
   who comes.
   We bless you from the house of the Lord;
   I will thank you for you have given answer
   and you are my saviour.
   Give thanks to the Lord for he is good;
   for his love has no end.

Gospel Acclamation John 10:14

Alleluia. I am the good shepherd, says the Lord; I know my own sheep and my own know me. Alleluia.

953

4th Easter (C)
Psalm 99:1-3, 5. R℣ v.3

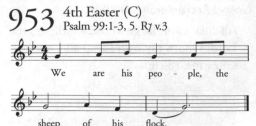

We are his peo - ple, the

sheep of his flock.

1. Cry out with joy to the Lord, <u>all</u> the earth.
   Serve the <u>Lord</u> with gladness.
   Come before him, <u>sing</u>ing for joy.

2. Know that he, the <u>Lord</u>, is God.
   He made us, we bel<u>ong</u> to him,
   we are his people, the sheep <u>of</u> his flock.

3. Indeed, how good <u>is</u> the Lord,
   eternal his mer<u>ci</u>ful love.
   He is faithful from <u>age</u> to age.

Gospel Acclamation John 10:14

Alleluia. I am the good shepherd, <u>says</u> the
Lord; I know my own sheep and my <u>own</u>
know me. Alleluia.

954

5th Easter (A)
Psalm 32:1-2, 4-5, 18-19. R℣ v.22

May your love be up - on us, O Lord,

as we place all our hope in you.

1. Ring out your joy to the Lord, <u>O</u> you just;
   for praise is fitting for <u>loy</u>al hearts.
   Give thanks to the Lord up<u>on</u> the harp,
   with a ten-stringed lute <u>sing</u> him songs.

2. For the word of the <u>Lord</u> is faithful
   and all his works <u>to</u> be trusted.
   The Lord loves jus<u>tice</u> and right
   and fills the earth <u>with</u> his love.

3. The Lord looks on those <u>who</u> revere him,
   on those who hope <u>in</u> his love,
   to rescue their <u>souls</u> from death,
   to keep them a<u>live</u> in famine.

Gospel Acclamation John 14:6

Alleluia. Jesus said: 'I am the Way, the
Truth <u>and</u> the Life. No one can come to
the Father ex<u>cept</u> through me.' Alleluia.

955

5th Easter (B)
Psalm 21:26-28, 30-32. R℣ v.26

You are my praise, O Lord, in the

great as - sem - bly.

1. My vows I will pay before <u>those</u> who fear
   him.
   The poor shall eat and shall <u>have</u> their fill.
   They shall praise the Lord, <u>those</u> who
   seek him.
   May their hearts live for <u>ev</u>er and ever!

2. All the earth shall remember and return
   <u>to</u> the Lord,
   all families of the nations wor<u>ship</u> before
   him.
   They shall worship him, all the mighty <u>of</u>
   the earth;
   before him shall bow all who go down <u>to</u>
   the dust.

3. And my soul shall live for him, my
   <u>chil</u>dren serve him.
   They shall tell of the Lord to generations
   <u>yet</u> to come,
   declare his faithfulness to peoples <u>yet</u>
   unborn:
   'These things the <u>Lord</u> has done.'

Gospel Acclamation John 15:4-5

Alleluia. Make your home in me, as I
make <u>mine</u> in you. Whoever remains in
me bears <u>fruit</u> in plenty. Alleluia.

956 5th Easter (C)
Psalm 144:8-13. R℣ cf. v.1

I will bless your name for e - ver, O God my King.

1. The Lord is kind and full of compassion,
   slow to anger, abounding in love.
   How good is the Lord to all,
   compassionate to all his creatures.

2. All your creatures shall thank you,
   O Lord,
   and your friends shall repeat their
   blessings.
   They shall speak of the glory of your reign
   and declare your might, O God.

3. They will make known to all your
   mighty deeds
   and the glorious splendour of your reign.
   Yours is an everlasting kingdom;
   your rule lasts from age to age.

Gospel Acclamation John 13:34

Alleluia. Jesus said: 'I give you a new
commandment: love one another, just as
I have loved you.' Alleluia.

957 6th Easter (A)
Psalm 65:1-7, 16, 20. R℣ cf. v.1

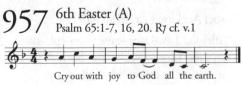

Cry out with joy to God all the earth.

1. Cry out with joy to God all the earth,
   O sing to the glory of his name.
   O render him glorious praise,
   Say to God: 'How tremendous your
   deeds!'

2. 'Before you all the earth shall bow;
   shall sing to you, sing to your name!'
   Come and see the works of God,
   tremendous his deeds among men.

3. He turned the sea into dry land,
   they passed through the river dry-shod.
   Let our joy then be in him;
   he rules for ever by his might.

4. Come and hear, all who fear God.
   I will tell what he did for my soul:
   Blessed be God who did not reject my
   prayer
   nor withhold his love from me.

Gospel Acclamation John 14:23

Alleluia. Jesus said: 'If anyone loves me
they will keep my word, and my Father
will love them and we shall come to
them.' Alleluia.

958 6th Easter (B)
Psalm 97:1-4. R℣ cf. v.2

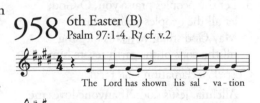

The Lord has shown his sal - va - tion
to all the na - tions.

1. Sing a new song to the Lord
   for he has worked wonders.
   His right hand and his holy arm
   have brought salvation.

2. The Lord has made known his salvation;
   has shown his justice to the nations.
   He has remembered his truth and love
   for the house of Israel.

3. All the ends of the earth have seen
   the salvation of our God.
   Shout to the Lord all the earth,
   ring out your joy.

Gospel Acclamation John 14:23

Alleluia. Jesus said: 'If anyone loves me
they will keep my word, and my Father
will love them and we shall come to
them.' Alleluia.

959 6th Easter (C)
Psalm 66:2-3, 5-6, 8. R℣ v.4

Let the peo - ples praise you, O God; let
all the peo - ples praise you.

1. O God, be gracious and bless us
   and let your face shed its light upon us.
   So will your ways be known upon earth.
   and all nations learn your saving help.

2. Let the nations be glad and exult
   for you rule the world with justice.
   With fairness you rule the peoples,
   you guide the nations on earth.

3. Let the peoples praise you, O God;
   let all the peoples praise you.
   May God still give us his blessing
   till the ends of the earth revere him.

Gospel Acclamation John 14:23

Alleluia. Jesus said: 'If anyone loves me
they will keep my word, and my Father
will love them and we shall come to
them.' Alleluia.

960 The Ascension of the Lord (A, B, C)
Psalm 46:2-3, 6-9. R℣ v.6

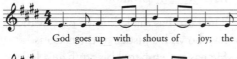

God goes up with shouts of joy; the
Lord goes up with trum-pet blast.

1. All peoples, clap your hands,
   cry to God with shouts of joy!
   For the Lord, the Most High, we must
   fear,
   great king over all the earth.

2. God goes up with shouts of joy;
   the Lord goes up with trumpet blast.
   Sing praise for God, sing praise,
   sing praise to our king, sing praise.

3. God is king of all the earth.
   Sing praise with all your skill.
   God is king over the nations;
   God reigns on his holy throne.

Gospel Acclamation Matthew 28:19, 20

Alleluia. Go, make disciples of all the
nations; I am with you always; yes, to the
end of time. Alleluia.

961 7th Easter (A)
Psalm 26:1, 4, 7-8. R℣ v.13

I am sure I shall see the Lord's
good - ness in the land of the liv - ing.

1. The Lord is my light and my help;
   whom shall I fear?
   The Lord is the stronghold of my life;
   before whom shall I shrink?

2. There is one thing I ask of the Lord,
   for this I long,
   to live in the house of the Lord,
   all the days of my life.

3. O Lord, hear my voice when I call;
   have mercy and answer.
   Of you my heart has spoken;
   'Seek his face.'

Gospel Acclamation cf. John 14:18

Alleluia. I will not leave you orphans,
says the Lord; I will come back to you,
and your hearts will be full of joy.
Alleluia.

962 7th Easter (B)
Psalm 102:1-2, 11-12, 19-20. R℣ v.19

The Lord has set his sway in
hea - ven.

1. My soul, give thanks to the Lord;
   all my being, bless his holy name.
   My soul, give thanks to the Lord
   and never forget all his blessings.

2. For as the heavens are high above the earth
   so strong is his love for those who fear him.
   As far as the east is from the west
   so far does he remove our sins.

3. The Lord has set his sway in heaven
   and his kingdom is ruling over all.
   Give thanks to the Lord, all his angels,
   mighty in power, fulfilling his word.

Gospel Acclamation cf. John 14:18

Alleluia. I will not leave you orphans,
says the Lord; I will come back to you,
and your hearts will be full of joy.
Alleluia.

963 7th Easter (C)
Psalm 96:1-2, 6-7, 9. R℟ vv.1, 9

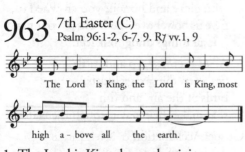

The Lord is King, the Lord is King, most high a-bove all the earth.

1. The Lord is King, let earth rejoice,
   the many coastlands be glad.
   His throne is justice and right.

2. The skies proclaim his justice;
   all peoples see his glory.
   All you spirits, worship him.

3. For you indeed are the Lord
   most high above all the earth
   exalted far above all spirits.

Gospel Acclamation cf. John 14:18

Alleluia. I will not leave you orphans,
says the Lord; I will come back to you,
and your hearts will be full of joy.
Alleluia.

964 Pentecost Sunday (A, B, C)
Psalm 103:1, 24, 29-31, 34. R℟ cf. v.30

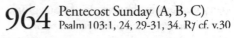

Send forth your spi-rit, O Lord, and re-

new the face of the earth.

1. Bless the Lord, my soul!
   Lord God, how great you are.
   How many are your works, O Lord!
   The earth is full of your riches.

2. You take back your spirit, they die,
   returning to the dust from which they
      came.
   You send forth your spirit, they are
      created;
   and you renew the face of the earth.

3. May the glory of the Lord last for ever!
   May the Lord rejoice in his works!
   May my thoughts be pleasing to him.
   I find my joy in the Lord.

Gospel Acclamation

Alleluia. Come, Holy Spirit, fill the
hearts of your faithful and kindle in them
the fire of your love. Alleluia.

965 The Most Holy Trinity (A)
Daniel 3:52-56. R℟ v.22

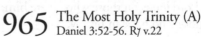

To you glo-ry and

praise for e-ver-more.

1. You are blest, Lord God of our fathers.
   To you glory and praise for evermore.
   Blest your glorious holy name.
   To you glory and praise for evermore.

Continued overleaf

2. You are blest in the temple <u>of</u> your glory.
   To you glory and praise for evermore.
   You are blest on the throne <u>of</u> your kingdom.
   To you glory and praise for evermore.

3. You are blest who gaze in<u>to</u> the depths.
   To you glory and praise for evermore.
   You are blest in the firm<u>ament</u> of heaven.
   To you glory and praise for evermore.

Gospel Acclamation cf. Revelation 1:8

   Alleluia. Glory be to the Father, and to the Son, and to the <u>Holy</u> Spirit, the God who is, who was, and who <u>is</u> to come. Alleluia.

966 The Most Holy Trinity (B)
Psalm 32:4-6, 9, 18-20, 22. R℣ v.12

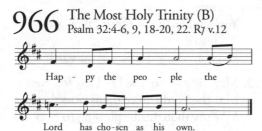

1. The word of the <u>Lord</u> is faithful
   and all his works <u>to</u> be trusted.
   The Lord loves jus<u>tice</u> and right
   and fills the earth <u>with</u> his love.

2. By his word the hea<u>vens</u> were made,
   by the breath of his mouth <u>all</u> the stars.
   He spoke; and they <u>came</u> to be.
   He commanded; they sprang <u>into</u> being.

3. The Lord looks on those <u>who</u> revere him,
   on those who hope <u>in</u> his love,
   to rescue their <u>souls</u> from death,
   to keep them a<u>live</u> in famine.

4. Our soul is waiting <u>for</u> the Lord.
   The Lord is our help <u>and</u> our shield.
   May your love be upon <u>us</u>, O Lord,
   as we place all our <u>hope</u> in you.

Gospel Acclamation cf. Revelation 1:8

   Alleluia. Glory be to the Father, and to the Son, and to the <u>Holy</u> Spirit, the God who is, who was, and who <u>is</u> to come. Alleluia.

967 The Most Holy Trinity (C)
Psalm 8:4-9. R℣ v.2

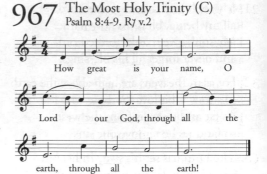

1. When I see the heavens, the work <u>of</u> your hands,
   the moon and the stars which <u>you</u> arranged,
   what are we that you should keep <u>us</u> in mind,
   mortals <u>that</u> you care for us?

2. Yet you have made us little <u>less</u> than gods;
   with glory and hon<u>our</u> you crowned us,
   gave us power over the works <u>of</u> your hand,
   put all things un<u>der</u> our feet.

3. All of them, <u>sheep</u> and cattle,
   yes, even the <u>savage</u> beasts,
   birds of the <u>air</u>, and fish
   that make their way <u>through</u> the waters.

Gospel Acclamation cf. Revelation 1:8

   Alleluia. Glory be to the Father, and to the Son, and to the <u>Holy</u> Spirit, the God who is, who was, and who <u>is</u> to come. Alleluia.

968 The Body and Blood of Christ (A)
Psalm 147:12-15, 19-20. R℣ v.12

1. O Praise the <u>Lord</u>, Jerusalem!
   Zion, <u>praise</u> your God!
   He has strengthened the bars <u>of</u> your gates,
   he has blessed the chil<u>dren</u> within you.

2. He established peace <u>on</u> your borders,
he feeds you with <u>fin</u>est wheat.
He sends out his word <u>to</u> the earth
and swiftly runs <u>his</u> command.

3. He makes his word <u>known</u> to Jacob,
to Israel his laws <u>and</u> decrees.
He has not dealt thus with <u>oth</u>er nations;
he has not taught them <u>his</u> decrees.

Gospel Acclamation John 6:51-52

Alleluia. I am the living bread which has
come down from heaven, <u>says</u> the Lord.
Anyone who eats this bread will <u>live</u> for
ever. Alleluia.

969 The Body and Blood of Christ (B)
Psalm 115:12-13, 15-18. R⁊ v.13

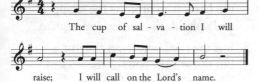

The cup of sal-va-tion I will
raise; I will call on the Lord's name.

1. How can I re<u>pay</u> the Lord
for his good<u>ness</u> to me?
The cup of salvation <u>I</u> will raise;
I will call on <u>the</u> Lord's name.

2. O precious in the eyes <u>of</u> the Lord
is the death <u>of</u> his faithful.
Your servant, Lord, your ser<u>vant</u> am I;
you have loos<u>ened</u> my bonds.

3. A thanksgiving sacri<u>fice</u> I make:
I will call on <u>the</u> Lord's name.
My vows to the Lord I <u>will</u> fulfil
before <u>all</u> his people.

Gospel Acclamation John 6:51-52

Alleluia. I am the living bread which has
come down from heaven, <u>says</u> the Lord.
Anyone who eats this bread will <u>live</u> for
ever. Alleluia.

970 The Body and Blood of Christ (C)
Psalm 109:1-4. R⁊ v.4

You are a priest for e-ver, a
priest like Mel-chi-ze-dek of old.

1. The Lord's revelation <u>to</u> my Master:
'Sit <u>on</u> my right:
I will put your foes be<u>neath</u> your feet.'

2. The Lord will <u>send</u> from Zion
your scep<u>tre</u> of power:
rule in the midst of <u>all</u> your foes.

3. A prince from the day <u>of</u> your birth
on the <u>holy</u> mountains;
from the womb before the daybreak
<u>I</u> begot you.

4. The Lord has sworn an oath he <u>will</u> not
change.
'You are a <u>priest</u> for ever,
a priest like Melchize<u>dek</u> of old.'

Gospel Acclamation John 6:51-52

Alleluia. I am the living bread which has
come down from heaven, <u>says</u> the Lord.
Anyone who eats this bread will <u>live</u> for
ever. Alleluia.

971 2nd in Ordinary Time (A)
Psalm 39:2, 4, 7-10. R⁊ vv.8, 9

Here I am, Lord! I
come to do your will.

1. I waited, I waited for the Lord and <u>he</u>
stooped down to me;
he <u>heard</u> my cry.
He put a new song in<u>to</u> my mouth,
praise <u>of</u> our God.

Continued overleaf

2. You do not ask for sacrifice and offerings,
   but an open ear.
   You do not ask for holocaust and victim.
   Instead, here am I.

3. In the scroll of the book it stands written
   that I should do your will.
   My God, I delight in your law
   in the depth of my heart.

4. Your justice I have proclaimed
   in the great assembly.
   My lips I have not sealed;
   you know it, O Lord.

Gospel Acclamation

   Alleluia. Blessings on the King who comes,
   in the name of the Lord! Peace in heaven
   and glory in the highest heavens! Alleluia.

or John 1:14, 12

   Alleluia. The Word was made flesh and
   lived among us; to all who did accept
   him he gave power to become children of
   God. Alleluia.

972 3rd in Ordinary Time (A)
Psalm 26:1, 4, 13-14. R⁊ v.1

1. The Lord is my light and my help;
   whom shall I fear?
   The Lord is the stronghold of my life;
   before whom shall I shrink?

2. There is one thing I ask of the Lord,
   for this I long,
   to live in the house of the Lord,
   all the days of my life.

3. I am sure I shall see the Lord's goodness
   in the land of the living.
   Hope in him, hold firm and take heart.
   Hope in the Lord!

Gospel Acclamation Matthew 4:23

   Alleluia. Jesus proclaimed the Good News
   of the kingdom, and cured all kinds of
   sickness among the people. Alleluia.

973 4th in Ordinary Time (A)
Psalm 145:7-10. R⁊ Matthew 5:3

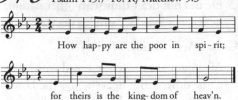

1. It is the Lord who keeps faith for ever,
   who is just to those who are oppressed.
   It is he who gives bread to the hungry,
   the Lord, who sets prisoners free.

2. It is the Lord who gives sight to the blind,
   who raises up those who are bowed down,
   the Lord, who protects the stranger
   and upholds the widow and orphan.

3. It is the Lord who loves the just
   but thwarts the path of the wicked.
   The Lord will reign for ever,
   Zion's God, from age to age.

Gospel Acclamation Matthew 11:25

   Alleluia. Blessed are you, Father, Lord of
   Heaven and earth, for revealing the
   mysteries of the kingdom to mere
   children. Alleluia.

or Matthew 5:12

   Alleluia. Rejoice and be glad: your reward
   will be great in heaven. Alleluia.

974 5th in Ordinary Time (A)
Psalm 111:4-9. R⁊ v.4

The good will be a light in the dark-ness.

1. They are a light in the darkness for the
   upright:
   they are generous, merciful and just.

The good take pity and lend,
They conduct their affairs with honour.

2. The just will never waver:
they will be remembered for ever.
They have no fear of evil news;
with a firm heart they trust in the Lord.

3. With a steadfast heart they will not fear;
open-handed, they give to the poor;
their justice stands firm for ever.
Their heads will be raised in glory.

Gospel Acclamation John 8:12

Alleluia. I am the light of the world, says
the Lord, anyone who follows me will
have the light of life. Alleluia.

975 6th in Ordinary Time (A)
Psalm 118:1-2, 4-5, 17-18, 33-34. R℣ v.1

They are hap-py who fol-low God's law!

1. They are happy whose life is blameless,
who follow God's law!
They are happy those who do his will,
seeking him with all their hearts.

2. You have laid down your precepts
to be obeyed with care.
May my footsteps be firm
to obey your statutes.

3. Bless your servant and I shall live
and obey your word.
Open my eyes that I may consider
the wonders of your law.

4. Teach me the demands of your statutes
and I will keep them to the end.
Train me to observe your law,
to keep it with my heart.

Gospel Acclamation 1 Sam. 3:9; John 6:68

Alleluia. Speak, Lord, your servant is
listening; you have the message of eternal
life. Alleluia.

976 7th in Ordinary Time (A)
Psalm 102:1-4, 8, 10, 12-13. R℣ v.8

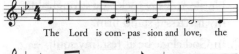

The Lord is com-pas-sion and love, the

Lord is com-pas-sion and love.

1. My soul, give thanks to the Lord,
all my being, bless his holy name.
My soul, give thanks to the Lord
and never forget all his blessings.

2. It is he who forgives all your guilt,
who heals every one of your ills,
who redeems your life from the grave,
who crowns you with love and
compassion.

3. The Lord is compassion and love,
slow to anger and rich in mercy.
He does not treat us according to our sins
nor repay us according to our faults.

4. As far as the east is from the west
so far does he remove our sins.
As a father has compassion on his sons,
the Lord has pity on those who fear him.

Gospel Acclamation John 14:23

Alleluia. If anyone loves me they will keep
my word, and my Father will love them
and we shall come to them. Alleluia.

or 1 John 2:5

Alleluia. When anyone obeys what Christ
has said, God's love comes to perfection in
him. Alleluia.

977 8th in Ordinary Time (A)
Psalm 61:2-3, 6-9. R℣ v.6

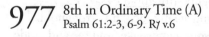

In God a - lone is my

soul at rest, at rest.

Continued overleaf

1. In God alone is my <u>soul</u> at rest;
   my help <u>comes</u> from him.
   He alone is my <u>rock</u>, my stronghold,
   my fortress: <u>I</u> stand firm.

2. In God alone be at <u>rest</u>, my soul;
   for my hope <u>comes</u> from him.
   He alone is my <u>rock</u>, my stronghold,
   my fortress: <u>I</u> stand firm.

3. In God is my safe<u>ty</u> and glory,
   the rock <u>of</u> my strength.
   Take refuge in God <u>all</u> you people.
   Trust him <u>at</u> all times.

Gospel Acclamation John 17:17

   Alleluia. Your word is <u>truth</u>, O Lord,
   consecrate us <u>in</u> the truth. Alleluia.

or Hebrews 4:12

   Alleluia. The word of God is something
   <u>alive</u> and active; it can judge secret
   emo<u>tions</u> and thoughts. Alleluia.

978   9th in Ordinary Time (A)
Psalm 30:2-4, 17, 25. R℔ v.3

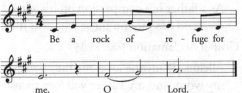

Be a rock of re - fuge for me, O Lord.

1. In you, O Lord, <u>I</u> take refuge.
   Let me never be <u>put</u> to shame.
   In your justice, <u>set</u> me free,
   hear me and spee<u>dily</u> rescue me.

2. Be a rock of re<u>fuge</u> to me,
   a mighty strong<u>hold</u> to save me,
   for you are my <u>rock</u>, my stronghold.
   For your name's sake, lead <u>me</u> and guide
   me.

3. Let your face shine <u>on</u> your servant.
   Save me <u>in</u> your love.
   Be strong, let your <u>heart</u> take courage,
   all who hope <u>in</u> the Lord.

Gospel Acclamation John 14:23

   Alleluia. If anyone loves me they will <u>keep</u>
   my word, and my Father will love them
   and <u>we</u> shall come to them. Alleluia.

or John 15:5

   Alleluia. I am the vine, you are the
   branches, <u>says</u> the Lord. Whoever
   remains in me, with me in him, bears
   <u>fruit</u> in plenty. Alleluia.

979   10th in Ordinary Time (A)
Psalm 49:1, 8, 12-15. R℔ v.23

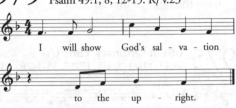

I will show God's sal - va - tion to the up - right.

1. The God of gods, the Lord, has spoken
   and sum<u>moned</u> the earth,
   from the rising of the sun <u>to</u> its setting.
   'I find no fault <u>with</u> your sacrifices,
   your offerings are al<u>ways</u> before me.'

2. 'Were I hungry, I <u>would</u> not tell you,
   for I own the world and <u>all</u> it holds.
   Do you think I eat the <u>flesh</u> of bulls,
   or drink the <u>blood</u> of goats?'

3. 'Pay your sacrifice of thanks<u>giving</u> to God
   and render him your <u>votive</u> offerings.
   Call on me in the day <u>of</u> distress.
   I will free you and <u>you</u> shall honour me.'

Gospel Acclamation cf. Acts 16:14

   Alleluia. Open our <u>heart</u>, O Lord, to
   accept the words <u>of</u> your Son. Alleluia.

or Luke 4:18

   Alleluia. The Lord has sent me to bring
   the good news <u>to</u> the poor, to proclaim
   liber<u>ty</u> to captives. Alleluia.

980   11th in Ordinary Time (A)
Psalm 99:2-3, 5. R/ v.3

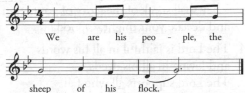

We are his peo - ple, the

sheep of his flock.

1. Cry out with joy to the Lord, all the earth.
   Serve the Lord with gladness.
   Come before him, singing for joy.

2. Know that he, the Lord is God.
   He made us, we belong to him,
   we are his people, the sheep of his flock.

3. Indeed, how good is the Lord,
   eternal his merciful love.
   He is faithful from age to age.

Gospel Acclamation John 10:27

Alleluia. The sheep that belong to me
listen to my voice, says the Lord, I know
them and they follow me. Alleluia.

or Mark 1:15

Alleluia. The kingdom of God is close at
hand. Repent, and believe the Good
News. Alleluia.

981   12th in Ordinary Time (A)
Psalm 68:8-10, 14, 17, 33-35. R/ v.14

In your great love, in your great love,

ans - wer me, O God,

ans - wer me, O God, in your love.

1. It is for you that I suffer taunts,
   that shame covers my face,
   that I have become a stranger to my
   brothers,

---

an alien to my own mother's sons.
I burn with zeal for your house
and taunts against you fall on me.

2. This is my prayer to you,
   my prayer for your favour.
   In your great love, answer me, O God,
   with your help that never fails:
   Lord, answer, for your love is kind;
   in your compassion, turn towards me.

3. The poor when they see it will be glad
   and God-seeking hearts will revive;
   for the Lord listens to the needy
   and does not spurn his servants in their
   chains.
   Let the heavens and the earth give him
   praise,
   the sea and all its living creatures.

Gospel Acclamation John 1:14, 12

Alleluia. The Word was made flesh and
lived among us; to all who did accept
him he gave power to become children of
God. Alleluia.

or John 15:26, 27

Alleluia. The Spirit of truth will be my
witness; and you too will be my
witnesses. Alleluia.

982   13th in Ordinary Time (A)
Psalm 88:2-3, 16-19. R/ v.2

I will sing for e - ver of your

love, O Lord.

1. I will sing for ever of your love, O Lord;
   through all ages my mouth will proclaim
   your truth.
   Of this I am sure, that your love lasts for
   ever,
   that your truth is firmly established as the
   heavens.

Continued overleaf

2. Happy the people who acclaim <u>such</u> a king,
who walk, O Lord, in the light <u>of</u> your face,
who find their joy every day <u>in</u> your name,
who make your justice the source <u>of</u> their bliss.

3. For it is you, O Lord, who are the glory <u>of</u> their strength;
it is by your favour that our might <u>is</u> exalted;
for our ruler is in the keeping <u>of</u> the Lord;
our king in the keeping of the Holy <u>One</u> of Israel.

Gospel Acclamation cf. Acts 16:14

Alleluia. Open our <u>heart</u>, O Lord, to accept the words <u>of</u> your Son. Alleluia.

or 1 Peter 2:9

Alleluia. You are a chosen race, a royal priesthood, a people set apart to sing the pra<u>ises</u> of God who called you out of darkness into his wond<u>er</u>ful light. Alleluia.

983 14th in Ordinary Time (A)
Psalm 144:1-2, 8-11, 13-14. R7 v.1

I will bless your name for e-ver, O God my King.

1. I will give you glory, O <u>God</u> my King,
I will bless your <u>name</u> for ever.
I will bless you day <u>after</u> day
and praise your <u>name</u> for ever.

2. The Lord is kind and full <u>of</u> compassion,
slow to anger, aboun<u>ding</u> in love.
How good is the <u>Lord</u> to all,
compassionate to <u>all</u> his creatures.

3. All your creatures shall thank <u>you</u>, O Lord,
and your friends shall re<u>peat</u> their blessing.
They shall speak of the glory <u>of</u> your reign
and declare your <u>might</u>, O God.

4. The Lord is faithful in <u>all</u> his words
and loving in <u>all</u> his deeds.
The Lord supports <u>all</u> who fall
and raises all who <u>are</u> bowed down.

Gospel Acclamation cf. Matthew 11:25

Alleluia. Blessed are you, Father, Lord of hea<u>ven</u> and earth, for revealing the mysteries of the kingdom <u>to</u> mere children. Alleluia.

984 15th in Ordinary Time (A)
Psalm 64:10-14. R7 Luke 8:8

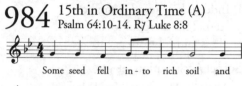

Some seed fell in-to rich soil and

yield-ed a rich har-vest.

1. You care for the earth, <u>give</u> it water,
you fill <u>it</u> with riches.
Your river in hea<u>ven</u> brims over
to pro<u>vide</u> its grain.

2. And thus you provide <u>for</u> the earth;
you <u>drench</u> its furrows,
you level it, soften <u>it</u> with showers,
you <u>bless</u> its growth.

3. You crown the year <u>with</u> your goodness.
Abundance flows <u>in</u> your steps,
in the pastures of the wild<u>erness</u> it flows.

4. The hills are gir<u>ded</u> with joy,
the meadows co<u>vered</u> with flocks,
the valleys are <u>decked</u> with wheat.
They shout for joy, <u>yes</u>, they sing.

Gospel Acclamation 1 Samuel 3:9; John 6:68

Alleluia. Speak, Lord, your ser<u>vant</u> is listening; you have the message of eternal life. Alleluia.

or

Alleluia. The seed is the word of God, Christ the sower; whoever finds this seed will remain for ever. Alleluia.

985 16th in Ordinary Time (A)
Psalm 85:5-6, 9-10, 15-16. R℣ v.5

O Lord, you are good and for-giv - ing.

1. O Lord, you are good and forgiving,
   full of love to all who call.
   Give heed, O Lord, to my prayer
   and attend to the sound of my voice.

2. All the nations shall come to adore you
   and glorify your name, O Lord:
   for you are great and do marvellous deeds,
   you who alone are God.

3. But you, God of mercy and compassion,
   slow to anger, O Lord,
   abounding in love and truth,
   turn and take pity on me.

Gospel Acclamation cf. Ephesians 1:17, 18

Alleluia. May the Father of our Lord Jesus Christ enlighten the eyes of our mind, so that we can see what hope his call holds for us. Alleluia.

or cf. Matthew 11:25

Alleluia. Blessed are you, Father, Lord of heaven and earth, for revealing the mysteries of the kingdom to mere children. Alleluia.

986 17th in Ordinary Time (A)
Psalm 118:57, 72, 76-77, 127-130. R℣ v.97

Lord, how I love your law!
Lord, how I love your law!

1. My part, I have resolved, O Lord,
   is to obey your word.
   The law from your mouth means more to me
   than silver and gold.

2. Let your love be ready to console me
   by your promise to your servant.
   Let your love come to me and I shall live
   for your law is my delight.

3. That is why I love your commands
   more than finest gold.
   That is why I rule my life by your precepts;
   I hate false ways.

4. Your will is wonderful indeed;
   therefore I obey it.
   The unfolding of your word gives light
   and teaches the simple.

Gospel Acclamation John 15:15

Alleluia. I call you friends, says the Lord, because I have made known to you everything I have learnt from my Father. Alleluia.

or cf. Matthew 11:25

Alleluia. Blessed are you, Father, Lord of heaven and earth, for revealing the mysteries of the kingdom to mere children. Alleluia.

987 18th in Ordinary Time (A)
Psalm 144:8-9, 15-18. R℣ v.16

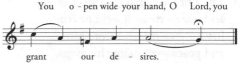

You o-pen wide your hand, O Lord, you grant our de - sires.

1. The Lord is kind and full of compassion,
   slow to anger, abounding in love.
   How good is the Lord to all,
   compassionate to all his creatures.

Continued overleaf

2. The eyes of all creatures <u>look</u> to you
and you give them their food <u>in</u> due time.
You open <u>wide</u> your hand,
grant the desires of <u>all</u> who live.

3. The Lord is just in <u>all</u> his ways
and loving in <u>all</u> his deeds.
He is close to <u>all</u> who call him,
call on him <u>from</u> their hearts.

Gospel Acclamation Luke 19:38

Alleluia. Blessings on the King who comes
in the name <u>of</u> the Lord! Peace in heaven
and glory in the <u>high</u>est heavens! Alleluia.

or Matthew 4:4

Alleluia. Man does not live on <u>bread</u>
alone, but on every word that comes
from the <u>mouth</u> of God. Alleluia.

988 19th in Ordinary Time (A)
Psalm 84:9-14. R℣ v.8

1. I will hear what the Lord God <u>has</u> to say,
a voice that <u>speaks</u> of peace.
His help is near for <u>those</u> who fear him
and his glory will dwell <u>in</u> our land.

2. Mercy and faithful<u>ness</u> have met;
justice and peace <u>have</u> embraced.
Faithfulness shall spring <u>from</u> the earth
and justice look <u>down</u> from heaven.

3. The Lord will <u>make</u> us prosper
and our earth shall <u>yield</u> its fruit.
Justice shall <u>march</u> before him
and peace shall fo<u>llow</u> his steps.

Gospel Acclamation Luke 19:38

Alleluia. Blessings on the King who comes,
in the name <u>of</u> the Lord! Peace in heaven
and glory in the <u>high</u>est heavens! Alleluia.

or Psalm 129:5

Alleluia. My soul is waiting <u>for</u> the Lord,
I count <u>on</u> his word. Alleluia.

989 20th in Ordinary Time (A)
Psalm 66:2-3, 5-6. 8. R℣ v.4

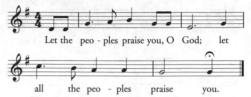

1. O God, be gra<u>cious</u> and bless us
and let your face shed its <u>light</u> upon us.
So will your ways be known <u>upon</u> earth
and all nations learn your <u>saving</u> help.

2. Let the nations be glad <u>and</u> exult
for you rule the <u>world</u> with justice.
With fairness you <u>rule</u> the peoples,
you guide the na<u>tions</u> on earth.

3. Let the peoples praise <u>you</u>, O God;
let all the <u>peoples</u> praise you.
May God still give <u>us</u> his blessing
till the ends of the <u>earth</u> revere him.

Gospel Acclamation John 10:27

Alleluia. The sheep that belong to me
listen to my voice, <u>says</u> the Lord, I know
them <u>and</u> they follow me. Alleluia.

or cf. Matthew 4:23

Alleluia. Jesus proclaimed the Good News
<u>of</u> the kingdom, and cured all kinds of
sickness a<u>mong</u> the people. Alleluia.

990 21st in Ordinary Time (A)
Psalm 137:1-3, 6, 8. R℣ v.8

1. I thank you, Lord, with <u>all</u> my heart,
   you have heard the words <u>of</u> my mouth.
   Before the angels <u>I</u> will bless you.
   I will adore before your <u>holy</u> temple.

2. I thank you for your faithful<u>ness</u> and love
   which excel all we <u>ever</u> knew of you.
   On the day I <u>called</u>, you answered;
   you increased the strength <u>of</u> my soul.

3. The Lord is high yet he looks <u>on</u> the
     lowly
   and the haughty he knows <u>from</u> afar.
   Your love, O Lord, <u>is</u> eternal,
   discard not the work <u>of</u> your hands.

Gospel Acclamation 2 Corinthians 5:19

   Alleluia. God in Christ was reconciling
   the world <u>to</u> himself, and he has
   entrusted to us the news that <u>they</u> are
   reconciled. Alleluia.

or Matthew 16:18

   Alleluia. You are Peter and on this rock I
   will <u>build</u> my Church. And the gates of
   the underworld can never hold <u>out</u>
   against it. Alleluia.

991 22nd in Ordinary Time (A)
Psalm 62:2-6, 8-9. R℣ v.2

1. O God, you are my God, for <u>you</u> I long:
   for you my <u>soul</u> is thirsting.
   My body <u>pines</u> for you
   like a dry, weary land <u>without</u> water.

2. So I gaze on you <u>in</u> the sanctuary
   to see your strength <u>and</u> your glory.
   For your love is bet<u>ter</u> than life,
   my lips will <u>speak</u> your praise.

3. So I will bless you <u>all</u> my life,
   in your name I will lift <u>up</u> my hands.
   My soul shall be filled as <u>with</u> a banquet,
   my mouth shall praise <u>you</u> with joy.

4. For you have <u>been</u> my help;
   in the shadow of your wings <u>I</u> rejoice.
   My soul <u>clings</u> to you:
   your right hand <u>holds</u> me fast.

Gospel Acclamation cf. Ephesians 1:17, 18

   Alleluia. May the Father of our Lord
   Jesus Christ enlighten the eyes <u>of</u> our
   mind, so that we can see what hope his
   call <u>holds</u> for us. Alleluia.

992 23rd in Ordinary Time (A)
Psalm 94:1-2, 6-9. R℣ v.8

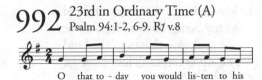

1. Come, ring out our joy <u>to</u> the Lord;
   hail the <u>rock</u> who saves us.
   Let us come before him, giving thanks,
   with songs let us <u>hail</u> the Lord.

2. Come in; let us bow <u>and</u> bend low;
   let us kneel before the <u>God</u> who made us
   for he is our God, and we the people
     who belong <u>to</u> his pasture,
   the flock that is led <u>by</u> his hand.

3. O that today you would listen <u>to</u> his
     voice!
   Harden not your hearts as <u>at</u> Meribah,
   as on that day at Massah in the desert,
     when your fathers put me <u>to</u> the test;
   when they tried me, though they <u>saw</u> my
     work.

Gospel Acclamation John 17:17

   Alleluia. Your word is <u>truth</u>, O Lord,
   consecrate us <u>in</u> the truth. Alleluia.

Continued overleaf

or 2 Corinthians 5:19

Alleluia. God in Christ was reconciling the world to himself, and he has entrusted to us the news that they are reconciled. Alleluia.

993 24th in Ordinary Time (A)
Psalm 102:1-4, 9-12. R⁄ v.8

The Lord is com-pas-sion and love, the

Lord is com-pas-sion and love.

1. My soul, give thanks to the Lord,
   all my being, bless his holy name.
   My soul, give thanks to the Lord
   and never forget all his blessings.

2. It is he who forgives all your guilt,
   who heals every one of your ills,
   who redeems your life from the grave,
   who crowns you with love and
      compassion.

3. His wrath will come to an end;
   he will not be angry for ever.
   He does not treat us according to our sins
   nor repay us according to our faults.

4. For as the heavens are high above the earth
   so strong is his love for those who fear him.
   As far as the east is from the west
   so far does he remove our sins.

Gospel Acclamation 1 Samuel 3:9. John 6:68

Alleluia. Speak, Lord, your servant is listening: you have the message of eternal life. Alleluia.

or John 13:34

Alleluia. I give you a new commandment: love one another, just as I have loved you, says the Lord. Alleluia.

994 25th in Ordinary Time (A)
Psalm 144:2-3, 8-9, 17-18. R⁄ v.18

The Lord is close to all who call him.

1. I will bless you day after day
   and praise your name for ever.
   The Lord is great, highly to be praised,
   his greatness cannot be measured.

2. The Lord is kind and full of compassion,
   slow to anger, abounding in love.
   How good is the Lord to all,
   compassionate to all his creatures.

3. The Lord is just in all his ways
   and loving in all his deeds.
   He is close to all who call him,
   who call on him from their hearts.

Gospel Acclamation Luke 19:38

Alleluia. Blessings on the King who comes, in the name of the Lord! Peace in heaven and glory in the highest heavens! Alleluia.

or cf. Acts 16:14

Alleluia. Open our heart, O Lord, to accept the words of your Son. Alleluia.

995 26th in Ordinary Time (A)
Psalm 24:4-9. R⁄ v.6

Re - mem-ber, re - mem-ber

your mer - cy, O Lord.

1. Lord, make me know your ways.
   Lord teach me your paths.
   Make me walk in your truth, and teach me;
   for you are God my saviour.

2. Remember your <u>mercy</u>, Lord,
and the love you have shown <u>from</u> of old.
Do not remember the sins <u>of</u> my youth.
In your <u>love</u> remember me.

3. The Lord is <u>good</u> and upright.
He shows the path to <u>those</u> who stray,
he guides the humble in <u>the</u> right path;
he teaches his way <u>to</u> the poor.

Gospel Acclamation John 14:23

Alleluia. If anyone loves me they will
<u>keep</u> my word, and my Father will love
them and <u>we</u> shall come to them.
Alleluia.

or John 10:27

Alleluia. The sheep that belong to me
listen to my voice <u>says</u> the Lord, I know
them and they <u>follow</u> me. Alleluia.

4. And we shall never forsake <u>you</u> again:
give us life that we may call <u>upon</u> your
name.
God of hosts, <u>bring</u> us back;
let your face shine on us and we <u>shall</u> be
saved.

Gospel Acclamation John 15:15

Alleluia. I call you friends, <u>says</u> the Lord,
because I have made known to you
everything I have learnt <u>from</u> my Father.
Alleluia.

or cf. John 15:16

Alleluia. I chose you from the world to
go out <u>and</u> bear fruit, fruit that will last,
<u>says</u> the Lord. Alleluia.

996 27th in Ordinary Time (A)
Psalm 79:9, 12-16, 19-20. R/ Isaiah 5:7

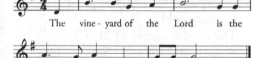

The vine-yard of the Lord is the

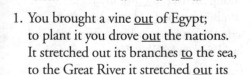

House of Is-ra-el.

1. You brought a vine <u>out</u> of Egypt;
to plant it you drove <u>out</u> the nations.
It stretched out its branches <u>to</u> the sea,
to the Great River it stretched <u>out</u> its
shoots.

2. Then why have you broken <u>down</u> its walls?
It is plucked by all <u>who</u> pass by.
It is ravaged by the boar <u>of</u> the forest,
devoured by the beasts <u>of</u> the field.

3. God of hosts, turn again, <u>we</u> implore,
look down from hea<u>ven</u> and see.
Visit this vine <u>and</u> protect it,
the vine your right <u>hand</u> has planted.

997 28th in Ordinary Time (A)
Psalm 22. R/ v.6

The Lord is my shep-herd; there is
no-thing I shall want, the Lord is my
shep-herd; there is no-thing I shall want.

1. The Lord <u>is</u> my shepherd;
there is nothing <u>I</u> shall want.
Fresh and green <u>are</u> the pastures
where he gives <u>me</u> repose.

2. Near restful wa<u>ters</u> he leads me,
to revive my <u>drooping</u> spirit.
He guides me along <u>the</u> right path;
he is true <u>to</u> his name.

3. If I should walk in the val<u>ley</u> of darkness
no evil <u>would</u> I fear.
You are there with your crook <u>and</u> your
staff;
with these you <u>give</u> me comfort.

Continued overleaf

4. You have prepared a banquet for me
   in the sight of my foes.
   My head you have anointed with oil;
   my cup is overflowing.

5. Surely goodness and kindness shall follow
      me
   all the days of my life.
   In the Lord's own house shall I dwell
   for ever and ever.

   Note: Verse 3 may be omitted.

Gospel Acclamation John 1:12,14

Alleluia. The Word was made flesh and
lived among us; to all who did accept
him he gave power to become children of
God. Alleluia.

or cf. Ephesians 1:17, 18

Alleluia. May the Father of our Lord
Jesus Christ enlighten the eyes of our
mind, so that we can see what hope his
call holds for us. Alleluia.

998 29th in Ordinary Time (A)
Psalm 95:1, 3-5, 7-10. R℣ v.7

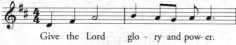

Give the Lord glo-ry and pow-er.

1. O sing a new song to the Lord,
   sing to the Lord all the earth.
   Tell among the nations his glory
   and his wonders among all the peoples.

2. The Lord is great and worthy of praise,
   to be feared above all gods;
   the gods of the heathens are naught.
   It was the Lord who made the heavens.

3. Give the Lord, you families of peoples,
   give the Lord glory and power,
   give the Lord the glory of his name.
   Bring an offering and enter his courts.

4. Worship the Lord in his temple.
   O earth, tremble before him.
   Proclaim to the nations: 'God is king.'
   He will judge the peoples in fairness.

Gospel Acclamation John 17:17

Alleluia. Your word is truth, O Lord,
consecrate us in the truth. Alleluia.

or Philippians 2:15-16

Alleluia. You will shine in the world like
bright stars because you are offering it the
word of life. Alleluia.

999 30th in Ordinary Time (A)
Psalm 17:2-4, 47, 51. R℣ v.2

I love you, Lord, O God, my
strength, I love you, Lord, my strength.

1. My God is the rock where I take refuge;
   my shield, my mighty help, my
      stronghold.
   The Lord is worthy of all praise.
   when I call I am saved from my foes.

2. Long life to the Lord, my rock!
   Praised be the God who saves me.
   He has given great victories to his king
   and shown his love for his anointed.

Gospel Acclamation cf. Acts 16:14

Alleluia. Open our heart, O Lord,
to accept the words of your Son. Alleluia.

1000 31st in Ordinary Time (A)
Psalm 130

Keep my soul in peace be-fore you, Lord.

1. O Lord, my heart is not proud
   nor haughty my eyes.
   I have not gone after things too great
   nor marvels beyond me.

2. Truly I have set my soul in silence and
      peace.
   A weaned child on its mother's breast,
      even so is my soul.
   O Israel, hope in the Lord
   both now and for ever.

Gospel Acclamation 1 Samuel 3:9. John 6:68

   Alleluia. Speak, Lord, your servant is
   listening; you have the message of eternal
   life. Alleluia.

1001   32nd in Ordinary Time (A)
        Psalm 62:2-8. R̷ v.2

1. O God, you are my God, for you I long;
   for you my soul is thirsting.
   My body pines for you
   like a dry, weary land without water.

2. So I gaze on you in the sanctuary
   to see your strength and your glory.
   For your love is better than life,
   my lips will speak your praise.

3. So I will bless you all my life,
   in your name I will lift up my hands.
   My soul shall be filled as with a banquet,
   my mouth shall praise you with joy.

4. On my bed I remember you.
   On you I muse through the night
   for you have been my help;
   in the shadow of your wings I rejoice.

Gospel Acclamation Matthew 24:42, 44

   Alleluia. Stay awake and stand ready,
   because you do not know the hour when
   the Son of Man is coming. Alleluia.

1002   33rd in Ordinary Time (A)
        Psalm 127:1-5. R̷ v.1

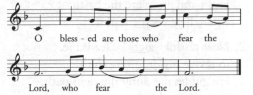

1. O blessed are those who fear the Lord
   and walk in his ways!
   By the labour of your hands you shall eat.
   You will be happy and prosper.

2. Your wife like a fruitful vine
   in the heart of your house;
   your children like shoots of the olive,
   around your table.

3. Indeed thus shall be blessed
   those who fear the Lord.
   May the Lord bless you from Zion
   in a happy Jerusalem.

Gospel Acclamation Revelation 2:10

   Alleluia. Even if you have to die, says the
   Lord, keep faithful, and I will give you
   the crown of life. Alleluia.

or John 15:4, 5

   Alleluia. Make your home in me, as I
   make mine in you, says the Lord.
   Whoever remains in me bears fruit in
   plenty. Alleluia.

1003 Our Lord Jesus Christ, Universal King (A)

Psalm 22. R/ v.1

The Lord is my shep-herd; there is no-thing I shall want, the Lord is my shep-herd; there is no-thing I shall want.

1. The Lord is my shepherd;
   there is nothing I shall want.
   Fresh and green are the pastures
   where he gives me repose.

2. Near restful waters he leads me,
   to revive my drooping spirit.
   He guides me along the right path;
   he is true to his name.

3. If I should walk in the valley of darkness
   no evil would I fear.
   You are there with your crook and your
       staff;
   with these you give me comfort.

4. You have prepared a banquet for me
   in the sight of my foes.
   My head you have anointed with oil;
   my cup is overflowing.

5. Surely goodness and kindness shall follow
       me
   all the days of my life.
   In the Lord's own house shall I dwell
   for ever and ever.

   Note: Verse 3 may be omitted.

Gospel Acclamation Mark 11:10

   Alleluia. Blessings on him who comes in
   the name of the Lord! Blessings on the
   coming kingdom of our father David!
   Alleluia.

1004 2nd in Ordinary Time (B)

Psalm 39:2, 4, 7-10. R/ vv.8, 9

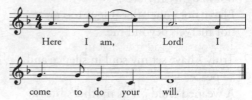

Here I am, Lord! I come to do your will.

1. I waited, I waited for the Lord and he
       stooped down to me;
   he heard my cry.
   He put a new song into my mouth,
   praise of our God.

2. You do not ask for sacrifice and offerings,
   but an open ear.
   You do not ask for holocaust and victim.
   Instead, here am I.

3. In the scroll of the book it stands written
   that I should do your will.
   My God, I delight in your law
   in the depth of my heart.

4. Your justice I have proclaimed
   in the great assembly.
   My lips I have not sealed;
   you know it, O Lord.

Gospel Acclamation 1 Samuel 3:9; John 6:68

   Alleluia. Speak, Lord, your servant is
   listening: you have the message of eternal
   life. Alleluia.

or

   Alleluia. We have found the Messiah –
   which means the Christ – grace and
   truth have come through him. Alleluia.

1005 3rd in Ordinary Time (B)

Psalm 24:4-9. R/ v.4

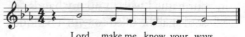

Lord, make me know your ways.

1. Lord, make me <u>know</u> your ways.
   Lord, teach <u>me</u> your paths.
   Make me walk in your <u>truth</u>, and teach
      me:
   for you are <u>God</u> my saviour.

2. Remember your <u>mercy</u> Lord,
   and the love you have shown <u>from</u> of old.
   In your <u>love</u> remember me,
   because of your good<u>ness</u>, O Lord.

3. The Lord is <u>good</u> and upright.
   He shows the path to <u>those</u> who stray,
   he guides the humble in <u>the</u> right path;
   he teaches his way <u>to</u> the poor.

Gospel Acclamation Mark 1:15

   Alleluia. The kingdom of God is <u>close</u> at
   hand; believe <u>the</u> Good News. Alleluia.

1006 4th in Ordinary Time (B)
Psalm 94:1-2, 6-9. R/ v.9

O that to-day you would lis-ten to his

voice: 'Har - den not your hearts.'

1. Come, ring out our joy <u>to</u> the Lord;
   hail the <u>rock</u> who saves us.
   Let us come before him, giving thanks,
   with songs let us <u>hail</u> the Lord.

2. Come in; let us kneel <u>and</u> bend low;
   let us kneel before the <u>God</u> who made us
   for he is our God, and we the people
      who belong <u>to</u> his pasture,
   the flock that is led <u>by</u> his hand.

3. O that today you would listen <u>to</u> his
      voice!
   'Harden not your hearts as <u>at</u> Meribah,
   as on that day at Massah in the desert,
      when your fathers put me <u>to</u> the test;
   when they tried me, though they <u>saw</u> my
      work.'

Gospel Acclamation cf. Matthew 11:25

   Alleluia. Blessed are you, Father, Lord of
   hea<u>ven</u> and earth, for revealing the
   mysteries of the kingdom <u>to</u> mere
   children. Alleluia.

or Matthew 4.16

   Alleluia. The people that lived in
   darkness have seen <u>a</u> great light; on those
   who dwell in the land and shadow of
   death a <u>light</u> has dawned. Alleluia.

1007 5th in Ordinary Time (B)
Psalm 146:1-6. R/ v.3

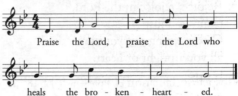

Praise the Lord, praise the Lord who

heals the bro - ken - heart - ed.

1. Praise the Lord for <u>he</u> is good;
   sing to our God for <u>he</u> is loving:
   to him our <u>praise</u> is due.

2. The Lord builds <u>up</u> Jerusalem
   and brings back Israel's exiles,
   he heals the <u>broken</u>-hearted,
   he binds up <u>all</u> their wounds.

3. Our Lord is great <u>and</u> almighty;
   his wisdom can ne<u>ver</u> be measured.
   The Lord rai<u>ses</u> the lowly;
   he humbles the wicked <u>to</u> the dust.

Gospel Acclamation John 8:12

   Alleluia. I am the light of the world, <u>says</u>
   the Lord, anyone who follows me will
   have the <u>light</u> of life. Alleluia.

or Matthew 8:17

   Alleluia. He took our sick<u>nesses</u> away,
   and carried our dis<u>eases</u> for us. Alleluia.

1008 6th in Ordinary Time (B)
Psalm 31:1-2, 5, 11. R℣ v.7

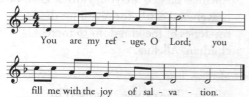

You are my ref - uge, O Lord; you fill me with the joy of sal - va - tion.

1. Happy are those whose offence is forgiven,
   whose sin is remitted.
   O happy are those to whom the Lord
   imputes no guilt.

2. But now I have acknowledged my sins;
   my guilt I did not hide.
   and you, Lord, have forgiven
   the guilt of my sin.

3. Rejoice, rejoice in the Lord,
   exult, you just!
   O come, ring out your joy,
   all you upright of heart.

Gospel Acclamation cf. Ephesians 1:17, 18

Alleluia. May the Father of our Lord
Jesus Christ enlighten the eyes of our
mind, so that we can see what hope his
call holds for us. Alleluia.

or Luke 7:16

Alleluia. A great prophet has appeared
among us; God has visited his people.
Alleluia.

1009 7th in Ordinary Time (B)
Psalm 40:2-5, 13-14. R℣ v.5

Heal my soul for I have sinned a - gainst you, Lord, heal my soul.

---

1. Happy are those who consider the poor
   and the weak.
   The Lord will save them in the day of evil,
   will guard them, give them life, make
   them happy in the land
   and will not give them up to the will of
   their foes.

2. The Lord will give them strength in their
   pain,
   he will bring them back from sickness to
   health.
   As for me, I said: 'Lord, have mercy on
   me,
   heal my soul for I have sinned against
   you.'

3. If you uphold me I shall be unharmed
   and set in your presence for evermore.
   Blessed be the Lord, the God of Israel
   from age to age. Amen. Amen.

Gospel Acclamation John 1:12, 14

Alleluia. The Word was made flesh and
lived among us; to all who did accept
him he gave power to become children of
God. Alleluia.

or Luke 4:18

Alleluia. The Lord has sent me to bring
the good news to the poor, to proclaim
liberty to captives. Alleluia.

1010 8th in Ordinary Time (B)
Psalm 102:1-4, 8, 10, 12-13. R℣ v.8

The Lord is com-pas-sion and love, the

Lord is com-pas-sion and love.

1. My soul, give thanks to the Lord,
   all my being, bless his holy name.
   My soul, give thanks to the Lord
   and never forget all his blessings.

2. It is he who forgives <u>all</u> your guilt,
   who heals every one <u>of</u> your ills,
   who redeems your life <u>from</u> the grave,
   who crowns you with love <u>and</u>
      compassion.

3. The Lord is compa<u>ssion</u> and love,
   slow to anger and <u>rich</u> in mercy.
   He does not treat us according <u>to</u> our sins
   nor repay us according <u>to</u> our faults.

4. So far as the east is <u>from</u> the west
   so far does he re<u>move</u> our sins.
   As a father has compassion <u>on</u> his sons,
   the Lord has pity on <u>those</u> who fear him.

Gospel Acclamation John 10:27

   Alleluia. The sheep that belong to me
   listen to my voice, <u>says</u> the Lord, I know
   them <u>and</u> they follow me. Alleluia.

or James 1:18

   Alleluia. By his own choice the Father
   made us his children by the message <u>of</u>
   the truth, so that we should be a sort of
   first-fruits of all that <u>he</u> created. Alleluia.

1011 9th in Ordinary Time (B)
Psalm 80:3-8, 10-11. R℣ v.2

Ring out your joy to God our strength.

1. Raise a song and <u>sound</u> the timbrel,
   the sweet-sounding harp <u>and</u> the lute,
   blow the trumpet at <u>the</u> new moon,
   when the moon is full, <u>on</u> our feast.

2. For this is Israel's law,
   a command of the <u>God</u> of Jacob.
   He imposed it as a <u>rule</u> on Joseph,
   when he went out against the <u>land</u> of
      Egypt.

3. A voice I did not know <u>said</u> to me:
   'I freed your shoulder <u>from</u> the burden;
   your hands were freed <u>from</u> the load.
   You called in distress <u>and</u> I saved you.

4. 'Let there be no foreign <u>god</u> among you,
   no worship of an a<u>lien</u> god.
   I am the <u>Lord</u> your God,
   who brought you from the <u>land</u> of Egypt.'

Gospel Acclamation cf. John 6:63, 68

   Alleluia. Your words are spirit, Lord, and
   <u>they</u> are life: you have the message of
   eternal life. Alleluia.

or cf. John 17:17

   Alleluia. Your word is <u>truth</u>, O Lord,
   consecrate us <u>in</u> the truth. Alleluia.

1012 10th in Ordinary Time (B)
Psalm 129. R℣ v.7

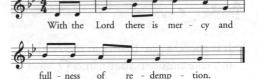

With the Lord there is mer - cy and
full - ness of re - demp - tion.

1. Out of the depths I cry to <u>you</u>, O Lord,
   Lord, <u>hear</u> my voice!
   O let your ears <u>be</u> attentive
   to the voice <u>of</u> my pleading.

2. If you, O Lord, should <u>mark</u> our guilt,
   Lord, who <u>would</u> survive?
   But with you is <u>found</u> forgiveness:
   for this <u>we</u> revere you.

3. My soul is waiting <u>for</u> the Lord,
   I count <u>on</u> his word.
   My soul is longing <u>for</u> the Lord
   more than watch<u>man</u> for daybreak.

4. Because with the Lord <u>there</u> is mercy
   and fullness <u>of</u> redemption,
   Israel indeed he <u>will</u> redeem
   from all <u>its</u> iniquity.

Gospel Acclamation John 14:23

   Alleluia. If anyone loves me they will <u>keep</u>
   my word, and my Father will love them
   and <u>we</u> shall come to them. Alleluia.

Continued overleaf

or John 12:31, 32

Alleluia. Now the prince of this world is to be overthrown, <u>says</u> the Lord. And when I am lifted up from the earth, I shall draw all men <u>to</u> myself. Alleluia.

1013 11th in Ordinary Time (B)
Psalm 91:2-3, 13-16. R/ cf. v.2

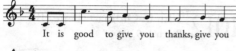

It is good to give you thanks, give you

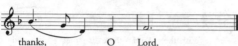

thanks, O Lord.

1. It is good to give thanks <u>to</u> the Lord
   to make music to your name, <u>O</u> Most
      High,
   to proclaim your love <u>in</u> the morning
   and your truth in the watches <u>of</u> the night.

2. The just will flourish <u>like</u> the palm-tree
   and grow like a <u>Leb</u>anon cedar.
   Planted in the house <u>of</u> the Lord
   they will flourish in the courts <u>of</u> our God.

3. Still bearing fruit when <u>they</u> are old,
   still full of <u>sap</u>, still green,
   they will proclaim that the <u>Lord</u> is just.
   In him, my rock, there <u>is</u> no wrong.

Gospel Acclamation John 15:15

Alleluia. I call you friends, <u>says</u> the Lord, because I have made known to you everything I have learnt <u>from</u> my Father. Alleluia.

or

Alleluia. The seed is the word of God, <u>Christ</u> the sower; whoever finds the seed will re<u>main</u> for ever. Alleluia.

1014 12th in Ordinary Time (B)
Psalm 106:23-26, 28-31. R/ v.1

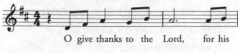

O give thanks to the Lord, for his

love en - dures for e - ver.

1. Some sailed to the <u>sea</u> in ships
   to trade on the <u>migh</u>ty waters.
   These have seen <u>the</u> Lord's deeds,
   the wonders he does <u>in</u> the deep.

2. For he spoke; he summ<u>oned</u> the gale,
   tossing the waves <u>of</u> the sea
   up to heaven and back in<u>to</u> the deep;
   their soul melted away in <u>their</u> distress.

3. Then they cried to the Lord <u>in</u> their need
   and he rescued them from <u>their</u> distress.
   He stilled the storm <u>to</u> a whisper:
   all the waves of the <u>sea</u> were hushed.

4. They rejoiced because <u>of</u> the calm
   and he led them to the haven <u>they</u>
      desired.
   Let them thank the Lord <u>for</u> his love,
   the wonders he does <u>for</u> his people.

Gospel Acclamation cf. Ephesians 1:17, 18

Alleluia. May the Father of our Lord Jesus Christ enlighten the eyes <u>of</u> our mind, so that we can see what hope his call <u>holds</u> for us. Alleluia.

or Luke 7:16

Alleluia. A great prophet has a<u>ppeared</u> among us; God has visi<u>ted</u> his people. Alleluia.

1015 13th in Ordinary Time (B)
Psalm 29:2, 4-6, 11-13. R/ v.2

I will praise you, Lord,

you have res - cued me.

1. I will praise you, Lord, <u>you</u> have rescued
   me
   and have not let my enemies rejoice <u>o</u>ver
   me.
   O Lord, you have raised my soul <u>from</u>
   the dead,
   restored me to life from those who sink
   in<u>to</u> the grave.

2. Sing psalms to the Lord, <u>you</u> who love
   him,
   give thanks to his <u>ho</u>ly name.
   His anger lasts but a moment; his fa<u>vour</u>
   through life.
   At night there are tears, but joy <u>comes</u>
   with dawn.

3. The Lord listened <u>and</u> had pity.
   The Lord came <u>to</u> my help.
   For me you have changed my mourning
   <u>in</u>to dancing,
   O Lord my God, I will thank <u>you</u> for ever.

Gospel Acclamation cf. John 6:63, 68

   Alleluia. Your words are spirit, Lord, and
   <u>they</u> are life: you have the message of
   e<u>ter</u>nal life. Alleluia.

1016 14th in Ordinary Time (B)
Psalm 122. R℣ v.2

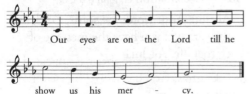

1. To you have I lifted <u>up</u> my eyes,
   you who dwell <u>in</u> the heavens:
   my eyes, like the <u>eyes</u> of slaves
   on the hand <u>of</u> their lords.

2. Like the eyes <u>of</u> a servant
   on the hand <u>of</u> his mistress,
   so our eyes are on the <u>Lord</u> our God
   till he show <u>us</u> his mercy.

3. Have mercy on us, <u>Lord</u>, have mercy.
   We are filled <u>with</u> contempt.
   Indeed all too full <u>is</u> our soul
   with the scorn <u>of</u> the rich.

Gospel Acclamation John 1:12, 14

   Alleluia. The Word was made flesh and
   <u>lived</u> among us; to all who did accept
   him he gave power to become chil<u>dren</u> of
   God. Alleluia.

or Luke 4:18

   Alleluia. The Lord has sent me to bring
   the good news <u>to</u> the poor, to proclaim
   liber<u>ty</u> to captives. Alleluia.

1017 15th in Ordinary Time (B)
Psalm 84:9-14. R℣ v.8

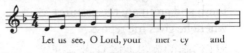

1. I will hear what the Lord God <u>has</u> to say,
   a voice that <u>speaks</u> of peace.
   His help is near for <u>those</u> who fear him
   and his glory will dwell <u>in</u> our land.

2. Mercy and faithful<u>ness</u> have met;
   justice and peace <u>have</u> embraced.
   Faithfulness shall spring <u>from</u> the earth
   and justice look <u>down</u> from heaven.

3. The Lord will <u>make</u> us prosper
   and our earth shall <u>yield</u> its fruit.
   Justice shall <u>march</u> before him
   and peace shall fo<u>llow</u> his steps.

Gospel Acclamation cf. John 6:63, 68

   Alleluia. Your words are spirit, Lord, and
   <u>they</u> are life: you have the message of
   e<u>ter</u>nal life. Alleluia.

Continued overleaf

or cf. Ephesians 1:17, 18

Alleluia. May the Father of our Lord
Jesus Christ enlighten the eyes of our
mind, so that we can see what hope his
call holds for us. Alleluia.

1018 16th in Ordinary Time (B)
Psalm 22. R/ v.2

The Lord is my shep-herd; there is
no-thing I shall want, the Lord is my
shep-herd; there is no-thing I shall want.

1. The Lord is my shepherd;
   there is nothing I shall want.
   Fresh and green are the pastures
   where he gives me repose.

2. Near restful waters he leads me,
   to revive my drooping spirit.
   He guides me along the right path;
   he is true to his name.

3. If I should walk in the valley of darkness
   no evil would I fear.
   You are there with your crook and your
      staff;
   with these you give me comfort.

4. You have prepared a banquet for me
   in the sight of my foes.
   My head you have anointed with oil;
   my cup is overflowing.

5. Surely goodness and kindness shall follow
      me
   all the days of my life.
   In the Lord's own house shall I dwell
   for ever and ever.

   Note: Verse 3 may be omitted.

Gospel Acclamation John 10:27

Alleluia. The sheep that belong to me
listen to my voice, says the Lord, I know
them and they follow me. Alleluia.

1019 17th in Ordinary Time (B)
Psalm 144:10-11, 15-18. R/ v.16

You o - pen wide your hand, O Lord, you
grant our de - sires.

1. All your creatures shall thank you,
      O Lord,
   and your friends shall repeat their blessing.
   They shall speak of the glory of your
      reign
   and declare your might, O God.

2. The eyes of all creatures look to you
   and you give them their food in due time.
   You open wide your hand,
   grant the desires of all who live.

3. The Lord is just in all his ways
   and loving in all his deeds.
   He is close to all who call him,
   who call on him from their hearts.

Gospel Acclamation cf. John 6:63, 68

Alleluia. Your words are spirit, Lord, and
they are life: you have the message of
eternal life. Alleluia.

or Luke 7:16

Alleluia. A great prophet has appeared
among us; God has visited his people.
Alleluia.

1020 18th in Ordinary Time (B)
Psalm 77:3-4, 23-25, 54. R/ v.24

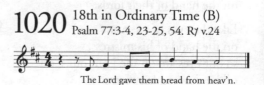

The Lord gave them bread from heav'n.

1. The things we have heard and <u>under</u>stood,
   the things our fore<u>bears</u> have told us,
   we will tell to the next ge<u>ner</u>ation:
   the glories of the Lord <u>and</u> his might.

2. He commanded the <u>clouds</u> above
   and opened the <u>gates</u> of heaven.
   He rained down manna <u>for</u> their food,
   and gave them <u>bread</u> from heaven.

3. Mere mortals ate the <u>bread</u> of angels.
   He sent them abun<u>dance</u> of food.
   He brought them to his <u>holy</u> land,
   to the mountain which his right <u>hand</u>
   had won.

Gospel Acclamation John 14:5

Alleluia. I am the Way, the Truth and the
Life, <u>says</u> the Lord; no one can come to
the Father ex<u>cept</u> through me. Alleluia.

or Matthew 4:4

Alleluia. Man does not live on <u>bread</u>
alone, but on every word that comes
from the <u>mouth</u> of God. Alleluia.

3. Look towards him <u>and</u> be radiant;
   let your faces not <u>be</u> abashed.
   When the poor cry out <u>the</u> Lord hears
   them
   and rescues them from all <u>their</u> distress.

4. The angel of the Lord <u>is</u> encamped
   around those who revere <u>him</u>, to rescue
   them.
   Taste and see that the <u>Lord</u> is good.
   They are happy who seek re<u>fuge</u> in him.

Gospel Acclamation John 14:23

Alleluia. If anyone loves me they will <u>keep</u>
my word, and my Father will love them,
and <u>we</u> shall come to them. Alleluia.

or John 6:51

Alleluia. I am the living bread which has
come down from heaven, <u>says</u> the Lord.
Anyone who eats this bread will <u>live</u> for
ever. Alleluia.

1022 20th in Ordinary Time (B)
Psalm 33:2-3, 10-15. R/ v.9

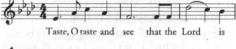
Taste, O taste and see that the Lord is

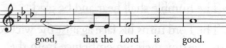
good, that the Lord is good.

1. I will bless the Lord <u>at</u> all times,
   his praise always <u>on</u> my lips;
   in the Lord my soul shall <u>make</u> its boast.
   The humble shall hear <u>and</u> be glad.

2. Revere the Lord, <u>you</u> his saints.
   They lack nothing, those <u>who</u> revere him.
   Strong lions suffer want <u>and</u> go hungry
   but those who seek the Lord <u>lack</u> no
   blessing.

3. Come, child<u>ren</u>, and hear me
   that I may teach you the fear <u>of</u> the Lord.
   Who are they who <u>long</u> for life
   and many days, to enjoy <u>their</u> prosperity?

1021 19th in Ordinary Time (B)
Psalm 33:2-9. R/ v.9

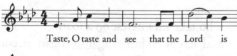
Taste, O taste and see that the Lord is

good, that the Lord is good.

1. I will bless the Lord <u>at</u> all times,
   his praise always <u>on</u> my lips;
   in the Lord my soul shall <u>make</u> its boast.
   the humble shall hear <u>and</u> be glad.

2. Glorify the <u>Lord</u> with me.
   Together let us <u>praise</u> his name.
   I sought the Lord and <u>he</u> answered me;
   from all my terrors he <u>set</u> me free.

Continued overleaf

4. Then keep your <u>tongue</u> from evil
   and your lips from spea<u>king</u> deceit.
   Turn aside from evil <u>and</u> do good;
   seek and strive <u>after</u> peace.

Gospel Acclamation John 1:12, 14

Alleluia. The Word was made flesh and
<u>lived</u> among us; to all who did accept
him he gave power to become child<u>ren</u> of
God. Alleluia.

or John 6:56

Alleluia. They who eat my flesh and
<u>drink</u> my blood live in me, and I live in
them, <u>says</u> the Lord. Alleluia.

1023 21st in Ordinary Time (B)
Psalm 33:2-3, 16-23. R/ v.9

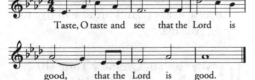

Taste, O taste and see that the Lord is
good, that the Lord is good.

1. I will bless the Lord <u>at</u> all times,
   his praise always <u>on</u> my lips;
   in the Lord my soul shall <u>make</u> its boast.
   The humble shall hear <u>and</u> be glad.

2. The Lord turns his face a<u>gainst</u> the wicked
   to destroy their remembrance <u>from</u> the
   earth.
   The Lord turns his eyes <u>to</u> the just
   and his ears to <u>their</u> appeal.

3. They call and <u>the</u> Lord hears
   and rescues them in all <u>their</u> distress.
   The Lord is close to the <u>broken</u>-hearted;
   those whose spirit is crushed <u>he</u> will save.

4. Evil brings death <u>to</u> the wicked;
   those who hate the <u>good</u> are doomed.
   The Lord ransoms the souls <u>of</u> his
   servants.
   Those who hide in him shall not <u>be</u>
   condemned.

Gospel Acclamation cf. John 6:63, 68

Alleluia. Your words are spirit, Lord, and
<u>they</u> are life: you have the message of
<u>eternal</u> life. Alleluia.

1024 22nd in Ordinary Time (B)
Psalm 14:2-5. R/ v.1

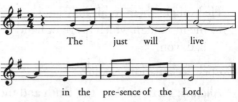

The just will live
in the pre-sence of the Lord.

1. Lord, who shall dwell on your <u>holy</u>
   mountain?
   Those who walk <u>without</u> fault;
   those who <u>act</u> with justice
   and speak the truth <u>from</u> their hearts.

2. Those who do no wrong <u>to</u> their
   kindred,
   who cast no slur <u>on</u> their neighbours,
   who hold the godless <u>in</u> disdain,
   but honour those who <u>fear</u> the Lord.

3. Those who keep their pledge, <u>come</u> what
   may;
   who take no interest <u>on</u> a loan
   and accept no bribes a<u>gainst</u> the innocent.
   Such people will stand <u>firm</u> for ever.

Gospel Acclamation cf. John 6:63, 68

Alleluia. Your words are spirit, Lord, and
<u>they</u> are life: you have the message of
<u>eternal</u> life. Alleluia.

or James 1:18

Alleluia. By his own choice the Father
made us his children by the message <u>of</u>
the truth, so that we should be a sort of
first-fruits of all that <u>he</u> created. Alleluia.

1025 23rd in Ordinary Time (B)
Psalm 145:7-10. R℣ v.1

My soul, give praise to the Lord.

1. It is the Lord who keeps <u>faith</u> for ever,
   who is just to those who <u>are</u> oppressed.
   It is he who gives bread <u>to</u> the hungry,
   the Lord, who sets pris<u>on</u>ers free.

2. It is the Lord who gives sight <u>to</u> the blind,
   who raises up those who <u>are</u> bowed down,
   the Lord who <u>loves</u> the just,
   the Lord, who pro<u>tects</u> the stranger.

3. The Lord upholds the wi<u>dow</u> and orphan,
   but thwarts the path <u>of</u> the wicked.
   The Lord will <u>reign</u> for ever,
   Zion's God, from <u>age</u> to age.

Gospel Acclamation 1 Samuel 3:9; John 6:68

Alleluia. Speak, Lord, your ser<u>vant</u> is
listening: you have the message of e<u>ter</u>nal
life. Alleluia.

or cf. Matthew 4:23

Alleluia. Jesus proclaimed the Good News
<u>of</u> the kingdom, and cured all kinds of
sickness a<u>mong</u> the people. Alleluia.

1026 24th in Ordinary Time (B)
Psalm 114:1-6, 8-9. R℣ v.9

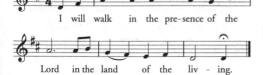

I will walk in the pre-sence of the

Lord in the land of the liv - ing.

1. I love the Lord for <u>he</u> has heard
   the cry of <u>my</u> appeal;
   for he <u>turned</u> his ear to me
   in the day <u>when</u> I called him.

2. They surrounded me, the <u>snares</u> of death,
   with the anguish <u>of</u> the tomb;
   they caught me, sorrow <u>and</u> distress.
   O Lord my <u>God</u>, deliver me!

3. How gracious is the <u>Lord</u>, and just;
   our God <u>has</u> compassion.
   The Lord protects the <u>simple</u> hearts;
   I was helpless <u>so</u> he saved me.

4. He has kept my soul from death, my <u>eyes</u>
      from tears
   and my <u>feet</u> from stumbling.
   I will walk in the presence <u>of</u> the Lord
   in the land <u>of</u> the living.

Gospel Acclamation John 14:5

Alleluia. I am the Way, the Truth and the
Life, <u>says</u> the Lord; no one can come to
the Father ex<u>cept</u> through me. Alleluia.

or Galatians 6:14

Alleluia. The only thing I can boast
about is the cross <u>of</u> our Lord, through
whom the world is crucified to me, and I
<u>to</u> the world. Alleluia.

1027 25th in Ordinary Time (B)
Psalm 53:3-6, 8. R℣ v.6

The Lord up - holds my

life, up - holds my life.

1. O God, save me <u>by</u> your name;
   by your power, up<u>hold</u> my cause.
   O God, <u>hear</u> my prayer;
   listen to the words <u>of</u> my mouth.

2. For the proud have ri<u>sen</u> against me,
   ruthless foes <u>seek</u> my life.
   They have no re<u>gard</u> for God.

Continued overleaf

3. But I have God for my help.
   The Lord upholds my life.
   I will sacrifice to you with willing heart
   and praise your name for it is good.

Gospel Acclamation John 8:12

Alleluia. I am the light of the world, says
the Lord, anyone who follows me will
have the light of life. Alleluia.

or cf. 2 Thessalonians 2:14

Alleluia. Through the Good News God
has called us to share the glory of our
Lord Jesus Christ. Alleluia!

1028 26th in Ordinary Time (B)
Psalm 18:8, 10, 12-14. R℣ v.9

The pre-cepts of the
Lord glad - den the heart.

1. The law of the Lord is perfect,
   it revives the soul.
   The rule of the Lord is to be trusted,
   it gives wisdom to the simple.

2. The fear of the Lord is holy,
   abiding for ever.
   The decrees of the Lord are truth
   and all of them just.

3. So in them your servant finds instruction;
   great reward is in their keeping.
   But who can detect all their errors?
   From hidden faults acquit me.

4. From presumption restrain your servant
   and let it not rule me.
   Then shall I be blameless,
   clean from grave sin.

Gospel Acclamation cf. John 17:17

Alleluia. Your word is truth, O Lord
consecrate us in the truth. Alleluia.

1029 27th in Ordinary Time (B)
Psalm 127. R℣ v.5

May the Lord bless us all the days of our life.

1. O blessed are those who fear the Lord
   and walk in his ways!
   By the labour of your hands you shall eat.
   You will be happy and prosper.

2. Your wife will be like a fruitful vine
   in the heart of your house;
   your children like shoots of the olive,
   around your table.

3. Indeed thus shall be blessed
   those who fear the Lord.
   May the Lord bless you from Zion
   in a happy Jerusalem.

Gospel Acclamation cf. John 17:17

Alleluia. Your word is truth, O Lord,
consecrate us in the truth. Alleluia.

or 1 John 4:12

Alleluia. As long as we love one another
God will live in us and his love will be
complete in us. Alleluia.

1030 28th in Ordinary Time (B)
Psalm 89:12-17. R℣ v.14

Fill us with your love, fill us with your love that
we may re - joice.

1. Make us know the shortness of our life
   that we may gain wisdom of heart.
   Lord, relent! Is your anger for ever?
   Show pity to your servants.

2. In the morning, fill us <u>with</u> your love;
   we shall exult and rejoice <u>all</u> our days.
   Give us joy to balance <u>our</u> affliction
   for the years when we <u>knew</u> misfortune.

3. Show forth your work <u>to</u> your servants;
   let your glory shine <u>on</u> their children.
   Let the favour of the Lord <u>be</u> upon us:
   give success to the work <u>of</u> our hands.

Gospel Acclamation cf. Matthew 11:25

Alleluia. Blessed are you, Father, Lord of
hea<u>ven</u> and earth, for revealing the
mysteries of the kingdom <u>to</u> mere
children. Alleluia.

or Matthew 5:3

Alleluia. How happy are the <u>poor</u> in spirit;
theirs is the king<u>dom</u> of heaven. Alleluia.

1031 29th in Ordinary Time (B)
Psalm 32:4-5, 18-20, 22. R/ v.22

May your love be up - on us, O Lord,

as we place all our hope in you.

1. The word of the <u>Lord</u> is faithful
   and all his works <u>to</u> be trusted.
   The Lord loves jus<u>tice</u> and right
   and fills the earth <u>with</u> his love.

2. The Lord looks on those <u>who</u> revere him,
   on those who hope <u>in</u> his love,
   to rescue their <u>souls</u> from death,
   to keep them a<u>live</u> in famine.

3. Our soul is waiting <u>for</u> the Lord.
   The Lord is our help <u>and</u> our shield.
   May your love be upon <u>us</u>, O Lord,
   as we place all our <u>hope</u> in you.

Gospel Acclamation John 14:15

Alleluia. I am the Way, the Truth and the
Life, <u>says</u> the Lord; no one can come to
the Father ex<u>cept</u> through me. Alleluia.

or Mark 10:45

Alleluia. The Son of Man <u>came</u> to serve,
and to give his life as a ran<u>som</u> for many.
Alleluia.

1032 30th in Ordinary Time (B)
Psalm 125. R/ v.3

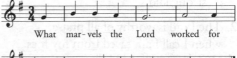

What mar-vels the Lord worked for

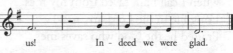

us! In - deed we were glad.

1. When the Lord delivered <u>Zion</u> from
   bondage,
   it seemed <u>like</u> a dream.
   Then was our mouth <u>filled</u> with laughter,
   on our lips <u>there</u> were songs.

2. The heathens themselves <u>said</u>: 'What
   marvels
   the Lord <u>worked</u> for them!'
   What marvels the Lord <u>worked</u> for us!
   Indeed <u>we</u> were glad.

3. Deliver us, O Lord, <u>from</u> our bondage
   as streams <u>in</u> dry land.
   Those who are so<u>wing</u> in tears
   will sing <u>when</u> they reap.

4. They go out, they go out, <u>full</u> of tears,
   carrying seed <u>for</u> the sowing:
   they come back, they come back, <u>full</u> of
   song,
   carry<u>ing</u> their sheaves.

Gospel Acclamation John 8:12

Alleluia. I am the light of the world, <u>says</u>
the Lord, anyone who follows me will
have the <u>light</u> of life. Alleluia.

1033 31st in Ordinary Time (B)
Psalm 17:2-4, 47, 51. R℣ v.2

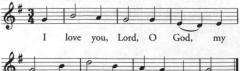

I love you, Lord, O God, my

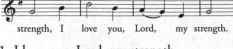

strength, I love you, Lord, my strength.

1. I love you, <u>Lord</u>, my strength,
my rock, my for<u>tress</u>, my saviour.
My God is the rock where <u>I</u> take refuge;
my shield, my mighty <u>help</u>, my
stronghold.

2. The Lord is worthy <u>of</u> all praise:
when I call I am saved <u>from</u> my foes.
Long life to the <u>Lord</u>, my rock!
Praised be the <u>God</u> who saves me.

Gospel Acclamation cf. John 6:63, 68

Alleluia. Your words are spirit, Lord, and
<u>they</u> are life: you have the message of
e<u>ter</u>nal life. Alleluia.

or John 14:23

Alleluia. If anyone loves me they will <u>keep</u>
my word, and my Father will love them
and <u>we</u> shall come to them. Alleluia.

1034 32nd in Ordinary Time (B)
Psalm 145:7-10. R℣ v.2

My soul, give praise to the Lord.

1. It is the Lord who keeps <u>faith</u> for ever,
who is just to those who <u>are</u> oppressed.
It is he who gives bread <u>to</u> the hungry,
the Lord, who sets pris<u>on</u>ers free.

2. It is the Lord who gives sight <u>to</u> the blind,
who raises up those who <u>are</u> bowed down.
It is the Lord who <u>loves</u> the just,
the Lord, who pr<u>otects</u> the stranger.

3. The Lord upholds the wi<u>dow</u> and orphan
but thwarts the path <u>of</u> the wicked.
The Lord will <u>reign</u> for ever,
Zion's God, from <u>age</u> to age.

Gospel Acclamation Revelation 2:10

Alleluia. Even if you have to die, <u>says</u> the
Lord, keep faithful, and I will give you
the <u>crown</u> of life. Alleluia.

or Matthew 5:3

Alleluia. How happy are the <u>poor</u> in spirit;
theirs is the king<u>dom</u> of heaven. Alleluia.

1035 33rd in Ordinary Time (B)
Psalm 15:5, 8-11. R℣ v.1

Pre-serve me, God, I take ref-uge in you.

1. O Lord, it is you who are my por<u>tion</u>
and cup;
it is you yourself who <u>are</u> my prize.
I keep the Lord ever <u>in</u> my sight:
since he is at my right hand, I <u>shall</u> stand
firm.

2. And so my heart rejoices, my <u>soul</u> is glad;
even my body shall <u>rest</u> in safety.
For you will not leave my soul a<u>mong</u> the
dead,
nor let your beloved <u>know</u> decay.

3. O Lord, <u>you</u> will show me
the <u>path</u> of life,
the fullness of joy <u>in</u> your presence,
at your right hand happ<u>iness</u> for ever.

Gospel Acclamation Matthew 24:42, 44

Alleluia. Stay awake <u>and</u> stand ready,
because you do not know the hour when
the Son of <u>Man</u> is coming. Alleluia.

or Luke 21:36

Alleluia. Stay awake, praying <u>at</u> all times
for the strength to stand with confidence
before the <u>Son</u> of Man. Alleluia.

1036 Our Lord Jesus Christ, Universal King (B)
Psalm 92:1-2, 5. R/ v.1

The Lord is King, with ma-je-sty en-robed.

1. The Lord is King, with majesty enrobed;
   the Lord has robed himself with might,
   he has girded himself with power.

2. The world you made firm, not to be moved;
   your throne has stood firm from of old.
   From all eternity, O Lord, you are.

3. Truly your decrees are to be trusted.
   Holiness is fitting to your house,
   O Lord, until the end of time.

Gospel Acclamation Mark 11:9, 10

Alleluia. Blessings on him who comes in the name of the Lord! Blessings on the coming kingdom of our father David! Alleluia.

1037 2nd in Ordinary Time (C)
Psalm 95:1-3, 7-10. R/ v.3

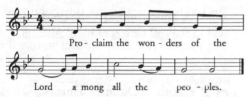

Pro-claim the won-ders of the
Lord a-mong all the peo-ples.

1. O sing a new song to the Lord,
   sing to the Lord all the earth.
   O sing to the Lord, bless his name.

2. Proclaim his help day by day,
   tell among the nations his glory
   and his wonders among all the peoples.

3. Give the Lord, you families of peoples,
   give the Lord glory and power,
   give the Lord the glory of his name.

4. Worship the Lord in his temple.
   O earth, tremble before him.
   Proclaim to the nations: 'God is king.'

Gospel Acclamation cf. John 6:63, 68

Alleluia. Your words are spirit, Lord, and they are life: you have the message of eternal life. Alleluia.

or cf. 2 Thessalonians 2:14

Alleluia. Through the Good News God has called us to share the glory of our Lord Jesus Christ. Alleluia.

1038 3rd in Ordinary Time (C)
Psalm 18:8-10, 15. R/ John 6:63

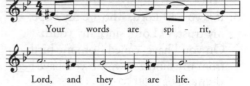

Your words are spi - rit,
Lord, and they are life.

1. The law of the Lord is perfect,
   it revives the soul.
   The rule of the Lord is to be trusted,
   it gives wisdom to the simple.

2. The precepts of the Lord are right,
   they gladden the heart.
   The command of the Lord is clear,
   it gives light to the eyes.

3. The fear of the Lord is holy,
   abiding for ever.
   The decrees of the Lord are truth
   and all of them just.

4. May the spoken words of my mouth,
   the thoughts of my heart,
   win favour in your sight, O Lord,
   my rescuer, my rock!

Gospel Acclamation Luke 4:18

Alleluia. The Lord has sent me to bring the good news to the poor, to proclaim liberty to captives. Alleluia.

1039 4th in Ordinary Time (C)
Psalm 70:1-6, 15, 17. R⁄ v.15

My lips will tell of your help.

1. In you, O Lord, I take refuge;
   let me never be put to shame.
   In your justice rescue me, free me;
   pay heed to me and save me.

2. Be a rock where I can take refuge,
   a mighty stronghold to save me;
   for you are my rock, my stronghold.
   Free me from the hand of the wicked.

3. It is you, O Lord, who are my hope,
   my trust, O Lord, since my youth.
   On you I have leaned from my birth,
   from my mother's womb you have been
       my help.

4. My lips will tell of your justice
   and day by day of your help.
   O God, you have taught me from my
       youth
   and I proclaim your wonders still.

Gospel Acclamation John 14:5

   Alleluia. I am the Way, the Truth and the
   Life, says the Lord; no one can come to
   the Father except through me. Alleluia.

or Luke 4:18

   Alleluia. The Lord has sent me to bring
   the good news to the poor, to proclaim
   liberty to captives. Alleluia.

1040 5th in Ordinary Time (C)
Psalm 137:1-5, 7-8. R⁄ v.1

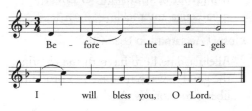

Be-fore the an-gels I will bless you, O Lord.

1. I thank you, Lord, with all my heart,
   you have heard the words of my mouth.
   Before the angels I will bless you.
   I will adore before your holy temple.

2. I thank you for your faithfulness and love
   which excel all we ever knew of you.
   On the day I called, you answered;
   you increased the strength of my soul.

3. All earth's kings shall thank you
   when they hear the words of your mouth.
   They shall sing of the Lord's ways:
   'How great is the glory of the Lord!'

4. You stretch out your hand and save me,
   your hand will do all things for me.
   Your love, O Lord, is eternal,
   discard not the work of your hand.

Gospel Acclamation John 15:15

   Alleluia. I call you friends, says the Lord,
   because I have made known to you
   everything I have learnt from my Father.
   Alleluia.

or Matthew 4:19

   Alleluia. Follow me, says the Lord, and I
   will make you fishers of men. Alleluia.

1041 6th in Ordinary Time (C)
Psalm 1:1-4, 6. R⁄ Psalm 39:5

Hap-py are those, hap-py are those who have

placed their trust in the Lord.

1. Happy indeed are those
   who follow not the counsel of the wicked;
   nor linger in the way of sinners
   nor sit in the company of scorners,
   but whose delight is the law of the Lord
   and who ponder his law day and night.

2. They are like a tree <u>that</u> is planted
   beside the <u>flow</u>ing waters,
   that yields its fruit <u>in</u> due season
   and whose leaves shall <u>never</u> fade;
   and all that they <u>do</u> shall prosper.

3. Not so are the wic<u>ked</u>, not so!
   For they like <u>win</u>nowed chaff
   shall be driven away <u>by</u> the wind.
   For the Lord guards the way <u>of</u> the just
   but the way of the wicked <u>leads</u> to doom.

Gospel Acclamation cf. Matthew 11:25

Alleluia. Blessed are you, Father, Lord of
hea<u>ven</u> and earth, for revealing the
mysteries of the kingdom <u>to</u> mere
children. Alleluia.

or Luke 6:23

Alleluia. Rejoice <u>and</u> be glad: your reward
will be <u>great</u> in heaven. Alleluia.

1042 7th in Ordinary Time (C)
Psalm 102:1-4, 8, 10, 12-13. R/ v.8

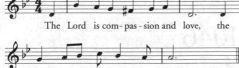

The Lord is com-pas-sion and love, the
Lord is com-pas-sion and love.

1. My soul, give thanks <u>to</u> the Lord,
   all my being, bless his <u>holy</u> name.
   My soul, give thanks <u>to</u> the Lord
   and never forget <u>all</u> his blessings.

2. It is he who forgives <u>all</u> your guilt,
   who heals every one <u>of</u> your ills,
   who redeems your life <u>from</u> the grave,
   who crowns you with love <u>and</u>
      compassion.

3. The Lord is compas<u>sion</u> and love,
   slow to anger and <u>rich</u> in mercy.
   He does not treat us according <u>to</u> our sins
   nor repay us according <u>to</u> our faults.

4. As far as the east is <u>from</u> the west
   so far docs hc re<u>move</u> our sins.
   As a father has compassion <u>on</u> his sons,
   the Lord has pity on <u>those</u> who fear him.

Gospel Acclamation cf. Acts 16:14

Alleluia. Open our <u>heart</u>, O Lord, to
accept the words <u>of</u> your Son. Alleluia.

or John 13:34

Alleluia. I give you a new commandment:
love <u>one</u> another, just as I have loved you,
<u>says</u> the Lord. Alleluia.

1043 8th in Ordinary Time (C)
Psalm 91:2-3, 13-16. R/ cf. v.2

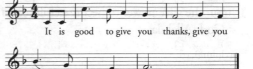

It is good to give you thanks, give you
thanks, O Lord.

1. It is good to give thanks <u>to</u> the Lord
   to make music to your name, <u>O</u> Most
      High,
   to proclaim your love <u>in</u> the morning
   and your truth in the watches <u>of</u> the night.

2. The just will flourish <u>like</u> the palm-tree
   and grow like a Le<u>ba</u>non cedar.
   Planted in the housc <u>of</u> the Lord
   they will flourish in the courts <u>of</u> our God.

3. Still bearing fruit when <u>they</u> are old,
   still full of <u>sap</u>, still green,
   they will proclaim that the <u>Lord</u> is just.
   In him, my rock, there <u>is</u> no wrong.

Gospel Acclamation cf. Acts 16:14

Alleluia. Open our <u>hearts</u>, O Lord, to
accept the words <u>of</u> your Son. Alleluia.

or Philippians 2:15-16

Alleluia. You will shine in the world <u>like</u>
bright stars because you are offering it the
<u>word</u> of life. Alleluia.

1044 9th in Ordinary Time (C)
Psalm 116:1-2. R℟ Mark 16:15

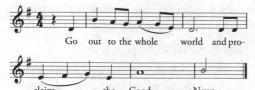

Go out to the whole world and proclaim the Good News.

1. O praise the Lord, <u>all</u> you nations,
   acclaim him <u>all</u> you peoples!

2. Strong is his <u>love</u> for us;
   he is faith<u>ful</u> for ever.

Gospel Acclamation John 1:14, 12

Alleluia. The Word was made flesh and
<u>lived</u> among us; to all who did accept
him he gave power to become chil<u>dren</u> of
God. Alleluia.

or John 3:16

Alleluia. God loved the world so much
that he gave his <u>only</u> Son so that
everyone who believes in him may have
et<u>ern</u>al life. Alleluia.

1045 10th in Ordinary Time (C)
Psalm 29:2, 4-6, 11-13. R℟ v.2

I will praise you, Lord,
you have res - cued me.

1. I will praise you, Lord, <u>you</u> have rescued
   me
   and have not let my enemies rejoice <u>over</u>
   me.
   O Lord, you have raised my soul <u>from</u>
   the dead,
   restored me to life from those who sink
   in<u>to</u> the grave.

2. Sing psalms to the Lord, <u>you</u> who love
   him,
   give thanks to his <u>holy</u> name.
   His anger lasts a moment; his fa<u>vour</u>
   through life.
   At night there are tears, but joy <u>comes</u>
   with dawn.

3. The Lord listened <u>and</u> had pity.
   The Lord came <u>to</u> my help.
   for me you have changed my mourning
   <u>into</u> dancing;
   O Lord my God, I will thank <u>you</u> for ever.

Gospel Acclamation cf. Ephesians 1:17, 18

Alleluia. May the Father of our Lord
Jesus Christ enlighten the eyes <u>of</u> our
mind, so that we can see what hope his
call <u>holds</u> for us. Alleluia.

or Luke 7:16

Alleluia. A great prophet has app<u>eared</u>
among us; God has vis<u>ited</u> his people.
Alleluia.

1046 11th in Ordinary Time (C)
Psalm 31:1-2, 5, 7, 11. R℟ cf. v.5

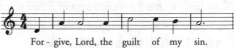

For - give, Lord, the guilt of my sin.

1. Happy are those whose offence <u>is</u> forgiven
   whose sin <u>is</u> remitted.
   O happy are those to <u>whom</u> the Lord
   im<u>putes</u> no guilt.

2. But now I have acknow<u>ledged</u> my sins:
   my guilt I <u>did</u> not hide.
   And you, Lord, <u>have</u> forgiven
   the guilt <u>of</u> my sin.

3. Rejoice, rejoice <u>in</u> the Lord,
   ex<u>ult</u>, you just!
   O come, ring <u>out</u> your joy,
   all you up<u>right</u> of heart.

Gospel Acclamation John 14:5

Alleluia. I am the Way, the Truth and the Life, <u>says</u> the Lord; no one can come to the Father ex<u>cept</u> through me. Alleluia.

or 1 John 4:10

Alleluia. God so loved us when he <u>sent</u> his Son to be the sacrifice that takes our <u>sins</u> away. Alleluia.

1047 12th in Ordinary Time (C)
Psalm 62:2-6, 8-9. R℣ v.2

For you my soul is thirst - ing, O Lord my God.

1. O God, you are my God, for <u>you</u> I long;
   for you my <u>soul</u> is thirsting.
   My body <u>pines</u> for you
   like a dry, weary land with<u>out</u> water.

2. So I gaze on you <u>in</u> the sanctuary
   to see your strength <u>and</u> your glory.
   For your love is be<u>tter</u> than life,
   my lips will <u>speak</u> your praise.

3. So I will bless you <u>all</u> my life,
   in your name I will lift <u>up</u> my hands.
   My soul shall be filled as <u>with</u> a banquet,
   my mouth shall praise <u>you</u> with joy.

4. For you have <u>been</u> my help;
   in the shadow of your wings <u>I</u> rejoice.
   My soul <u>clings</u> to you;
   your right hand <u>holds</u> me fast.

Gospel Acclamation John 8:12

Alleluia. I am the light of the world, <u>says</u> the Lord, anyone who follows me will have the <u>light</u> of life. Alleluia.

or John 10:27

Alleluia. The sheep that belong to me listen to my voice, <u>says</u> the Lord, I know them <u>and</u> they follow me. Alleluia.

1048 13th in Ordinary Time (C)
Psalm 15:1-2, 5, 7-11. R℣ v.1

Pre-serve me, God, I take ref-uge in you.

1. Preserve me, God, I take re<u>fuge</u> in you.
   I say to the Lord: 'You <u>are</u> my God.'
   O Lord, it is you who are my por<u>tion</u>
        and cup;
   it is you yourself who <u>are</u> my prize.

2. I will bless the Lord who <u>gives</u> me counsel,
   who even at night di<u>rects</u> my heart.
   I keep the Lord ever <u>in</u> my sight:
   since he is at my right hand, I <u>shall</u> stand
        firm.

3. And so my heart rejoices, my <u>soul</u> is glad;
   even my body shall <u>rest</u> in safety.
   For you will not leave my soul a<u>mong</u> the
        dead,
   nor let your beloved <u>know</u> decay.

4. O Lord, <u>you</u> will show me
   the <u>path</u> of life,
   the fullness of joy <u>in</u> your presence,
   at your right hand happ<u>iness</u> for ever.

Gospel Acclamation 1 Samuel 3:9; John 6:68

Alleluia. Speak, Lord, your <u>servant</u> is listening: you have the message of e<u>ternal</u> life. Alleluia.

1049 14th in Ordinary Time (C)
Psalm 65:1-7, 16, 20. R℣ v.1

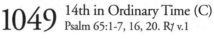

Cry out with joy to God all the earth.

1. Cry out with joy to God <u>all</u> the earth,
   O sing to the glory <u>of</u> his name.
   O render him <u>glorious</u> praise.
   Say to God: 'How tremen<u>dous</u> your
        deeds!'

Continued overleaf

2. 'Before you all the <u>earth</u> shall bow;
shall sing to you, sing <u>to</u> your name!'
Come and see the <u>works</u> of God,
tremendous his deeds <u>a</u>mong men.

3. He turned the sea in<u>to</u> dry land,
they passed through the ri<u>ver</u> dry-shod.
Let our joy then <u>be</u> in him;
he rules for ever <u>by</u> his might.

4. Come and hear, all <u>who</u> fear God.
I will tell what he did <u>for</u> my soul.
Blessed be God who did not re<u>ject</u> my
prayer
nor with<u>hold</u> his love from me.

Gospel Acclamation John 15:15

Alleluia. I call you friends, <u>says</u> the Lord,
because I have made known to you
everything I have learnt <u>from</u> my Father.
Alleluia.

or Colossians 3:15, 16

Alleluia. May the peace of Christ reign <u>in</u>
your hearts, because it is for this that you
were called together as parts <u>of</u> one body.
Alleluia.

1050
15th in Ordinary Time (C)
Psalm 68:14, 17, 30-31, 33-34, 36-37.
R℣ cf. v.33

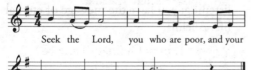

Seek the Lord, you who are poor, and your
hearts will re - vive.

1. This is my prayer to you, my prayer <u>for</u>
your favour.
In your great love, answer <u>me</u>, O God,
with your help that <u>never</u> fails:
Lord, answer, for your <u>love</u> is kind.

2. As for me in my pover<u>ty</u> and pain
let your help, O God, <u>lift</u> me up.
I will praise God's name <u>with</u> a song;
I will glorify him <u>with</u> thanksgiving.

3. The poor when they see it <u>will</u> be glad
and God-seeking hearts <u>will</u> revive;
for the Lord listens <u>to</u> the needy
and does not spurn his servants <u>in</u> their
chains.

4. For God will bring <u>help</u> to Zion
and rebuild the ci<u>ties</u> of Judah.
The sons of his servants <u>shall</u> inherit it;
those who love his <u>name</u> shall dwell there.

Alternative Responsorial Psalm

Psalm 18:8-11. R℣ v.9

The pre - cepts of the
Lord glad - den the heart.

1. The law of the <u>Lord</u> is perfect,
it re<u>vives</u> the soul.
The rule of the Lord is <u>to</u> be trusted,
it gives wisdom <u>to</u> the simple.

2. The precepts of the <u>Lord</u> are right,
they glad<u>den</u> the heart.
The command of the <u>Lord</u> is clear,
it gives light <u>to</u> the eyes.

3. The fear of the <u>Lord</u> is holy,
abi<u>ding</u> for ever.
The decrees of the <u>Lord</u> are truth
and all <u>of</u> them just.

4. They are more to be de<u>sired</u> than gold,
than the pu<u>rest</u> of gold
and sweeter are <u>they</u> than honey,
than honey <u>from</u> the comb.

Gospel Acclamation John 10:27

Alleluia. The sheep that belong to me
listen to my voice, <u>says</u> the Lord, I know
them <u>and</u> they follow me. Alleluia.

or cf. John 6:63, 68

Alleluia. Your words are spirit, Lord, and
<u>they</u> are life: you have the message of
e<u>ter</u>nal life. Alleluia.

1051 16th in Ordinary Time (C)
Psalm 14:2-5. R/ v.1

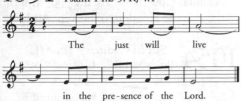

The just will live in the pre-sence of the Lord.

1. Lord, who shall dwell on your holy
   mountain?
   Those who walk without fault;
   Those who act with justice
   and speak the truth from their hearts.

2. They who do no wrong to their kindred
   who cast no slur on their neighbour,
   who hold the godless in disdain,
   but honours those who fear the Lord.

3. Those who keep their pledge, come what
   may;
   who take no interest on a loan
   and accept no bribes against the innocent.
   Such people will stand firm for ever.

Gospel Acclamation cf. Acts 16:14

Alleluia. Open our heart, O Lord, to
accept the words of your Son. Alleluia.

or cf. Luke 8:15

Alleluia. Blessed are those who, with a
noble and generous heart, take the word
of God to themselves and yield a harvest
through their perseverance. Alleluia.

1052 17th in Ordinary Time (C)
Psalm 137:1-3, 6-8. R/ v.3

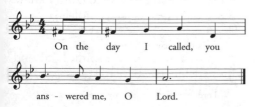

On the day I called, you
ans - wered me, O Lord.

1. I thank you, Lord, with all my heart,
   you have heard the words of my mouth.
   Before the angels I will bless you.
   I will adore before your holy temple.

2. I thank you for your faithfulness and love
   which excel all we ever knew of you.
   On the day I called, you answered;
   you increased the strength of my soul.

3. The Lord is high yet he looks on the
   lowly
   and the haughty he knows from afar.
   Though I walk in the midst of affliction
   you give me life and frustrate my foes.

4. You stretch out your hand and save me,
   your hand will do all things for me.
   Your love, O Lord, is eternal,
   discard not the work of your hands.

Gospel Acclamation John 1:12,14

Alleluia. The Word was made flesh and
lived among us; to all who did accept
him he gave power to become children of
God. Alleluia.

or Romans 8:15

Alleluia. The spirit you received is the
spirit of children, and it makes us cry
out, 'Abba, Father!' Alleluia.

1053 18th in Ordinary Time (C)
Psalm 89:3-6, 12-14, 17. R/ v.1

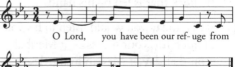

O Lord, you have been our ref-uge from
one gen-er-a-tion to the next.

1. You turn us back into dust
   and say: 'Go back children of the earth.'
   To your eyes a thousand years are like
   yesterday, come and gone,
   no more than a watch in the night.

Continued overleaf

2. You sweep us away <u>like</u> a dream,
   like grass which springs up <u>in</u> the
        morning.
   In the morning it springs <u>up</u> and flowers:
   by evening it wi<u>thers</u> and fades.

3. Make us know the shortness <u>of</u> our life
   that we may gain wis<u>dom</u> of heart.
   Lord, relent! Is your an<u>ger</u> for ever?
   Show pity <u>to</u> your servants.

4. In the morning, fill us <u>with</u> your love;
   we shall exult and rejoice <u>all</u> our days.
   Let the favour of the Lord <u>be</u> upon us:
   give success to the work <u>of</u> our hands.

Alternative Responsorial Psalm

Psalm 94:1-2, 6-9. R℣ vv.7-8

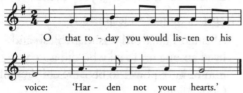

O that to - day you would lis-ten to his

voice: 'Har - den not your hearts.'

1. Come, ring out our joy <u>to</u> the Lord;
   hail the <u>rock</u> who saves us.
   Let us come before him, <u>giving</u> thanks,
   with songs let us <u>hail</u> the Lord.

2. Come in; let us bow <u>and</u> bend low;
   let us kneel before the <u>God</u> who made us
   for he is our God, and we the people
        who belong <u>to</u> his pasture,
   the flock that is led <u>by</u> his hand.

3. O that today you would listen <u>to</u> his voice!
   'Harden not your hearts as <u>at</u> Meribah,
   as on that day at Massah in the desert,
        when your fathers put me <u>to</u> the test;
   when they tried me, though they <u>saw</u> my
        work.'

Gospel Acclamation cf. John 17:17

   Alleluia. Your word is <u>truth</u>, O Lord,
   consecrate us <u>in</u> the truth. Alleluia.

or Matthew 5:3

   Alleluia. How happy are the <u>poor</u> in spirit;
   theirs is the <u>kingdom</u> of heaven. Alleluia.

1054   19th in Ordinary Time (C)
Psalm 32:1, 12, 18-20, 22. R℣ v.12

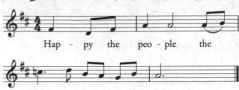

Hap - py the peo - ple the

Lord has cho-sen as his own.

1. Ring out your joy to the Lord, <u>O</u> you just;
   for praise is fitting for <u>loyal</u> hearts.
   They are happy, whose God <u>is</u> the Lord,
   the people he has chosen <u>as</u> his own.

2. The Lord looks on those <u>who</u> revere him,
   on those who hope <u>in</u> his love,
   to rescue their <u>souls</u> from death,
   to keep them a<u>live</u> in famine.

3. Our soul is waiting <u>for</u> the Lord.
   The Lord is our help <u>and</u> our shield.
   May your love be upon <u>us</u>, O Lord,
   as we place all our <u>hope</u> in you.

Gospel Acclamation cf. Matthew 11:25

   Alleluia. Blessed are you, Father, Lord of
   hea<u>ven</u> and earth, for revealing the
   mysteries of the kingdom <u>to</u> mere
   children. Alleluia.

or Matthew 24:42, 44

   Alleluia. Stay awake <u>and</u> stand ready,
   because you do not know the hour when
   the Son of <u>Man</u> is coming. Alleluia.

1055   20th in Ordinary Time (C)
Psalm 39:2-4, 18. R℣ v.14

Lord, come to my aid,

Lord, come to my aid!

1. I waited, I waited for the Lord
   and he stooped down to me;
   he heard my cry.

2. He drew me from the deadly pit,
   from the miry clay.
   He set my feet upon a rock
   and made my footsteps firm.

3. He put a new song into my mouth,
   praise of our God.
   Many shall see and fear
   and shall trust in the Lord.

4. As for me, wretched and poor,
   the Lord thinks of me.
   You are my rescuer, my help,
   O God, do not delay.

Gospel Acclamation cf. Acts 16:14

Alleluia. Open our heart, O Lord, to
accept the words of your Son. Alleluia.

or John 10:27

Alleluia. The sheep that belong to me
listen to my voice, says the Lord, I know
them and they follow me. Alleluia.

1056 21st in Ordinary Time (C)
Psalm 116. R/ Mark 16:15

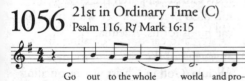

Go out to the whole world and proclaim the Good News.

1. O praise the Lord, all you nations,
   acclaim him all you peoples!

2. Strong is his love for us;
   he is faithful for ever.

Gospel Acclamation John 14:23

Alleluia. If anyone loves me they will
keep my word, and my Father will love
them and we shall come to them.
Alleluia.

or John 14:6

Alleluia. I am the Way, the Truth and the
Life, says the Lord; no one can come to
the Father except through me. Alleluia.

1057 22nd in Ordinary Time (C)
Psalm 67:4-7, 10-11. R/ cf. v.11

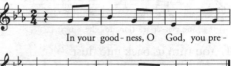

In your good-ness, O God, you prepared a home for the poor.

1. The just shall rejoice at the presence of
   God,
   they shall exult and dance for joy.
   O sing to the Lord, make music to his
   name;
   rejoice in the Lord, exult at his presence.

2. Father of the orphan, defender of the
   widow,
   such is God in his holy place.
   God gives the lonely a home to live in;
   he leads the prisoners forth into freedom.

3. You poured down, O God, a generous
   rain:
   when your people were starved you gave
   them new life.
   It was there that your people found a
   home,
   prepared in your goodness, O God, for
   the poor.

Gospel Acclamation John 14:23

Alleluia. If anyone loves me they will
keep my word, and my Father will love
them and we shall come to them.
Alleluia.

Continued overleaf

or Matthew 11:29

Alleluia. Shoulder my <u>yoke</u> and learn from me, for I am gentle and hum<u>ble</u> in heart. Alleluia.

1058 23rd in Ordinary Time (C)
Psalm 89:3-6, 12-14, 17. R/ v.1

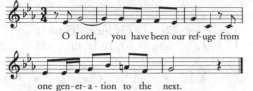

O Lord, you have been our ref-uge from

one gen-er-a-tion to the next.

1. You turn us back <u>into</u> dust
and say: 'Go back, children <u>of</u> the earth!'
To your eyes a thousand years are like
yesterday, <u>come</u> and gone,
no more than a watch <u>in</u> the night.

2. You sweep us away <u>like</u> a dream,
like grass which springs up <u>in</u> the
morning.
In the morning it springs <u>up</u> and flowers:
by evening it wi<u>thers</u> and fades.

3. Make us know the shortness <u>of</u> our life
that we may gain wis<u>dom</u> of heart.
Lord, relent! Is your <u>anger</u> for ever?
Show pity <u>to</u> your servants.

4. In the morning, fill us <u>with</u> your love;
we shall exult and rejoice <u>all</u> our days.
Let the favour of the Lord <u>be</u> upon us:
give success to the work <u>of</u> our hands.

Gospel Acclamation John 15:15

Alleluia. I call you friends, <u>says</u> the Lord,
because I have made known to you
everything I have learnt <u>from</u> my Father.
Alleluia.

or Psalm 118:135

Alleluia. Let your face shine <u>on</u> your
servant, and teach me <u>your</u> decrees.
Alleluia.

1059 24th in Ordinary Time (C)
Ps 50:3-4, 12-13, 17, 19. R/ Lk 15:18

I will leave this place and

go to my Fa - ther.

1. Have mercy on me, God, <u>in</u> your
kindness.
In your compassion blot out <u>my</u> offence.
O wash me more and more <u>from</u> my guilt
and cleanse me <u>from</u> my sin.

2. A pure heart create for <u>me</u>, O God,
put a steadfast spi<u>rit</u> within me.
do not cast me away <u>from</u> your presence,
nor deprive me of your <u>ho</u>ly spirit.

3. O Lord, o<u>pen</u> my lips
and my mouth shall de<u>clare</u> your praise.
My sacrifice is a <u>contrite</u> spirit;
a humbled, contrite heart you <u>will</u> not
spurn.

Gospel Acclamation cf. Ephesians 1:17, 18

Alleluia. May the Father of our Lord
Jesus Christ enlighten the eyes <u>of</u> our
mind, so that we can see what hope his
call <u>holds</u> for us. Alleluia.

or 2 Corinthians 5:19

Alleluia. God in Christ was reconciling
the world <u>to</u> himself, and he has
entrusted to us the news that <u>they</u> are
reconciled. Alleluia.

1060 25th in Ordinary Time (C)
Psalm 112:1-2, 4-8. R/ cf. vv.1, 7

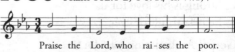

Praise the Lord, who rai-ses the poor.

1. Praise, O servants <u>of</u> the Lord,
praise the name <u>of</u> the Lord!
May the name of the <u>Lord</u> be blessed
both now and for <u>ever</u>more.

2. Who is like the <u>Lord</u>, our God,
   who has risen on high <u>to</u> his throne
   yet stoops from the heights <u>to</u> look down,
   to look down upon hea<u>ven</u> and earth?

3. From the dust he lifts <u>up</u> the lowly,
   from the dungheap he rai<u>ses</u> the poor
   to set them in the com<u>pany</u> of rulers,
   yes, with the rulers <u>of</u> his people.

Gospel Acclamation cf. Acts 16:14

Alleluia. Open our <u>heart</u>, O Lord, to
accept the words <u>of</u> your Son. Alleluia.

or 2 Corinthians 8:9

Alleluia. Jesus <u>Christ</u> was rich, but he
became poor for your sake, to make you
rich out <u>of</u> his poverty. Alleluia.

1061 26th in Ordinary Time (C)
Psalm 145:6-10. R℣ v.2

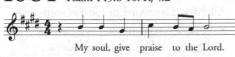

My soul, give praise to the Lord.

1. It is the Lord who keeps <u>faith</u> for ever,
   who is just to those who <u>are</u> oppressed.
   It is he who gives bread <u>to</u> the hungry,
   the Lord, who sets pri<u>soners</u> free.

2. It is the Lord who gives sight <u>to</u> the blind,
   who raises up those who <u>are</u> bowed down.
   It is the Lord who <u>loves</u> the just,
   the Lord, who pro<u>tects</u> the stranger.

3. He upholds the wi<u>dow</u> and orphan
   but thwarts the path <u>of</u> the wicked.
   The Lord will <u>reign</u> for ever,
   Zion's God, from <u>age</u> to age.

Gospel Acclamation John 10:27

Alleluia, alleluia! The sheep that belong
to me listen to my voice, <u>says</u> the Lord,
I know them <u>and</u> they follow me.
Alleluia!

or 2 Corinthians 8:9

Alleluia. Jesus <u>Christ</u> was rich, but he
became poor for your sake, to make you
rich out <u>of</u> his poverty. Alleluia.

1062 27th in Ordinary Time (C)
Psalm 94:1-2, 6-9. R℣ v.9

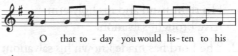

O that to - day you would lis - ten to his

voice: 'Har - den not your hearts.'

1. Come, ring out our joy <u>to</u> the Lord;
   hail the <u>rock</u> who saves us.
   Let us come before him, giving thanks,
   with songs let us <u>hail</u> the Lord.

2. Come in; let us bow <u>and</u> bend low;
   let us kneel before the <u>God</u> who made us
   for he is our God, and we the people
       who belong <u>to</u> his pasture,
   the flock that is led <u>by</u> his hand.

3. O that today you would listen <u>to</u> his
       voice!
   'Harden not your hearts as <u>at</u> Meribah,
   as on that day at Massah in the desert,
       when your fathers put me <u>to</u> the test;
   when they tried me, though they <u>saw</u> my
       work.'

Gospel Acclamation 1 Samuel 3:9; John 6:68

Alleluia. Speak, Lord, your ser<u>vant</u> is
listening: you have the message of e<u>ternal</u>
life. Alleluia.

or 1 Peter 1:25

Alleluia. The word of the Lord re<u>mains</u>
for ever: What is this word? It is the
Good News that <u>has</u> been brought to
you. Alleluia.

1063 28th in Ordinary Time (C)
Psalm 97:1-4. R/ cf. v.2

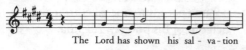

The Lord has shown his sal-va-tion

to all the na-tions.

1. Sing a new song to the Lord
   for he has worked wonders.
   His right hand and his holy arm
   have brought salvation.

2. The Lord has made known his salvation;
   has shown his justice to the nations.
   He has remembered his truth and love
   for the house of Israel.

3. All the ends of the earth have seen
   the salvation of our God.
   Shout to the Lord all the earth,
   ring out your joy.

Gospel Acclamation cf. John 6:63, 68

Alleluia. Your words are spirit, Lord, and
they are life; you have the message of
eternal life. Alleluia.

or 1 Thessalonians 5:18

Alleluia. For all things give thanks,
because this is what God expects you to
do in Christ Jesus. Alleluia.

1064 29th in Ordinary Time (C)
Psalm 120. R/ cf. v.2

Our help is in the name of the Lord who

made heav-en and earth.

1. I lift up my eyes to the mountains:
   from where shall come my help?
   My help shall come from the Lord
   who made heaven and earth.

2. May he never allow you to stumble!
   Let him sleep not, your guard.
   No, he sleeps not nor slumbers,
   Israel's guard.

3. The Lord is your guard and your shade;
   at your right side he stands.
   By day the sun shall not smite you
   nor the moon in the night.

4. The Lord will guard you from evil,
   he will guard your soul.
   The Lord will guard your going and
       coming
   both now and for ever.

Gospel Acclamation cf. Ephesians 1:17, 18

Alleluia. May the Father of our Lord
Jesus Christ enlighten the eyes of our
mind, so that we can see what hope his
call holds for us. Alleluia.

or Hebrews 4:12

Alleluia. The word of God is something
alive and active; it can judge secret
emotions and thoughts. Alleluia.

1065 30th in Ordinary Time (C)
Psalm 32:2-3, 17-19, 23. R/ v.7

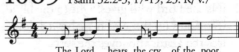

The Lord hears the cry of the poor.

1. I will bless the Lord at all times,
   his praise always on my lips;
   in the Lord my soul shall make its boast.
   The humble shall hear and be glad.

2. The Lord turns his face against the
       wicked
   to destroy their remembrance from the
       earth.
   The just call and the Lord hears
   and rescues them in all their distress.

3. The Lord is close to the broken-hearted;
   those whose spirit is crushed he will save.
   The Lord ransoms the souls of his
      servants.
   Those who hide in him shall not be
   condemned.

Gospel Acclamation cf. Matthew 11:25

   Alleluia. Blessed are you, Father, Lord of
   heaven and earth, for revealing the
   mysteries of the kingdom to mere
   children. Alleluia.

or 2 Corinthians 5:19

   Alleluia. God in Christ was reconciling
   the world to himself, and he has
   entrusted to us the news that they are
   reconciled. Alleluia.

1066   31st in Ordinary Time (C)
Psalm 144:1-2, 8-11, 13-14. R℣ cf. v.1

1. I will give you glory, O God my King,
   I will bless your name for ever.
   I will bless you day after day
   and praise your name for ever.

2. The Lord is kind and full of compassion,
   slow to anger, abounding in love.
   How good is the Lord to all,
   compassionate to all his creatures.

3. All your creatures shall thank you,
      O Lord,
   and your friends shall repeat their blessing.
   They shall speak of the glory of your reign
   and declare your might, O God.

4. The Lord is faithful in all his words
   and loving in all his deeds.
   The Lord supports all who fall
   and raises all who are bowed down.

Gospel Acclamation Luke 19:38

   Alleluia. Blessings on the King who
   comes in the name of the Lord! Peace in
   heaven and glory in the highest heavens!
   Alleluia.

or John 3:16

   Alleluia. God loved the world so much
   that he gave his only Son, so that
   everyone who believes in him may have
   eternal life. Alleluia.

1067   32nd in Ordinary Time (C)
Psalm 16:1, 5-6, 8, 15. R℣ v.15

1. Lord, hear a cause that is just,
   pay heed to my cry.
   Turn your ear to my prayer:
   no deceit is on my lips.

2. I kept my feet firmly in your paths;
   there was no faltering in my steps.
   I am here and I call, you will hear me,
      O God.
   Turn your ear to me; hear my words.

3. Guard me as the apple of your eye.
   Hide me in the shadow of your wings.
   As for me, in my justice I shall see your
      face
   and be filled, when I awake, with the
      sight of your glory.

Gospel Acclamation Luke 21:36

   Alleluia. Stay awake, praying at all times
   for the strength to stand with confidence
   before the Son of Man. Alleluia.

or Revelation 1:5, 6

   Alleluia. Jesus Christ is the First-born
   from the dead; to him be glory and
   power for ever and ever. Alleluia.

1068   33rd in Ordinary Time (C)
Psalm 97:5-9. R℣ cf. v.9

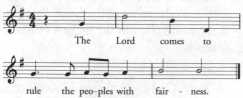

The Lord comes to rule the peo-ples with fair-ness.

1. Sing psalms to the Lord <u>with</u> the harp
   with the <u>sound</u> of music.
   With trumpets and the sound <u>of</u> the horn
   acclaim the <u>King</u>, the Lord.

2. Let the sea and all with<u>in</u> it, thunder;
   the world, and <u>all</u> its peoples.
   Let the rivers <u>clap</u> their hands
   and the hills ring <u>out</u> their joy.

3. Rejoice at the presence <u>of</u> the Lord,
   for he comes to <u>rule</u> the earth.
   He will rule the <u>world</u> with justice
   and the <u>peoples</u> with fairness.

Gospel Acclamation Luke 21:36

Alleluia. Stay awake, praying <u>at</u> all times
for the strength to stand with confidence
before the <u>Son</u> of Man. Alleluia.

or Luke 21:28

Alleluia. Stand erect, hold <u>your</u> heads
high, because your liberation is <u>near</u> at
hand. Alleluia.

1069   Our Lord Jesus Christ, Universal King (C)
Psalm 121:1-5. R℣ cf. v.2

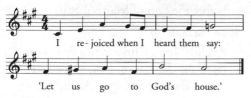

I re-joiced when I heard them say:
'Let us go to God's house.'

1. I rejoiced when I <u>heard</u> them say:
   'Let us go <u>to</u> God's house.'
   And now our <u>feet</u> are standing
   within your gates, <u>O</u> Jerusalem.

2. Jerusalem is built <u>as</u> a city
   strong<u>ly</u> compact.
   It is there that the <u>tribes</u> go up,
   the tribes <u>of</u> the Lord.

3. For Israel's <u>law</u> it is,
   there to praise <u>the</u> Lord's name.
   There were set the <u>thrones</u> of judgement
   of the <u>house</u> of David.

Gospel Acclamation Mark 11:9, 10

Alleluia. Blessings on him who comes in
the name <u>of</u> the Lord! Blessings on the
coming kingdom of our <u>father</u> David!
Alleluia.

1070   The Presentation of the Lord (A, B, C)
Psalm 23:7-10. R℣ v.8

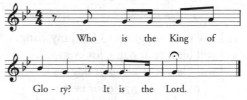

Who is the King of Glo-ry? It is the Lord.

1. O gates, lift <u>up</u> your heads;
   grow higher, <u>ancient</u> doors.
   Let him enter, the <u>King</u> of Glory!

2. Who is the <u>King</u> of Glory?
   The Lord, the <u>mighty</u>, the valiant,
   the Lord, the <u>valiant</u> in war.

3. O gates, lift <u>high</u> your heads;
   grow higher, <u>ancient</u> doors.
   Let him enter, the <u>King</u> of Glory!

4. Who is he, the <u>King</u> of Glory?
   He, the <u>Lord</u> of armies,
   he is the <u>King</u> of Glory.

Gospel Acclamation Luke 2:32

Alleluia. The light to enlighten the Gentiles and give glory to Israel, your people. Alleluia.

1071 The Birth of St John the Baptist (A, B, C)

Psalm 138:1-3, 13-15. R℣ v.14

I thank you, Lord, for the won-der of my be - ing.

1. O Lord, you search me and you know me, you know my resting and my rising,
you discern my purpose from afar.
You mark when I walk or lie down,
all my ways lie open to you.

2. For it was you who created my being, knit me together in my mother's womb.
I thank you for the wonder of my being,
for the wonders of all your creation.

3. Already you knew my soul,
my body held no secret from you
when I was being fashioned in secret
and moulded in the depths of the earth.

Gospel Acclamation cf. Luke 1:76

Alleluia. As for you, little child, you shall be called a prophet of God, the Most High. You shall go ahead of the Lord to prepare his ways before him. Alleluia.

1072 SS Peter and Paul, Apostles (A, B, C)

Psalm 33:2-9. R℣ v.5. Alt. R℣ v.8

From all my ter - rors the Lord has set me free.

1. I will bless the Lord at all times,
his praise always on my lips;
in the Lord my soul shall make its boast.
The humble shall hear and be glad.

2. Glorify the Lord with me.
Together let us praise his name.
I sought the Lord and he answered me;
from all my terrors he set me free.

3. Look towards him and be radiant;
let your faces not be abashed.
When the poor cry out the Lord hears them,
and rescues them from all their distress.

4. The angel of the Lord is encamped
around those who revere him, to rescue them.
Taste and see that the Lord is good.
They are happy who seek refuge in him.

Gospel Acclamation Matthew 16:18

Alleluia. You are Peter and on this rock I will build my church. And the gates of the underworld can never hold out against it. Alleluia.

1073 The Transfiguration of the Lord (A, B, C)

Psalm 96:1-2, 5-6, 9. R℣ vv.1, 9

The Lord is King, the Lord is King, most

high a - bove all the earth.

1. The Lord is king, let earth rejoice,
let all the coastlands be glad.
His throne, justice and right.

2. The mountains melt like wax
before the Lord of all the earth.
All peoples see his glory.

Continued overleaf

3. For you indeed <u>are</u> the Lord
   most high above <u>all</u> the earth
   exalted far a<u>bove</u> all spirits.

Gospel Acclamation Matthew 17:5

   Alleluia. This is my Son, <u>the</u> Beloved, he
   enjoys my favour; lis<u>ten</u> to him. Alleluia.

1074
The Assumption of the Blessed
Virgin Mary (A, B, C)
Psalm 44:10-12, 16. R℣ v.10

On your right hand stands the queen, in gar - ments of gold.

1. The daughters of kings are a<u>mong</u> your
   loved ones.
   On your right stands the queen in <u>gold</u>
   of Ophir.
   Listen, O daughter, give ear <u>to</u> my words:
   forget your own people and your <u>father's</u>
   house.

2. So will the king de<u>sire</u> your beauty.
   He is your lord, pay ho<u>mage</u> to him.
   They are escorted amid glad<u>ness</u> and joy;
   they pass within the palace <u>of</u> the king.

Gospel Acclamation

   Alleluia. Mary has been taken up <u>into</u>
   heaven; all the choirs of angels <u>are</u>
   rejoicing. Alleluia.

1075
The Triumph of the Cross
(A, B, C)
Psalm 77:1-2, 34-38. R℣ v.7

Ne-ver for-get, ne-ver for- get the deeds of the Lord.

1. Give heed, my people, <u>to</u> my teaching;
   turn your ear to the words <u>of</u> my mouth.
   I will open my mouth <u>in</u> a parable
   and reveal hidden lessons <u>of</u> the past.

2. When he slew them then <u>they</u> would
      seek him,
   return and seek <u>him</u> in earnest.
   They would remember that God <u>was</u>
      their rock,
   God the Most High <u>their</u> redeemer.

3. But the words they spoke <u>were</u> mere
      flattery;
   they lied to him <u>with</u> their lips.
   For their hearts were not <u>truly</u> with him;
   they were not faithful <u>to</u> his covenant.

4. Yet he who is full <u>of</u> compassion
   forgave their <u>sin</u> and spared them.
   So often he held <u>back</u> his anger
   when he might have stirred <u>up</u> his rage.

Gospel Acclamation

   Alleluia. We adore you, O Christ, <u>and</u> we
   bless you; because by your cross you have
   re<u>deemed</u> the world. Alleluia.

1076
All Saints (A, B, C)
Psalm 23:1-6. R℣ cf. v.6

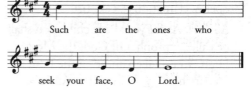

Such are the ones who seek your face, O Lord.

1. The Lord's is the earth <u>and</u> its fullness,
   the world and <u>all</u> its peoples.
   It is he who set it <u>on</u> the seas;
   on the waters he <u>made</u> it firm.

2. Who shall climb the mountain <u>of</u> the
      Lord?
   Who shall stand in his <u>holy</u> place?
   Those with clean hands <u>and</u> pure heart,
   who desire not <u>worth</u>less things.

3. They shall receive blessings <u>from</u> the Lord
   and reward from the <u>God</u> who saves
      them.
   Such are the <u>ones</u> who seek him,
   seek the face of the <u>God</u> of Jacob.

Gospel Acclamation Matthew 11:28
   Alleluia. Come to me, all you who labour
   and are <u>over</u>burdened, and I will give you
   rest, <u>says</u> the Lord. Alleluia.

1077 The Commemoration of all the
Faithful Departed (A, B, C)
Ps 26:1, 4, 7-9, 13-14. R℣ v.1. Alt. R℣ v.13

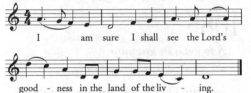

I am sure I shall see the Lord's

good - ness in the land of the liv - ing.

1. The Lord is my light <u>and</u> my help;
   whom <u>shall</u> I fear?
   The Lord is the stronghold <u>of</u> my life;
   before whom <u>shall</u> I shrink?

2. There is one thing I ask <u>of</u> the Lord,
   for <u>this</u> I long,
   to live in the house <u>of</u> the Lord,
   all the days <u>of</u> my life.

3. O Lord, hear my voice <u>when</u> I call;
   have mer<u>cy</u> and answer.
   It is your face, O Lord, <u>that</u> I seek;
   hide <u>not</u> your face.

4. I am sure I shall see <u>the</u> Lord's goodness
   in the land <u>of</u> the living.
   Hope in him, hold firm <u>and</u> take heart.
   Hope <u>in</u> the Lord!

Gospel Acclamation John 6:39
   Alleluia. It is my Father's will, says the
   Lord, that I should lose nothing of all
   that <u>he</u> has given me, and that I should
   raise it up on <u>the</u> last day. Alleluia.

1078 The Dedication of a Church
Psalm 45:2-3, 5-6, 8-9. R℣ v.5

The wa-ters of a ri - ver

give joy, give joy to God's ci - ty.

1. God is for us a <u>refuge</u> and strength,
   a helper close at hand, in time <u>of</u> distress:
   so we shall not fear though the <u>earth</u>
      should rock,
   though the mountains fall into the
   depths <u>of</u> the sea.

2. The waters of a river give joy <u>to</u> God's city,
   the holy place where the <u>Most</u> High
      dwells.
   God is within, it can<u>not</u> be shaken;
   God will help it at the dawning <u>of</u> the day.

3. The Lord of <u>hosts</u> is with us:
   the God of Jacob <u>is</u> our stronghold.
   Come, consider the works <u>of</u> the Lord
   the redoubtable deeds he has done <u>on</u> the
      earth.

Gospel Acclamation 2 Chronicles 7:16
   Alleluia. I have chosen and consecrated
   this house, <u>says</u> the Lord, for my name to
   be <u>there</u> for ever. Alleluia.

EUCHARISTIC ADORATION

1079-82
St Thomas Aquinas
trans. John Mason Neale

1. O salutaris hostia,
   quae cæli pandis ostium,
   bella premunt hostilia,
   da robur, fer auxilium.

2. Uni trinoque Domino
   sit sempiterna gloria,
   qui vitam sine termino
   nobis donet in patria. Amen.

English version

1. O saving victim, op'ning wide
   the gate of heav'n to man below;
   our foes press on from ev'ry side;
   thine aid supply, thy strength bestow.

2. To thy great name be endless praise,
   immortal Godhead, One in Three;
   O grant us endless length of days
   in our true native land with thee. Amen.

1083-84
St Thomas Aquinas, trans. James Quinn
© Geoffrey Chapman, imprint of Cassell plc

1. Tantum ergo Sacramentum
   veneremur cernui:
   et antiquum documentum
   novo cedat ritui;
   præstet fides supplementum
   sensuum defectui.

2. Genitori, genitoque
   laus et jubilatio,
   salus, honor, virtus, quoque
   sit et benedictio;
   procedenti ab utroque
   compar sit laudatio. Amen.

English version

1. Come, adore this wondrous presence,
   bow to Christ, the source of grace.
   Here is kept the ancient promise
   of God's earthly dwelling-place.
   Sight is blind before God's glory,
   faith alone may see his face.

2. Glory be to God the Father,
   praise to his co-equal Son,
   adoration to the Spirit,
   bond of love, in Godhead one.
   Blest be God by all creation
   joyously while ages run.

1085

*Adoremus in æternum
sanctissimum sacramentum.*

1. Laudate Dominum, omnes gentes;
   laudate eum, omnes populi.

2. Quoniam confirmata est super
   nos misericordia ejus;
   et veritas Domini manet
   in æternum.

3. Gloria Patri et Filio;
   et Spiritui Sancto.

4. Sicut erat in principio
   et nunc et semper;
   et in sæcula sæculorum. Amen.

Index of Authors and Sources of Text

Scriptural Index

6:25-34	779	24:42-44	704, 721, 1001, 1035, 1054	11:9-10	3, 4, 5, 7, 8, 59, 60, 61, 62, 63, 64, 65, 66, 67, 253, 274, 344, 750, 772, 861, 1003, 1036, 1069	3:21-22	631

6:25-34 779
6:26 477, 770
6:30 839
6:33 604, 897
7:7 96, 562, 604
7:9 189
7:11 718
7:14 144
7:24-27 780, 847
8:2 740
8:17 1002
8:20 259, 350, 477
8:23-27 635, 706
8:26 166, 243, 245, 351, 751, 836, 863
9:9 259, 350, 451, 483, 740, 840
9:36 677
9:38 270
10:8-9 286, 297
10:29-31 842, 853
10:38 259, 429
11:5 152, 487, 706
11:25 973, 983, 985, 986, 1006, 1030, 1041, 1054, 1065
11:28-30 127, 222, 223, 224, 351, 451, 483, 525, 553, 642, 725, 757, 1057, 1076
12:8 452
13:1-23 565
13:4 350, 509
13:8 228
13:24-30 670
13:25 226
13:41 147, 226
13:47-50 670
14:13-21 272
14:22-33 379
14:25 243
14:29 483
15:31 706
16:18 271, 990, 1072
16:24 259
16:27 306
17:1-8 711
17:5 55, 927, 928, 929, 1073
17:20 245
18:12-14 99, 131, 310, 350, 677
19:14 784
20:12 790
20:28 267, 394, 668
21:1-11 113, 487, 593
21:9 3, 4, 5, 7, 8, 59, 60, 61, 62, 63, 64, 65, 66, 67, 253, 274, 344, 750, 772, 861
22:37-40 464, 762
24:30-31 13, 316, 438, 521, 529, 686, 708

24:42-44 704, 721, 1001, 1035, 1054
25:4 274
25:31 13, 147, 306
25:31-46 228, 595, 726, 730, 766
26:6-11 595
26:26-29 225, 273, 295, 459, 509, 523, 539, 570, 642, 681, 715, 732
26:36-42 888, 889
26:36-27:56 188
26:39 267, 582, 876
26:41 544, 849
27:22 487
27:29 551, 552
27:32-61 719
27:46 482
28:1-10 678, 747, 761
28:6-7 184, 703
28:9 649
28:18 286
28:19-20 110, 270, 273, 345, 379, 459, 467, 623, 631, 708, 781, 831, 960

MARK
1:1-8 541, 721
1:3 897
1:4 99, 220
1:8 120
1:9-11 631
1:12-13 264, 363, 458, 462
1:15 980, 1005
1:16 234
1:17 259, 451, 483, 740
1:18 350
1:40 740
2:14 259, 350, 483, 537, 740, 840
2:28 452
4:1-20 565
4:3 350, 509
4:26-29 180, 226, 261, 351
4:35-41 635, 706
4:39 166, 243, 245, 351, 751, 836, 863
6:31 483
6:32-44 272
6:34 677
6:45-52 379
6:48 243
7:37 125
8:34 259, 429
8:38 306
9:2-8 711
9:7-8 55, 920
10:14 784
10:21 451
10:45 267, 394, 668, 1031
11:1-11 113, 487, 593

11:9-10 3, 4, 5, 7, 8, 59, 60, 61, 62, 63, 64, 65, 66, 67, 253, 274, 344, 750, 772, 861, 1003, 1036, 1069
12:28-31 464, 762
13:11 297, 779
13:25-26 13, 316, 438, 521, 529, 708
13:33 704, 721
14:3-9 595
14:22-25 225, 273, 295, 459, 462, 509, 523, 539, 570, 642, 681, 715, 732
14:32-15:41 188
14:34-36 267, 582, 876, 888, 889
14:38 544, 849
15:13 487
15:17 551, 552
15:21-47 719
15:34 482
16:1-8 184, 678, 747, 761
16:7 703
16:15-18 459, 1044

LUKE
1-2 646
1:26-38 343, 508
1:28 128, 141, 313, 360, 550, 632, 795
1:32 387, 910, 911
1:35 629
1:38 524, 733
1:42 597, 618
1:46 49, 877, 886
1:46-55 109, 285, 488, 489, 491, 644, 679, 907
1:52 257
1:76 1071
1:79 679
2:1-7 472, 536
2:1-20 229, 296, 601, 603, 723
2:7 208, 725, 819
2:10-11 912
2:8-20 134, 135, 155, 302, 354, 365, 501, 614, 651, 739
2:13-14 1, 3, 7, 20, 21, 22, 23, 24, 25, 26, 27, 28, 29, 30, 31, 32, 100, 130, 152, 238, 317, 375, 399, 526, 676, 776
2:29-32 599, 752, 1070
2:35 145
3:1-18 541, 721
3:3-4 99, 221, 897, 903, 904, 905
3:16 120, 922

3:21-22 631
4:1-13 264, 363, 458, 462, 811
4:4 604
4:18 216, 297, 413, 471, 673, 740, 771, 906, 907, 908, 979, 1009, 1016, 1038, 1039
4:34 166
5:11-12 234, 740
5:27 259, 350, 451, 483, 740, 840
6:5 452
6:20-23 589, 654, 757, 1041
6:27 828
6:47-49 780, 847
7:6 139
7:16 1008, 1014, 1019, 1045
7:22 395, 487
7:34 110
8:4-15 565
8:5 350, 509
8:8 984
8:15 1051
8:22-25 166, 243, 245, 351, 635, 706, 751, 836, 863
9:10-17 272
9:23 259, 429
9:28-36 711
9:35 55
9:58-59 259, 350, 451, 477, 740
10:2 270
10:6 286
10:25-29 362, 464, 762
10:39 691
11:1 447
11:2-4 83, 84, 85, 86, 87, 189, 470, 718
11:9 96, 562
12:6-7 842, 853
12:22-32 779
12:24 477, 770
12:28 839
12:31 897
13:10-17 353
14:12-24 376
14:13 235, 327, 706
15:4-6 99, 131, 241, 310, 350, 656, 677
15:11-32 99, 620
15:18 935
15:20 293
15:32 714
16:22 241
18:15 784
19:1-10 857
19:5 483
19:10 672
19:28-38 113, 487, 593

Index of Uses

Index of Sunday and Feastday Themes

234	Dear Lord and Father of mankind		307	Guide me, O thou great Redeemer		448	Lord Jesus, think on me
350	I am the Light					514	O God, our help in ages past
453	Lord, the light of your love		390	Jesus Christ is waiting		647	The Church's one foundation
665	The race that long in darkness pined		654	The kingdom of heaven		847	The wise man
			738	Where true love is present			

234 Dear Lord and Father of mankind
350 I am the Light
453 Lord, the light of your love
665 The race that long in darkness pined

Year B *Follow me*
234 Dear Lord and Father of mankind
259 Follow me, follow me
451 Lord of life
483 My God said to me, 'Follow'
740 Will you come and follow me

Year C *Good News*
297 God's Spirit is in my heart
471 Make way, make way
673 The Spirit of the Lord
735 Where love and charity endure
736 Where the love of Christ unites us

4th SUNDAY
Year A *Good News for the poor*
158 Be blessed, pure of heart
174 Blest are the pure in heart
654 The kingdom of heaven
717 We hold a treasure
749 You are salt for the earth

Year B *The crowds stare*
163 Be still and know I am with you
333 Holy God, we praise thy name
529 O Lord, my God
561 Our God sent his Son long ago
582 Praise to the Holiest

Year C *Persecuted love*
194 Christ be beside me
355 If I am lacking love
463 Love is patient
557 O, the love of my Lord
644 Tell out, my soul

5th SUNDAY
Year A *Light*
350 I am the Light
439 Longing for light
467 Lumen Christi
672 The Spirit lives to set us free
749 You are salt for the earth

Year B *Healing the broken*
164 Be still and know that I am God
202 Colours of day
319 Healer of our every ill
320 Healer of the sick
413 Lay your hands gently upon us

Year C *Called by the Holy God*
234 Dear Lord and Father of mankind
259 Follow me, follow me
333 Holy God, we praise thy name
376 I, the Lord of sea and sky
740 Will you come and follow me

6th SUNDAY
Year A *What God demands*
224 Come to me, come, my people

307 Guide me, O thou great Redeemer
390 Jesus Christ is waiting
654 The kingdom of heaven
738 Where true love is present

Year B *Healing*
283 God be in my head
413 Lay your hands gently upon us
447 Lord Jesus Christ
620 Sing, my soul
740 Will you come and follow me

Year C *Good News for the poor*
174 Blest are the pure in heart
589 Rejoice, all heavenly powers
654 The kingdom of heaven
757 You shall cross the barren desert
1041 Happy indeed (Psalm 1)

7th SUNDAY
Year A *Love your enemies*
186 Brother, sister, let me serve you
425 Let there be love
462 Love is his word
464 Love is the only law
828 O Lord, all the world

Year B *Forgiven and healed*
131 Amazing grace
170 Blessed assurance
195 Christians, lift up your hearts
286 God forgave my sin
304 Grant to us, O Lord

Year C *Compassion*
94 Abba, Abba, Father
425 Let there be love
464 Love is the only law
470 Make me a channel of your peace
726 Whatsoever you do

8th SUNDAY
Year A *At rest in God*
382 I will never forget you
445 Lord, for tomorrow and its needs
604 Seek ye first
688 Though the mountains may fall
779 Do not worry over what to eat

Year B *Wedded to God*
133 A new commandment
169 Bind us together, Lord
207 Come back to me
562 Our hearts were made for you
724 What feast of love

Year C *Giving yourself away*
194 Christ be beside me
385 I will sing, I will sing
431 Like a sea without a shore
558 O the word of my Lord
678 Thine be the glory

9th SUNDAY
Year A *Building on rock*
119 All my hope on God is founded

448 Lord Jesus, think on me
514 O God, our help in ages past
647 The Church's one foundation
847 The wise man

Year B *Freedom from slavery*
266 Freedom for my people
299 Go in peace
355 If I am lacking love
711 We behold the splendour of God
717 We hold a treasure

Year C *Outsiders are welcome*
139 As bread my Lord comes to me
164 Be still and know that I am God
197 Christ is made the sure foundation
240 Do not be afraid
395 Jesus is Lord! In love he came

10th SUNDAY
Year A *I want love not ritual*
355 If I am lacking love
376 I, the Lord of sea and sky
462 Love is his word
463 Love is patient
562 Our hearts were made for you

Year B *Adam and Satan*
168 Be thou my vision
186 Brother, sister, let me serve you
299 Go in peace
582 Praise to the Holiest
746 Ye choirs of new Jerusalem

Year C *The dead raised to life*
220 Come, praise the Lord
348 I am the bread of life (Konstant)
520 O, how good is the Lord
561 Our God sent his Son long ago
564 Ours were the sufferings he bore

11th SUNDAY
Year A *Spread the Good News*
206 Come and praise him
286 God forgave my sin
289 God is love
303 Go, the Mass is ended
546 Open your ears, O Christian people

Year B *Growth of the Kingdom*
120 All over the world
123 All the earth proclaim the Lord
180 Bread from the earth
226 Come, ye thankful people, come
351 I cannot tell

Year C *God forgives*
131 Amazing grace
237 Deep within my heart
258 Firmly I believe
620 Sing, my soul
862 Bless the Lord, my soul

12th SUNDAY
Year A *Do not be afraid*
240 Do not be afraid

21st SUNDAY

Year A *Built on rock*
197 Christ is made the sure foundation
324 He brings us into his banqueting table
647 The Church's one foundation
654 The kingdom of heaven
690 Thy hand, O God, has guided

Year B *To whom else would we go?*
97 Abide with me
110 Alleluia, sing to Jesus
165 Be still, for the presence of the Lord
379 I will be with you
755 You have the message of eternal life

Year C *No east or west*
115 All God's people, here together
120 All over the world
262 For the healing of the nations
330 He's got the whole world in his hand
420 Let all the world in every corner sing

22nd SUNDAY

Year A *A living sacrifice*
94 Abba, Abba, Father
259 Follow me, follow me
331 He who would valiant be
483 My God said to me, 'Follow'
544 Onward, Christian pilgrims

Year B *Submit to God's Word*
304 Grant to us, O Lord
390 Jesus Christ is waiting
558 O the word of my Lord
658 The Lord hears the cry of the poor
675 The temple of the living God

Year C *The heavenly Jerusalem for the humble*
224 Come to me, come, my people
285 God fills me with joy
327 Here in this place
373 I saw the Holy City
387 Jerusalem the golden

23rd SUNDAY

Year A *Responsibility for brothers and sisters*
186 Brother, sister, let me serve you
289 God is love
470 Make me a channel of your peace
736 Where the love of Christ unites us
738 Where true love is present

Year B *The deaf hear again*
158 Be blessed, pure of heart
395 Jesus is Lord! In love he came
413 Lay your hands gently upon us
669 The Saviour will come, resplendent in joy
771 Christ is our king

Year C *Counting the cost*
259 Follow me, follow me
483 My God said to me, 'Follow'
697 Unless a grain of wheat
740 Will you come and follow me
754 You have called us

24th SUNDAY

Year A *As forgiving as God*
164 Be still and know that I am God
186 Brother, sister, let me serve you
286 God forgave my sin
449 Lord, make me a means of your peace
862 Bless the Lord, my soul

Year B *What faith entails*
189 By the cross
259 Follow me, follow me
354 If God is for us
483 My God said to me, 'Follow'
754 You have called us

Year C *The prodigal Father*
99 Across the years there echoes still
131 Amazing grace
293 God of mercy and compassion
517 O God, your people gather
700 Vaster far than any ocean

25th SUNDAY

Year A *Generous to a fault*
173 Bless the Lord, my soul
178 Blest be the Lord
290 God is love: his the care
520 O, how good is the Lord
620 Sing, my soul

Year B *Servants of each other*
174 Blest are the pure in heart
186 Brother, sister, let me serve you
470 Make me a channel of your peace
533 O my Lord, within my heart
571 Peace I leave with you

Year C *The right use of money*
123 All the earth proclaim the Lord
262 For the healing of the nations
286 God forgave my sin
512 O God of earth and altar
658 The Lord hears the cry of the poor

26th SUNDAY

Year A *Humble repentance*
147 At the name of Jesus
325 He is Lord
338 Holy Jesus, in our likeness born
385 I will sing, I will sing
475 Meekness and majesty

Year B *Whatsoever you do to the least*
262 For the healing of the nations
512 O God of earth and altar
658 The Lord hears the cry of the poor
726 Whatsoever you do

730 When I needed a neighbour

Year C *Riches corrupt you*
224 Come to me, come, my people
255 Fight the good fight
390 Jesus Christ is waiting
448 Lord Jesus, think on me
604 Seek ye first

27th SUNDAY

Year A *Sour grapes*
236 Deep peace of the running wave to you
534 O my people, what have I done to you?
571 Peace I leave with you
675 The temple of the living God
782 Each of us is a living stone

Year B *Man and wife, one body*
133 A new commandment
147 At the name of Jesus
289 God is love
421 Let love be real
1029 O blessed are those who fear the Lord

Year C *Increase our faith*
119 All my hope on God is founded
245 Faith in God
416 Lead us, heavenly Father, lead us)
417 Leave your country and your people
1062 Come ring out our joy

28th SUNDAY

Year A *Everyone is invited*
146 At the Lamb's high feast we sing
256 Fill my house
480 My God, and is thy table spread
661 The Lord's my shepherd
690 Thy hand, O God, has guided

Year B *The Kingdom is worth every sacrifice*
259 Follow me, follow me
417 Leave your country and your people
451 Lord of life
558 O the word of my Lord
717 We hold a treasure

Year C *Gratitude*
111 Alleluia, thank you for fathers
320 Healer of the sick
407 Keep in mind
697 Unless a grain of wheat
1063 Sing a new song to the Lord

29th SUNDAY

Year A *God as Supreme King*
119 All my hope on God is founded
120 All over the world
361 Immortal, invisible, God only wise
696 Turn to me
998 O sing a new song

Responsorial Psalm Index

A complete set of Responsorial Psalms will be found at numbers 900-1078.

Those suggested below are either alternative translations, paraphrases or songs based on the appropriate psalm.

The Lectionary also provides for common psalms for each season which are also noted here.

ADVENT

Index of First Lines

This index is in five parts:

1. Mass Music
2. Hymns and Songs
3. Children's Hymns and Songs
4. Chants
5. Eucharistic Adoration with Benediction

Responsorial Psalms at numbers 900-1078 are not included in this index.

This index gives the first line of each hymn. If a hymn is known also by a title (e.g. As gentle as silence) this is given as well, but indented and in italic.

MASS MUSIC

HYMNS and SONGS

A

CHANTS

EUCHARISTIC ADORATION WITH BENEDICTION

Acknowledgements

The publishers wish to express their gratitude to the following for permission to include copyright material in this publication. Details of copyright owners are given underneath each individual hymn.

Ateliers et Presses de Taizé, F-71250 Taizé-Communauté, France.

The Benedictine Foundation of the State of Vermont Inc., Weston Priory, 58 Priory Hill Road, Weston, VT 05161, USA.

Boosey & Hawkes Music Publishers Ltd, 295 Regent Street, London W1R 8JH.

Canon J. E. Bowers.

Central Board of Finance of the Church of England, Church House, Great Smith Street, London SW1P 3NZ.

Geoffrey Chapman (an imprint of Cassell plc), Wellington House, 125 Strand, London WC2R 0BB.

CopyCare Ltd, P.O. Box 77, Hailsham, East Sussex, BN27 3EF, on behalf of Birdwing Music/EMI Christian Music Publishing; Bud John Songs/EMI Christian Music Publishing; Deep Fryed Music/Word Music/Maranatha! Music; Hope Publishing; Lillenas Publishing Co./Maranatha! Music; Mercy/Vineyard Publishing/Music Services; Mission Hills Music; People of Destiny International; The Rodeheaver Co/Word Music; Salvationist Publishing & Supplies; Word's Spirit of Praise Music; Word of God Music and Paul Booth.

J. Curwen & Sons Ltd, 8/9 Frith Street, London W1V 5TZ.

Daybreak Music Ltd, Silverdale Road, Eastbourne, East Sussex, BN20 7AB.

Mr Noel Donnelly.

Downside Abbey Trustees, Stratton-on-the-Fosse, Bath, BA3 4RH.

The Rt. Revd. Timothy Dudley-Smith, 9 Ashlands, Ford, Salisbury, Wiltshire, SP4 6DY.

Sister Delores Dufner, OSB, Sisters of the Order of St Benedict, 104 Chapel Lane, St Joseph, MN 56374-0220, USA.

The Archdiocese of Durban, 408 Innes Road, Durban 4001, S. Africa.

Editions Musicales SM, 54 Rue Michel Ange, 75016 Paris, France.

Faber Music Ltd, 3 Queen Square, London WC1N 3AU.

GIA Publications Inc., 7404 S. Mason Avenue, Chicago, IL 60638, USA.

The Revd. M. J. Hancock.

David Higham Associates Ltd, 5-8 Lower John Street, Golden Square, London W1R 4HA.

Mr Michael Hodgetts.

Revd. Pierre-Marie Hoog, SJ, Eglise Saint Ignace, 75006 Paris, France.

International Music Publications, Griffin House, 161 Hammersmith Road, London W6 8BS.

Iona Community (The Wild Goose Resource Group), Pearce Institute, 840 Govan Road, Glasgow G51 3UU.

Rev. W. F. Jabusch, Calvert House, 5735 University Avenue, Chicago, IL 60637, USA.

Mr James G. Johnson, Eighth Day Creations Music, Box 375, Red Lodge, Montana 59068, USA.

Jubilate Hymns, 4 Thorne Park Road, Chelston, Torquay, TQ2 6RX.

Kingsway's Thankyou Music, P.O. Box 75, Eastbourne, East Sussex, BN23 6NW, on behalf of Kingsway's Thankyou Music; Scripture in Song (UK only); Integrity's Hosanna! Music (UK only); Fred Boch Music Co. (Europe, excl. Germany, and British Commonwealth, excl. Canada); Celebration (Europe and British Commonwealth, excl. Canada, Australasia and Africa); Glorie Music and Stuart K. Hine (Worldwide, excl. USA and Canada).

Mr Greg Leavers.

Father Jean-Paul Lecot, 'Espélugues', 1 Ave. Mgr. Théas, 65100 Lourdes, France.

Leosong Copyright Service, Independent House, 54 Larkshall Road, Chingford, London E4 6PD.

Make Way Music, P.O. Box 263, Croydon, CR9 5AP.

McCrimmon Publishing Co Ltd, 10-12 High Street, Great Wakering, Southend-on-Sea, Essex, SS3 0EQ.

Mrs Francesca McEvoy.

Sister Mary E. McGann RSCJ, 5 Acacia Avenue, Berkeley, CA 94708, USA.

The Medical Mission Sisters, 92 Sherman Street, Hartford, CT 06105, USA.

Every effort has been made to trace the owners of copyright material, and we hope that no copyright has been infringed. Pardon is sought and apology made if the contrary be the case, and a correction will be made in any reprint of this book.

By the same token we would remind the users of this book that many of the songs in this collection are copyright: further reproduction of any kind without prior permission of the copyright owner is both illegal and immoral.

Our Lady, Help of Christians

1.On this our journey to your Son we need you, Mother
To help us love ourselves and also one another,
And show this love by doing what he asks,
As we perform our routine daily tasks
And so we ask,
Our Lady, help of Christians, Pray for us.

2. When trials come and on our own we seem to falter,
Our Mother guides us to Him at the holy altar.
She tells us that to Him we all must pray,
To fast and do good deeds is what she'll say,
And so we ask,
Our Lady, Help of Christians, Pray for us.

3. By giving her whole life to God and His desire
She gives the Christians all the help that they require.
She listened to His Word and showed the way
That we should follow when to him we pray,
And so we ask,
Our Lady, Help of Christians, Pray for us.

4. Our Lady dear, whom God has chosen as His Mother
Is guide and help for every sister and her brother
On each and every step that they've been given
To everlasting life with God in heaven,
And so we ask,
Our Lady, Help of Christians, Pray for us.

1. They are waiting for our petitions,
Silent and calm;
Their lips no prayer can utter,
No suppliant psalm;
We have made them all too weary
With long delay,
For the souls in their still agony,
Good Christian pray.

    Requiescant in Pace.

2. For the soul thou holdest dearest
Let prayer arise.
The voice of love is mighty
And will pierce the sky;
Waste not in selfish weeping
One precious day,
But speeding the soul to heaven,
Good Christian pray.

    Requiescat in Pace.

3. For the soul by all forgotten,
Even its own;
By its nearest and dearest,
Left all alone;
Whisper a De Profundis
Or gently lay
Alms in some beggar's
outstretched Palm,
Good Christian pray.

    Requiescat in Pace.

1. I rise from Dreams of time.
And an angel guides my feet,
To the sacred altar-throne,
Where Jesus' heart doth beat,
   Ever pleading day and night
   Thou canst not from us part;
   O veiled and wond'rous Son,
   O love of the Sacred Heart.

2. The lone lamp softly burns,
And a wondrous silence reigns,
Only with a low still voice,
The Holy One complains.
   Ever pleading...

3. Long, long, I've waited here,
And though thou heedest not Me,
The Heart of God's own Son,
Beats ever on for thee.
   Ever pleading...

4. In the womb of Mary meek,
In the cradle, on the tree,
Heart of pure undying love,
It lived, loved, bled for me.
   Ever pleading...

Guardian Angel, from Heaven so bright,

Watching beside me, to lead me aright,

Fold thy wings round me, O guard me with love,

Softly sing songs to me, of heav'n above.

Chorus:Beautiful angel, my guardian so mild,

Tenderly guide me, for I am thy child.

Angel so holy, whom God sends to me,

Sinful and lowly, my guardian to be.

Wilt thou not cherish the child of thy care?

Let me not perish, my trust is my prayer.

Chorus.

Oh! May I never forget thou art near;

But keep me for ever in love and in fear.

Waking and sleeping, in labour and rest,

In thy sweet keeping my life shall be blessed.

Chorus.

Lord, you have come to the sea shore,
Neither searching for the rich nor the wise,
Desiring only that I should follow,
O Lord, with your eyes set upon me,
Gently smiling, you have spoken my name.
All I long for I have found by the water,
At your side I will seek other shores.
Lord, see my goods, my possessions,
In my boat, you find no power, no wealth.
Will you accept then, my nets my labour?
O Lord, with your eyes set upon me... ...
Lord, take my hands and direct them,
Help me spend myself in seeking the lost,
Returning love for the love you gave me,
O Lord, with your eyes set upon me... ...
Lord, as I drift on the waters
Be the resting place of my restless heart,
My life's companion, my friend and refuge,
O Lord, with your eyes set upon me... ...